dig

dedication

For my mother, who first led me into the garden, and for my husband, who joins me while I potter.

Published in 2003 by Murdoch Books®, a division of Murdoch Magazines Pty Ltd.

Murdoch Books® Australia
GPO Box 1203
Sydney NSW 1045
Phone: + 61 (0) 2 4352 7000
Fax: + 61 (0) 2 4352 7026

Murdoch Books UK Limited
Ferry House
51–57 Lacy Road
Putney, London SW15 1PR
Phone: + 44 (0) 20 8355 1480
Fax: + 44 (0) 20 8355 1499

Design Concept: Marylouise Brammer
Designers: Marylouise Brammer and Vivien Valk
Design Assistant: Genevieve Huard
Editorial Director: Diana Hill
Project Editor: Sarah Baker
Production Editor, UK edition: Sue Read
UK Consultant, Adapting Editor: Alan Toogood
Production Manager: Kylie Kirkwood
Production Controller: Janis Barbi
Photo Library Manager: Anne Ferrier

Chief Executive: Juliet Rogers
Publisher: Kay Scarlett

Cover photographs: Sue Stubbs

ISBN 1 90399 249 4
A catalogue record for this book is available from the British Library

Printed by Tien Wah Press. PRINTED IN SINGAPORE.
Printed 2003.

dig
modern seasonal gardening

Meredith Kirton

Adapted by Alan Toogood

MURDOCH
B O O K S

contents

contents

preface

Creating a garden, growing plants and watching them closely to absorb their detail is a rewarding pursuit. This book was written with the intention of providing something for everyone. Whether you have a moment, an hour or a week, I hope this book illuminates and inspires you and, in doing so, enriches your knowledge of hands-on techniques in modern gardening.

The text of *Dig* was written and photographed over a year, season by season. The result is a book that contains not just researched information, but also a lot of first-hand observations and experience. It is the essence of a year in my garden and also provides glimpses of gardens belonging to friends and neighbours, many other wonderful private gardens and nurseries.

The layered effect of text, photography, tips and interesting facts, step-by-step techniques, projects, cultivation advice, special pictorial spreads of groups of plants and quotes are similar in a way to the layers that a garden is built upon — the successes and failures of personal attempts, knowledge gleaned from others and years of growth. A microcosm of evolution itself.

Many people would have you believe that gardening is 'dead easy'. Well, it's not. Gardens require patience, care and, indeed, affection. Gardeners possess these attributes to varying degrees. Experience helps but it rarely provides all the answers. I have been gardening as a professional for more than fifteen years, but I am only just beginning to apply expertise in my field. There is a world beyond — of plant breeding, market gardens and landscapes in remote places with plants very different to those that are familiar to me. Gardens are a source of constant challenge and, consequently, of infinite satisfaction.

Pay careful attention to magazines and garden books, and be alert to what grows well in your neighbourhood. Learn from your own experiences and gardening will become more of an art and less of a mystery. It will always keep you on your toes though: unusual weather, insect attack and wildlife — all factors beyond your control — are just around the corner.

It is this pursuit of the elusive 'perfect' garden, where it all comes together by accident or design, that keeps us all striving. This blend of science (how to get plants to grow well) and art (combining plants and other features together to achieve the best effect) which first attracted me to gardening. Remember, a garden starts but never finishes.

introduction

The gardening year naturally divides into the four seasons, each characterized by certain events, cycles of life and the weather. For obvious reasons, this book is divided into spring, summer, autumn and winter. Each of the four chapters begins with an overview, a synopsis of what the season has in store.

The further divisions — such as 'Shrubs & trees' — are based on a plant's function and form in the garden. Delving further into these will give you a deeper understanding of the mainstays of traditional gardening, including some old favourites, and introduce you to some exciting new developments in horticulture.

Weather and climate

There is a worldwide agricultural zone system which is based on minimum temperatures, as this is the greatest limiting factor when it comes to plant growth. There are, however, many factors that affect the climate of an area, including latitude, altitude, wind direction and velocity, as well as the proximity to physical features such as mountains or the sea.

Climate affects plant growth, most obviously by determining how many months per year plants can actually grow. Generally, the cooler the climate, the shorter the growth period, but extremely high temperatures or low rainfall can also be limiting factors. In addition, climate affects when seeds germinate or plants flower.

Microclimates can be created by such factors as the slope of the land, depressions creating 'frost pockets', modifying breezes and the position of the sun. Planting trees or building structures such as pergolas can also help plants to grow in areas outside their optimum zones, as can conservatories. A heated conservatory greatly increases the range of plants that can be grown in frost-prone climates. Various conditions may be maintained in conservatories: cool, with a minumum temperature of 4.5°C, intermediate (or temperate), with a minimum of 10°C, and warm, with a minimum of 15.5°C.

Each plant has evolved to suit its particular zone, so changing its climate can result in spectacular growth or miserable failure. Many plants have evolved with some adaptations to suit their conditions: succulent foliage or grey leaves to help cope with dry, hot conditions, or large leaves with drip points that help rainforest plants survive low light levels and high humidity. Many grey-leaved plants will therefore rot in humid areas and, likewise, rainforest plants will burn in too much sun.

Weather is the day-to-day prevailing condition. This seasonally changes, with spring and autumn characterized by milder temperatures, summer by hotter temperatures and winter by cooler ones. These seasonal changes are most noticeable away from the equator, where temperature changes little but rainfall patterns are normally grouped into wet and dry seasons.

Phenology

How do you know it's spring? Just because the calendar reads 1 March doesn't mean that spring has arrived. The answer will depend not on the date but on the weather in your area.

Continents and many countries are so vast that climatic conditions vary enormously from one area to another. They will enjoy spring at different times, so look for nature's clues — if the birds are singing loudly, bare branches are budding and daffodils and forsythia are flowering, spring is in the air.

These observations are known as 'phenology'. This is a field of science concerned with the influence of climate on the recurrence of biological phenomena, such as plant flowering. Some years may be cooler or warmer than others, yet the unfurling of leaves, the bloom of a wild flower or the appearance of a particular insect occurs in the same order.

Meteorologists measure this in degree days or number of daylight hours, and each plant has its own set number of how many of these it needs before it will react either out of dormancy or into flower.

For hundreds of years farmers and gardeners have observed that the best time to plant or harvest depends on the timing of other plants in their area. Native Americans, for example, planted corn when oak leaves had unfurled to the size of a squirrel's ear. As we reach a greater understanding of nature's signals, the better we will be able to interpret them for better management in agriculture and backyard gardening.

Author's note

The term 'bulb' refers to a modified underground bud, with a compressed stem and fleshy scale-like leaves, that stores food and water when growing conditions are unfavourable, then sends leaves upwards and roots downwards when conditions improve. In this book, all storage organs — such as corms, tubers, certain rhizomes and true bulbs — are categorized as 'bulbs'.

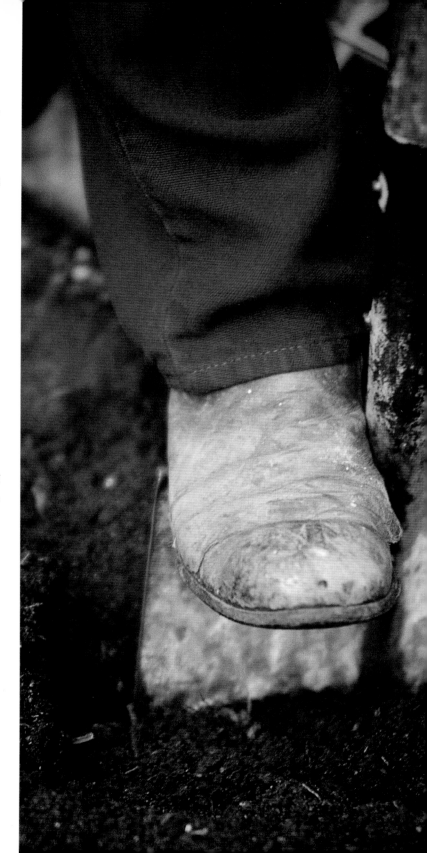

Bud swell and blossom.
The warbling of magpies
and fleeting moments
of delight. Frenzy.
Sniffles and sneezes.
Fresh. Fragile. Handle
with care.

spring

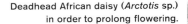

Deadhead African daisy (*Arctotis* sp.) in order to prolong flowering.

spring overview of the season

Spring evokes a feeling of renewal and excitement in all gardeners. Novices and enthusiasts alike cannot help but be inspired by the show nature puts on.

Lime-coloured new growth bursts from tired grey twigs, flowers come to life in even the most neglected beds — there is action everywhere in the garden.

If spring were to be summed up by one word, it would be 'busy'. Everything happens at once at this time of the year. New season's vegetables, herbs and annuals need planting, it is a great time for blossom trees, and a wonderful selection of hybrid natives become available. Trees, weeds, flowers, birds and insects are all experiencing a frenzy of growth. This explosion of life can leave you feeling either a little bewildered about where to start in the garden, or inspired by nature's extravagance and keen to make progress

Rhododendron 'Kirin' is covered in flowers from mid-spring.

To own a bit of ground, to scratch it with a hoe, to plant seeds, and watch their renewal of life — this is the commonest delight of the race, the most satisfactory thing. . .

Charles Dudley Warner

The new leaves of Japanese maple and *Spiraea japonica* 'Goldflame' and the pretty blooms of chaenomeles signal the arrival of spring.

with your own patch of ground. Don't be overwhelmed: tackle each task in bite-sized chunks and the rewards will come. Make the most of glorious days in the sunshine by walking around a nursery, visiting an open garden or simply getting your hands dirty in your own backyard.

In the temperate months of spring, garden chores don't seem too arduous, so you should go outside and enjoy the garden before the weather becomes too hot.

• If you have been feeding plants regularly with compost, manure and fertilizer, your soil will start to become more acid — that is, the pH will be below 7 (see 'Soil pH' on page 23 for more information on pH). Unless your garden consists only of acid-loving plants, such as camellias and azaleas, you should lime your soil to compensate.

• Give plants enough food to achieve maximum results. Slow-release fertilizers are a good way of ensuring all trace elements and macronutrients are supplied. Seaweed solutions act like a plant 'tonic' and are proven performers.

• Happy plants are healthy, so give your garden an all-over application of complete fertilizer and you will be rewarded with a cheerful response.

• Top up your mulch in time for the summer heat.

• The sunshine also wakes up your weeds, so one day spent weeding now saves a week of hard work further down the track when the weeds have seeded.

• Insects are out and about feeding and breeding, so be vigilant and smart in dealing with them. You can deal with sapsuckers such as thrips, fruit fly, aphids, scale and mealy bugs easily and safely by vigorous hosing, before using a systemic insecticide such as white oil.

• Clean up scale and sooty mould on camellias, citrus, oleander and any other damaged plants.

• Whatever you resolve to grow, don't rush into things. Premature plantings put in before the soil warms up won't mature any sooner, so use the time to think about your selections and prepare the soil. You'll be rewarded for your patience!

Did you know? The Roman writer Pliny described the mulberry, the last to come into leaf, as the wisest tree. Traditionally gardeners regarded their plants as safe from frost once a mulberry was in leaf.

weather**watch**

How do you know that it is spring? The answer will depend not on the date but on the weather in your area. Look for nature's clues — if the birds are singing loudly, bare branches are budding and someone you know is suffering from hay fever, spring is in the air.

HOSING ON FERTILIZER

Revive a dull lawn with some liquid lawn fertilizer.

1 Pour concentrated liquid fertilizer into the bottle of a fertilizer diluter attached to a hose.

2 Following the manufacturer's instructions on application rates, hose the fertilizer onto your lawn.

Chicken manure Fertilize shrubs and trees with pelletized chicken manure.

Spring into action

Why not spring clean your garden and give it the facelift it deserves? There are lots of jobs to do.

Rake up any fallen leaves still around from autumn and put them in the compost; the old adage 'a new broom sweeps clean' is very much the case in the garden! Hire a high-pressure water blaster and clean paved surfaces. Spot-spray weeds in garden beds, pathways and paved areas, then grab the secateurs and get stuck into any wayward shrubs (avoid pruning spring- and early summer-flowering shrubs now, as you may be removing flower buds). Plants are quick to recover in spring, and can easily be trimmed down a size or two without any harmful effect.

A dose of pelletized manure may bring around the neighbour's dog, but it will also do wonders for trees and shrubs. Spread some fresh mulch on garden beds for an instant effect, and use a liquid lawn fertilizer to restore the greenness of a tired-looking lawn.

Once the hard work is done, it is time for a bit of fun. A trip to a local nursery during spring should inspire even the most inactive gardeners. When visiting these plant havens check the longevity of the shrubs and examine their form and foliage to gauge whether they will be good-value year-round specimens or one-day wonders.

If you are after a quick fix, annuals are among the best investments. They are cheap and cheery, and can be massed to fill any bare spots without great expense. Plant some annuals where they will make most impact: a display in pots by entrance ways, in pockets in garden beds either side of the

driveway and massed in a border along the front boundary will give people the impression that you have spent weeks working on the garden.

Time-saving ideas

If you know you won't have time to work in the garden every day or each night when you get home from work, don't plant a high-maintenance garden. Planting roses, perennials such as Michaelmas daisies, that need regular lifting and dividing, and very fast growers might seem like a good idea at the time, but they will eventually make you a slave to your garden.

Choose low-maintenance plants that are drought tolerant, cope with a bit of neglect and are suited to your conditions. Include plenty of shrubs, as generally speaking they

require the least amount of care. The following are good low-maintenance plants: bougainvillea (for frost-free climates), hardy bulbs, shrubby cinquefoils, ornamental grasses, hebes, hellebores, ivies, junipers, mahonias, dwarf pines and yarrows. Avoid large areas of lawn, vegetables and flowers, as these plants require the most effort to cultivate and demand more of your time. Group together any demanding plants, such as fruit trees, so that feeding, spraying and watering can all be done in one go.

Paving is a good alternative to lawn. It is a good surface for entertaining, relaxation and children's play, and, unlike lawn, it dries quickly after the rain.

The best tip is to do a little work often. Just ten minutes a day weeding and tidying up will save hours of work in the long run.

Choosing a good plant at the nursery

1 First of all, check that the leaves are uniformly green.
2 Look for a specimen of balanced proportions, one that is not lopsided or top-heavy.
3 See if you can spot insect damage, weeds or fungus rots. Leave any contaminated plants alone.
4 Never buy a pot-bound plant. You can tell these from the roots growing out of the base of the pot or packing the compost. Don't hesitate to remove the pot to have a good look at the root system, but remember to replace it!
5 Don't just be seduced by the flowers, ask how long these last and picture what the plant will look like when they finish.

Clockwise from above: Massed annuals provide a quick fix while hebes and bougainvilleas are low-maintenance plants.

Below: The potting compost should be just held together by the roots, not packed with roots as in this plant.

Planting tips

New plantings need special attention until they have become established.

- Water at least weekly from the time you plant until the end of the first summer if necessary. This should give the plant enough time to grow roots into the surrounding soil, where they can then start to source water for themselves.
- Often rain doesn't provide enough water. Before deciding whether plants need an extra drink, check below the surface of the soil to see if water has penetrated to the root zone.
- Planting time is an ideal opportunity for adding water-storing granules to dry soils. Mix these into the soil as you backfill around the planting hole.
- To help retain moisture, place a 'doughnut' shape of mulch around each plant, at least 10 cm thick and extending out twice as wide as the root ball.
- Never mulch up to the collar or trunk of a plant as this can cause both collar rot and ringbarking.
- Although strong fertilizers should never be used at planting time, most landscapers add a little slow-release food underneath a layer of soil to provide some much-needed nutrients at the source when new roots grow into the surrounding soil.
- However tempting it seems, don't allow fruiting plants to crop in their first year as it will be at the expense of new growth.

MULCHING

1 You'll need a generous amount of mulch. It will conserve moisture and suppress weeds.

2 Spread it 10 cm thick. The mulch should be twice as wide as the root ball.

3 Take care not to mulch up the collar or trunk of the tree or you'll end up with collar rot.

Great ideas for small gardens

If you love visiting open gardens in spring, you may return home feeling like you need another hectare or two to create a really satisfying garden. However, small spaces can be just as beautiful.

Confined garden spaces are becoming a fact of life for most city dwellers, but the courtyard or balcony can be a big challenge on a small scale. The contained garden can be intimate, with colourful creepers, evergreen hedges and scented screens. Small spaces can be converted into green, usable extensions of a living area, becoming outdoor rooms.

The following tricks of the trade might make the difference at your place.

- Focal points. Create a highlight such as a garden seat, potted urn or fountain — a focal point makes an outdoor space more inviting to explore.
- Illumination. Lighting helps create mood and gives a small garden depth.
- Ceilings and walls. Plant a tree, or build a pergola or raised garden beds to help enclose an area and convert it into an outdoor room.
- Pattern and texture. Decking and paving, unusual types of foliage and architectural shapes can add interest, definition and substance to small spaces.
- Trickery and illusion. Mirrors, hedges, trompe l'oeil and manipulation of perspective can all make a space appear larger than it is.

Above: Here the indoors appears larger by 'borrowing' the exterior landscape: the arch of the wall fountain echoes the fanlight over the French doors.

Below: The tubbed citrus trees obscure the boundaries, making this garden seem like an outdoor room.

Bring your soil to life too

With the frenzy of spring-time growth in the garden it is easy to overlook your soil: after all, brown earth is not as appealing as a pretty blossom. Many gardeners put all their efforts into the above-ground parts of their garden, forgetting what is going on below soil level. Half of every plant lies hidden in the soil, feeding and supporting the leaf and flower growth above.

To cater for your whole plant, it is important to understand soil, compost, mulching, fertilizing and the organisms that make it all happen. There are three main factors in improving the soil in your garden: mulch, compost and fertilizers.

Instead of putting out green waste for the council collection, consider buying a shredder to convert prunings into mulch.

Mulch

Mulch provides a blanket layer over your soil. Normally about 10 cm thick, it:

• regulates soil temperature, by keeping roots cool in summer and warm in winter;
• conserves moisture and cuts down on watering requirements by reducing evaporation from the soil surface and increasing water penetration; and
• controls weeds by preventing weed seeds from germinating.

Mulches are available in many forms, both organic and inorganic. Organic mulches include leaf mould, chipped bark (especially pine bark), wood chips, straw, newspaper, garden compost, and well-rotted animal or poultry manure. An effective mulch should not be dislodged by wind and rain and should have a loose enough structure to allow water to soak through easily.

Some mulches — for example, garden compost and animal or poultry manure — have a high nitrogen content. These mulches improve the soil fertility, but they rot down quickly and so need to be topped up annually. Never use peat as a mulch as it repels water once it is dry.

Inorganic mulches — such as black plastic, weed control mat and decorative gravels — are not really 'garden friendly': they add nothing to the soil structure, and once these mulches are in place, soil

Pebble mulch Use decorative pebbles as mulch dressings in pots.

additives are difficult to incorporate. They tend to raise the soil temperature and some can even stop your soil from breathing, which can lead to serious problems.

Depending on the time of year at which you mulch, you can influence soil temperatures. For example, if you mulch at the end of autumn, you will keep the soil warmer for longer, while mulching in early spring will keep the soil cooler and prevent overheating in summer.

Composting

Organic matter in the process of breaking down is referred to as compost. This organic content brings your soil to life by adding humus and is essential for sustaining living plants. Without organic matter your soil is 'dead'. The breakdown and decay of both animal and vegetable materials produces compost, which is rich in the essential elements that are needed for plant growth.

The composting process is a complex one, employing countless micro-organisms to bring about chemical changes in organic waste matter (see page 24 for information about how to establish a compost heap). These microscopic workers like plenty of air, a little moisture and heat in order to perform their composting duties; they also rely on a good carbon/nitrogen ratio. You can achieve this ratio in your compost heap by incorporating a balanced mix of wet (vegetables and grass) and dry (for example, leaf litter) ingredients, as well as by regularly turning the mix.

Adding compost to the garden is a natural way of aiding water retention and maintaining a rich, quality soil. Compost is in effect nature's miracle tonic. Composting can convert bulky 'rubbish' into a fertilizer that is of great benefit to the soil. If you add organic matter to your soil in the form of compost on a regular basis, even a poor soil can be transformed into a rich, friable organic loam which in no time will be teeming with worms.

Some organic mulches:

1 Coarse wood chip.

2 Fine wood chip.

3 Wood chip (stained redwood).

4 Leaf litter.

5 Pine bark.

6 Finely chipped pine.

All the fertile areas of this planet have at least once passed through the bodies of earthworms.

Charles Darwin

Worms

Worms are natural recyclers, converting vegetative matter into nutrient-rich worm castings. Once introduced, worms will multiply rapidly and greatly increase the aeration of the soil and the nitrogen content. Compost worms will eat their way through kitchen scraps and garden waste and produce castings that can be used on the garden.

A worm farm full of compost worms is even better than a compost heap. A typical worm farm comprises three different layers: the top layer of paper scraps and organic matter, a centre layer where worms nest, and a bottom layer of castings (worm poo). Add food scraps to the top layer and, as the worms consume them, keep adding more food. Note, however, that worms do not like banana, citrus, onion or garlic.

You can keep adding layers and the worms will migrate to the new layer and begin the process again. As chambers fill with waste, empty them into the garden or into pots.

If you occasionally pour water into the farm, it will filter through the worm castings and can be collected via a tap that allows you to drain off and use the liquid waste. (See 'Worms' in 'Autumn'.) Use this waste diluted to 1:10 with water.

Right (top to bottom): Blood, fish and bone, milled cow manure, slow-release fertilizer, complete plant food, soluble fertilizer and pelletized chicken manure.

Fertilizers

Even if they are growing in great soil with added compost and mulch, plants sometimes need supplementary feeding. With so many different fertilizers on the market, it is hard to know what to use and when to use it.

Fertilizers can be separated into 'natural' fertilizers, such as seaweed extract and animal manures, and artificial combinations or chemical fertilizers. Each type of fertilizer offers benefits, but they are of different kinds. Organic fertilizers can encourage the growth of soil organisms and lead to better structured soils. Chemical fertilizers can be fast acting and balanced, and many are designed to cater for the specific needs of certain plants such as tomatoes, flowers, roses and fruit trees.

Fertilizers are classified according to their component ratio of nitrogen, potassium and phosphorus (known as the NPK ratio). These are particularly important elements, as they are needed for basic plant growth and function and are used in relatively large quantities. The 'big three' are all highly soluble, so if you are overly generous and apply an excess of fertilizer it washes straight into waterways and will eventually cause algal growth. It is particularly important to remember this when you are feeding your lawn.

Handy feeding hints

- Always fertilize when the soil is moist and water thoroughly after you have completed the application.
- If in doubt, apply fertilizer at half-strength twice as often.
- Plants don't use much food in winter, so don't bother feeding then. Spring, summer and autumn feeds are generally better value.
- Nitrogen is responsible for leaf growth, but too much nitrogen can cause floppy growth and poor flowers.
- Phosphorus is vital for strong roots and stems but is often deficient in soils. In this case apply a dressing of either superphosphate or a complete fertilizer containing this element. If you are growing plants in the Proteaceae family, bear in mind that they do not like high levels of phosphorus in the soil.
- Potassium maintains the rigidity of plants and is important in promoting flowering.

Soil pH

Gardening books often speak of the pH range. The pH is a measure of acidity and alkalinity, based on a scale of 1 to 14, with 1 being extremely acid and 14 being extremely alkaline. Test your soil to see if your plants are compatible with the pH. Some plants, including rhododendrons, camellias, pieris, kalmias, heathers and hydrangeas (where blue flowers are

wanted) require a range of 4.5 to 5.5 (acid). Most garden plants — including roses, bedding plants, annuals, mints, grasses and ferns — prefer soils that are slightly acid to neutral.

Nearly all members of the pea family (wisteria, peas, beans, sweet peas and clovers), iris, lilac, hydrangeas (where pink flowers are wanted) and many rockery plants and herbs prefer alkaline soils with a pH range of 6.5 to 7.5.

Foliar feeding works regardless of soil pH and is handy in some cases. Use diluted liquid fertilizer over the leaves so they can absorb the nutrients directly.

TESTING SOIL pH

1 Place the soil sample in a tube (the tube should be about ⅕ full).

2 Pour in the chemical solution supplied.

3 Shake.

4 Let the sample settle. The colour change indicates whether the soil is alkaline or acidic. This test shows that the soil is alkaline.

For washing and storing the test kit, follow the manufacturer's instructions.

worm farm

Worm farms are ideal for households with small amounts of waste which can then be turned into a nutritious plant food or mulch. The system harnesses the natural capacity of compost worms to consume green waste, the by-products being worm castings and a liquid manure. You can buy worm farms from some garden supply companies but you may have to hunt around for a supplier.

Build up your compost heap with alternate layers of wet and dry material. Wet material is high in nitrogen and low in carbon and thus helps to break down dry material, which is low in nitrogen and high in carbon. A compost heap works faster if some things are already broken down – that is, if the material already has organisms in it. Lime helps to balance pH, as the other materials are very acid. Both blood, fish and bone and chicken manure also help to break down other materials as they are both high in nitrogen.

How to manufacture compost

You can build a basic compost heap by spreading a 10 cm layer of leaves, kitchen waste or other vegetative matter over a square metre or so of bare earth. Cover this with a layer of soil, then with a layer of animal manure. Repeat the layers as vegetative matter becomes available. You can use shredded prunings, leaves and grass clippings, and keep the pile topped with straw to shed rain water.

A more sophisticated method is to use multiple bins. Three bins used in rotation are ideal: use the first bin for filling, the second for maturing and the third for holding the usable completed compost.

However, you can build many different multiple-bin systems. A two-bin system such as the one shown opposite is ideal. Concrete blocks, preferably the breeze block sort if you can get hold of some, can be used to construct the back wall. You could place a concrete slab at the base of the bins or build them on well-firmed soil, which is the preferred method.

Compost should be composed of a mixture of materials. A compost heap or bin won't work if only cut grass or only kitchen scraps are used. You should layer the compost materials with prunings, vegetable peelings, cut grass, a bucket of soil and a handful of blood and bone to encourage the

All really grim gardeners possess a keen sense of humus.

W. C. Sellar and R. J. Yeatman

rapid multiplication of soil bacteria and fungal decomposers. When a bin has been filled, spread 2 cm of soil on top and press it down to help keep the heat in and the rain out.

Compost tumblers are possibly the quickest way to make compost. Manufacturers of compost tumblers claim the tumbling process takes just fourteen days to convert a load of fresh organic matter into rich crumbly compost. You do not add material day by day — instead, completely fill the tumbler with four parts of moist organic material to one part of dry. Make sure the mixture is not too wet (add more dry material such as straw if it is). Turn the tumbler five or six times each day to aerate the mixture so that the heat builds through the centre.

MAKING A COMPOST HEAP

1—3 Collect the 'ingredients'.

4 Kitchen scraps.

5 Mushroom compost.

6 Prunings.

7 Lime.

8 Liquid compost.

9 Applying manure.

10 Chicken manure.

11 Leaf mulch.

12 Cross-section of heap.

compost bins

This wooden bin has removable doors and two compartments; when one is full but not ready, use the other. The boards along the back are permanently fixed, while the side and front boards are removable. These boards fit into slots formed by rails nailed on to the posts, and are spaced 3 cm apart to allow air to circulate. Each bin measures 1.5 x 1.5 x 1.5 m which is a good workable size. Treated pine is the best material for the timber sections.

All creatures great and small

Make your garden a place everyone and everything can enjoy. It is an unexpected delight to find lizards basking on a rock or butterflies flittering about from blossom to blossom.

Birds and non-domestic animals need three essential creature comforts to make your place their home.

- Food. For a supply of nectar in your garden to attract bees and butterflies plant asters, buddlejas, heathers, lavenders and monarda; to attract birds (with seeds and berries) try cotoneasters, ornamental grasses, hollies, poppies, shrub roses and sunflowers.
- Water. Birdbaths need to be shallow with a depth of only a few centimetres or birds can drown — place some rocks in deeper water containers so that birds have something to perch on.
- Shelter. Hollow logs, thickets of holly and rhododendron, and low branching shrubs provide excellent shelter. Remember, dogs and cats will act as a great deterrent.

Bug watch

Spring is normally quiet on the bug front, but sometimes you will find black sooty mould on the leaves of your plants (that black substance which can be rubbed or scraped off the leaves with a little effort). You may be inclined to think it is a fungus; however, the problem is actually a secondary one related to insects such as scale or aphids. Spray the insects with a

suitable insecticide, and wash the leaves with washing soda or soapy water (made with pure soap flakes).

It can be very difficult to treat large trees that are infested or diseased, but you can reduce the stress they undergo and help them rectify problems naturally by giving adequate water and by hosing down the foliage.

Not so creepy crawlies

Encourage the good guys: nature hates any imbalance in the environment, so destroying all insects could leave your plants vulnerable to other problems. A better way is to encourage balance.

- Attract beneficial insects by dotting parsley, dill and Queen Anne's lace about, and by planting perfumed shrubs.
- Birds eat lots of grubs, but will only venture into your garden if there is water to drink and some low-growing bushes for them to perch on in safety. Growing some plants that produce seed and nectar will also encourage birds to stay.
- Lizards eat snails and slugs, but will be frightened away by dogs and cats. Rocks, hollow logs and sections of pipe will help to make them feel safe.
- Spiders eat insects too, so try to control the urge to kill them unless, of course, they are known to be harmful to humans.
- Plant some flowers in your vegetable garden to attract pollinators such as bees.
- The young juicy foliage of seedlings is delicious to snails and slugs. Guard seedlings with snail bait, or try putting beer in shallow containers around the garden. The slugs and snails drown in the yeasty brew.
- Tall new growth is attacked by aphids, so be vigilant and hose them off. Alternatively, spray accessible foliage with a pyrethrum-based insecticide.

Far left and left: Nectar-laden plants, such as these kniphofias, and birdbaths, attract beneficial insects and grub-eating birds.

Above, top to bottom: Aphids secrete sticky honeydew on which unsightly sooty mould grows; the delicate flowers of Queen Anne's lace attract beneficial insects such as bees; and the grubs of ladybirds or ladybugs devour huge quantities of aphids.

Spring fever

With millions of people suffering from seasonal hay fever or asthma each spring and summer, it makes sense to know more about the plants in your garden, and which ones may be harmful. Allergies to plants are quite common, and usually run in a family.

Allergies are hypersensitive reactions of the body's immune system to specific substances called allergens, which include pollen. The most common allergies are those that involve skin and breathing problems. In fact, most people will suffer from some sort of allergic reaction at some time in their life, even if it is just a lump from a bee sting!

A frightening fact is that an increasing number of children are asthmatic, and skin allergies, including eczema and contact dermatitis, are also on the increase. Therefore it makes sense to understand how problems can be avoided through careful planting and the development of a low-allergen garden.

Allergy triggers

Pollen has been shown to be a major cause of allergy-related breathing problems. All flowering plants produce pollen at some time in their life, but those that rely on wind for dispersal produce so much pollen

that it can easily enter our lungs and trigger a response.

Grasses are among the worst flowering plants for hay fever. Depending on species, they start flowering in spring in some areas and continue into summer. So avoid meadows when grasses are in flower. In the garden, avoid planting ornamental grasses such as pampas grass and miscanthus varieties. Lawn grasses are not a problem as regular mowing prevents their flowering.

Similarly, spores from ferns, fungi and mosses float freely in the air, and can create problems. Some fragrant plants can also act as an irritant, giving rise to an attack of asthma or hay fever. Common perpetrators include honeysuckle, carnations, lilies and sweet Williams. The pollen of plants in the daisy family, including chrysanthemums, marigolds and zinnias, can be a hazard.

Wind-pollinated trees, including native species, should be avoided as they produce masses of pollen. Examples include beech and oaks, but do check at your garden centre before buying as not all trees cause problems. Many of the smaller ornamentals are pollinated by insects and therefore the pollen does not generally cause a problem for hay fever sufferers.

Some plants are so toxic that if they come into contact with the skin they cause allergic responses, and not just in people with allergic tendencies. These plants, which should be excluded from all gardens, include the rhus tree (*Toxicodendron succedaneum*) and poison ivy (*Rhus radicans*). Other plants that should be avoided if you are prone to allergies include daphne, lily-of-the-valley, oleander, gloriosa lily, castor oil plant and deadly nightshade.

Strategies for healthy gardening

Wearing protective clothing such as gloves, a hat, long sleeves and sunglasses is a good way of avoiding problems. The time of the year you choose to garden is also important —·choose sunny days in winter, when pollen numbers are down, to do big tidy-ups in the garden.

Spring is a bad time of year as this is when many wind-pollinated trees such as poplars, willows, liquidambars, oaks and many conifers are in flower. Do not create wildflower meadows in your garden (a practice which is a current fashion) as the native flowering grasses and wildflowers that are used in such meadows will affect hay fever sufferers.

Hot summer days seem to be worse for skin allergies and summer nights worse for fungal spores, so be mindful of this when you are outside.

Many of our gardening practices can also cause problems. Mulch, especially pine bark, can harbour fungal spores that trigger attacks. Although not the best for the garden, black plastic and gravel mulches are the easiest on sufferers' respiratory systems. Other fine organic materials such as blood, fish and bone fertilizer can also cause problems and are best avoided if you or your neighbours react.

Once you have gone to all this trouble, don't then spoil your efforts by spraying with garden chemicals. Always try organic methods first.

Whatever the time of year, apply sunscreen if necessary and wear a hat, long sleeves and good work boots.

Planting your new, low-allergen garden

Having eliminated many plants from the garden, you'll probably want to replace them with more suitable species.

- Annuals and biennials: snapdragons, begonias, impatiens, forget-me-not, petunias, salvia, pansies, phlox and love-in-a-mist
- Perennials: bear's breeches, agapanthus, Japanese windflower, columbine, daylily, penstemon, oriental poppy and Jacob's ladder
- Ground covers: bugle, lady's mantle, cranesbill, hosta, lamium, catmint and periwinkle
- Climbers: clematis, Virginia creeper, passion flower, ornamental grape and 'Iceberg' rose
- Shrubs: camellias, deutzia, escallonia, fuchsias, hebes, hydrangeas, smoke tree, viburnums, weigela and photinia
- Trees: bottlebrush, tupelo (*Nyssa*), Irish strawberry tree, magnolias, crab apples, ornamental pears and tulip trees

Plants for containers

Many plants work well in confined spaces and some won't upset the allergy sufferer. Choose from agapanthus, camellias, convolvulus, cordyline, fuchsia, hebe, hydrangea, iris, floribunda roses, salvia and petunia. You can choose virtually any container, from a plastic tub to an old chimney pot — perfect for those gardeners limited by age, ill health or lack of space.

Top: Irish strawberry tree.

Bottom: Chinese forget-me-not (*Cynoglossum*).

spring
annuals,
perennials & bulbs

Spring is certainly the time to admire your hard work in the garden. In fact, nature puts on such a wonderful display during spring that even the laziest gardener has something to delight in, even if it's just the sunshine!

Admired most are spring flowers — the bulbs, annuals and perennials that produce such a fanfare, celebrating the sunshine and this fair season. Sow new seeds for summer now and also consider bulbs which flower then too; gladioli, for example, need to be planted in spring.

Annuals

Planting annuals is the best way to revitalize a tired, lifeless garden. Annuals are cheap, take only about six weeks to flower from seedlings and come in a huge range of colours and varieties.

Geranium cinereum
'Lawrence Flatman'.

People from a planet without flowers would think we must be mad with joy the whole time, to have such things about us.

Iris Murdoch

Bedding plants, as they are also known, only live for one season (hence the name 'annual'), which means you can change colour schemes to create different effects each season.

This spring, for example, you could effectively paint a picture in your garden with pansies, primroses and Iceland poppies. For a bold and bright statement, try a mix of orange sweeping across plush purple to create a flamboyant effect, using wallflowers and pansies. A mix of butter yellow and snowy white mingled with shades of sky blue flowers, using double daisies, primroses, forget-me-nots and violas, will add cheer to your garden. Alternatively, choose the exotic colours of the orient, perhaps a spicy mix of cinnamon and soft rose, using pansies and wallflowers.

A river of colour

High light intensity calls for the use of strong colour in the garden. Try using single, bold colours such as royal blue, dark velvety green and sunny yellow, or rich combinations, to create an impact.

For a different look, plant your seedlings in 'rivers' of colour rather than in rows. Simply prepare the soil with added compost and a slow-release pelletized organic fertilizer. Rake this into a fine bed, then map out rivers using a stick. Transplant your raised seedlings into these swirls in thick bands.

To make the effect as striking as possible use contrasting colours such as purple and orange, or even foliage colour contrast such as the green leaves of parsley mixed with red flowers. Another striking combination can be achieved by mixing opal-leaved basil with golden yellow flowers. Choose plants of similar height, so that one variety doesn't tower over another, and limit your selection to three or four plants.

For bright spring colour plant annuals such as wallflowers (strictly a biennial) and sweet peas. The latter normally bloom from early summer but in warm climates or under glass they will flower earlier.

Viola tricolor.

White alyssum, blue violas and parsley.

White gardens

A white garden is the essence of simplicity, yet reveals in its detail a myriad of possibilities and intricacies.

The overall effect of a white garden is fresh and pure, yet a closer examination will reveal creams, soft pink centres, pale yellows and off-whites all blending with the various greens of foliage in a calm and natural harmony.

White is especially useful for night gardens, because the colour glows under moonlight, and also for small gardens as it can make a space feel larger than it really is.

Black gardens

Much has been written about white, but rarely does its flip side, black, get a mention. Black flowers do exist, and can be quite beautiful. Pansies, tulips, scabiosa, carnations, hollyhocks, columbines, hellebores, cranesbills and iris all have black or purplish black varieties.

Some of these darker flowers rely on flies to pollinate their blooms and so have unpleasant odours, such as the *Dracunculus vulgaris*. The brown-maroon chocolate cosmos (*Cosmos atrosanguineus*) doesn't fall into this category, however; it has a delicious chocolate scent.

Another interesting addition to a black garden is the globe artichoke 'Violetto di Chioggia', which has silver leaves and almost black edible flower heads. The black rose continues to elude breeders!

Clockwise from left: Queen Anne's lace (anthriscus); *Geranium phaeum*, a 'black' flower; and a refreshing armful of white and green flowers.

poppies

Delicate, silken, crepe-like blooms sway in the breeze held high on slender, downy stalks . . . such apparent fragility masks the true nature of these brilliant survivors which grow wild in the fields of Europe, Asia and North Africa. Poppy flowers add brilliant splashes of colour to the garden, and look stunning grown as a mass planting or among perennials. In mild and warm climates some poppies, particularly the Iceland poppies, start flowering in spring. In colder areas, flowering starts from early summer.

The Iceland poppy, *Papaver nudicaule*, is just one of a group containing many famous plants. The dried latex of the opium poppy (*P. somniferum*) is made into a narcotic; its seed is used to flavour curries or decorate cakes and bread. The Flanders or field poppy (*P. rhoeas*) has a single scarlet flower with a black blotch. Growing wild in the fields of Flanders it has become a symbol of the lives lost in World War I. The Shirley poppy is a cultivar of *P. rhoeas*.

Vital statistics

Scientific name: *Papaver* sp.
Family: Papaveraceae.
Climate: Grow best in areas with cool winters.
Culture: Cut back withering poppy heads to the base.
Colours: Flowers come in reds, pinks, oranges, yellow, white.
Height: Grow to 40 cm to 1 m in height, depending on species.
Planting time: Sow annuals and biennials in spring (the latter will flower in the following year).
Soil: Grow in free-draining fertile soil kept on the dry side.
Position: Poppies love sun and protection from strong winds.
Planting spacing: Plant at 20–30 cm intervals.
Fertilizer: Top dress with complete fertilizer in spring once roots have established.
Pests/diseases: There are occasional fungal problems in humid areas, so water plants early in the day.
Cutting: Poppies make great cut flowers if their stems are plunged into hot water or scorched over a flame. Seed pods of some species can make decorative dried arrangements.
Propagation: Grow from seed.

two **basket plants**

Plan now for summer by planting a basket – either orchid cactus or begonia (*Begonia fuchsioides* shown above). Choose a dappled shade position protected from wind for begonia (but not outside until frosts are over), and a conservatory for the orchid cactus. *Epiphyllum*, a spineless cactus, is ideal. Many flower earlier in the season, but the spectacular 'Lady of the Night', *E. oxypetalum*, has large white nocturnal flowers that are intensely fragrant, especially on nights with a full moon. The foliage is confused with Christmas cactus (formerly *Zygocactus* sp., but now *Schlumbergera* sp.) which flower in winter. The ultimate greenhouse plant, begonias are really succulent perennials, great for growing in bare patches under camellias or azaleas, but also terrific for hanging baskets in sheltered patios. Choose from the double rose-like blooms of tuberous begonias and the stunning stained-glass leaves of Rex types.

check list

jobs to do now

- With so much flowering occurring at this time of year, it is important to remove spent blossoms. This 'deadheading' not only makes plants look fresher, it also encourages second and third flushes.

- Plant over yellowing bulbs with fast-growing flowers such as lobelias and sweet alyssum and apply liquid fertilizer fortnightly. Never cut back or plait bulb leaves while there is any green pigment left as it will stop them flowering next year.

- Divide water plants and water lilies, and clean the pond or any other water features if you are feeling really energetic.

- Don't neglect your potted plants. All repotting should be carried out by the end of spring. Don't forget to repot, fertilize and replant hanging baskets and wall pots.

- Taste-test citrus before harvesting. Some may have coloured well already but it will be some time before they are sweet enough to eat. A dose of fertilizer won't go astray either.

plant now

- New season seedlings such as marigolds, cleomes, cosmos, dahlias and salvias can all be put in now once frosts are over.

- Annuals such as sunflowers and California poppies are easy to grow, and they have cheery flowers that make them perfect for children's gardens.

- Plant summer-flowering perennials such as agapanthus, delphiniums and border phlox.

- Dahlia tubers can be planted now and are great for cut flowers until late autumn.

- There are many other bulbs besides spring-flowering daffodils and tulips. Check out some of the stunning summer-flowering bulbs that are planted at this time of year.

A mixture of gladioli (both the large-flowered and the small-flowered varieties), lilies, pineapple flowers (eucomis) and the frost-tender tiger flower (tigridia) will make a good display and the gladioli are particularly good for cutting.

flowering now

- Colourful annuals and biennials such as sweet alyssum in mild areas, primulas (especially polyanthus and coloured primroses), some poppies, wallflowers, forget-me-nots, snapdragons in mild areas, English or double daisies, pot marigolds, pansies and violas, honesty (lunaria) and nigellas or love-in-a-mist in mild areas.

- Perennials flowering in spring include Solomon's seal, irises (including bearded), aquilegias or columbines, some species of foxglove, peonies, red valerian, perennial candytuft, violets, primulas, thrift, some species of speedwell, bleeding heart, some geraniums or cranesbills, lupins in very mild areas, bugle, hellebores, leopard's bane, lungwort, aubrieta, bergenias, epimediums, lily-of-the-valley and saxifrages.

- Bulbs that flower in spring include tuberous windflowers or anemones, ranunculus or Persian buttercup, bluebells, Dutch irises, daffodils, tulips, hyacinths, crocuses, ornamental alliums, baboon flower (frost tender), star of Bethlehem, fritillaries, grape hyacinth, harlequin flower (half-hardy), ipheion or spring star flower, scilla, glory of the snow, snowdrops and snowflakes.

Perennials

The emergence of the garden from winter dormancy into the full flush of spring growth is part of the magic of the season.

The perennials in your garden can easily be overlooked when many of them are sleeping during winter, but they in fact remain alive for a number of years. Although some perennials have foliage that dies back, the rootstock is permanent, a bit like a bulb. Like annuals, perennials can provide a colourful display, but they have the advantage that they don't need to be replanted each year.

Perennials can be planted among shrubs or used as a backdrop to annuals. The classic perennial border is a bed wide enough to display a range of plants, and long enough for some repetition of plantings to create a lovely flow and rhythm. Perennials vary widely in size, shape and colour, and there are plants to suit every climate, aspect and soil.

The value of the vertical

Although a sea of colour can be spectacular, you could create contrast by punctuating the horizontal level with spear-like plants that spire into the sky. Apart from some irises and early foxgloves and lupins, there are few perennials that give this effect in spring — you will have to wait for summer-flowering kinds, including foxgloves and lupins, delphiniums, verbascums, hollyhocks and acanthus.

A selection of popular spring-flowering perennials (clockwise from top left): Solomon's seal, bleeding heart, pulmonaria and bergenia.

peony

It seems unfair that we have to wait a whole year between a show of blooms, but unfortunately the peony only flowers in late spring/early summer. The peony (a perennial), a rhizome native to China, Tibet and Siberia, is the classic inclusion for a cool-climate border. There is probably no more important or rewarding flower than the peony, which has been grown in China for 2500 years.

One great asset peonies have is a very long life — there are specimens more than 100 years old in Asian temple gardens. One reason for their long life is that they are so resistant to pests and disease — they have no natural enemies. Peonies have been a symbol of beauty through the centuries, and their forms and great range of colours are sublime.

Vital statistics

Scientific name: *Paeonia* sp.

Family: Paeoniaceae.

Climate: Best suited to cooler and cold areas.

Colours: Pink, rose, red, white, purple.

Height: Bushes grow to around 1 m.

Planting time: Plant during autumn.

Soil and culture: Soil should be rich, well-drained, well-dug, neutral to slightly alkaline, and on the heavy side. Enrich the soil with compost and well-rotted farm manure (fowl is best) as these plants are gross feeders. If the soil is acid a handful of lime mixed with the prepared soil will help them along (a handful of lime per square metre). Do not use peat or cow manure. Mix in a large bucket of screened compost and add to this 500 g of bone meal or other general fertilizer.

Position: Open aspect, good light and shelter from strong winds; if they have a cool root run these plants will grow freely in most soils in sun or partial shade. Peonies sulk if grass grows too closely around them, but recover quickly when it is removed.

Planting depth and spacing: Plant with the crown at soil level and 60 cm apart.

Watering: Water well in dry weather and generously while they are flowering.

Fertilizer: Top dress annually after blooming with blood, fish and bone or old manure, or mulch with compost or add leaf mould and bone meal. The occasional addition of a handful of wood ash is also a good idea.

Pests/diseases: *Botrytis paeoniae* or peony wilt may attack stems causing wilt. Cut out affected stems.

Cutting: Remove spent blooms. Do not let peonies seed. While bushes are young cut few flowers; with plants four years old and over cut up to two thirds of the blooms.

Propagation: Propagate by division in autumn. Plant the divisions with the buds at soil level, firming the soil well around the roots without damaging the buds.

Storage: Divide and replant as soon as possible.

Meadow magic

Spring lends itself to a haphazard planting style, with the plants themselves driving the design. If you are not the neat, obsessive type, then don't succumb to a clipped, manicured garden. Instead give your creativity free rein by planting a selection of spillovers, cover-ups and wild things.

Many annuals and even some perennials have adapted perfectly to our climate. They will pop up in any little crevice, put on a show and then fade away as quickly as they came. This self-seeding process creates a delightful link with nature and can often produce chance associations that are far more effective than anything you could design. Often these little treasures are the plants that remain in old gardens. What are they, how can you obtain them and how are they best used in your garden?

If you want to create a relaxed, cottage feeling in your garden, try to encourage plants to self-seed. This may mean putting up with some messy plants as you wait for the seed heads to form fully. It also means weeding and disturbing the soil as little as possible, as tiny plants are hard to see and can easily be damaged. Try to keep the garden moist, and wait until spring before mulching so that young seedlings are large enough to be noticed and left undisturbed.

Annual favourites include forget-me-nots with their pink or eggshell blue flowers, marvellous plants if kept in check, and Johnny-jump-up, a self-seeding viola sometimes called heartsease. Various other

Johnny-jump-ups (top) and forget-me-nots (above) are two self-seeding favourites in the spring garden.

More grows in the garden than was sown there.

Traditional saying

annual and perennial self-seeders include columbines, also known as granny's bonnets, sweet alyssum, primulas and honesty. *Erigeron karvinskianus* — which goes by various names such as fleabane and Mexican daisy — can also be a lovely ground cover, but be warned, it will overtake everything if given the chance.

The columbines, stone blue,
or deep night brown,
Their honey-comb like blossoms
hanging down;
Each cottage garden's fond
adopted child,
Though heaths still claim them,
where they yet grow wild.

John Clare

Many perennials propagate themselves asexually, spreading into massive clumps. These plants can be great for stifling weeds. Lungwort and epimediums work well under established trees, as does the arum lily. The bugle (*Ajuga reptans*) is another vigorous grower in difficult semi-shaded areas and comes in lovely cultivars, including variegated and large-leaved types. Don't forget that old-fashioned sweet violets can be used in these conditions as well.

Quite surprisingly many spring-flowering perennials are more suited to positions in partial shade, but spring-flowering kinds for more open, sunny spots include irises of all kinds, early flowering

Top to bottom: *Aquilegia vulgaris* 'Black Barlow', *A. vulgaris* 'Nora Barlow' and *A. flabellata*.

geraniums (also taking partial shade), aubrieta and leopard's bane. Vigorous clump-forming perennials flowering at other times of year include the autumn-flowering asters or Michaelmas daisies, with masses of varieties, as have summer-flowering campanulas or bellflowers.

Aquilegias

These enchanting spring-flowering perennials are a delightful addition to any shaded, moist garden spot. Although each plant lasts only a few years, aquilegias or columbines tend to self-seed, creating new and interesting colour combinations and popping up where you least expect.

Aquilegias flower in spring, but their foliage is attractive for most of the year: it has a fine, delicate look to it, not unlike maidenhair fern or rue. Divide each plant in autumn when it looks scruffy, and keep well watered in dry weather.

Many named varieties are now available. Mostly large-flowered hybrids, they have long- and short-spurred forms and vary in colour from purest white, through to lemon, burgundy, blue and various bicolours.

The Ranunculaceae family

The buttercup family contains about fifty genera, including perennial herbs, such as aquilegia, meadow rue (*Thalictrum*), windflowers (*Anemone*), hellebores and buttercups; annuals such as larkspur, delphinium and love-in-a-mist; climbers such as clematis; or tuberous perennials (often regarded as bulbs by gardeners) such as ranunculus. Happiest in cooler temperate regions, many members of this family are poisonous when eaten.

Top to bottom: *Aquilegia* 'Blue Peat', *A. chrysantha* var. *chaplinei* 'Yellow Queen' and *A. alpina*.

Did you know? Columbine, the common name of *Aquilegia*, comes from the Latin word for dove. It refers to the flying spurs behind the flower's face.

MASHING BERRIES

1 Some flax lily (*Dianella* sp.) seeds.

2 With your hand inside a large jar, mash the berries with your fingers.

3 Add some water to the jar, replace the lid and give it a good shake.

4 Remove the pulp, which should have floated to the top, and retrieve the seeds once they have settled on the bottom of the jar.

Gone to seed

All seeds have an optimum temperature range at which they germinate best. This range is mostly between 15°C and 25°C, so spring and early autumn generally make the most appropriate times to sow seeds.

A seed is a miniaturized plant, packed and stored within a protective coat, waiting for the perfect conditions that will give it its start in life. Some plants will easily self-seed, others may need collecting, treating, sowing and transplanting. Seeds from dry seed heads can be shaken or rubbed from the plant, with any debris removed. In many cases, collecting seed heads in paper bags will help contain the seed as it falls.

Seeds enclosed in fleshy fruits or berries need more vigorous treatment. First mash the fruit, then place the results in a jar with water and shake. The pulp that floats to the top can be removed, leaving behind the seeds, which can then be dried and stored in paper bags.

Certain seeds need to be stimulated out of dormancy before they will germinate. Some cold climate plants need an artificial cool time (called stratification) for germination to occur. This is an adaptation to prevent seeds from germinating until the last of the cold weather is over, so that late frosts or snow don't harm the young seedlings. Other seeds respond to heat and smoke (which is in effect the simulation of a bushfire) or drought. Hard seed coats can prevent plants from germinating by keeping out air and water, two vital ingredients in the process, and the seeds will therefore need to be chipped or rubbed with abrasive paper (a process called scarification) before sowing. (See 'Seed treatment' opposite.)

All are most interesting, whether feathered like the polished silvery shuttlecocks of the Cornflower, to whirl in the wind abroad and settle presently, point downward, into the hospitable ground; or oared like the Maple, to row out upon the viewless tides of the air.

Celia Thaxter

Once you have treated your seeds in the appropriate way, sow them in containers. Most seeds should be sown in a seed tray initially, then pricked out and planted into larger containers as the seedling develops.

When sowing very fine seed, such as that of rhododendron, campanula, gloxinia, impatiens, lobelia, polyanthus, African violets and primulas, add fine dry sand to make spreading the seeds easier. Just tamp these seeds down slightly after sowing, rather than covering them over. Add sand to hairy seeds to stop them sticking.

Slightly larger seed can be sown straight from the packet or container. Draw a line (called a 'drill') with a pencil, sow the seed, then backfill slightly. Most seed can be handled like this, including seeds of asparagus, broccoli, cauliflower, chives, dianthus, eggplant, freesia, fuchsia, lettuce, onions, parsley, penstemon, phlox, salvia, tomato, verbena and violas. Even larger seed can be sown directly into clumps, while very large seed should be sown individually into pots.

Pricking out, or removing seedlings from trays, can be done after the first set of true leaves appears (these are the baby pair of leaves, or cotyledons) and before the third set has arrived, to minimize root damage. The more leaves a seedling grows, the more roots they also develop; and these roots might be disturbed by transplanting. Always harden plants off before planting them out.

A spell in an open, shaded position toughens them up and is particularly important if you have covered your seedling tray with glass to keep the warmth and moisture in. Try to gradually acclimatize the seedlings to cooler growing conditions, and watch that your seedlings don't dry out or get eaten by pests at this stage. (See 'Sowing seeds: Five steps to success' on page 107.)

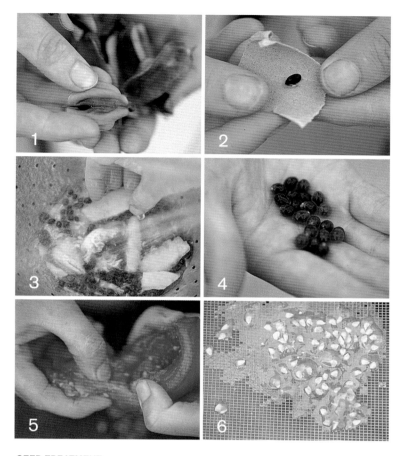

SEED TREATMENT

1 Hard seeds, such as these wattle seeds, need to be scarified.

2 Simply rub the seeds with some abrasive paper. Alternatively, soak wattle or other native Australian or South African seeds in some smoky water: the smoke in the water mimics a bushfire and stimulates the seeds to germinate.

3 With large seeds, such as paw paw seeds, use a hose and your fingers to push the pulp through the holes of a colander.

4 Dry the seeds before sowing them.

5 Remove the pulp and seeds from tomatoes.

6 Push the pulp through a fine mesh and then dry the tomato seeds on some kitchen paper.

the **pros** and **cons** of seeds

The advantages of raising plants from seed are cost, access to interesting new genetic material, variation and variety, ready availability, and minimal storage and space requirements. This must be weighed against the possible loss of particular characteristics (such as flower colour) which may change in the second generation, particularly in the case of annuals and biennials.

Stocks are loved for their spicy, clove-scented blooms. They also provide the gardener with a vast array of colours.

Growing plants for cut flowers

Although it is easy to have flowers in the garden during spring, filling your house with homegrown arrangements is rewarding too. Bringing flowers inside is a sure path to enormous pleasure.

Flowers for all seasons

The capacity of a garden to produce flowers will wax and wane with the weather, the time available for gardening, its inherent potential and other variables. The following selection of late winter and spring bloomers will reward your efforts reliably and are just perfect for the cutting garden.

Columbine (*Aquilegia*) self-seeds readily, popping up in unexpected places in a way that is so rewarding for the carefree gardener. Easily grown in sun or partial shade, it looks best in posies. Other great selections if you like making posies include sweet violet (*Viola odorata*) which blooms in late winter and early spring. The blue or sometimes white flowers are very sweetly scented. It self-seeds prolifically so you will never be without plants in the garden. Forget-me-nots or myosotis are great for posies as are the perennial cynoglossums or hound's tongue, similar to forget-me-nots, some of which flower in spring.

Borage is an annual herb and is the type of plant that is a friend for life as it self-sows freely. Unfortunately it can become almost weed-like in some gardens. Seeds are sown in spring where they are to flower and plants may start blooming later in the season in mild areas, but summer is the main flowering period. The pendulous, starry, bright blue flowers are excellent for cutting. They are edible and can be crystallized for cake decoration. Borage thrives in any well-drained soil and even tolerates dry or drought conditions.

One of the earliest and longest flowering plants (late spring and summer) is known as red valerian (*Centranthus*). It thrives with little care in a sunny or partially shaded, well-drained position and produces masses of flowering spikes up to 1 m tall in pink, white or red. Plants like this one are great for tall, free-form arrangements.

Wallflowers (*Erysimum*) are great cut flowers as their botanical synonym, *Cheiranthus*, indicates — in Latin it literally means 'hand flower'. They add scent and colour to the garden in spring. The winter wallflower, *Erysimum* x *kewense*, is an excellent low-growing evergreen perennial which produces clusters of yellow and mauve flowers from winter to summer; these last well in a vase if the water is changed regularly.

Closely related to wallflowers are stocks, which have spicy clove-scented blooms. Although they usually need to be replaced each year, they are worth the effort for the vast array of colours you can choose from: from white to apple blossom, peach, pink, lilac, lavender and lemon tones.

Green, the new white!

Green has become fashionable! There are green chrysanthemums, green bells of Ireland, and green varieties of the late winter- and spring-flowering hellebores (*Helleborus*) and spurge (*Euphorbia*).

Finally, don't forget about beautiful blossoms. Many work well in oriental-style ikebana arrangements, and the spring-flowering magnolias and ornamental quince (*Chaenomeles*) are particular favourites.

Tips for cut flowers

- Pick flowers early in the morning.
- Stand blooms in a deep container of water in a darkened, cool room.
- Burn the ends of milky or mucilaginous sappy plants such as poppy, euphorbia, dahlia and hydrangea; this will prolong their life as it seals in the vital sap. You may either apply a burning taper to the cut end for a few seconds or immerse the tip of the cut end in boiling water.
- Keep water sweet with charcoal or oil of peppermint (one drop for 1 L).
- Alstroemerias last best in a few centimetres of water — too much water can rot them.

Clockwise from above: Spurge (*Euphorbia*), bells of Ireland or *Molucella laevis* (sow now for summer flowers) and *Helleborus argutifolius*.

Below: Burn the ends of milky plants to prolong their lives as cut flowers.

- Daisy flowers such as erigeron and chamomile (*Anthemis*) are best soaked overnight in a full sink of water.
- Waterlilies look lovely in float bowls but they close up in the late afternoon. To keep them open, carefully drop a spot of paraffin wax at the base of each petal.
- Use warm water in cold weather.
- A vase with a lot of stems in it needs to be regularly refilled with water.

Bulbs

Bulbs are an essential part of spring and there is a wealth of hardy kinds suitable for cool and cold climates. Easily grown, newly bought bulbs are almost guaranteed to flower as the flower buds are already formed in the bulbs.

Bulbs are a delightful addition to a garden, make excellent container plants and are among the easiest plants to grow. Each bulb is a surprise package — it appears from previously bare ground to excite the eye, and adds a touch of spring to the garden in a way no other plant can achieve.

Potted bulbs

If you forgot to plant your spring bulbs last autumn, don't despair. Most garden centres stock potted bulbs ready to flower. Either plant them outside for an instant touch of spring, or bring them indoors to enjoy.

Choose plants in full bud, rather than in flower, to extend the season, and spell them outdoors at night so that they last longer. Once the flowers are past their prime, simply plant them outside. The perfect spot is under the shade of a deciduous tree, but anywhere with at least half a day's sun and protection from summer winds is fine.

Feed your bulbs with liquid fertilizer as soon as flowering is over. Apply fertilizer weekly until the leaves die down. Use a general-purpose or flower-garden fertilizer, especially one based on seaweed. Feeding encourages the bulbs to grow large and this results in more flowers the following year.

display gardens

Although spring is not the time to plant most bulbs, it is a good time to visit a display garden for ideas on what to plant next autumn. Check where these gardens are in garden-visiting books. The Keukenhof at Lisse in The Netherlands is a world-famous bulb garden. Admittedly, display gardens are few and far between so the next best thing is to visit botanical or other large gardens open to the public where there should be good displays of bulbs. Again, garden-visiting books often indicate if gardens are noted for bulb displays. Many public parks also have good displays of spring bulbs.

Red tulips traditionally meant a declaration of love while yellow ones signalled 'hopeless love'.

Daffodils

Daffodils belong to the genus *Narcissus* with hundreds of varieties. They are split into groups, each with particular characteristics. Flowers come in shades of yellow, gold, white, orange or pink or in a combination of these colours. Heights vary from about 8 cm to 30 or 45 cm. Many varieties have one large flower per stem with a prominent trumpet or cup. Some have charming markings, like the old pheasant's eye daffodil (*N. poeticus* var. *recurvus*), ideal for naturalizing and cutting. The miniatures — hoop-petticoat daffodils (*N. bulbocodium* and *N. cantabricus*) and *N. cyclamineus* — only grow to 15 or 20 cm in height. Some daffodils have clusters of flowers on each stem and in some cases they are very fragrant. Good examples are the Jonquilla and Tazetta groups.

The Amaryllidaceae family

The Amaryllidaceae family contains many bulbs and perennials such as daffodils, clivia, amaryllis, snowdrops, snowflakes, crinums, nerines and spider lily (hymenocallis). Most of these plants are widely grown for garden display in spring, summer or autumn depending on genus.

The members of this family are widely distributed, with genera ranging from the tropics and subtropics to temperate climates. Many are perfect choices for bulb plantings in heated greenhouses or conservatories in cool and cold climates (they grow well in pots), while many others are perfectly hardy in these climates.

Did you know? The name daffodil is a corruption of the Old English word 'affodyle', meaning 'that which comes early'.

Top to bottom: Double daffodil, potted hyacinths and crocus.

1 'Phar Lap'. 2 'Dolomite'. 3 'Modern Art'. 4 'Professor Einstein'. 5 'Mopsy'. 6 'Memento'. 7 'Halvose'. 8 'Trim'. 9 'Avalon'. 10 'Jenny'. 11 'Flower Parade'. 12 'Glenfarclas'. 13 'Coppertone'. 14 'Moondah'.

daffodils

15 'Matador'. 16 'Phantom'. 17 'Beryl'. 18 'Dolly Mollinger'. 19 'Ethel Breen'. 20 'Gold Sprite'.
21 'Tweedle Dee'. 22 'Seagull'. 23 'Grand Monarque'.

The beauty of all iris is their unusual flower, comprising the 'standards' and 'falls' — that is, upright or drooping petals, respectively.

Iris

Named after the Greek goddess of the rainbow, the iris was also the French Royal family's emblem, known as the fleur-de-lis.

Some of these irises are spring-flowering; others bloom in early summer. Some grow from fat rhizomes or horizontal stems, including the most popular bearded irises. Many make excellent border plants, especially among perennials, while others, such as the Japanese irises, grow in shallow water or very moist conditions.

The flowers vary from red, yellow, pink, blue, purple and orange, to near black and pure white. There are over 200 species and hundreds of hybrids and cultivars.

Bearded iris

The modern garden bearded irises are hybrids and come in an amazing range of single colours and bicolours. Their graceful, elegant flowers open one or two at a time on stems held well above the fans of stiff leaves. Planted en masse they can be a breathtaking sight. Two species of iris are grown for the production of orris, used in perfumery. They are *Iris* x *germanica*, especially its variety 'Florentina', which is a major source of orris, and *I. pallida*. *Iris germanica* is the 'fleur-de-lis' (literally 'lily flower') of French history.

Louisiana iris

Bred from iris native to Louisiana and Florida in the United States, these iris have a rather flat form. Hybrids available today from specialist nurseries display colours of astonishing depth and richness. They love moist or wet, neutral to acid soil and full sun.

Japanese iris

Although these irises were grown in Japan for centuries, their origin is obscure. They are known for their beautiful flat flowers, some having wavy or frilled margins. Many have flowers that are veined or netted in deep colours. The colour range covers all the shades of blue, red and purple. Grow in shallow water or moist soil (neutral to acid).

Siberian iris

This is a group of border irises that multiply well in the right conditions. The foliage is narrower than that of some other groups and the colour range is confined mainly to white and shades of blue or purple. New varieties are heading towards pinks and reds.

Dutch iris

These bulbous irises die back after flowering in spring or summer. The stately blooms are borne singly; come in white, blue, purple and yellow; and make elegant cut flowers.

In the Spring a livelier iris changes on the burnish'd dove;
In the Spring a young man's fancy lightly turns to thoughts of love.

Alfred, Lord Tennyson

Dutch hybrid, 'Professor Blaauw'.

Spring in miniature

Why not pot up a miniature spring garden? Any container, provided it has a drainage hole, will do. Wheelbarrows, wine barrels or large pieces of broken pottery can all look great once planted with a selection of spillovers, annuals and shrubs.

Simply pick coordinating plants with various heights to achieve a staggered planting that looks great. When choosing suitable plants group together those with similar cultivation and aspect requirements, such as amount of sun.

A pretty pot could be made from grey-foliaged plants such as *Senecio cineraria* 'Silver Dust', the trailing variegated ground ivy, and brachyscome, mixed with the white-flowered *Convolvulus cneorum*, which has silvery foliage. Add some coordinating spring bulbs to make a garden microcosm.

Pot planting tips

- Windbreaks are important for balcony gardeners. Pots and hanging baskets can dry out very quickly if they are not protected by larger plants, or by a lattice or reinforced glass panelling.
- If you choose your plant material to suit the position, maintenance will be easier.
- If you are unsure of your ability to mix and match, choose uniform pots made of one material, such as sandstone.
- Check weight restrictions before buying pots — plastic may be your only choice.
- Rather than dot pots about aimlessly, place them in a logical order, perhaps grouped around a large central pot or other feature.
- To keep your potted plants perfect, use good-quality, proprietary potting compost. Feed annually with slow-release fertilizer and monthly with liquid fertilizer.
- Don't put gravel or crockery in the bottom of pots. This does very little, if anything,

POTTING A MINIATURE SPRING GARDEN

1 Plant generously and make sure you have some things that 'froth over' the pot.

2 Top up with good quality potting compost.

3 We chose *Senecio cineraria*, ground ivy, brachyscome and *Convolvulus cneorum*.

to improve drainage; in any case, it is quite unnecessary if a good-quality potting mix is used.

The language of flowers

Throughout the ages flowers have always had special significance. In the flower language of Victorian times yellow roses were associated with jealousy and white roses were said to mean secrecy. Black flowers were meant to be bad omens, and the orchid signified good business. Forget-me-nots were symbolic of lovers being true to each other despite the separation of years, and six-petalled primroses (they normally have five petals) signified that if you were in love your love was returned.

Different cultures sometimes view the same flower differently. For example, in Europe chrysanthemums are often thought of as funeral flowers, yet in Australia they are traditional Mother's Day flowers (it is autumn then in the Southern Hemisphere). Some cultures associate arum lilies with death, while for others they are attractive cut flowers, or fine plants for the garden or conservatory. Acacias or wattles, familiar in florists' shops, are a symbol of hidden love.

Above: *Helleborus* x *hybridus*, a 'black flower'.

feature bulb
snow**flake**

Snowflakes are often confused with snowdrops (*Galanthus* sp.) as both bulbs have dainty, white, bell-shaped flowers. Snowflakes differ in that each petal on the bell has a green spot at the tip.

Vital statistics

Scientific name: *Leucojum vernum*.
Family: Amaryllidaceae.
Plant/bulb type: They are true bulbs.
Climate: Warm and cold areas.
Culture: A great bulb for shady areas, even in warmer climates.
Height: 30 cm.
Planting time: Plant in late summer to autumn.
Soil: Friable, moist but well drained, moderately fertile.
Position: Grow in full sun to half shade.
Planting depth and spacing: 10 cm deep and 8–10 cm apart.
Watering: Start watering when growth appears and keep the soil slightly moist until the foliage dies off after flowering. Ideally, keep bulbs relatively dry while they are dormant.
Fertilizer: Mulch annually with decayed manure after bulbs die down.
Flowering time: Early spring.
Pests/diseases: None.
After-flowering care: Bulbs need lifting and dividing every five years. Lift congested clumps immediately after flowering, divide and replant.

spring
grasses, ground covers & climbers

If a garden is like an outdoor room, then grasses, ground covers and climbers are the sort of furnishings that add a finishing touch.

A sweeping expanse of lawn, a wall with spillover plants cascading gently, a lovely ground cover or an arbour draped in fragrant climbers — it looks as beautiful as it sounds. These elements are charming in their own right, but also help to link buildings to their surrounds and soften hard landscaping features such as paths.

Grasses

With the arrival of the warm weather your grass has a surge of energy and makes new growth. Spring is therefore an ideal time to smother weeds and repair bare patches.

Lightly fork over worn areas and mossy patches in the lawn, then give the whole area a vigorous raking over. An application of a 'weed and feed' product that clicks onto your hose will work wonders. Finally, sow some grass seed of the appropriate type on those bare patches and the job is done.

Like daffodils and new leaves, beautiful wisteria is one of the signals of spring.

Greener pastures

Most lawns look a little tired after winter. To have a really good spring lawn, the type that reminds you of a billiards table or makes you want to set up a picnic, you need to put in more work than simply remembering to mow it when you can't get to the letter box anymore.

A lovely lawn sets off most gardens. The amount of time and care you give a lawn depends on the type of grass you choose and the degree to which it becomes an obsession. No plant grows as relentlessly as grass, and the time spent behind a lawn mower is torture for some and relaxing therapy for others.

Cutting a lawn too short weakens the grass, which gradually becomes thinner. Weeds soon take over, worn patches develop, and the ground becomes compacted before hardening in the heat of summer. You should set the mower higher, so that the grass stems are left at least 2.5 cm long. When grass is left longer it will grow vigorously to form a thick healthy turf. This in turn will allow the grass to grow much stronger as the roots will penetrate deeper into the soil.

When you mow it is best to dispose of most of the clippings into the compost, leaving just a small amount for use as mulch. Piles of dead grass can create fungus problems. Once a year, usually in late winter, it is a good idea to thoroughly rake the entire lawn to remove dead grass (a process known as scarifying). This helps to rejuvenate the lawn and should be done before weed control and fertilizing are carried out.

Nothing disfigures a lawn more than bare patches, especially at gateways and other entranceways. To fix this problem you can use either a hollow-tined roller or a strong fork to work lots of holes deep into the soil to allow air and water to penetrate. You might also find aerating shoes at your

Grass, the world's most popular plant, makes a show — either as a featured plant like this meadow grass (above left) or as a manicured lawn (above).

You fight dandelions all weekend,
and late Monday afternoon there they are, pert as all get out,
in full and gorgeous bloom, pretty as can be,
thriving as only dandelions can in the face of adversity.

Hal Borland

Above: Aerate your lawn with a strong fork.

Right: A spring lawn bordered by box hedges.

local hardware store or garden centre (see 'Autumn'). Areas of lawn that experience heavy use should be aerated several times a year. Whichever method you use, be sure to scatter coarse, dry sand over the surface before watering — this will flow into the holes to provide long-lasting drainage plugs.

There are two types of gardener: those who feed their gardens regularly and neglect the lawn, and those who feed their lawn so much that fertilizer washes away.

Hungry, impoverished lawns quickly become infested with weeds. It is a good idea to feed your lawn twice a year, in spring and autumn. The trick is to use a specially formulated, slow-acting lawn food that will sink down past shallow roots, inducing the roots to grow downwards after the food. If you have big trees growing in your lawn, the grass will need more fertilizer, as the tree will be constantly robbing nutrients from the ground around. Never apply fertilizer to dry soil as this can severely burn the grass. Feed your lawn immediately after rain or a good watering.

In hot areas it is wise to sprinkle your lawn with a soil-wetting agent once at the beginning of summer to help moisture penetrate. It works wonders on any type of soil and is possibly the best thing you can do for your lawn. If a lawn is watered too frequently there is no need for the grass to make good long roots — this means that shallow roots will be cooked in very hot weather and the turf will further deteriorate.

When weeds appear, use a small-pronged hand tool known as a daisy grubber to remove them. If that sounds too hard, use a lawn weedkiller. This is recommended if the lawn is heavily infested with weeds. Use this weedkiller strictly according to the manufacturer's instructions to avoid damaging the lawn.

types of **grass**

There are many different lawn grasses available today. They are divided into cool season and warm season grasses. Cool season grasses, the ones grown throughout much of the northern hemisphere, are perennial and mostly of tufted habit, although some of them have a running habit. They are suited to cool temperate climates and are not recommended for warm climates. Major cool season grasses include browntop bent, fescues (particularly Chewings fescue), perennial rye grass and smooth-stalked meadow grass (also known as Kentucky blue grass). Tall fescue (also known as meadow fescue) is generally grown as a meadow grass and is good for wildflower meadows. In warm climates the warm season grasses perform best. These are also perennial grasses and have a running habit. They are best suited to climates that are frost-free. Many of the warm climate grasses lose their colour in winter but gardeners should not panic when this happens as they do not die, but resume their normal colour in spring. Major warm season grasses include Queensland blue couch, buffalo grass (also known as St Augustine grass), carpet grass, Bermuda or couch grass and Kikuyu. Lawn grass seed, especially for temperate climates, generally comes in a mixture of different grasses.

top **lawn tips**

- Always water well before feeding.
- Mowing close to ground level increases the risk of weed invasion.
- Mow frequently, not severely — try raising the height of the mower blades.
- Areas of lawn that experience heavy use, such as gateways and the track to the clothesline, should be aerated each year.
- Top dressing in autumn, using a mix of peat, sand and loam, can improve the surface of the soil.
- If your lawn has been incorrectly fed over the years it may have become quite acid. A pH test (kits are available from your local garden centre) could help you diagnose this, and the problem can be rectified by an application of lime.

Grasses (top to bottom): Queensland blue couch, buffalo, carpet grass, Bermuda or couch, browntop bent, smooth-stalked meadow grass (Kentucky blue grass), Kikuyu, perennial rye grass and tall fescue.

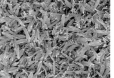
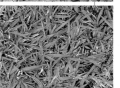
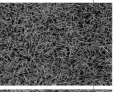
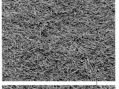
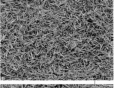

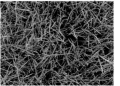

A river of mown grass draws the eye through this garden and acts as a visual contrast to the beds on either side.

growing grass

You can grow a lawn by sowing seed or by laying turf – ready-grown grass which comes in rolls that can be laid over a well-prepared soil bed. It depends on what you can afford.

Starting afresh

Springtime is great for establishing new lawns. The longer days are perfect for lots of leaf growth, and coolish nights help roots to establish before the summer heat. Laying a lawn is a once-only job, so it is a good idea to prepare the soil bed well before you start. It is extremely expensive and difficult to improve soil quality, drainage or levels after you have laid the lawn. Follow the steps outlined below when preparing the site.

1 For poor drainage, lay land drainage pipes.
2 Remove old grass and any debris and eradicate weeds (use glyphosate weedkiller for perennial weeds).
3 Once the weeds are dead, rotary hoe the soil bed, rake the surface smooth, even out any hollows and remove lumps.
4 The top 2 cm of soil should be especially well cultivated and fine textured. You may need some top-quality loam for this.
5 Rake in a lawn starter fertilizer, specially formulated for accelerating growth.

Sowing seed

Spring is a great time to grow a new lawn from seed. Spread the lawn seed evenly over the prepared soil surface. Firm the seed into the soil with a lawn roller or tamp it down with the back of a metal rake — or just walk gently over the area in flat-soled shoes.

Keep the seeds just damp, not too wet, from the time of sowing until they germinate. Continue to water carefully: too much water and the seedlings will rot, too little water and they will dry out. Make sure you give the lawn deep watering until it is established so the roots will grow deeply.

Mow your grass once it reaches a height of 8–10 cm, and don't shave it too close. Place the mower on its highest setting and mow frequently to stimulate root growth.

LAYING TURF

1 First, remove all the old turf, weeds and debris from the site. Make sure there are no runners under the surface of the soil.

2 Level the site by eye.

3 Rake washed river sand over the site and re-level.

4 Compact the sand by tamping it down with a levelling or flat board.

5 Apply starter fertilizer.

6 Rolls of turf as they are delivered by the supplier. Lay them immediately.

7 Lay the rolls of turf and be careful to leave no gaps.

8 Water in.

Laying turf

Once your turf rolls are delivered they must be laid immediately or they will quickly dry out and deteriorate.

Lay the turf in lines, butting the edges together. Using an old knife, cut the turf to fit the required shape. Push the edges down with the back of a metal rake so that they make good contact with the prepared soil bed, then water the turf until it is soaking.

Don't allow pedestrians on the new lawn for two days. Keep the lawn moist as it establishes roots in the soil, and water new turf regularly for the first few months.

Protect new turf If you're laying turf over a large area which will be subject to a lot of pedestrian traffic, lay down some boards to spread the load across turves.

Ornamental grasses

Don't restrict grass to the lawn. Create interesting textures and accents in the garden with a group that is as versatile as any shrub.

Ornamental grasses have increased in popularity enormously over the last ten years, with new awareness of their beauty and design possibilities. They are great for massed plantings, as a foil for perennials, or as accent plants. The new spring growth of ornamental grasses is often overlooked with so much else in flower, but they have a beauty all their own.

Grasses are a way of introducing some textural interest into a garden, with their soft strap leaves contrasting with the round form of shrubs. For something a little different, grow the fabulous red Japanese blood grass, which looks sensational with black ophiopogon, acorus and zebra grass.

Other grass-like plants such as white-variegated irises, variegated sweet flag, striped ophiopogon, variegated liriope or lily turf, and variegated agapanthus such as 'Tinkerbell', are worthy additions to your garden and give the same design effect. As

Above: Bamboos are actually grasses with woody stems.

Above right: Sweet flag (*Acorus calamus* 'Variegatus') is a grass-like evergreen perennial which grows easily in any moist spot or shallow water.

well as being attractive, ornamental grasses require little maintenance. They don't need staking, spraying or deadheading, and most grasses grow in a variety of climates and look good throughout the year.

Always check with a horticulturist first to make sure your selection won't seed readily and become invasive.

How to beat lawn weeds

Weeds are best dealt with in spring before they set seed over summer. So, to have a luscious green lawn underfoot that not only looks and feels great but also sets off the appearance of your house and garden, get out the gear and start work. Weeds shouldn't be a big problem in well-maintained, well-established turf; most serious problems result from low mowing and scalped patches where weeds can gain a foothold.

If your lawn looks more like a paddock, transform it this spring. Keeping weeds out of your grass used to mean hours of backbreaking hand weeding, but modern treatments have made the 'bowling green' effect attainable for the weekend gardener. The first step is to feed. Hungry grass is slow to repair damage caused by pets, insect attack and active children. Liquid 'weed and feed' hose-on products will give your lawn an instant pick-me-up and help to control the majority of lawn weeds. After weeding and fertilizing, use a slow-release lawn food to continue giving a safe, sustained supply of nutrients over the rest of the growing season.

Clear up single perennial weeds such as daisies or dandelions by treating them individually with a spot lawn weedkiller, applying it according to the instructions given by the manufacturer.

ten common
lawn weeds

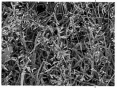

1   Clover (spring and summer)

2   Ribwort or narrow-leaved plantain (perennial, flowering in summer)

3   Creeping oxalis (perennial weed, flowering spring to autumn, seeding summer and autumn)

4   Common or broad-leaved plantain (perennial, summer-flowering)

5   Common cat's ear (perennial, summer-flowering)

6   English daisy (perennial, flowers spring to autumn)

7   Annual meadow grass or annual bluegrass (an annual grass)

8   Creeping buttercup (perennial, flowers spring and summer)

9   Dandelion (perennial herb, flowering spring and summer)

10 Common yarrow (perennial, summer-flowering)

Common lawn weeds (from top): Clover, oxalis, dandelion, common yarrow, annual meadow grass and English daisy.

Cut thistles in May, they grow in a day;
Cut them in June, that is too soon;
Cut them in July, then they die.

English rhyme

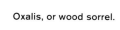

Oxalis, or wood sorrel.

project
potted **grass garden**

Grass gardens can be fun additions to the smallest spaces. Dabble with your own miniature grass garden. A low bowl with pebble mulch and contrasting grasses makes a sensational feature.

1 Gently tease out the root ball and separate the clump slightly. This is ribbon grass (*Phalaris arundinaceae* var. *picta*).

2 Remove any weed seedlings and mound up the potting mix to cover the roots.

3 Mulch with decorative gravel.

OTHER IDEAS Coloured foliage works well as a potted specimen. Below *Ophiopogon planiscapus* 'Nigrescens', *Dianella* species (good for mild climates or conservatory) and bold tufts of sedge (*Carex* species) add impact to your container.

check list

jobs to do now

- Use weed and feed products to control weeds in lawns before they gain a foothold.

- Lawns really take off in spring so treat them to a proprietary, slow-release lawn fertilizer to produce a strong, healthy carpet that will last through summer.

- Using climbers is a lovely way to soften the look of verandah posts and pergolas, but now is the time to stop them invading your roof and gutters. Prune back long stems of wisteria and other climbers if they are growing beyond their allotted space.

plant now

- Create new lawns by sowing an appropriate grass seed mixture or by laying turf.

- Lots of shrubs, climbers and perennials can be propagated from cuttings of soft shoots in the spring.

- Choose wisteria and clematis in flower to ensure the desired variety.

- Raise Spanish flag (*Ipomoea lobata*) from seeds for vivid red and yellow flowers or plant coral vine (*Antigonon* sp.) seedlings for cerise-pink bracts in summer. In frost-prone climates grow the coral vine in a heated conservatory.

flowering now

- Some ornamental grasses and grass-like plants such as various fescues, milium (especially *Milium effusum* 'Aureum'), carex or sedges and luzula or woodrush

- Ground-cover plants such as bugle (*Ajuga* species and varieties), bergenias, saxifrages, aubrieta, violets, some species of rock or alpine phlox, lesser or dwarf periwinkle, rock cress, snow-in-summer, thrift and some geraniums (most flower in summer)

- Climbers such as wisteria, many clematis species and varieties including *C. montana*, banksia rose (*Rosa banksiae*) and its varieties, *Bougainvillea spectabilis* (in a conservatory in frost-prone climates), chocolate vine, jasmines (some species such as *Jasminum humile*, *J. mesnyi* and *J. polyanthum*), various honeysuckles including *Lonicera* x *tellmanniana*, glory pea or parrot beak, holboellia, and Carolina jasmine (grow in a conservatory in frost-prone climates)

What a man needs in gardening is a cast-iron back with a hinge in it.

Charles Dudley Warner

japanese blood grass

This grass has sensational red leaf blades, the brilliant colour lasting from spring to late autumn. It is a slow-growing rhizomatous plant which makes a beautiful accent in the garden, especially in a shaded woodland location. Growing to about 45 cm, it looks particularly handsome in contrast with black ophiopogon, or planted with red-tinged shrubs, such as dwarf nandina. It can also be used in pots and, like most grasses, copes better than many other plants with neglect — perfect for the absent-minded gardener!

Vital statistics

Scientific name: *Imperata cylindrica* 'Rubra'.
Family: Poaceae.
Climate: Grows in cool temperate to warm temperate areas.
Culture: Divide every 5–6 years to encourage new clumps and fresh red leaves.
Colours: Has blood red leaves.
Height: Grows 30–45 cm, quite upright.
Planting time: Plant in spring.
Soil: Requires soil that is moist but well drained.
Position: Grow in partial shade.
Plant spacing: Plant 30 cm apart for a striking massed effect.
Fertilizer: Feed in spring with well-rotted manure.
Pests/diseases: Generally is not affected by pests or disease.
Cutting: Prune out dead foliage as necessary.
Propagation: Propagate by division of rhizomes.

Ground covers

Are your weekends spent slaving away maintaining the lawn and weeding garden beds? If you don't need a putting green, why not replant your lawn with an easier alternative?

Above: Various thymes make a scented carpet around this stone bench.

Below: A bunch of thyme.

Give away this backbreaking work forever — once the warm spring weather arrives, plant ground covers, the plants that lie low and let you lie in.

They smother bare soil so that weed seeds cannot find space to germinate. Low-maintenance gardens are the fashion and many landscapers use ground-cover plants liberally, sometimes creating large 'mosaics' or patchworks of ground covers. This is attractive and makes a refreshing change from conventional lawns.

Ground covers are, as the name suggests, plants that carpet the ground. This carpeting effect has a multitude of benefits.

Ground covers squeeze out the weeds, carpet the ground leaving no space for weed seeds to take hold and are less demanding than lawn in terms of water, fertilizer and labour requirements. They provide the seasonal interest, flowers or coloured foliage that turf lacks. If you plant in spring these carpet-like plants will be well established by summer so that your garden will need very little attention next year. This garden is so much more restful than one that requires a great deal of labour for its upkeep.

Some useful ground cover plants for partially shady places (clockwise from above): the autumn-flowering Japanese windflower or anemone, lesser or dwarf periwinkle, bugle and rock cress.

Hiding in the dark

Shady or partially shady gardens do not need to miss out on ground covers. The variegated rock cress (*Arabis caucasica* 'Variegata') is generally thought of as a sun lover and recommended for a position in full sun, but it will perform quite well in partial shade, and indeed in climates with hot dry summers some shade is particularly recommended. Where winters are mild or on the warm side this arabis may be rather short-lived.

Golden creeping Jenny (*Lysimachia nummularia* 'Aurea') has golden yellow foliage all the year round so it can be recommended for combining with spring-flowering ground cover plants, particularly varieties of bugle (*Ajuga*) such as 'Burgundy Glow' with red-flushed leaves. In summer it produces bright yellow flowers. It is very vigorous and will soon cover the soil. Indeed, you will need to make sure it does not outgrow its allotted space or smother nearby plants, but surplus growth is easily pulled out.

Possibly the most difficult place for plants is dry shade under large trees where there are masses of roots. Japanese windflower or anemone is tough enough to cope with these harsh conditions and has no trouble with the root competition. It features quite attractive mid-green, lobed leaves in the spring and summer, and in autumn produces delicate flowers in soft pink and white, on tall stems.

In impoverished soils, bugle (*Ajuga reptans*) is a tough, obliging ground cover with deep blue flowers. It is indispensable for its ability to grow in impossible places — in rich soils it will romp away at such an alarming rate you will have trouble keeping up with it. In addition to 'Burgundy Glow', there is the white-variegated 'Variegata'. Very popular is 'Atropurpurea', also sold as 'Purpurea' with rich purple foliage. There are many varieties of bugle; the range varies from country to country. Some are classed as giant kinds with extra large foliage and taller flower spikes, a good example being 'Catlin's Giant' with purple-flushed leaves.

Sunlovers

Another foliage contrast is provided by the ground cover lamb's ear (*Stachys byzantina*), which will grow anywhere as long as the soil is well drained. Lamb's ear needs a sunny spot to keep its leaves attractive and silvery. Divide the clumps any time through spring to multiply your supply.

Another useful grey ground cover is snow-in-summer (*Cerastium tomentosum*). Its charm is provided by its silver-grey carpet of leaves, but white flowers are a bonus in late spring and summer. Use it cascading over walls like grey froth.

Lighten up an expanse of green ground covers with white. For example, in late spring once frosts are over plant some ivy-leaved pelargonium 'Ekva' with clotted-cream variegated foliage and, in summer, red flowers. The variety 'L'Elégante' has white variegated leaves and, during summer, white flowers. A very attractive plant to use as ground cover is the variegated star jasmine, *Trachelospermum jasminoides* 'Tricolor', with pink tips to its leaves. This is a climber but it makes good ground cover when allowed to trail over the ground or down banks. It has white flowers in summer.

Mild traffic areas, such as side pathways, need robust ground covers. For these places try *Vinca minor* (lesser or dwarf periwinkle) varieties, creeping thymes which flower in late spring and summer, creeping mints, *Mazus reptans*, and ground-hugging grevilleas (for mild and frost-free gardens).

Rose of Sharon (*Hypericum calycinum*) is an old-fashioned ground cover with large clear yellow flowers from midsummer to mid-autumn, each flower featuring a fluffy mass of stamens. This ground cover is tough enough to grow under trees.

Other suitable ground cover plants for sunny spots are the many varieties of sun rose, derived mainly from *Helianthemum nummularium*, which start flowering in late spring and continue well into summer. Evergreen or partially evergreen, they form carpets of growth studded with masses of small, single or double, rose-like flowers in a range of brilliant and pastel colours.

TOP 10 SPRING-FLOWERING GROUND COVERS

1 Snow-in-summer

2 Thrift

3 *Thymus praecox*

4 *Aurinia saxatilis*

5 *Grevillea* 'Poorinda Royal Mantle'

6 Cranesbill

7 *Helianthemum* 'Supreme' (rock rose)

8 Alpine phlox

9 Viola

10 Epimedium

Lawn impersonators

Low traffic areas, such as garden beds where weed seeds rather than trampling feet are a problem, look great with the addition of bugle, campanula, lamb's ear, snow-in-summer, verbena, arabis, dianthus, bergenia, windflowers, lamium and catmint.

High traffic zones, such as those where children play, call for tough plants. In these areas only the toughest will survive. Hardy selections include dwarf ornamental grasses like fescues (festuca), particularly those with greyish or bluish foliage, and the blue oat grass (*Helictotrichon sempervirens*). Erigerons or fleabane are suitable, especially *E. karvinskianus* or Mexican daisy.

For a green lawn look, try these:
- Hot, dry areas: *Coprosma* x *kirkii* (only for frost-free gardens and good near the sea), gazanias (for summer only in gardens prone to frost), prostrate rosemaries, and prostrate cytisus or brooms
- Under trees: lily turf (*Liriope muscari*) and its varieties, ophiopogon species (also known as lily turf), spider plant or chlorophytum (frost-tender), bugle (*Ajuga reptans* varieties), and ground ivy (*Glechoma hederacea*)
- Sunny spots: African daisy or arctotis (frost-tender), prostrate sedums or stonecrops, and sempervivums or houseleeks
- Shady spots: Australian violet (*Viola hederacea*), especially for mild climates, English ivy (*Hedera helix* varieties), pratia species, dead nettle (*Lamium maculatum*) varieties, and lesser or dwarf periwinkle (*Vinca minor*) varieties

Clockwise from far left: *Festuca ovina* var. *glauca*, *Ophiopogon jaburan* (variegated), *Liriope muscari* 'Munroe White', ivy, *Lamium maculatum* 'White Nancy' and spider plant.

lily-of-the-valley

In the old language of flowers, 'the return of happiness' was the meaning given to this bewitching plant which flowers in mid-spring. Lily-of-the-valley makes excellent ground cover in moist, shady places with its carpet of lush foliage, even though it dies down for the winter. Plant it generously under deciduous trees or among shrubs in a border. Spread is usually quite vigorous, by means of creeping rhizomes. There are numerous varieties, including one with pink flowers.

Vital statistics

Scientific name: *Convallaria majalis.*
Family: Convallariaceae.
Climate: Frost hardy, drought sensitive.
Height: Plants grow 20–30 cm high.

Planting time: Plant rhizomes in autumn.
Soil: Easily grown in permanently moist soil. Dig in an ample supply of compost or leaf mould before planting.
Position: Prefers full shade but tolerates partial sun under trees.
Planting depth and spacing: Plant the rhizomes 5 cm deep and 5–8 cm apart.
Watering: Keep moist throughout growing season. Poor drainage during their autumn and winter dormancy may rot their root system.
Fertilizer: There is no need to apply fertilizer, but instead mulch the plants in autumn with leaf mould or well-rotted garden compost.
Flowering time: Flowers in spring.
Pruning: Remove old foliage in autumn once it has completely died down.

Climbers

Some climbers are so closely associated with spring that a spring garden would be incomplete without them. The classic example is wisteria. Other climbers start flowering in spring and continue into summer, including clematis.

Spring-flowering climbers

Spring heralds some fragrant climbers including wisteria and the earliest of the honeysuckles. However, it is worth thinking about other less well-known spring-flowering climbers, such as the dusky coral pea (*Kennedia rubicunda*), and the bower vine (*Pandorea jasminoides*). In frost-prone climates these make superb specimens for the cool conservatory.

Chocolate vine

Also known as the five-leaf akebia, this unusual semi-evergreen twining vine has purple-brown flowers with a chocolate scent. *Akebia quinata* is vigorous, especially in milder climates, and capable of reaching 10 m. It grows more slowly in cooler areas. The five-fingered leaves are attractive, so this is a pleasant plant even when out of flower. Strong-growing climbing roses make good companions as they will take over from the spring display. Grow the chocolate vine over a trellis screen or pergola.

Clockwise from bottom left: *Clematis montana* var. *rubens*, chocolate vine, pergola shrouded in grape vine, Carolina jasmine (double cv.) and honeysuckle.

Clematis

The best-known of the spring-flowering clematis is the vigorous *Clematis montana*. The species carries white single flowers but varieties are usually grown including var. *rubens* and 'Tetrarose', both with pink flowers and purple-flushed foliage. Another excellent spring-flowering clematis is *C. armandii*. An evergreen species with leaves divided into three long, shiny, deep green leaflets, it has white, fragrant flowers.

Gelsemium

Carolina jasmine is an attractive climber which doesn't become too vigorous. Bell-shaped, sunny yellow flowers appear twice a year, first in late winter and spring and then again in autumn. It has green glossy foliage. Grow in a cool conservatory in frost-prone climates.

Honeysuckle

The earliest honeysuckles include *Lonicera japonica* (the Japanese honeysuckle) with fragrant white flowers and *L.* x *tellmanniana* with yellowish orange blooms. Both continue into summer, when they are joined by other species including the fragrant woodbine, *L. periclymenum*, and its varieties. Some species of honeysuckle grow as a shrub rather than as a climber. *Lonicera nitida* has become extremely popular for hedging, while *L. fragrantissima* is great for winter perfume. You should prune climbing honeysuckles annually after flowering as they can become a tangled mass of growth.

I will wind thee in my arms.
So doth the woodbine, the sweet honeysuckle,
Gently entwist.

William Shakespeare

The graceful racemes of Japanese wisteria showering down from a rustic arbour.

Wisteria

This plant evokes the magic of late spring and early summer. Its long racemes of pea-shaped flowers hang like fragrant decorations, then the plant bursts into a mass of shading green foliage. This display is followed by a subtler autumn show of golden leaves and pendulous pods, which finally fall to reveal twisted, gnarled stems of great character and strength.

Wisteria originates from either Asia or North America, depending on the species. The Japanese (*Wisteria floribunda*) has the longest flowers, with racemes hanging down 1.5 m. The Chinese (*W. sinensis*) is the most commonly grown. The Chinese wisteria has shorter, plumper flowers than does the Japanese species, but it is equally beautiful.

The easiest way for the amateur to tell the two species apart is by looking at how they climb, with the Japanese growing up clockwise and the American and Chinese growing anticlockwise.

There has been plenty of crossbreeding and cultivation of these species. Worth hunting out are *W. floribunda* cultivars 'Violacea Plena' (for its double flowers of violet colour), and 'Rosea' (also known as 'Hon-beni') with pink flowers in long racemes. *W. brachybotrys* 'Shiro Kapitan', sometimes called white silky wisteria, is probably the most pure, sparkling white.

Be sure to prune back wayward tendrils as they grow or wisteria can quickly get out of hand and cause damage to roofs, guttering and woodwork.

wisteria
lookalikes

If you have no room for a vigorous climber, there are other plants with features similar to wisteria that may be more suitable. For example, if a small-growing clumping shrub would suit your garden, try *Indigofera* (left). This semi-deciduous plant has pink flowers in short racemes like wisteria, and suckers to form a clump. The pinnate foliage is also very attractive. *Indigofera* is hardy and can be grown as a free-standing shrub or trained flat against a sunny wall.

jasmine

Some jasmines start flowering in the spring, including hardy *Jasminum humile* 'Revolutum', yellow jasmine, and *J. mesnyi*, primrose jasmine, also with yellow flowers, which makes a good cool conservatory plant in frost-prone climates. *J. polyanthum* is another excellent plant for the cool conservatory in frost-prone climates, producing white, highly fragrant flowers.

Other jasmines follow in the summer, including the hardy and very popular *J. officinale*, common jasmine. This vigorous climber produces highly fragrant, white flowers through summer and into autumn. There are several varieties of the common jasmine including *affine* with flowers tinged with pink. There are also several with attractive variegated foliage. The species shown here, *J. sambac*, the Arabian jasmine, produces its highly fragrant flowers in summer as well as at other times of the year. Unfortunately it is tender so in frost-prone climates grow it in a warm conservatory.

Vital statistics

Scientific name: *Jasminum* sp.

Family: Oleaceae.

Climate: There are species suited to cold and frost-free climates. In cold climates, grow frost-sensitive species in a heated conservatory.

Culture: Shelter jasmine from strong winds. Remove straggly growth after flowering.

Colours: Flowers are white, pink and yellow.

Height: Plants grow as climbers or shrubs up to 7 m.

Soil: Grow jasmine in free-draining soil.

Position: Plants require a sunny position.

Fertilizer: Mulch around the stems in spring with well-rotted manure.

Pests/diseases: Plants are not commonly affected.

spring
shrubs & trees

Spring is a time of renewal. Many trees and shrubs blossom now and all have a flurry of growth that will transform your garden with translucent green leaves and delicate blooms.

The simple elegance of magnolia blossoms lingers on in early spring.

He told of the magnolia spread
High as a cloud, high overhead.

William Wordsworth

However, this may mean rethinking areas, pruning back over-zealous plants or filling in gaps that still need something. The choice at this time is enormous. Garden centres are stocked to capacity and it is the busiest time of the year for them. Spring is quite a good season to plant, as the weather isn't too hot, so feel free to succumb to the odd temptation; after all, it will probably be snapped up by autumn.

Unlike autumn purchases, spring plantings only have three months to establish themselves into the surrounding soil before the summer heat. Help them grow roots with a seaweed-based liquid fertilizer which will stimulate this area, and ensure that the soil stays moist with a thick layer of mulch and regular water.

The other danger with spring planting is that new growth can be out of sync with the microclimate of your area, and may fall victim to late frosts. Address this problem with covers at night for the first month or so, or spray with a foliage stress guard.

Shrubs

Shrubs give a garden its strength, with the colour, form and flowers creating a distinctive character.

Shrubs can screen out an unwanted view, provide privacy and even perfume an outdoor living area. A garden can be created entirely out of carefully planted contrasting shrubs, and be a beautiful place every month of the year.

Deciduous spring-flowering shrubs

Most people are aware of spring-flowering trees — apples, peaches and cherries to name a few. Not everyone thinks about including deciduous flowering shrubs in their garden, and therefore miss out on some of the most delightful and fragrant blossoms of all. Noteworthy inclusions are the buttercup yellow forsythia, the underrated spiraeas, hardy weigela (which flowers pink, white or red), deutzia with its pink or white bells, and *Kerria japonica* 'Pleniflora' with double yellow flowers.

Many of these spring-flowering beauties have the added bonus of coloured foliage, which extends their usefulness throughout summer and autumn. There are stunning golden-leaved varieties of dwarf spiraea and weigela, and white-variegated weigela.

One beautiful plant worth hunting down and including in your garden is white forsythia (*Abeliophyllum distichum*), which looks just like a white version of forsythia but grows like an abelia with gracefully arching branches. The late winter and early spring blooms are wonderfully fragrant, and last well indoors where the scent can be easily appreciated. It is happy in any spot as long as the summers aren't too hot and dry, as it prefers a cool temperate climate.

hawthorn

Deciduous, with shapely lobed leaves, *Crataegus* sp. are useful screening plants. In spring they are a mass of white blossom, and in autumn and winter they are adorned with bright red berries. Hawthorns prefer full sun but tolerate wind.

For range of colour, profuse flowering habit and sheer flamboyance, few spring-flowering shrubs can compete with azaleas and rhododendrons.

Azaleas and rhododendrons

A flowering azalea is a sight to behold, with blooms so plentiful that they almost mask the foliage. Azaleas come from mountainous regions where they occur naturally among rock crevices and on the sides of ravines, so they are very shallow rooting and need good drainage. They are understorey plants, happiest in broken sunlight and mulched heavily by leaves which have fallen from the canopy above. This makes them ideal for growing in broad shallow pots and in rockery pockets.

Today they are equally at home in garden beds of improved, rich soil with an acid pH, and breeding has extended their vigour and toughness.

Botanists used to distinguish azaleas from rhododendrons by classifying those with five stamens as azaleas and those with ten as rhododendrons. Azaleas are now classified as *Rhododendron* sp. Few plants make such a sea of colour, ranging through pink and white through to lilac, red, orange and yellow. They belong to the family Ericaceae, which includes the heathers (see 'Heaths and heathers' in 'Winter'), kalmias and blueberries.

Few of the evergreen garden azaleas are fragrant although there are exceptions. The tall hybrids between evergreen rhododendrons and deciduous azaleas, known as azaleodendrons, are fragrant in some varieties. The plants are semi-evergreen and very hardy but not very well known. You really have to look to the deciduous azaleas for fragrance.

The dwarf evergreen Kurume azaleas have masses of small flowers, small foliage and are ideal for shrub borders and edges of woodland gardens. There are hundreds of modern hybrids with ruffled edges, double flowers and even variegated foliage, and these come in a multitude of colours.

Deciduous azaleas occur naturally in Asia and North America. The flower colours include shades of yellow, orange, pink and red, plus white, and quite a few are fragrant, including the Ghent, Knap Hill-Exbury and Occidentale hybrids.

The evergreen hybrid rhododendrons range from dwarf to large shrubs and come in a very wide range of colours including shades of blue and violet, the flowers being produced mainly in large trusses. They are generally very hardy and take hard frosts.

In frost-prone areas the tropical rhododendrons are excellent plants for a cool conservatory and deserve to be more widely grown. Known as Vireyas, they tend to flower spasmodically throughout the year, with a major flush in late winter. Their foliage is glossy green, and the flowers range from red, pink, salmon and yellow through to white. Some are even epiphytic, growing in nooks of trees in nothing but leaf mould.

Silk rose

For some reason, the silk rose (*Rhodoleia* sp.) is not as popular as *Rhododendron* sp., which it resembles. This beautiful shrub has thick, shining green leaves and pendulous flower clusters of rose red. Native to Southeast Asia, it likes woodland conditions in frost-free areas. If you can find it, it is a worthwhile plant for the conservatory in areas prone to frost.

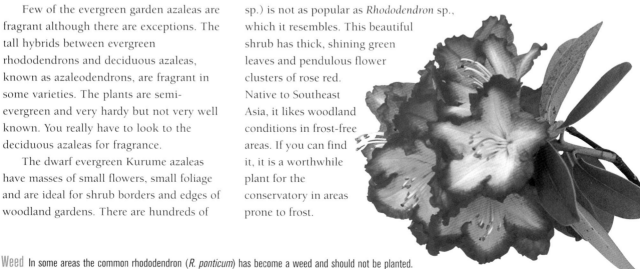

Weed In some areas the common rhododendron (*R. ponticum*) has become a weed and should not be planted.

Above: *Rhododendron yakushimanum.*

Above right: A Vireya rhododendron called 'Island Splendour'.

Gifts from the Orient

The enchanted forest of Asia — where towering maples protect rhododendron and camellia bushes from harsh sun and cold, and leaf litter collects and forms a nutrient rich layer of moist humus — contains much of what we plant in our gardens today.

It is in these special places that magnolias, camellias, rhododendrons, azaleas, hydrangeas, to name just a few, originated.

Spring is flowering time for many of these beauties, with bare branches from the canopy above allowing the sun to awaken their blossoms.

Now gardeners in the West can enjoy some of these Eastern marvels by planting them in their own gardens.

Camellias

Camellias grow happily in cool climates and are among the staples for gardens with acid or lime-free soil. By planting the main types — sasanquas, japonicas, reticulatas and the hybrids (*Camellia* x *williamsii*) – you can enjoy their flowers from autumn to the end of spring, with the dainty flowers of *C. sasanqua* starting off the show.

Grow camellias in large tubs for patio and courtyard gardens, or train them against walls and fences as espalier (great for narrow beds). They are also ideal for shady gardens, although some varieties withstand full sunshine.

Camellias like a slightly acid soil that is rich in organic matter, and range in colour from the purest white through pinks and

The colours [of rhododendrons] leap at you...dripping in blood red rivers from the ledges, choppy sulphur seas breaking from a long, low surf of pink.

Frank Kingdon Ward

into purple and reds. They make great garden shrubs, pot specimens and even hedges, and have glossy green foliage that is attractive all year.

The most commonly grown type, *Camellia sinensis*, is actually not valued for its flowers. Rather, the leaves have boiling water poured over them to become the world's most consumed beverage — tea.

The sasanqua varieties can be recognized by their smaller, sharper leaves and open habit of growth. This feature, together with their long flowering period, makes them well suited for hedging.

Camellia japonica is the most popular of all the camellias, with thousands of named varieties dating back through the centuries, and a huge range of colours and forms in the flowers. The foliage, too, with its glossy texture and perfect shape, is probably superior. Some *C. japonicas* have remarkable foliage, such as the zig-zag camellia (*Camellia japonica* 'Unryu'). This charming camellia, which has a curious zig-zag branching pattern, originated in Japan. The name 'Unryu' means 'dragon in the clouds': to the Japanese the plant apparently looks like a dragon climbing up into the sky. The small, single flowers are crimson with deeper coloured veining.

The *Camellia* x *williamsii* varieties (*C. japonica* x *C. saluenensis*) are excellent shrubs with glossy elliptic leaves and flowers in shades of pink, plus white, mainly in mid- to late spring. Possibly the best-known variety is 'Donation' which

Blowzy, simple or formal, camellia blossoms suit any garden or taste. Clockwise from top: the unusual foliage of the fishtail camellia (*C. japonica* 'Kingyo-tsubaki'), *C. japonica* variety (striped), *C. japonica* 'Bokuhan', *C. japonica* variety (formal double) and *C. sasanqua* 'Early Pearly'.

A camellia seed (above) and the hybrid camellia, *C. x williamsii* 'Donation' (right).

Disbudding camellias

Camellias, mainly japonicas, tend to produce too many flower buds and cannot support them. This can cause the buds to drop and the flowers to fall prematurely. To disbud your camellias, remove excess buds, leaving only one or two buds at the end of each shoot. You may feel like a sadist, but doing this allows the plant to produce new growth as well as larger and longer-lasting blooms.

produces big, semi-double, pink flowers throughout spring. It is a compact, upright shrub, ideal where space is limited.

Camellia reticulata is generally regarded as the aristocrat of the camellia family by virtue of its large flowers, around 20 cm in diameter. This spring-flowering species and its varieties are less hardy than the other camellias and gardeners in regions with hard winters should grow plants in tubs and winter them in a cool conservatory.

Camellia hybrids

Apart from the all-time great, *Camellia* x *williamsii*, there are many other good camellia hybrids. 'Flower Girl' is especially well-known for its fragrant flowers, which are semi-double and bright pink in colour. 'Francie L' has semi-double red flowers and is good for training as an espalier against a wall. 'Freedom Bell' is a neat, small plant with bright red, semi-double flowers. All bloom from the middle of winter to spring.

Camellia species

The species have a charm all of their own, often with smaller flowers and foliage than the hybrids. Many are scented, such as *C. lutchuensis*. This produces small white single flowers towards the end of winter. It is not too hardy and needs to be grown in a tub and wintered in a cool conservatory in regions with hard winters. Good for training as an espalier in mild areas, it can also be grown as a standard, ideal for tub culture.

Camellia tsaii is quite a large shrub with a weeping habit of growth and like *C. lutchuensis* is not too hardy, being best in mild climates or with conservatory protection over winter. It produces tiny white single flowers during the winter.

The very hardy *C. rusticana* is popularly known as the snow camellia. Normally the varieties are grown and these produce small single or double flowers in colours of pink, red or white in the winter and spring.

Magnolias

Few flowering shrubs and trees can rival the elegance of magnolias. Their great goblets, often scented, are borne on bare grey branches, heralding the spring. These well known, spring-flowering shrubs boast many different varieties.

Most widely grown are the ones with goblet-shaped flowers. *Magnolia* x *soulangeana* varies in colour from almost white through to purple, and then there is the pure white yulan (*M. denudata*), a favourite species with its milky white, scented flowers. Most are mid-sized shrubs, looking their best with shelter from taller trees and protection from hot westerly winds. There are also the star-like flowers of *M. stellata* which grows into a large shrub.

Lastly, there are evergreen magnolias (*M. grandiflora*) which flower in summer and autumn, have a lemon fragrance and grow into a large park tree. Michelias are closely related, flowering in spring (see 'Michelias — the evergreen cousin of magnolia' in 'Spring' on page 82).

Magnolia seeds.

Did you know? The Chinese regard the yulan as a symbol of purity and candour.

ESPALIERED MICHELIA

1 *Michelia yunnanensis* 'Scented Pearl' can be grown as an espalier.

2 Use budding tape to tie the branches to a support.

3 Cut back any outward growing branches.

4 A freestyle espalier in the making.

Michelias — the evergreen cousin of magnolia

Michelias come from one of the most ancient of flowering plant families, Magnoliaceae. The bright colours of modern flowers are not their style. They rely on perfume to attract prehistoric insects such as beetles for pollination, and can throw their scent quite a distance to lure them. Even one plant will add to a 'scentscape'. However, they are suited only to frost-free climates so in frosty regions use them to scent out a cool conservatory.

The glossy green leaves are so beautiful they are used in floristry, and many have a handsome velvet brown underside. But their recent popularity is due to their perfume, with scents varying from light lemon to port wine or orange blossom.

Most people have probably only heard of *Michelia figo* or *M. doltsopa*, and these are certainly the most easily available. Like all of the genus they should be grown in acid to neutral soil. The showiest of these is a new cultivar of *M. doltsopa* called 'Silver Cloud'. During spring it has large white flowers which are heavily scented, and look like a cross between the Bull Bay magnolia

and the star magnolia. It grows to about 12 x 6 m and has a bushy, pyramidal shape, making it ideal for average-sized gardens as either a specimen tree or a large screen.

For perfume alone, few could resist the divine fragrance of 'Pak-lan' (*M. alba*). In summer the apple green leaves and creamy white flowers, which have slender pointed petals and a light orange blossom perfume, make them a heavenly tree for any garden. These white flowers are best known as the essence in Chanel No. 5. *Michelia longifolia*, or 'Buk-lan', is similar in habit.

The 'Cham-pak' (*M. champaca*) has a smallish (only about 3 cm) butterscotch yellow flower, but makes up for its size with the strength and reach of its heady scent. It grows into a medium-sized tree, has glossy foliage and creates year-round shade. Hard to come by, although worth the effort, is the rare species *M. maudiae*. Another medium-sized tree, in late winter it has large fragrant white flowers which are similar to *M. doltsopa*.

If your garden doesn't have the space for a tree, think about using *M. yunnanensis* 'Scented Pearl', which only grows 3–4 m and makes a lovely hedge or espaliered specimen. The foliage is comparatively small, and has chocolate-coloured felt-like hairs on the underside of the leaves. The 5 cm white cup-like flowers look striking against the green and brown background.

There are also new varieties of *M. figo*. Called 'Coco' and 'Lady of the Night', they seem to have similar characteristics: both flower eight months of the year, have slightly larger white flowers tinged with pink as they age, and a slightly bigger leaf. In the pipeline is another *figo*-like hybrid called 'Mixed Up Miss'. This is a bushy shrub growing to 4 m which has white flowers in spring. Some of these plants are not available in all countries, but it is worth growing those that are available.

Spring scents

Each spring we are tempted by a vast array of perfumed plants, such as lilac, viburnum and jasmine. These plants have developed this property in order to attract pollinating insects; unlike the blooms of bird-pollinated plants, the colour and size of the flowers are not very important. Perfumed plants can revive old memories, soothe the soul and uplift the spirit.

Some scents are at their strongest first thing in the morning and others at night. Many perfumes in a garden cannot be detected near the plant; in many cases the scent is dispersed and only develops into a full heady fragrance when it is 100 m away.

Orange jessamine

This evergreen has glossy foliage, an orange blossom-like fragrance and white flowers at least three times a year from spring through to early autumn, and makes a terrific screen, formal hedge or container specimen. *Murraya paniculata* grows to about 4 x 3 m in both full sun and shade. It

needs well-drained soil and in frost-prone areas a warm conservatory is required.

Mexican orange blossom

A much hardier shrub for cool and cold climates is *Choisya ternata* with wonderfully fragrant white flowers reminiscent of orange blossom, hence the common name. The blossoms appear in late spring and then more are produced in late summer and autumn. Bees find the flowers very attractive. The deep green leaves, which are aromatic, consist of three leaflets. Mexican orange blossom can be grown in the shrub border or used as an informal hedge. For best results provide well-drained soil and full sun.

Top: The wonderfully fragrant flowers of Mexican orange blossom.

Above: Orange jessamine.

Deliciously fragrant trusses of lilac blossom are one of the great delights of spring in cool temperate areas.

Lilac blossom

Lilac (*Syringa*), a 2.5 m upright suckering shrub, is best known for its fragrance, and is often sold as a cut flower in spring. (It should not be confused with the California lilac, *Ceanothus*, which produces intensely blue flowers in spring and early summer.)

These plants, with their trusses of spring blooms comprising tiny flowers in dense cylindrical spikes, are an excellent choice for small gardens, and come in white, purple, pink, mauve and bicolour forms. Only suited to cool temperate areas and requiring cool nights in order to flower properly in spring, they are tolerant of frosts and extreme cold. Lilac grows well in many soils, including chalky ones.

Plant care

Lilacs are at their best in deep, friable loams with regular rainfall and full sun exposure, but must have protection from strong winds. Encourage shoots produced above any graft union as potential new flowering wood, and remove dead flowers immediately after flowering.

Lilac look-a-likes and namesakes

California lilacs (*Ceanothus*) are native to the USA and Mexico, and known best for their showy blue flowers (although they also come in pink and white). Some hybrids are semiprostrate, but most grow to about 4 m and flower in spring and early summer. They prefer light, freely drained coarse soils in a mild climate with an open sunny position.

Hebe, also known as veronica, is a genus mainly native to New Zealand. It has a raceme of flowers similar to lilacs. Most are small rounded shrubs to about a metre or so, and make fabulous flowering plants, growing in any open, sunny, well drained position, even coping with strong salt-laden winds and temperatures to -5°C. Flowering time varies depending on the species, but most are at their best during the summer. They benefit from a light trim after each flush of blooms.

Other lilac look-a-likes include chaste tree (*Vitex* sp.) and butterfly bushes (*Buddleja* sp.) which both have flower spikes in the lilac, lavender, pink and white range. Vitex is a frost-hardy shrub taking a low of -5°C and buddlejas are fully hardy. Both relish well-drained soils in full sun.

The Oleaceae family

The olive family contains some of the most ancient cultivated plants, including olives, which date back to 2000 BC as a food source in Egypt, and jasmine which has been prized for its fragrance and oil for many hundreds of years by the Chinese.

Many genera are highly ornamental: lilacs, osmanthus, fringe tree (*Chionanthus*), forsythia and white forsythia (*Abeliophyllum*) are a few of the flowering plants, while ash are beautiful autumn foliage trees, and some, particularly privet, are widely used for creating formal garden hedges. Some genera are of considerable economic importance for food (olives and oil), timber (ash for lumber), perfumery (jasmine oil) and as a cut flower (lilac).

How slowly through the lilac-scented air
Descends the tranquil moon!

Henry Wadsworth Longfellow

check list

jobs to do now

• Prune banksia roses after flowering by removing only the oldest wood.

• Cut back deutzia, choisya and callistemon when blooms finish.

• Prune out old flowered stems of weigela, spiraea and kerria as soon as flowering is over.

• Prune *Clematis montana* and *C. armandii* after flowering by removing any dead or dying wood and reducing other stems if necessary.

• To prevent frost damage to young plants, surround them with hessian and don't prune them until all chance of late frosts has passed.

• Tie or train in long new shoots of wisteria but delay pruning back new side shoots until late summer.

• Mulch rhododendrons, azaleas and michelias with leaf mould, peat or shredded/chipped bark to help the soil to retain moisture. When rhododendrons have finished flowering remove the seed heads by gently twisting them off.

• When dwarf evergreen azaleas have finished flowering they can be very lightly trimmed with shears to remove dead flowers and to maintain a compact shape. Cut back any overlong shoots.

• Make sure that the soil remains steadily moist for those plants that need these conditions, including rhododendrons, azaleas and michelias.

• Remove the seeds heads from lilac by cutting them off just above the growth buds, using secateurs.

plant now

• Spring is the best time to plan and plant hedges. Look beyond the flowers and imagine how the planting will look like for the year.

• Buy spring-flowering shrubs now, while they are in flower.

flowering now

• Evergreen shrubs, including azaleas, rhododendrons, California lilac (ceanothus), orange jessamine and Mexican orange blossom

• Deciduous shrubs, such as chaenomeles, deutzia, forsythia, kerria, lilac, spiraea, viburnum, weigela and white forsythia (abeliophyllum)

• Trees, such as laburnum, hawthorn (crataegus), crab apples, michelia, ornamental pears, and ornamental cherries and other prunus species

Roses

The most important job early in the season is pruning, when the worst of the frosts are over (in mild areas prune in late winter). Bare-root roses can still be planted — early in the season before growth starts. Spring is also the best time to combat various pests and diseases that can really get out of hand in the warm weather if you leave them untreated now.

Rose pruning

Roses are pruned in order to grow bigger and better plants that will produce top quality blooms. Neglected, unpruned roses gradually lose vigour, and their branches become tangled and matted. This encourages disease because air can't circulate freely around the leaves, and they succumb to diseases like powdery mildew and black spot.

Pruning clears out the unwanted and dead branches and stimulates new vigorous growth. This channels the energy of the rose into just a few main branches, instead of many smaller ones, and results in bigger flowers. Pruning also helps to keep roses to a desired shape and manageable size.

For pruning you'll need a sharp, clean pair of secateurs (parrot-beaked blades are best), a sturdy pair of gloves, old gardening clothes or an apron and a pruning saw. Keep viral diseases in check by wiping the secateur blades with a cloth moistened with disinfectant or bleach after you prune each rose bush.

How to prune modern bush roses

Remove any dead branches and thin, weak and spindly growth. Remove any old branches (they'll look dull and grey while new growth is red/green and shiny). Cut the stem off at the bud union. If there are any shoots (called 'suckers') growing from below the bud union, remove these also.

Remove any crossing and crowded branches to open the centre of the bush and allow good air circulation. Prune any branches that are thinner than the thickness of a pencil.

Shorten the remaining branches by half and prune each one to a plump outward-facing bud. When making your cuts, cut on a 45 degree angle about 1 cm above an outward-facing bud (see step 5 in the sequence above).

Prune above the bud scar.

Pruning other rose types

Shrub roses, both modern and old, do not need pruning except for thinning and removal of very old or dead wood. Train climbing roses to a horizontal position to increase flowering. Reduce good stems to half. On weeping roses, remove the oldest stems and shorten the longest to just above ground level.

How hard to prune

1 **Hard pruning.** Cut stems back to only three or four buds. Hard pruning is recommended for newly planted roses or for rejuvenating neglected roses. It results in larger, but fewer, blooms.

2 **Moderate pruning.** Cut stems back to half their length. This method is recommended for all established roses.

3 **Light pruning.** Cut stems back to two thirds their length, so that the main stems are merely tipped. Use this method with very vigorous varieties. Light pruning generally results in a profusion of flowers.

Planting bare-rooted roses

1 Prior to planting, soak your roses in lukewarm water for 12–24 hours.

2 Choose a site that has 4–6 hours of sun per day and well drained soil.

3 Dig a hole large enough to easily fit the roots of the plants, and deep enough so that the bud union will be just above the soil level.

4 Before you backfill the hole, mix some rose food into the soil (follow the recommended dosage on the packet).

5 Trim off any broken roots or stems, then hold the plant in place (with bud union at ground level) and backfill the hole. Tread the soil firmly and leave a basin at the base of the plant for watering.

6 Soak the soil with a few buckets of water.

Transplanting Winter or very early spring is also a good time for transplanting roses. Simply prune them back first, then dig up as much root ball as you can and replant, following the instructions at left from step 2 onwards.

Pests If you have a problem with aphids and caterpillars because excessive spring feeding has resulted in soft, fleshy growth, try feeding your roses in winter with a rotted manure mulch, then feed them again in autumn to encourage late blooms. For the rest of the growing season, top up monthly with a liquid feed specifically formulated for roses.

beating rose pests

Roses inevitably suffer from black spot each summer, unless you are growing varieties that are resistant to this disease. To combat black spot, try to increase air circulation by pruning bushes into an open vase shape. Rake up all fallen leaves and dispose of them, ideally by composting them. As soon as pruning has been completed, start spraying with a combined rose spray (contains fungicide and insecticide) as directed by the maker. Repeat the application throughout the spring and summer.

viburnum

For showy flowers, heavenly perfume, bright berries and colourful autumn leaves, the various species of viburnum cover almost everything you could desire in an ornamental plant. Some — such as *Viburnum odoratissimum*, *V. tinus* and *V. japonicum* — are evergreen and make great screens or formal hedges. Deciduous species like the Japanese snowball bush (*V. plicatum*) and snowball tree (*V. opulus* 'Roseum', illustrated) have sensational late spring and early summer flowers. *V. x bodnantense* produces its fragrant pink flowers from autumn to spring.

Vital statistics

Scientific name: *Viburnum* sp.
Family: Caprifoliaceae.
Climate: There are viburnums which are suited to a wide range of climates, from warm or mild to cool and cold.

You are best advised to buy what is available in your local garden centre.
Culture: Moderate pruning after flowering.
Colours: Plants produce white or pink flowers; or white flowers from pink buds.
Height: Viburnums grow to 2–5 m.
Planting time: Plant any time from pots.
Soil: Require moist, fertile well-drained loam.
Position: Grow in full sun to part shade.
Fertilizer: Add lots of compost and mulch to the surrounding soil to help retain moisture over summer.
Pests/diseases: Aphids are often a problem in summer but are controlled with sprays of insecticidal soaps. If leaf spots appear spray with a systemic fungicide.
Propagation: Propagate evergreens from semi-ripe cuttings in summer or autumn, deciduous species from hardwood cuttings in winter.

Trees

Chosen carefully, trees can provide the essential elements of colour, seasonal interest and longevity in the garden. Their new growth is part of the magic of spring – acid yellow gleditsias, elms and robinia, purple splashes from many maples and the lettuce green of magnolias in young, tender growth all form part of the spell.

Fast finishes

If your garden is devoid of cover, check out these speedy growers which will provide fast shade. A tree doesn't just provide a refuge from the sun for you — it will also protect other plants growing underneath, allowing a calm, green garden oasis to develop.

Fiddlewood (*Citharexylum*) is a fast-growing evergreen tree reaching 10 m, with plenty of features to recommend it. First, the glossy green foliage gives great cover. The perfumed white flowers which appear in spring and summer also make it suitable for blending with green and white colour schemes. Fiddlewoods also have another unusual characteristic: the leaves change colour in spring and turn salmon orange, almost like an autumn display. Fiddlewoods are for warm and mild climates so in areas prone to hard frosts grow them in tubs and winter in a frost-free conservatory.

The weeping European ash (*Fraxinus excelsior* 'Pendula') is a handsome deciduous tree with weeping branches that sweep down to the ground. It is fully hardy but needs plenty of space to develop. Or, if you have the space, the common horse chestnut (*Aesculus hippocastanum*) is a vigorous deciduous tree with a spectacular late spring/early summer display of white flowers, and huge hand-shaped leaves.

Don't overlook gum trees. Most have sparse canopies, making them perfect for providing dappled shade, and many have beautiful flowers, mottled bark or scented foliage to add to their charm. Spring-flowering gums include the hardy snow gum (*Eucalyptus pauciflora* subsp. *niphophila*) with fluffy white flowers.

A tree for all seasons, fiddlewood has handsome foliage, very small white, scented flowers and seasonal colour.

When the root is deep, there is no reason to fear the wind.

Chinese proverb

There is a flowering blossom tree perfect for every garden. Position the smaller deciduous blossom trees for winter sun and summer shade. For small gardens consider weeping cherry trees that have been grafted onto a standard. They make excellent focal points. Here, the blossom and fragrance of a flowering cherry and *Choisya ternata* combine to create a pretty garden sanctuary.

Spring blossom trees

Nothing signals the end of winter more than spring blossom. Bursting from bare grey branches, the buds swell and then open to fill the air with fragrance and a white or pink haze of colour.

All blossom trees are deciduous. Most flower on bare branches before the leaves appear, some as early as midwinter. Many of these smaller deciduous trees are ideal for the home garden.

Soil and climate

All flowering fruit trees are adaptable to most soil types, but they benefit from regular feeding, summer watering and a heavy application of organic mulch.

Most tolerate a range of climates, although cherries and crab apples do perform better in areas with cold winters. If you live in a warm coastal area and still want the beauty of spring blossom, stick with flowering peaches, which are suitable even for seaside gardens provided they are sheltered from salt-laden winds.

Selection guide

Flowering apricots

The flowering apricots (*Prunus mume*) have a delicate profusion of flowers, more so than other blossoms. Varieties include white and pink, in either single or double forms, all of which are fragrant. Apricots have a broad, spreading shape and grow to approximately 4 x 4 m.

Flowering cherries

One of the first to flower is *Prunus subhirtella* 'Autumnalis' which starts in autumn and continues into spring. The Taiwan cherry, *Prunus campanulata*, prefers milder conditions and has pendulous, bell-shaped, deep pink blossoms throughout spring.

Different cherries have different requirements for cold temperatures; basically, without cold winters they won't flower or set fruit. The Taiwan cherry has the lowest chill requirement of all the cherries, which means it can tolerate warmer climates and is one of the first to flower, usually in early spring. The single, bell-shaped flowers are a deep cyclamen red and hang in pendulant clusters. This tree's mature dimensions of 4 x 3 m, with an upright, narrow habit, make it ideal for a small garden.

Other species, which are more suited to cooler areas, include the Japanese and Chinese cherries, which are usually grown as standards, creating a broad umbrella effect. Most cherries have the bonus of a brilliant autumn show of foliage, with colours ranging from yellows to brilliant reds.

Flowering peaches

The spring-flowering peaches, reliable small flowering trees, reach 4 m at maturity. These magnificent blossom trees grow well in warm temperate areas. Prune them immediately after flowering to prevent fruit formation and to encourage vigorous new growth for next season's flowers.

Particularly well-known peaches, varieties of *Prunus persica*, include 'Klara Meyer' and 'Helen Borchers'. Tending to flower mid-spring, the unusual crimson 'Magnifica' makes a strong splash of colour, while the equally unusual 'Versicolor' has multicoloured blooms which range from almost white to candy-striped and deep pink. The white-flowered 'Alboplena' is always popular, with its large white double flowers.

Flowering plums

Well suited to warm gardens, the flowering plums are the hardiest of all blossoms, tolerating a wide range of climatic conditions (to -28°C) and soil types. Foliage is one of their principal features, and the flowers, which appear in early spring, range from white through to pink in both single and double forms. Blossoms are followed by dark black-red foliage which provides a strong contrast.

The purple-leaved cherry plum (*Prunus cerasifera* 'Nigra') has delicately perfumed, shell pink flowers followed by deep purple foliage. *Prunus x blireana* is a cross between flowering plum and flowering apricot, with deeper pink double blossoms and reddish

Clockwise from above: *Malus floribunda*, *Prunus* 'Shirotae', *Prunus persica* and *Malus* 'Hopa'.

purple leaves. Flowering plums can grow to about 4 x 3 m.

Crab apples

Crab apples flower later in spring, with the blossoms appearing after the foliage. Closely related to eating apples, they have small, edible and often decorative fruit. Their moderate size and shapely spreading form make them ideal shade trees in small gardens. Once established, a crab apple flowers and fruits better if left undisturbed.

There are many varieties ranging from pink single-flowered trees, such as the Japanese crab apple (*Malus floribunda*), to spectacular double varieties such as 'Katherine' with light pink blossoms.

Above: *Robinia pseudoacacia.*

Below: *Gleditsia triacanthos* 'Sunburst'.

Favourite deciduous trees

If you have room, consider planting a deciduous tree. It will let in valuable winter sun but also provide summer shade.

Two locusts, *Robinia* x *slavinii* 'Hillieri' and *R.* x *ambigua* 'Decaisneana', grow quickly to 10 m and are smothered in pink flowers during late spring and early summer. Another beauty is the laburnum, or golden rain tree (golden chain tree), one of the most popular spring-flowering trees. It forms a curtain of golden yellow flowers when trained over a pergola, an impressive way of growing it to provide shade. Of course, it can also be grown as a normal tree, when it will reach a height of around 8 m. One of the best laburnums is *L.* x *watereri* 'Vossii' which has extra-long racemes of rich yellow flowers. Sennas (syn. cassias) also have yellow flowers but in frost-prone climates should be grown in tubs and wintered in a conservatory.

Many deciduous trees have stunning foliage. For a splash of yellow, choose between the golden robinia *Robinia pseudoacacia* 'Frisia', which has an upright habit, or the more graceful, weeping look of *Gleditsia triacanthos* 'Sunburst'. Another *Gleditsia*, which has bronze-claret new growth and can be a good contrast specimen, is *G.* 'Rubylace'.

An impressive deciduous tree is the *Catalpa bignonioides*, or Indian bean tree, which flowers in profusion in summer with white flowers, stained yellow and purple. Some cultivars, such as 'Aurea', have sensational large heart-shaped leaves.

He that plants trees loves others beside himself.

Traditional

dogwood

Tree dogwoods are spectacular, especially *Cornus florida* and its varieties from the eastern United States. The beautiful North American dogwood is a delightful tree. The simple flower head consists of an inconspicuous flower surrounded by showy white or rosy pink bracts. Its foliage is richly coloured in autumn, and its spring growth is sometimes flushed pink, depending on the variety.

Vital statistics

Scientific name: *Cornus* sp.
Family: Cornaceae.
Climate: Cool to cold climates.
Culture: Great small tree for cooler climates, requiring little pruning or feeding.
Colours: Produces snowy white to rosy pink flower-like bracts, followed by bright red clusters of fruits.
Height and spread: Grows to 6 x 8 m, taller in its native habitat.
Planting time: Plant in autumn and winter.
Soil: Dogwood will not be successful in poor, chalky soils, preferring free-draining soils enriched with organic matter.
Position: Grow in full sun with shelter from strong winds.
Fertilizer: Young trees can be fed with slow-release fertilizer in spring.
Pests/diseases: This tree can suffer from fungal wilts, anthracnose and fungal leaf spotting.

The Oak is called
the king of trees,
The Aspen quivers
in the breeze,
The Poplar grows up
straight and tall,
The Peach tree spreads
along the wall,
The Sycamore gives
pleasant shade,
The Willow droops
in watery glade,
The Fir tree useful
timber gives,
The Beech amid the
forest lives.

Sara Coleridge

spring
herbs, fruit & vegetables

The delicate flavours of spring finally make it to the dinner table: young lamb seasoned with fresh mint, and the earliest peas. The milder your climate, the more early fruit and vegetables that will be available.

There is a lot of concern these days about genetically modified food, and many experts are advancing the case for chemical-free produce. This is more than just a trend, and there is no better way to get on the right track than to grow your own food.

Indeed, there are already many people who are quiet participants in a backyard revolution, growing their own herbs, fruit and vegetables.

The possibilities are endless: a patch of taste-laden, vine-ripened tomatoes; an old-fashioned strawberry patch with its promise of succulent, sweet berries; the simple pleasure to be had from picking some parsley growing in a pot at your back door. No matter what your level of commitment, the idea of consuming produce that you have grown yourself has undeniable appeal. The dreary routine of waiting in supermarket queues in order to buy wilted lettuce and tasteless, waxy produce can become a thing of the past.

What was Paradise but a garden? An orchard of trees and herbs, full of pleasure, and nothing there but delights.

W. Lawson

Herbs

Spring is the perfect time to revive tired herbs, or pot up fresh supplies for your windowsill or verandah. Growth is fast, which means they taste tender and sweet.

Left to right: Chinese spinach, 'Sweet Bite' tomatoes and a lush vegetable garden planted with flowers.

Below left: A herb and vegetable garden.

Planting fresh crops of herbs in spring will ensure a summer harvest of annuals such as coriander and basil. Herb gardens can range in size from a garden dedicated to herb growing to a few ground-cover herbs in a rockery. In a small backyard or townhouse you can even keep your herb garden in pots on the back step, or hanging in a basket on a sunny verandah. If you live in a flat, herbs can be grown on a sunny windowsill. The more accessible the herbs are, the easier it becomes to make use of them in the kitchen.

growing tips

- Herbs grow naturally in many different soils and climates. Some thrive in extremely dry areas, others in tropical rainforests and temperate woodlands, so if you choose the appropriate herbs for the prevailing conditions you cannot go wrong.
- Most herbs prefer full sun and free-draining soil.
- Don't pick more than one third of a young plant or more than half of a mature specimen at the one time. The more often you pick, the bushier and healthier herbs become.
- Don't overfertilize — there will be too much soft leafy growth at the expense of essential oils.
- Many herbs grow better when planted next to other herbs, but some will struggle in the wrong combinations. For example, mint hates growing near parsley. If your herbs aren't doing well, and they are growing in the right conditions, maybe they are in with the wrong crowd.
- Snails and insects like herbs too. Be vigilant and pick off grubs by hand, and trap snails with small saucers of beer.
- Have you ever wondered what the difference is between a herb and a spice? Herbs are the leaves of plants; spices are produced from the other parts, such as flowers, seeds and roots.
- To develop full flavour, most herbs should have at least five hours of sunlight a day or sixteen hours under fluorescent lights (placed 5–10 cm above plants).

Saffron strands.

Some popular herbs you can easily grow yourself (left to right): parsley, chives, rosemary, sage, thyme and dill.

Top ten herbs

1 Parsley. The mostly widely grown herb, growing to 45 cm from a thick taproot. Rich in iron and vitamins A, B and C, it is great in salads, soups, stuffing and garnishes. Legend has it that you have to be wicked to be able to grow parsley successfully. Replace on a regular basis as this plant has a disconcerting habit of disappearing from the garden just when you think it is established for good.

2 Chives. A perennial herb with fine, hollow leaves, it adds onion flavour to food and can be used as a companion plant for roses.

3 Rosemary. A woody shrub that loves full sun and dry conditions. It is perfect with lamb.

4 Thyme. A symbol of courage and vitality. This herb is used for flavouring egg and cheese dishes. It is mostly grown as an aromatic ground cover for a sunny spot.

5 Dill. This herb is great for use in pickling, with fish and in soups. It has attractive fine foliage and needs to be forced with lots of nitrogen fertilizers.

6 Mint. A herb that grows well in cool, moist areas, even shade, although it can become a pest if it likes the conditions too much. It can be used in drinks and salads and for flavouring the traditional favourite, roast lamb.

7 and 8 Marjoram and oregano. These closely related, strongly flavoured herbs are excellent for flavouring soups and pasta. They make a great ground cover in a sunny spot.

9 Sage. A close relative of ornamental salvia, with grey leaves useful for stuffing, and for flavouring soups, veal and poultry.

10 Basil. An extremely popular cooking herb for use in soups, tomato dishes and pasta. This herb is a summer-growing annual and needs replanting each spring. It is also an effective companion plant for tomatoes, as it repels white fly and other pests.

Marjoram.

Indoor growing tips

Herbs really grow best in full sun, so while temporarily growing them indoors is an option, don't expect them to last forever.

- Select a pot with plenty of drainage holes.
- Use a well-drained potting mix suitable for shrubs.
- Incorporate a slow-release fertilizer at the highest rate.
- Water with liquid fertilizer regularly if growth is slow.
- Try for as much direct sunlight as possible to build in flavour.
- Try rotating your herbs with the same group outside.
- Choose herbs that cope with some shade, such as mint and 5-in-1 herb (*Plectranthus amboinicus*), also known as Spanish thyme or Indian mint.

Sweet basil.

check list

jobs to do now

- Prune passion fruit in early spring.
- Feed fruit trees in early spring with a balanced, general-purpose proprietary fertilizer.
- Consider erecting a fruit cage to protect ripening fruits from birds. It is a simple structure: a tubular-steel framework covered in plastic netting.

plant now

- Salad herbs and leafy greens — including lettuce, mustard, cress, radicchio, endive and rocket — should all go in now.
- Sow annual herbs such as basil, coriander, parsley and dill.
- Container-grown raspberries, gooseberries and strawberries can all be planted for delicious summer fruit. Plant in early spring if possible.
- Sow vegetables such as peas, beans (dwarf, broad or fava and climbing), eggplant (aubergine), courgettes (zucchini squash), carrots, cabbages, melons, sweet corn, beetroot, sweet peppers (capsicum), cucumbers, pumpkins, radishes and celery.
- Plant tomatoes — home-grown varieties are much tastier than shop-bought tomatoes and children will love them too.
- The onion family, called alliums, include chives and shallots and look great planted as a decorative border because of their tufting, grass-like foliage. Plant them now together with garlic.
- Do not overlook tall edibles such as Jerusalem and globe artichokes.

flowering now

- Rosemary and borage
- Ornamental cabbages and kale for their foliage colour in cool areas where low temperatures bring out the strongest pigmentation in the coloured leaves
- The earliest peas and broad or fava beans, especially those sown in autumn in mild climates

sweet **basil**

Many herbs die out over winter, needing replacement each spring. The most popular of all annual herbs is probably basil. The aromatic foliage is a superb companion to tomato-based dishes, and the many varieties mean it can look as good as it tastes.

Vital statistics

Scientific name: *Ocimum basilicum.*
Family: Lamiaceae.
Flower/foliage colour: Basil produces white flowers. Foliage can be purple or grass green, and is shiny and ornamental in its own right.
Height: Bushes grow to around 0.5 m.
Planting time: Plant during spring.
Soil: Grow in rich, well-drained, well-dug soil.
Position: Prefers an open aspect and full sun, but will tolerate partial shade.
Planting spacing: Space 20 cm apart.
Fertilizer: Top dress annually with blood, fish and bone or old manure.
Watering: Water well during dry weather.
Pests/diseases: Slugs and snails think basil is delicious! Watch out for them, particularly after rain.
Cutting: Don't cut more than a third of the plant at one time, and trim off flowers to promote leaf growth.
Uses: Leaves have a clove-like flavour and can be used fresh or dried. Basil tastes superb in Southeast Asian and Mediterranean cuisine, and is excellent in summer salads, tomato dishes, pesto sauce and stir-fries.
Ornamental varieties: Bush, camphor, cinnamon, 'Green Ruffles', 'Lemon Sweet Dani', lime, 'Purple Ruffles', 'Red Rubin', sacred, 'Spicy Globe', sweet and Thai. There are many more varieties. Availability depends on country or region. The best advice is to check out the mail-order seed catalogues or your local garden centre.

Fruit

Most of us live in a temperate climate so we can grow a range of fruit trees, from apples and pears to stone fruits and berries. In frost-prone areas these can be extended to tender fruits with a heated conservatory.

Position is all when it comes to fruit. If possible avoid low-lying areas which may be frost pockets. Improve soil before planting by deep digging and adding bulky organic matter. Drainage must be good so install land drains if waterlogging occurs.

Elderberry

Elderberry or *Sambucus* dates back to ancient Greek times, and is shrouded in mystery and folklore. It is said that Christ's cross was made of elderwood, and that elder would only grow where blood had been spilt!

In fact, elderberry grows happily in any temperate or cold climate and is very hardy. There are a few species, but if you intend to make elderberry wine, sorbet or jelly, be sure to plant the edible *Sambucus nigra* rather than the others, which are poisonous. This species bears large heads of tiny white flowers in late spring or early summer depending on climate, followed by clusters of purple-black berries.

A few highly ornamental cultivars are available, including the purple-leafed 'Guincho Purple', golden-leafed 'Aurea' and the white variegated form.

Of all our fruits, the apple is perhaps the most useful, and is appreciated by birds and beasts as well as by man. My bullfinch loves his slice of apple, my horse thanks me by many little signs for the gift of an apple and my cows delight to be offered one.

Nineteenth century gardening book

Beautiful berry fruits

Judicious planting of berries can supply fruit from late spring/early summer (particularly strawberries) through to autumn, with a glut midsummer for scrumptious pavlovas, fruit salads, jams and jellies. Berries are absolutely delicious when eaten fresh straight from the bush, or cooked in a little sugar and water and poured over ice cream, or meringue and cream.

The smallish nature of many types makes them perfect for the backyard orchard. They can be broadly separated into two groups: those with an upright bushy habit, and those that ramble and trail. The two exceptions of course are strawberries and mulberries.

Bush fruits include currants, blueberries and gooseberries. The most ornamental and adaptable of these is the blueberry, which ripens midsummer and has a piquant and unique taste. The blueberry bush has ball-shaped flowers that develop into green berries which gradually turn blue. The leaves change into vibrant autumn shades before falling, although in warmer climates the blueberry is not deciduous. It can be a very attractive addition to any garden. Growing to a height of up to 2 m, blueberries require moist, cool conditions and very acid soil. They should be planted in a sheltered position that receives morning sun and afternoon shade.

Gooseberries and currants have a high winter chilling requirement and therefore are best suited to cool or warm temperate regions. It is also advisable to shelter them from strong winds. They ripen in summer.

Clockwise from bottom left: Mulberries, raspberries, blueberries, strawberries and gooseberries.

The Cape gooseberry or ground cherry is quite an ornamental perennial but is not related at all to gooseberries — it is actually in the tomato family. The yellow globe-shaped fruit is held in a papery husk and ripens in summer. The ground cherry is treated as an annual in cool climates and grown like tomatoes, under glass in frost-prone areas.

Trailing berries and brambles include blackberries (some varieties do not become invasive), boysenberries, loganberries and youngberries. Raspberries, the latest berries to ripen, crop right into late autumn. Blackberries, boysenberries and youngberries will grow in both cool and warm areas, but loganberries as well as raspberries like it cold and crisp.

Mulberries are often overlooked these days as a summer fruit for the home garden. Maybe the memories of stained fingers and clothing has banished them from modern society's backyards, but this preoccupation with cleanliness is a sad loss to children everywhere. After all, what other tree could possibly be as much fun? They are great to climb, produce fruit all summer, and grow absolutely anywhere with ease. They are also the favourite diet for silkworms, which brings children all the delights of keeping silkworms and watching the process of metamorphosis.

In a smaller garden you can plant weeping standard mulberries, which make a beautiful specimen tree, and if you're still worried about the stains, remember you can either use green fruits to remove stubborn marks, or choose the white-fruited mulberry.

Did you know? According to medieval superstition, blackberries picked after Michaelmas Day were contaminated by the devil.

Care tips

- All berries should be picked when well coloured. They store in the fridge for up to three weeks, or you can freeze them for later. Well-grown berries will fruit for up to twenty years and produce 5 kg of berries each year.
- In general, fruit is produced on year-old wood, so carefully prune and remove older unproductive stems to ensure cropping from one year to the next, and a plant that can be harvested with ease.
- Prepare the soil before planting by adding organic matter and humus. Generous amounts of well-made compost will provide the plants with excellent nutrition. Do not add lime.
- It's best to plant out young trees during the autumn months when the bushes are dormant.
- When well established, mulch generously with leaves, woodchips or sawdust to a depth of 10 cm to provide protection and moisture for the surface roots. Thick mulch will also suppress weeds.
- Berries should appear in the year following planting, but only a few to start with. Feed all fruits in early spring by applying a general-purpose, balanced fertilizer followed by a mulch of garden compost or well-rotted manure.

potted
strawberries

Strawberries can be grown in garden beds or in containers, such as large terracotta strawberry pots specially designed for the purpose.

1 To plant a strawberry pot, half fill it with a premium quality potting mix to just below the level of the first holes. Add water-storing granules to the mix and make sure it drains well, as strawberries hate water-logged soil.

2 Carefully remove the plants from their containers so that you don't damage the roots.

3 Gently push each plant through a hole in the sides of the pot.

4 Cover the roots with more potting mix as you go, then fill the pot almost to the rim before planting another few strawberries in the top.

5 Top up with potting mix and water the plants in. Keep watering regularly during their growing season to encourage good quality fruit.

6 Place the pot in any sunny spot, keep it well watered and you'll have an ornamental feature for your garden as well as a source of delicious fruit. You can also grow strawberries in plastic 'blooming' bags which have holes in the sides.

cherries

Both sweet and sour cherries are grown but the former are by far the most popular. Cherries bloom in spring, and in warm areas fruits may start to appear in late spring, but this is the exception and gardeners in cooler areas will have to wait until the beginning of summer for the earliest fruits to ripen. The peak time for most cherries is midsummer. There are early, mid-season and late varieties to choose from. It is usually necessary to grow two varieties side by side for fruits to be produced.

Vital statistics

Scientific name: *Prunus* sp.
Family: Rosaceae.
Climate: Cherries need cool winters, with up to 1200 hours below 7°C.
Culture: They flower in the spring so blossoms are vulnerable to frost damage. Make sure the trees are not in a frost pocket.
Colours: Cherries produce white blossom. The fruit varies in colour from red to black.
Height: Grow to about 10 m. But cherries can also be trained as more manageable fans on a wall or fence.
Planting time: Plant in autumn when trees are dormant.
Soil: Grow in deep, well drained soil.
Position: Grow in full sun.
Fertilizer: Feed with complete fertilizer in early spring.
Pests/diseases: To protect from birds, trees need to be netted, more easily achieved with fan-trained trees. Cherries also suffer from aphids, brown rot and canker.
Cutting: Shaping is needed to form an open framework although this is normally stopped after the third season as cherries fruit on older spurs.
Storage: Fruit can be preserved or glacéed.

Vegetables

Spring is the time to start your vegie patch or rejuvenate a forgotten plot. Many delicious favourites are sown right now — from tomatoes to sweet corn, cucumbers and peppers.

Start a patch

It is quite simple to start your own vegie patch. It can be big enough to feed the family or as small as an old packing case. Start by selecting a sunny, sheltered spot. Clear away any unwanted grass and weeds, then add lots of organically rich anything to your soil — it can be home-made compost, spent mushroom compost, animal manure or composted bark. Next, apply some complete plant food and pelletized manure to ensure that your vegetables have plenty to eat. Vegetables are hungry plants and the faster they grow, the sweeter they'll taste.

Now you're ready for sowing. You can sow many larger seeds, such as beans and marrows, directly into the ground, but for other types you will need to raise them first in seedling trays then plant them out as you need them. Whichever method you try, stagger your sowings by a couple of weeks so that you have a continuous supply rather than a glut at one time.

Water young plants regularly and watch out for sapsucking insects like aphids and whitefly as well as hungry caterpillars which like tender young greens as much as we do. Be vigilant in patrolling for pests. Hand culling at dusk is an efficient method of controlling many grubs, while yellow sticky paper or petroleum jelly on pieces of plastic is a good way of trapping the sapsuckers.

Sow pumpkin seeds after the last frost, or indoors in cold regions for transplanting in warmer weather.

A well-designed patch such as this one uses the vertical space as well as the ground.

Space and conditions

The size of vegetable beds should be tailored to each family's requirements. If you eat lots of vegetables, have a big backyard and want to save money, go for broke with a large vegetable garden. An area of 80–100 m² can feed a family of four all year.

Where to locate your vegetable patch

The first step is to select the warmest and sunniest spot in the garden. The site should also have good drainage: pick a gently sloping area if you are on really heavy clay soils and raise the beds by adding lots of compost and manure to the soil.

Keep the beds accessible for planting, weeding and harvesting; many fruits, vegetables and herbs are highly decorative, so even if you don't have room to devote a whole patch to them, grow them in borders with your ornamental garden plants.

Space-saving plants

A small vegetable patch that is lovingly cared for will be more productive than a larger neglected patch. A wide variety of dwarf cultivars are now available. Perfect for pots, these establish themselves quickly and can be grown outside the conventional vegetable-planting seasons if they are placed in protected positions. Lettuce, cabbage, oriental vegetables and tomatoes are all ideal.

Fruit and vegetable care tips

- Always plant the right variety for the season.
- Prepare your soil with lots of organic material or compost.
- Only grow as much as you can eat and don't grow more than you can manage to look after.
- Control weeds, pick off any damaged fruit and remove diseased plants as soon as possible – these are all essential procedures for the organic gardener.
- Water and feed your vegetables regularly.
- Harvest them as soon as they are ripe, otherwise the birds or rabbits will do it for you.

SOWING FINE SEEDS

1 Before sowing, create a fine tilth in your vegetable patch. Draw a drill in the soil.

2 This paper strip is encrusted with carrot seeds. Simply lay the tape in the drill and the paper will eventually rot down into the soil.

3 Backfill lightly.

4 Water in the newly sown seeds.

Alternative vegetables

Heirloom vegetables

These old-fashioned types often have the best flavour. You can obtain low-acid, yellow striped tomatoes, red-skinned eggplant and rainbow chard (silver beet) to brighten up your dinner plate. Many other types are available, and seed-swapping or gardening clubs offer great selections.

Perpetual vegetables

Most vegetables are annuals and need replacing each season. Try to include some perennial kinds such as globe artichokes, Jerusalem artichokes, cardoons, asparagus and seakale (*Crambe maritima*).

Asian vegetables

Specialised cuisines have developed around the vegetables grown in Asia. Chinese broccoli, cabbage, radish, turnips and cabbage-like greens such as tatsoi and mizuna are delicious in stir-fries and salads.

Edible flowers

Appearance is an integral part of the enjoyment of food. Borage, calendula, elder flower, heartsease, nasturtium and sage flowers don't just have pretty faces, they also taste great. See page 314 in 'Autumn' for some ideas on how to use them.

Clockwise from above left: Nasturtiums, Chinese spinach and pot marigold (*Calendula officinalis*).

Right: 'Bull's Blood', a heritage variety of beetroot.

Sowing seeds:
five steps to success

Jump start spring by planting cold-sensitive crops into peat pots that can be planted straight into the ground once the frosty weather finishes.

Step 1

Fill the container (seed tray or pot) with seed-raising mix to 1 cm below the top of the container. Level the mix.

Step 2

You can plant tomatoes, aubergines, sweet peppers and chillies. For this step-by-step sequence, we planted tomato seeds.

Step 3

Sow two seeds per pot in order to allow for any losses.

Step 4

Sow seed to a depth that is roughly equivalent to the seed diameter. Lightly cover with seed-raising mix and firm it very gently with your fingers.

Step 5

Water in gently using a fine rose on the watering can. Seeds need warmth to germinate so place the container either in a heated propagating case with bottom heat, or on a warm windowsill indoors and cover with a sheet of clear plastic or glass. When germination starts remove any coverings.

Did you know? Pak choi, also known as bok choi, literally means 'white vegetable'.

SPRING SOWING

1 Fill some peat pots with seed-raising mix.

2 Sprinkle the seeds into your hand.

3 Sow two seeds per pot.

4 Sow seed to a depth that is roughly the same as the seed diameter. Cover lightly with seed-raising mix and firm it gently to ensure the seeds are in close contact with the compost.

5 Water in.

Fresh asparagus shoots are a delicious spring vegetable. White spears are the result of 'earthing up' or mounding the soil around the shoots.

inferior spears. Alternatively, plant out two-year-old crowns in autumn or early spring. Some people mound their plants to produce extra long white spears, but whatever your practice, ensure your soil is open and friable so that the shoots can spring up easily.

Garden legumes

Commercially frozen peas (and beans) are the most popular green vegetables, yet their flavour cannot compare with that of home-grown peas, especially when they are picked as 'petit pois' — tiny, sweet peas. For ease at home, why not plant a hanging basket of edible podded sugar peas (snow peas). For something a little different, try the asparagus pea, which is not a true pea and has winged seeds which are eaten whole and are flavoured like asparagus. For great colour, look for purple peas.

Beans are one of the first of the summer vegetables and will grow in just about anything! Colours will range from the traditional green, through to blue, white, yellow and purple cultivars. If you are growing haricot beans (which have edible seeds), leave the pods till they turn yellow on the bush before harvesting them. If you are growing runner beans you have a choice of climbing or bush varieties, the former bearing the heaviest crops.

The ultimate health food, peas and beans are tremendously good sources of protein, amino acids, fibre, vitamins and minerals, and are low in fat and sugar. They also contain phyto-oestrogens which are beneficial to women suffering from premenstrual tension or going through menopause, and help protect men against prostate cancer. Soak dried beans for at least an hour and rinse and cook thoroughly (normally an hour or so) to avoid flatulence.

Asparagus

Asparagus is actually the tender young shoots that emerge each spring from a fern-like plant. It is traditionally grown in a corner of the vegie patch where it can do its own thing, and be harvested once a year when the shoots are tasty and young. Twenty plants should feed a family and blanched spears keep well in the freezer.

Asparagus is best suited to mild and cold climates, as each winter it rests during the cold weather and dies back to crowns. It can be sown from seed, but cull any female (berry-producing) plants as they have

peas

Shelling peas and edible-podded sugar peas (known as snow peas) and mangetout types, are pretty, easy-to-grow annuals and are attractive in the vegetable garden. Don't confuse them with 'sweet pea', as it is their fragrance, not their seed, which is sweet. The ornamental *Lathyrus odoratus* is highly poisonous both raw and cooked and can cause paralysis if eaten.

Vital statistics

Scientific name: *Pisum sativum*.

Family: Fabaceae.

Climate: Peas can be grown in most climates but bear in mind that the seeds will not germinate if the soil is colder than 10°C. Although seedlings are not harmed by frosts, the flowers can certainly be damaged. Bear these points in mind when deciding on the best time to sow in your area.

Culture: Tall varieties need support. Keep the weeds down. Dig finished plants back into the soil to act as a green manure.

Colours: Peas produce white or purple flowers.

Height: Grow to 45 cm to 2 m depending on the variety.

Planting time: Main sowing period is spring and summer, but autumn sowings can be made in mild areas.

Soil: Grow in well-drained soil with a pH of 6.0 to 7.0.

Position: Peas grow in sun to partial shade.

Planting depth and spacing: Sow seed 3 cm deep, 5–10 cm apart.

Fertilizer: Peas don't need much feeding as they are nitrogen-fixing legumes. Slight additions of compound fertilizer and well-composted manure or organic matter prior to sowing should be adequate.

Pests/diseases: Peas have fewer problems than many vegetables, although mildew, blight, grubs and aphids can be a problem. Crop rotation will greatly reduce these.

Harvest: Regularly pick either immature or mature peas, when the pods are shiny and firm. Overripe peas lose their tenderness and flavour.

Propagation: Grow from seed.

Storage: Peas can be stored fresh, dried or frozen.

legumes

1 Dried French or snap beans.

2 Shelling pea 'Earlicrop Massey'.

3 French or snap bean 'Blue Lake'.

4 Broad bean seeds.

5 Edible-podded mangetout peas.

6 Seeds of French or snap beans.

7 Pea seeds 'Greenfeast'.

8 Lima or butter beans.

9 Sugar or snow pea seeds.

10 Snake bean seeds.

11 Broad bean seeds 'Crimson Flowered'.

12 Edible podded sugar pea 'Sugar Snap'.

13 Lima or butter beans.

14 Red French or snap bean seeds.

15 French or snap beans.

16 Runner bean seeds.

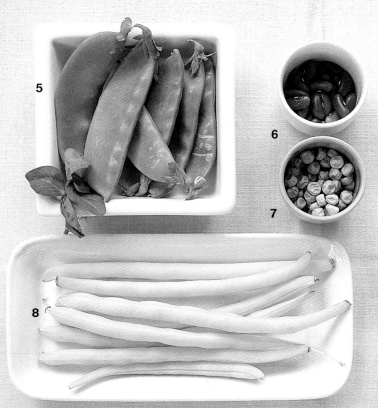

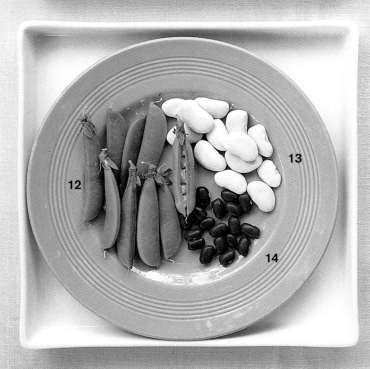

5

6

7

8

9   10   11

12

13

14

15

16

Sunburn. Glare. Sand, salt and sea breezes. Scorched leaves and faded flowers. Picnics, evening walks and heady scents. The drone of cicadas. Nature at full speed.

summer

summer
overview of the season

Summer is the season for using and enjoying your garden — cricket with the kids on the back lawn, barbecues with friends (and the mossies) or simply breakfast on the deck.

Agapanthus flower profusely throughout summer, and the cut blooms are long-lasting.

With holidays, relaxing with the family and hot weather dominating the agenda in summer, it's hard to fit in any gardening other than lawn mowing, watering and mulching. It's easy to see why...Gardeners often refer to summer as the forgotten season. But it can be easy if you choose plants that are reliable, flower generously and fit your lifestyle. So take the heat out of your gardening chores with our summer gardening tips.

Take time to wander around the garden, taking note which plants are unable to cope with summer weather patterns, such as reflected heat or drying winds. The impatiens that were pretty earlier on might now be suffering from dehydration, and need planting in a cooler, shadier position next year.

Summer is not a traditional time for planting, as the hot weather increases the stress on young root systems when they are planted out. This doesn't mean you can't put anything in, it just means you have to

be more careful with your watering, and make sure your purchases have a healthy (not pot-bound) root system (see 'Choosing a good plant at the nursery' on page 17).

A regular stroll through the entire garden will show you gaps that need summer colour. Fill these with annuals, potted colour or advanced plants and that way you'll have lots of flowers for summer. But remember, if your garden is hot and dry during the summer you will need to plant plenty of drought-tolerant plants such as many of the silver-leaved plants, plus achilleas, ceanothus, eryngiums, lavenders, Spanish broom (spartium) and verbascums.

For a head start to your spring flower garden, sow some seeds now, especially of hardy biennials used for spring bedding, such as wallflowers, English daisies and winter/spring flowering pansies, plus sweet Williams and Canterbury bells.

Whatever you do in the garden at this time of the year, do it gently. This is not the time to make major landscape alterations or to establish new garden beds. But that doesn't mean you can forget the garden. Even the most neglected garden looks okay in spring, but if you're lazy now, your summer garden will really start to struggle.

- Wake up early and take a walk outside to look for pests, and squish them.
- Before the summer heat takes its toll, check that your watering system is working and all the nozzles are clear.
- Prune any rampantly growing plants before they become a problem.
- Turn the compost, or start a new heap.
- Clean ponds and other water features.
- Keep weeds under control or by late summer you'll have a full harvest!
- With any luck you remembered to feed with complete fertilizer in spring, but if your garden needs a miracle or two, try some liquid feed.
- The warm, and maybe humid, summer weather can bring with it fungal diseases such as mildew that are liable to attack your plants. Try to water the roots of plants rather than the leaves as this is less likely to encourage diseases.

The boldness of summer blooms can make it easy to overlook the intricate, such as these dainty purple berries of flax lily (dianella), the graceful leaves of the silk tree (albizia) and, in the conservatory, the blooms of *Dais cotinifolia*.

weatherwatch
Last, but not least, remember to water. Deep soakings are the best, and if you haven't spread a thick layer of mulch around by now, you really should. It will save you litres of water and countless hours later in the season.

Tidy up   If friends are coming around and you're embarrassed about your lawn, get out with the edger and mower – it's amazing what a fresh haircut can do. Also, a blast with hose-on fertilizer will smarten up your grass by midsummer. But do not feed when the soil is dry.

Be prepared for extreme weather conditions in summer. If you live in a fire-risk area, always keep your gutters clear (top). Avoid damage from strong winds by pruning trees with brittle branches, such as this robinia (above).

Summer protection

Summer has its risks, not least of which are too much sun on our bodies and the possibility of bush, forest or heathland fires.

Over summer there is the risk of sunburn. But even more alarming, in recent years we have been told about the ever-increasing risk of skin cancer if we subject our bodies to too much sun without the protection of sunscreen. This is due to receiving ultra-violet radiation because of holes in the ozone layer in the upper atmosphere.

After years of 'slip, slop, slap' advertising, many people are still not heeding the warnings. If you're out and about, put on a hat and sunscreen. Roll down your shirt sleeves, and try and keep out of the sun at midday.

In the garden, the best protection from the sun is a tree, so why not plant one or two? It doesn't need to be a huge forest tree, a small tree will do. Ask your garden centre for a local tree species or select something exotic and attractive. Shade is so cool, you'll love it and so will the wildlife.

In the summer dangerous fires may sweep through some areas of Europe and North America, destroying homes, livestock, native plants and, in extreme cases, even taking human life.

If your home is close to a fire-risk area and you haven't already taken a few precautionary measures, you must carry out a few preventive steps now to lower the risk of becoming a victim. Make sure you clear away all flammable goods around the house and create a wide firebreak between the bush and your property. Many exotic plants have increased volumes of moisture in the leaves and around the canopy compared to native plants: ask your local fire authority and nursery which ones could help slow the speed of fire in your street.

Ensure that you have plenty of hoses close to the house or easy access to swimming pools and water. Check that your auxiliary pumps are in sound working order. Clear out the gutters around your house and be prepared to fill them with water in times of emergency.

On a personal level, place all photo albums and sentimental items together in a place that is easily accessible. Work out a fire procedure with household members so everyone knows what to do. And, of course, always keep a portable radio with fresh batteries handy.

In windy areas it makes sense not to have trees too close to the house, and to avoid those with brittle wood whose branches are liable to snap off during high winds, such as ash trees (fraxinus) and locusts (robinias). If you already have these, judicious pruning reduces potential damage.

Summer watering

Watering plants can be a difficult task for some gardeners to master — too much and the plant drowns, too little and it wilts.

If your water bill is very high, you might be wasting water on your garden and your lawn. When you're watering, check water doesn't run off down paths and driveways into the gutter: your sprinkler should be set to water the lawn and garden only. Watering systems save water. Sprayers and drippers apply water only where it's needed — at the roots of your plants — but do check their nozzles for any blockages.

In hot dry weather you only need to water your lawn for half an hour, twice a week. Anything more wastes water and money. Some clay soils actually repel water so it's a good idea to water your lawn (and your garden too) with one of the new generation soil wetters. These liquids reduce the waxy coating on soil particles, allowing water to penetrate further into the soil to the roots of plants. This helps to moisten pot and garden soils and to stop water wastage from runoff.

It is possible to add water-retaining granules to potting compost. These act as a reservoir so that when the soil dries out, water can be absorbed from the granules. Once you apply water the granules are hydrated again. They continue the swelling and shrinking process, providing plants with water for up to six years. Use them at planting time.

Hoses

Most quality garden hoses have ultraviolet stabilizers or protectors added to the plastic, but unless you take extra care, your garden hose is still only going to last a year or two in the hot summer sun.

The following tips will certainly extend its life by several years.

• It is sensible to put the hose away in the shade when it's not in use.

• Get it off the driveway. The weight of the car fractures the inner tubing, weakening the hose.

• Store your hose by rolling it up. This will remove kinks and bends, which cause wear. To roll up a hose easily and correctly for storage, run the hose out to its full length in a straight line. Then, starting at the tap end, pull the hose up into a circle or wind it on to a portable hose reel. Keeping it rolled up also makes it easy to roll out the hose kink free, next time.

When it's not in use, your hose should be rolled up and, preferably, stored in the shade. Always check the fittings in summer: if they're fitted loosely or worn out, the nozzles and joiners will leak, wasting precious water.

Watering tip Try not to water in the heat of the day, when much of the water will evaporate at once.

Pebbles complement a grey-leafed sedge.

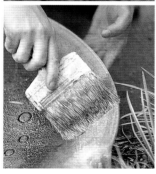

You can use any container for a water feature but make sure you waterproof it with sealant first.

Water features

The allure and charm of a water feature is one of summer's underrated garden essentials. The water reflects light and cools the air, and moving water creates a peaceful ambience.

A water feature can be as simple as a shallow bowl with duckweed or elaborate as a naturalistic pool with cascades.

Many people would love to have a water feature, but the thought of pumps, digging huge holes, liners and the like is off-putting. Installing a pond in the garden is also a fairly expensive business. The easiest and cheapest way is simply to use a large pot.

Wine barrels, stone and glazed pots, old coppers and plastic terracotta look-a-likes are all suitable candidates. Use any large container, but make sure the inside is waterproofed with a sealant and any drainage holes plugged (a cork, or acrylic polymer sealant used to seal around edges of sinks and baths, should do the trick).

Most flowering aquatic plants like the sun, with waterlilies, water irises and pickerel weed all suited to a sunny spot. If the water feature is in partial shade try marsh marigolds, water mint, water forget-me-not, arum lily or calla (*Zantedeschia aethiopica*) and sedges.

You can also use floating aquatics such as frogbit (*Hydrocharis morsus-ranae*) and although most grow quickly you can easily pull out the excess regularly in order to allow the other plants the room they need.

Ponds take time to install but, once established, require less work than garden beds. Position is everything. Avoid placing ponds under trees, as overhanging trees also

water**lilies**

Waterlilies have been featured in Arabic and Moorish gardens for centuries. In China, waterlilies are traditionally grown in large glazed pots raised on plinths in the middle of a courtyard, allowing them to be admired without any distractions. They really took off in Europe and then in the rest of the world in the late nineteenth century when heated glasshouses made it possible for the tropical species to be grown indoors.

The French Impressionist painter Claude Monet featured them in his 'Water Lily' series of paintings, set in his garden in Giverny, France. They are now the best known of all aquatic plants. There is a waterlily available to suit any climate, from tropical to cold zones. The miniature species *Nymphaea tetragona* (also known as *N. pygmaea*) is especially suited to pots. Very beautiful in flower, it is herbaceous, with leaves dying back to a permanent rootstock as the weather cools. Every two or three years established plants can be lifted in spring just as they are starting into growth, and divided.

drop leaves and flowers that upset the biological balance of the water. When selecting water plants, take the position of your water feature into consideration. Arum lilies cope with shade, are long flowering and evergreen. Waterlilies don't like splashing water, need lots of sun and die down over winter, making them suitable for bigger ponds and still pools. Small pots may only take a handful of floating weed.

The world's most popular aquatic plant is the waterlily. Nothing could be more exotic on a balcony or in the garden than a pond filled with waterlilies. The flowers are so elegant and the plants are easy to grow.

Growing waterlilies

You can grow waterlilies in either a large, shallow pond in the garden or in a pot on a verandah or sheltered rooftop garden, as long as it is a sunny position. There are shorter stemmed waterlilies available that

To grow yellow flag iris (*Iris pseudacorus*) successfully, your pond should be in a sunny position.

are perfect for pot culture. Select a tub or decorative pot, about 20–30 cm deep and at least 50 cm wide, without a hole. Lined half barrels are ideal.

Grow waterlilies in a plastic mesh aquatic basket lined with hessian to prevent the soil from falling through. Add a pinch of slow-release fertilizer to the compost and insert the waterlily root system. (Too much fertilizer will result in algal blooms in the water.) Then gently settle the basket into

the water on the bottom of the pot, or to a depth of about half a metre if you are planting in a pond. Keep the water clean; some fish will keep the mossies at bay. After several weeks large leaves will appear, then huge, plump flower buds. Once flowering, waterlilies keep blooming for months, and many are perfumed.

For fantastic flowers and foliage also consider Louisiana iris. They grow naturally in swamps and are great marginals around a

PLANTING WATERLILIES

1 A waterlily root with some new shoots.

2 Insert the waterlily root into compost.

3 Mulch with pebbles.

PLANTING LOUISIANA IRIS

1 Line a wire basket with coconut fibre.

2 Add garden soil.

3 Trim the leaves on your iris before potting.

4 Carefully divide the plant.

5 Top up with garden soil.

6 Finish with pebble mulch.

pond, or even as garden perennials as long as they are given plenty of water.

Go to a garden centre specializing in aquatic plants for best advice and biggest range of waterlilies and other water plants.

Bog gardens

In poorly drained areas where the soil is constantly saturated, most deep-rooted shrubs and trees can't get enough air. Some herbaceous plants, such as gunnera, moisture-loving irises, lysichitum, bog primulas, mimulus, astilbes and hostas, will flourish here, and look great teamed with

The lotus springs from the mud.

Chinese proverb

ferns, sedges and some bamboos that also thrive in these conditions. Other plants that like damp conditions include willows, alders, swamp cypress (large tree) and shrubby dogwoods (cornus).

It makes good sense to work with the conditions, so why not create a bog garden? They look fantastic and display a range of flowering perennials that can be difficult to grow in drier parts of the garden.

aquatics To keep the water clean in your ponds, keep sunlight off with a layer of floating aquatics covering 70 per cent of the surface area. This will stop the algae from growing and keep your fish fed with greens when you're away. Here, fairy moss (azolla) and other plants do the job. Include plenty of submerged oxygenating plants to help keep the water clear.

Free plants

Propagating plants from your garden is a very rewarding experience. So many plants are easy to propagate.

You can take cuttings and grow your own plants, and you don't even need a green thumb. Choose from lavender, box, camellia, fuchsia, rhododendron, pittosporum, osmanthus, azalea, hebe, hydrangea, viburnums and photinia.

Easy cuttings

At this time of year, most plants grow rapidly. Use this new growth to take softwood or semi-ripe cuttings. The best time to collect your cuttings is in the early morning before the sun heats up. Take a tip piece of stem (the 'soft' wood), about 8 cm long, from a healthy new shoot and put it in a moist plastic bag. Remove the lower leaves. If the remaining leaves are large, cut them in half to reduce the amount of water lost by transpiration. Dip the stem in hormone powder to encourage strong root growth. Fill a small pot with a free-draining potting compost, insert several cuttings around the edge and then water them in gently.

Cover the pot with plastic and keep it shaded until your cuttings have struck. Alternatively, you can make a mini glasshouse by inverting a used coffee jar over the cuttings. This will provide a humid, moist environment for your cuttings and help prevent them drying out.

In a few weeks, roots should have formed on each cutting. Then you can repot each cutting into its own pot.

Water young plants regularly to prevent their drying out, which retards growth.

PROPAGATING FUCHSIA

1 The roots of this fuchsia cutting are well established and ready for planting.

2 Plant the struck fuchsia in a suitable pot.

3 Add potting mix.

4 If you're growing your fuchsia as a standard, tie it to a stake with budding tape. If you're growing it as a bush, tip prune the leader and encourage side shoots.

Organic gardening

Summer can be a particularly devastating time for our environment, and gardeners should bear some of the blame.

After all, their desire to have lush greenery can result in indulgent overuse of water and fertilizers. But with organic gardening techniques you can have it both ways.

The word 'organic' has become a fashionable term, but what does it mean and how can you adopt organic ideas in your own garden? Organic gardening means putting back in the soil what has been taken out — in other words, using, not abusing, the environment. Organic gardeners use naturally occurring fertilizers and pest control methods, as well as lots of bulky, well-rotted material.

A thriving compost heap is essential in the organic garden, but you can also dig farmyard manure, leaf mould, seaweed and old mushroom compost into your beds. Any organic matter will feed your plants gently and encourage good soil organisms.

Keep the garden free of plant debris as many pests and diseases lurk among dying foliage. Encourage insects and birds — many of them are natural predators of garden pests. For example, ladybirds or ladybugs and lacewings eat aphids. And bees will pollinate your fruit and vegetables, which will set much better crops as a result. To attract bees, plant *Buddleja* (or butterfly bush) and sedum.

Finally, mulching your garden well conserves moisture and protects it from the summer heat.

Encouraging birds helps keep grubs and bugs to a minimum. This bird feeder has been made from 'junk'. One tray is used for seed and the other for water.

mulch The secret to a happy summer garden is mulch, the best strategy for getting the most from your garden and having it look fabulous over the holidays. It also maximizes your efforts in the garden.

The value of blanketing your garden in a 10 cm layer of organic matter to keep the soil moist and the weeds away cannot be overestimated. With the possibility of hot and dry periods in summer, your plants can really become stressed if the soil is not mulched.

Smother the soil around your plants with a thick layer of mulch to prevent the roots baking in hot summer sun and to conserve moisture.

Mulch can be made up of any organic material. Leaves make good mulch but work best once they have decomposed – run over them with the lawn mower to speed up this process. Pine bark is popular for mulching. Use it with pelletized chicken manure as the bark can absorb nitrogen from the soil and rob your plants of this nutrient, turning them yellow.

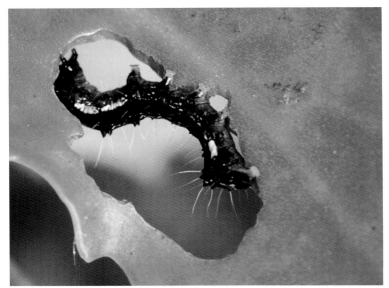

Plant problems

Summer can be a difficult time for plants in the garden. The butterflies and moths of spring have laid their eggs, and by now they have hatched into lots of grubs which are eating their way through your garden.

Do you reach for a spray at the first sign of a creepy crawly? Well, they may all give you the shivers, but there is a difference between friend and foe.

All creatures, great and small, have a part in the food chain, and a little understanding can go a long way towards coexisting with the insect world and still having a garden.

First, let's look at the way most people garden. We group plants together according to ways that suit us. While vegies in their own patch, roses in a rose bed and the annuals down the driveway might look attractive to us, to insects they're rather like neon signs pinpointing eating spots.

It would be much more sensible to mix everything up together. Hide your delicious vegetables in the garden and distribute the roses among other flowering shrubs.

This technique also encourages beneficial insects in the garden. These insects parasitize aphids, mites and the like, controlling the 'bad guy' numbers naturally. To coax more 'good guys' into your garden, try planting some insect and bird-attracting plants, including parsley, dill, elderberry, fennel, Queen Anne's lace (*Anthriscus sylvestris*) and nectar-rich flowering plants.

By practising all the principles of good plant cultivation (such as feeding, pruning, watering and mulching), in most cases you should minimize the opportunity for pests and diseases to take hold. Plants are often attacked because they are under other stresses, so always deal with the problem first, and the solution second.

If you still experience some outbreaks after taking these preventive measures, stop before you reach for the spray, and follow these simple steps to outwit the craftiest crawly and slimiest disease!

1 Correctly identify the pest or disease. This may mean a trip to your local nursery so you can ask a horticulturist to look at it.

2 At what stage is the pest or disease? In other words, will spraying catch the problem, or will it have flown away?

3 Not every problem will have a chemical solution: sometimes you'll have to rectify the way you care for your garden.

4 Don't overkill. Every time you use a spray to control a pest you may also be killing its natural predators.

attract the **good guys**

Flowers such as Queen Anne's lace (shown here) and elderberry attract beneficial insects to your garden. For example, ladybirds eat huge numbers of aphids, mites, mealy bugs and scales. Other insects, such as lacewings and parasitic wasps, also work for you but chemical sprays will kill them as well as the pests.

Common summer problems

Silvering foliage

A wide range of insects attack different plants but they all produce the same sort of damage — silvery leaves. These insects can be red spider, thrips and lace bugs. Most people jump to the conclusion that it is red spider (which is really not a spider at all but a mite), especially when this damage appears on an azalea.

In fact, this sort of damage occurs because of any insect known as a 'rasping feeder'. They scratch away at the undersurface of the leaf, causing it to bleed sap, which they then suck up. This rasping action permanently discolours leaves on azaleas, fuchsias, viburnum, roses and a host of commonly grown ornamentals.

To effectively control these pests, you must identify them correctly. Make sure you examine the underside of the foliage, and take a few leaves down to your local nursery, or the garden clinic, for identification.

The chemical control will vary (see, for example, 'Summer azalea care'), but one treatment is common to all — keep the underside of your plant well watered and hosed down. This will keep all these plants clean and healthy, and far less prone to significant attack. Large trees can be very difficult to treat, but adequate watering and hosing down the foliage will reduce stress in trees, and help them to rectify any problems naturally.

Millipedes

After summer rains you might notice that lots of insects are seeking the dryness of houses and verandahs. One such crawly is the millipede. At this time of the year they may come inside, especially one species, the black Portuguese millipede.

Millipedes are actually pretty harmless creatures. When their numbers build up in wet weather, they might eat soft fruit such as strawberries that grow close to the ground, but generally they feed on decomposing organic matter. If they become really hungry, they might eat some young roots, seedlings or seeds.

Millipedes have a long segmented body that has a hard external covering, but are famous for their multitude of legs. Many pairs line the sides of their bodies.

When disturbed they curl up in a flat spiral, and can be easily squashed or swept up. If they are really worrying you an insecticidal dust, such as ant killer type, may kill them.

Above: An adult lace bug.

Below: Millipedes attack seedlings and the roots of young plants.

Fruit flies

Fruit flies are a problem for commercial fruit growers and home gardeners in warmer climates. The insect is about the size of a small housefly and you often see the pest sitting on fruit with its transparent wings waving back and forth. It lays eggs in the fruit and these hatch into little maggots or grubs. During the warmer months of the year the fly attacks ripening citrus and stone fruits such as peaches, nectarines and cherries, and in the vegie patch, tomatoes and sweet peppers.

Here are some tricks for reducing the damage caused by this pest. Select early maturing varieties of fruit trees. This will mean you'll harvest the crop before the fruit fly arrives. Your nursery will know the special fruit varieties to ask for. Instead of spraying chemicals on the fruit, hang a fruit fly trap in the trees to catch the fly. An empty plastic soft drink bottle is ideal. Cut a few slits in the side of the bottle, near the top. Partly fill it with a solution of sugar or yeast extract spread mixed in warm water. The liquid acts as a lure, trapping the insect inside. Alternatively, if you are really keen, place a paper bag over the ripening fruit.

Thrips

Thrips are common summer pests in gardens and greenhouses. They are tiny insects that feed by sucking the sap from leaves, after scraping the surface of the leaf to release the sap. This action causes leaves to become finely mottled or streaked on the upper surface of a wide range of plants.

Some thrips go for flowers, such as roses, chrysanthemums and gladioli, causing pale mottling or flecking on the

MAKING A FRUIT FLY TRAP

1 Use a knife to make holes in a plastic drink bottle.

2 Add a dollop of yeast extract.

3 Pour in a few centimetres of water and replace the lid. Give the bottle a good shake and turn it upside down. Add a few drops of insecticide if you wish.

4 Make two holes in the bottom of the bottle, thread fine wire through them and tie it in a loop.

5 Hang your trap in a fruit tree just as the fruit is beginning to ripen.

petals; sometimes the buds fail to open. Western flower thrips are the main culprits here, both under glass and outdoors.

Other thrips go for vegetables such as onions, tomatoes and peas (here the pods are attacked). Adult thrips can be controlled by hanging sticky yellow traps among plants. Spray plants with water regularly. Use insecticidal soap in severe attacks. Biological control, using a special predatory mite, is recommended for western flower thrips, which are difficult to control with insecticides.

Disease alert

Summer is warm and, in some areas, humid — ideal conditions for many fungal diseases such as mildew, leaf spots and rust. Many plants are susceptible to these diseases. Careful garden hygiene is a good preventive measure — much better than resorting to chemical controls. Remove leaves affected by fungal spots or mildew and throw them away. Don't put them into the compost. Clear away fallen leaves. Allow good air circulation around your plants. This is very important, especially with roses. Remove any weed growth at ground level to discourage fungus diseases like black spot. Feed your roses now to encourage new growth that will flower in autumn.

Crape myrtle is in full flower now. These magnificent small flowering trees are susceptible to powdery mildew. It's pointless to spray larger trees, the chemical just drifts in the air. If your tree is healthy, the mildew will not affect either its growth or its flowering. Make sure that your tree gets enough sunshine...that will also discourage fungus.

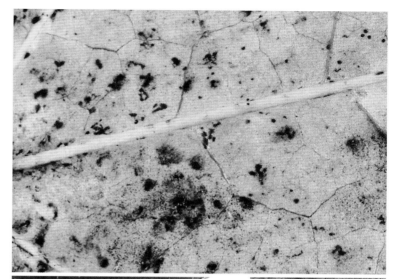

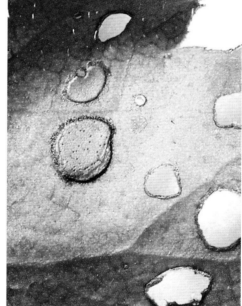

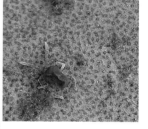

Clockwise from left: Leaf tissue destroyed by a fungus; a liquidambar leaf sucked dry by thrips; and red spider.

home-made **remedies**

Many insecticides now are synthesized forms of pyrethrum. To make your own spray, finely chop the flowers and leaves of the pyrethrum daisy and immerse in water overnight. Strain the water through a muslin cloth and store it in a container. Use the mixture as needed as a contact spray for aphids and other sapsuckers.

Other foul-tasting concoctions can be made from chilli, garlic, wormwood and quassia chips. See 'Chilli water' on page 239.

Before you go on holidays, prune lavender (above), stake tall perennials (top) and place all your indoor plants on a damp towel in the bath (above right).

We're all going on a summer holiday

While you're on holiday make sure you don't neglect your garden. A little forward planning will make sure it looks just as great when you get back.

Get things in order

- Stake and tie back taller perennials. Rake, edge and tidy up. Most weeds set seed in summer so it is vital that you weed before this happens.
- A light trim all over will help give hedges a lived-in look. Removing old flowers, and even flower buds, can promote bushy growth and help conserve energy.
- Water your garden with a wetting agent to help any light showers penetrate into the soil. Dig water-storing crystals into dry areas: they act as water reservoirs.
- Mulch the whole garden, pots included, with a thick (10–15 cm) layer of organic matter. Water everything thoroughly, as both the mulch and the soil below need to be wet. This will help keep the roots cool and moist, and reduce evaporation.

Protect pot plants

- Pots dry out quickly at the best of times, so summer holidays can spell disaster. Move them into a shady corner, and group them together, with the toughest on the perimeter. This will make it easier for your neighbour to water, and also reduce the impact of wind and sun on those plants in the centre.
- Saucers can also help, but remove them when you return so that roots don't rot. Any really precious pot plants should be plunged in a moist area of the garden, and dug back up when you get home.

A special tool makes weeding easier.

Pelargoniums (top) and gazanias can cope with dry weather when you go on holiday.

• Put indoor plants in the bath on an old towel, water them thoroughly, and leave the tap dripping slightly. Make sure the plug is not in place. Water will get sucked up along the towel to the root balls, and the room will stay cool and moist, further protecting your plants.

Keep your lawn controlled

• Cut the grass just before you leave, but not too short. Without regular watering scalped areas will burn and, if there's a heat wave while you're away, some patches will end up being badly damaged.
• Do not forget to cut the edges of the lawn before you go away as here the grass can quickly grow into flower beds. Long-handled edging shears make this job much easier than crouching down with a pair of ordinary garden shears.

When you return

• If the grass is really long, raise the blades of your mower to the highest setting and gradually reduce the height with each successive cut.
• Dig up any pots that you've heeled into the ground.
• Buy your neighbour a bunch of flowers or a pot plant as a thank you for keeping an eye on things.

Plants that thrive on neglect

• The key to success at this time of year is preparation, plant selection and maintenance. Prepare the bed with added organic matter, such as compost, to help the soil retain what little moisture it receives at this time of year.
• Buy small plants as these often establish and grow away much more quickly than larger plants.
• Plant ground covers to help shade the soil, suppress weeds, contain moisture and reduce evaporation.
• Drought-tolerant summer bedding plants include gazanias, pelargoniums, ice plant or lampranthus and Livingstone daisy.

Friendship garden Cut a big bunch of flowers and buds for any relatives you're visiting – after all, they'll go to waste in the garden!

Gardening in small areas

Small gardens can be very special additional rooms of the house — places for relaxing on sunny days and for eating on balmy evenings.

The direct warmth of the sun, small movements of the air, the sound of water, deep shadows and the dazzle of light on leaves, the fresh green of thriving plants — these are pleasures that no interior can achieve. But that is only half their charm, for they also form vivid backdrops to daily life, fascinating display cases to be enjoyed from the house.

The contained garden

With increasing pressure on the urban environment from growing populations, unit and townhouse dwelling is becoming a fact of life for more and more people. There are lots of ideas, plants and books being developed especially for small gardens.

Do you have a tiny garden? Perhaps it's only a balcony or courtyard. Well, we can show you just what can be achieved in a limited space with a bit of imagination. Small spaces can be transformed into pretty, usable green extensions of your home's living space to make an outdoor room. These can be intimate — with lattice smothered in perfumed creepers — or cheery and portable, ideal for renters.

Climate control

A difficulty facing courtyard and balcony gardeners is exposure to prevailing winds. Wind will dry out pots and hanging baskets very quickly so some form of protection is

Above: A small formal garden with a water feature makes an ideal outdoor 'room'.
Below: Alpine dianthus and various thymes soften this old stone sink.

required. For a balcony, a reinforced glass screen will give protection without obscuring views or blocking out the sun. In a courtyard, a panel of lattice supporting a hardy climber will stop the draughts.

The choice of plant material in a small garden will depend on the sunlight available. This will vary according to the aspect as well as height and proximity of neighbouring buildings. The ideal aspect is a southerly one which is warm and receives plenty of sun, but you may need some form of shading from strong midday sun.

Plants suitable for containers

Virtually any plant can be potted, as long as it is treated properly. This may require root pruning every few years (in effect 'bonsaiing'), or taking cores of the root ball out each year. This can often be an arduous task so it's probably better to choose dwarf or smaller-growing specimens if you can.

Some examples of these include:

- Fruit trees: Many citrus remain small in pots. In frost-prone climates winter them in a conservatory. There are dwarf varieties of peaches, and dwarf forms or pillar-like varieties of apple.
- Screening trees: Small-growing pittosporums are ideal for containers, as are camellias, particularly smaller-growing sasanquas. Remember that camellias must be grown in acid compost.
- Flowering shrubs: abutilons and brugmansias (these will both need conservatory protection in winter in frosty climates), *Camellia* x *williamsii* varieties, hardy fuchsias, hebes or shrubby veronicas, *Hydrangea macrophylla* varieties, *Leptospermum scoparium* varieties (winter in conservatory in hard winter

areas), oleander (winter in a conservatory in frost-prone areas), and rhododendrons, including azaleas (these require acid compost).

Pruning techniques for small gardens

Topiary, standardizing and espalier are all pruning techniques that can be used on a wide range of plants to keep them smaller.

Topiary, or clipping plants into shapes, can be a way of introducing formality or even whimsy. You could prune your favourite hedging plant into a bird, watering can or simply an obelisk. Easy, fast-growing plants suitable for topiary include privet, box, box honeysuckle (*Lonicera nitida*), yew and holly.

For the traditional standard, or 'ball on a stick' look, choose from fuchsias, roses, rhododendrons, grevilleas, sweet bay, grape vine, bougainvillea and even wisteria.

Espalier involves growing plants flat against a wall or frame. Plants that are often grown as espaliers include fruit trees such as apples and pears, plus ornamentals like camellias and firethorn.

potting with **unusual containers**

You don't have to use standard plastic or terracotta pots for your potted garden: collect some unusual containers and pot them up with quick growers such as verbena and lobelia. Check your kitchen cupboards or local garage sales for some suitable potting containers. Here, some colanders, an old bird cage and a watering can are being planted with verbena and lobelia. Just make sure you use good quality fresh potting compost.

Did you know? The term 'espalier' comes from the French word for trellis.

Above: Gerberas need full sun and in frost-prone climates will need wintering in a cool conservatory.

Above right: These hanging baskets complement the colour scheme of the house and brighten it up at the same time.

On the move If you're renting, make sure everything is portable. Often balconies are three flights of stairs up, so smaller items make potting and transportation possible.

Baskets for extra colour

Baskets are very decorative in courtyards and balconies but they dry out quickly, particularly in hot windy weather. As a rule, the bigger the basket the less often you'll have to water and the more scope there will be in plant selection, so choose something at least 300 mm wide or larger.

Which plant where?

The arrangement and placement of plants is important in achieving an overall, pleasant effect. Pots should be uniform, all terracotta or all plastic, not a mixture. Place them in some logical order, perhaps grouped around a large central pot with a feature plant.

When choosing plants, take into account the conditions in your garden. A sunny exposed site may be perfect for a Tuscan theme with bright red pelargoniums in terracotta troughs. Window boxes or troughs are the ideal shape for long narrow spaces. To add height, grow potted standard bougainvillea which flower for months and love the baking sun, as do potted gerberas.

For a damp and shady position, try dwarf arum lilies, begonias, ferns and impatiens.

Perfect potted plants

The biggest problem facing plants in pots is drying out. A good quality potting compost is essential, and some added peat will hold more water. If the potting compost does dry out, break up the surface with a small fork or the water will run off the soil without being absorbed. Use wetting agents and water-storing crystals to help with water absorption and retention. All potted plants are best fed with slow-release fertilizers. If you add some nutrient solution to the water your plants will thrive.

Maintenance tips

• Group your containers together to reduce the impact of exposure when you're away.
• Regularly pinch back shoots to help plants bush out.
• Deadheading is essential for most flowering plants to maintain flowering over a long period.

Wish list

Plants make wonderful gifts. They continue to grow and give pleasure long after the actual celebration is over, reminding us of the giver and their kind thoughts.

Living plants can contain special meanings, adding to the thoughtfulness of the present. Here are some ideas for giving flowers and plants as gifts.

Christmas ideas

There are so many things that make wonderful living gifts at Christmas time, but if you're bored with the usual choice of red poinsettias and Christmas trees, look out for the pretty small-flowered hardy rhododendron called 'Christmas Cheer'.

Birthdays, births and christenings

Many plants are named after people, and matching a plant's name with the recipient is a special touch. Some common examples include camellias such as 'Jennifer Susan', 'Vanessa' and 'Susan'; and roses such as 'Carla', 'Sexy Rexy' and 'Cecilia'. There are less common ones too, such as a magnolia called 'Elizabeth' and a tibouchina named 'Kathleen', so ask your local nursery for some ideas.

A special gift for a newborn or a christened child is a tree which can grow with them. If it is going to be planted in the garden, choose something that doesn't grow too big, such as flowering cherry. Alternatively, suggest that the local park may need greening up with a native tree.

If none of those options suits, you could choose the child's birth flower. There is a floral emblem that is traditionally associated with each month of the year.

birth flowers

The following list of birth flowers is not definitive – you'll find there are other combinations, depending on the source – but this is a start.

January . . . . . Carnation
February . . . Violet
March . . . . . . Daffodil
April . . . . Sweetpea
May . . . . Lily-of-the-valley
June . . . . Rose
July . . . . Larkspur
August . . . . . Gladiolus
September . Aster
October . . . . Marigold
November . . Chrysanthemum
December . . Holly

A potted chilli plant makes a decorative and useful Christmas present.

bulbs are great survivors at cemeteries. For indoors, peace lily (spathiphyllum) makes a thoughtful gift, or give rosemary, which is traditionally associated with remembrance.

House warmings

The happy plant (*Dracaena fragrans* Deremensis Group), like the jade plant (*Crassula ovata*), is supposed to be good feng shui and bring good fortune.

St Valentine's Day

For a low-kilojoule gift on this day of traditional chocolate indulgence, buy pots of chocolate cosmos and chocolate mint, both of which are chocolate scented, to accompany a red rose.

Father's Day and Mother's Day

Tomatoes are perfect Father's Day presents. Dads seem to love the competitive aspect of tomato growing, and early spring is just the right time to be planting young seedlings.

Chrysanthemums, affectionately known as 'Mums' in the cut flower industry, are given by the bucketful each Mother's Day, but do remember that to European mothers (or mothers-in-law), chrysanthemums are traditional funeral flowers.

Looking after live Christmas presents

- Acclimatize plants slowly from being indoors to a position in full sun by placing them in a shaded position for a few weeks.
- Don't let plants sit in saucers of water. Lift them up out of the tray with a brick or pebbles so that their roots don't rot.
- Feed Christmas trees in spring to ensure they look great for the next year.

Weddings and anniversaries

For weddings and anniversaries there is plenty to choose from in the plant department. Again, many plants have names that suit perfectly, like the azaleas named 'Silver Anniversary' and 'Ruby Glow' or the roses called 'Gold Medal' and 'Wedding Day'. Another nice idea is to plant up a basket with a matching colour scheme, such as a silver foliage combo for a silver wedding anniversary.

Remembrance

A living gift is a thoughtful way of remembering the loss of a loved one. It can be planted at the memorial site or at the home of a close relative. Pick something hardy and understated.

A pure white camellia or rhododendron is always nice, and old-fashioned roses and

White flowers

White borders or beds are becoming increasingly popular and provide a cool atmosphere in summer.

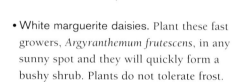

White dahlias.

White can give your garden a dazzling brilliance, lifting shady or partially shady areas and calming your spirit. So splash about some white, sit back and enjoy the sunshine.

- **Mock orange.** Mock orange or philadelphus are deciduous shrubs and they smell divine when in flower during early summer. There are numerous species and varieties ranging from tall to dwarf plants. These shrubs grow well in full sun or partial shade and in any reasonably good, well-drained soil. Prune annually after flowering, cutting out the old flowered wood. This encourages young shoots that will flower next year.
- **'Iceberg' rose.** 'Iceberg' has made a name for itself as a trouble-free, prolific flowerer grown as a shrub or a standard rose. The light green foliage is reasonably resistant to black spot. There is also a climbing version of 'Iceberg'. But 'Iceberg' is not the only white rose: many other modern and old varieties are worth considering.
- **White hydrangeas.** Plant masses of white, shade-loving hydrangeas for summer-long bunches of flowers.
- **Madonna lily.** *Lilium candidum* is one of the best white-flowered lilies. The trumpet-shaped blooms have a sweet fragrance and are carried on stems up to 1.8 m in height. This lily will grow in sun with the roots shaded and needs a neutral to alkaline soil.

- **White marguerite daisies.** Plant these fast growers, *Argyranthemum frutescens*, in any sunny spot and they will quickly form a bushy shrub. Plants do not tolerate frost.
- **Plantain lilies.** White-flowered hostas with their bold green foliage are excellent for white planting schemes. *H. plantaginea* with scented flowers is a good one and prefers a position in sun with moist soil.
- **White agapanthus.** There are now white miniature and standard agapanthus, perfect for clumps, lining paths and driveways or edging garden beds.
- **Potato vine.** Possibly the fastest, most prolific flowering vine for a warm, protected area. *Solanum jasminoides* 'Album' will grow in the sun or shade, and is seldom without flowers. In frost-prone climates grow in a conservatory.
- **Star jasmine.** A hardier climber, evergreen *Trachelospermum jasminoides* has white, sweetly scented blooms and reaches 9 m high. Grow in full sun or partial shade.
- **White annuals.** If there are any gaps left in your white border, cram the sunny spots with petunias and the shady areas with impatiens.

Hanging baskets

Every home, no matter how big or small, has a transition zone, the space that connects the inside to the outside. Whether it's a porch, verandah or a large pergola-covered entertaining area, this area can be the most exciting and enjoyable of all.

Ivy-leaved pelargoniums and white alyssum make a cheery combination.

A most satisfying gardening activity is to grow plants in a hanging basket in this space linking the house with the garden. Choose annuals filled with seasonal colour or a mass planting of mixed seedlings, pendulous plants and a small shrub or two.

In recent years many improvements have been made to moisture-retaining products, potting composts and fertilizers, making growing plants in baskets much easier. Water-absorbing granules act like a reservoir in the soil by holding water in the basket. Potting composts have improved enormously with premium quality ingredients made up to the highest standard. Controlled, slow-release fertilizer means plants need only be fed once every nine months, and generally that's sufficient for the life of the display. There is even a product that when watered on to the soil draws the moisture down into the compost.

Bear in mind that potting composts may not contain all of these products: for example, you may have to add water-absorbing granules and wetting agent.

There are also various products available for lining baskets, including coir fibre and wool waste. These are starting to replace traditional sphagnum moss. There are also various kinds of solid liner that can be used. Take a look around your local garden centre to see what's available.

blooming bag To brighten up a patio, balcony or balustrade, go down to your local garden centre and buy a 'blooming bag'. These are strong plastic bags, with slits cut down one side. Fill the bag up in levels, planting seedlings in the pockets as you go. Impatiens look great planted in this way, as do lobelia, nasturtium and strawberries or mixed cottage selections. Choose the right seedlings for each spot, and you'll have colour in the sun or shade.

make a **ball basket**

Baskets filled with colourful flowering plants look fabulous. You can hang them from the walls of your home and use them to decorate your patio, pergola, courtyard or verandah, or hang them from established trees in your garden.

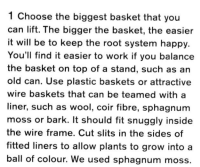

1 Choose the biggest basket that you can lift. The bigger the basket, the easier it will be to keep the root system happy. You'll find it easier to work if you balance the basket on top of a stand, such as an old can. Use plastic baskets or attractive wire baskets that can be teamed with a liner, such as wool, coir fibre, sphagnum moss or bark. It should fit snugly inside the wire frame. Cut slits in the sides of fitted liners to allow plants to grow into a ball of colour. We used sphagnum moss.

2 Line the basket with sphagnum moss.

3 Use a premium quality potting mix that contains water-absorbing granules and slow-release fertilizer.

4 As you fill the basket, position the seedlings and then plant the top.

5 Planted with wishbone flower (*Torenia* sp.), viola and alyssum, this basket will be a mass of flowers in a few weeks.

A posy from the garden

High summer and the garden is at its flowering peak. Your home should be filled with fresh flowers.

- Dahlias, flowering from midsummer to autumn, are top of the list. Liquid feed them now for more flowers. Stake them to support the heavy summer growth.
- Shasta daisies are tough and drought-hardy. They love the sun. Pick them for posies and you'll encourage more flowers.
- Lavender is another favourite cut flower. All lavender species and varieties love hot, dry conditions as they come from Mediterranean regions. The swing towards reduced water use in gardens has made lavenders very popular.
- Hydrangeas are lovely in vases. Pick them early in the morning and submerge them in water for an hour before you arrange them. Modern varieties are more compact and don't require much pruning. Buy them now while they're in flower and plant them in partial shade.
- Lilies and bulbs, from agapanthus to Jacobean lilies, from liliums to tuberoses, are uniquely beautiful.

tussie mussie

A tussie mussie or nosegay is a posy of flowers and herbs that convey some meaning or purpose. Originally tussie mussies were intended to ward off disease, but their purpose evolved throughout the eighteenth century, and eventually came to spell out a message using the language of flowers. Most often this message was an expression of love for one's sweetheart, but it could also be other things, such as hate, grief or thankfulness.

Here are some examples:

- angelica – inspiration
- balm – sympathy
- basil – good wishes
- forget-me-not – true love

- lavender – distrust
- mint – virtue
- parsley – festivity
- rose bud – pre-love

- tansy – war
- violet – modesty
- zinnia – thoughts of absent friends

A couple of tips for cut flowers Recut the stems just before you place your flowers in the vase. Change the water daily or add some preserving liquid to the water.

Sensuous summer

Fragrant plants are particularly lovely in summer when you're actually outside, with night scents wafting by, or even when you are dining in the conservatory.

Some of these plants need a heated conservatory in a frost-prone climate, so do check with your garden centre. Shrubs like gardenias and buddleja are invaluable for daytime, while *Cestrum nocturnum*, or night jessamine, will cast its magic spell at night.

An often overlooked flowering shrub with a delightful perfume is *Bouvardia longiflora*. This small shrub tends to be a bit floppy, and may require some support and protection, but its wonderful, pure white tubular flowers are worth the extra effort.

Train climbers over pergolas, on trellises near windows or on tripods in pots. Hoya, stephanotis, common white jasmine and honeysuckle give delicious daytime scent; the moonflower will charm you at night.

Although most bulbs have finished in spring, the Easter lily (*Lilium longiflorum*) and the oriental lilies are both highly perfumed and worth keeping in pots both inside and out when they are in flower.

Trees are easily forgotten, especially when it comes to planting for perfume. If you have room in a warm conservatory, frangipani is a wonderful old favourite. *Eucryphia lucida* is a hardy evergreen tree to 8 m with bowl-shaped white flowers. It should be grown in neutral to acid soil, in sun but with the root area shaded.

The breath of flowers is far sweeter in the air…than in the hand.

Francis Bacon

Clockwise from above: Three for the conservatory if you live in a frost-prone climate – gardenia, hoya and frangipani. Each has a delicious fragrance.

Above: The silver and blue shades of this garden provide respite from summer's frantic pace.

Below: Bog sage, or *Salvia uliginosa*.

Singing the blues

There's nothing like a good dose of the blues to cheer up your garden. In the world of flowers, blue is the ultimate cool colour.

It takes only a glimpse of sparkling blue water to offer relief from the heat of summer, and blue flowers in the garden create the same feeling.

Blue is a distant ethereal colour, and planted en masse can seem sombre. Coming from the cool side of the colour wheel and traditionally associated with spiritual things, blue conjures a mood of innermost peace.

Along with green, blue is the most agreeable of colours in the garden, combining readily with hot or cool colours. Blue comes in many flowering forms from late spring and through summer: the clouds of ceanothus or California lilac, agapanthus or African blue lily (also known as lily-of-the-Nile), cornflowers, love-in-a-mist, many clematis and many varieties of hydrangea.

A good approach is to use blue as a base for highlights such as white, contrasting yellow or with harmonies of pinks and violets. It's a delight with pink, cream, lemon yellow and silver, vibrant with orange, but dull and flat in red and purple partnerships. Use silver foliage plants — such as lamb's ears, wormwood, artichokes and cotton lavender — to add to the effect of your flower colour. To enhance the blueness of foliage, combine it with plants that have yellow-green leaves or creamy flowers, such as various hostas, *Sisyrinchium striatum*, some kniphofia varieties, *Philadelphus coronarius* 'Aureus' and goatsbeard (*Aruncus dioicus*).

Blues, silvers and greys seem to recede into the distance, suggesting a larger space. You can make small gardens appear bigger by planting cool colours at the back of the garden and warmer shades — such as reds, yellows and oranges — in the foreground.

At dusk blue flowers have special value. Together with whites they remain visible longer than any other colour. You can take advantage of this effect by concentrating blue and white flowers around the areas where you like to sit on summer evenings.

Blue and white agapanthus make sensational border planting in areas exposed to hot full sun. Their neat mounds of strap-like leaves look good from spring to autumn. The blue and white flowers decorate the summer garden and should be pruned as soon as they finish if you want your display of agapanthus to remain one colour as this stops the seeds from forming, and germinating throughout your bed.

True blue

Plenty of plants describe themselves as blue, but are actually shades of lilac and mauve. However, there are a few plants that fall into that elusive category of 'true blue'.

- **Plumbago.** Originally from South Africa, *Plumbago auriculata* grows best in warm climates, to 2 m, and smothers itself in sky blue flowers through the warm months. Grow it as an informal hedge or trimmed as a formal hedge. In frost-prone gardens grow it in a cool conservatory; place pot-grown plants outside for the summer.
- **Gentians.** Some gentians have pure blue flowers including *Gentiana asclepiadea*, the willow gentian, a herbaceous perennial for moist borders. It takes full sun in cool, moist climates but needs shade from strong sun where summers are warmer.

Blues for all occasions

Many blue-flowering plants are easy to grow and disease-free. In the panel beside are some you may like to try. Most of these plants are hardy but some are frost tender and in frost-prone climates should be grown in a conservatory or used for garden display only in the summer.

Get the **look**

Annuals
Forget-me-not, love-in-a-mist (*Nigella*), salvia, pansy, lobelia, viola, verbena, cornflower, petunia, baby-blue eyes

Perennials

Aster × frikartii, Michaelmas daisy, delphinium, perennial salvia, Stokes' aster, campanula, balloon flower, iris, *Geranium* 'Johnson's Blue', Russian sage (*Perovskia atriplicifolia*), agapanthus, borage, globe thistle, gentian, meconopsis

Bulbs

Most blue-flowered bulbs are spring-flowering, but for summer there are some alliums and camassias.

Ground covers

Periwinkle, fan flower (*Scaevola*), catmint (*Nepeta*), bugle (*Ajuga*), convolvulus, evolvulus, dampiera, leschenaultia, prostrate rosemary, perennial verbena, brachyscome

Climbers

Clematis (various), potato vine (*Solanum crispum* 'Glasnevin') and blue trumpet vine or sky flower (*Thunbergia grandiflora*)

Shrubs

Buddleja, lavender, hydrangea, California lilac (ceanothus), rosemary, *Hibiscus syriacus* (rose of sharon, shrub althaea), plumbago, *Clerodendrum ugandense*, bluebeard (caryopteris), ceratostigma and hebes

summer

annuals, perennials & bulbs

No plants give your garden a splash of colour quite like annuals, perennials and bulbs. More than any other season, summer yields the festive feel of flowers — from sunny yellows to cool blues — and lots of them.

As summer is generally a stressful time for young plants, with the heat affecting their immature root systems, protect your young charges under shade cloth or, alternatively, leave them under a tree to acclimatize slowly.

Various biennials for spring bedding can be sown in early summer, such as wallflowers, winter- and spring-flowering pansies and English daisies, plus sweet Williams and Canterbury bells.

Annuals

Summer annuals can be big, bold and blowzy perfumed affairs.

Gaudy reds, pinks and tangerines can be found in succulents such as Livingstone daisies and portulaca, and in upright growers such as sunflowers and zinnias. Softer, cooler colours for subdued background plantings can be found in spider flower (*Cleome* sp.), foxgloves (*Digitalis* sp.) and cosmos, while asters, phlox, lobelia and floss flower provide long-lasting foreground selections.

Seedlings

Growing seedlings, whether they're flowers or vegetables, can be a bit tricky. So, when choosing your punnets of seedlings at the nursery, always select fresh young stock. Avoid tired, root-bound plants that are past their prime – they will grow slowly and will neither perform well nor fend off disease.

Select the coolest part of the day for planting and plant the young plants in well-prepared soil. Firm them in moderately with your fingers: excess firming is liable to damage the delicate roots.

Water them in well to settle the soil around the young plants. To avoid too much disturbance, use a watering can fitted with a fine rose. Thereafter apply water whenever the soil starts to become dry on

the surface. Keep this up until the plants are well established.

Feeding summer flowers

Don't pull out plants which have already been flowering for a few months. You can revive them to perform again before summer ends.

If petunias have been damaged or look tired and lifeless, prune them back by at least half, then feed them up with a liquid fertilizer. They'll bloom within ten days.

Dahlias can also be fed but use an organic feed like blood, fish and bone or one of the pelleted manures before applying a complete liquid fertilizer. Remove any spent flowers so you'll have a mass of dahlias in flower during autumn.

Summer prune hybrid tea roses that have finished their spring flush: remove about 25 per cent of the bush. Spray with Pest Oil®, feed with pelleted manures and a handful of rose food, water thoroughly and then mulch with lucerne hay or sugar cane.

Left to right: Pansy (*Viola* x *wittrockiana* cv.), rose moss (*Portulaca grandiflora*) and spider flower (*Cleome hassleriana*).

Opposite: Pineapple lily.

Summer set lip to earth's bosom bare, and left the flushed print in a poppy there.

Francis Thompson

PLANTING SEEDLINGS

1 Dig a hole large enough to accommodate each plant.

2 Gently separate the seedlings, taking care not to damage the roots.

3 Plant each seedling and then backfill.

Perfect potted colour

Ever wondered how those glossy magazines get wonderful pictures of potted plants filled with colour and perfect growth? Of course they employ very skilled photographers, but the secret lies in the selection and quantity of the plants being used in the first place.

At home most of us tend to be a bit stingy and plant only one shrub or a couple of seedlings in each pot, and then we expect them to perform like the one in the magazine. Look closely at the photograph. You will see that there are always several plants in one container, sometimes one or two main shrubs with a dozen annuals of a complementary colour. Leaf colour can also be used with dramatic results.

Fill a pot or trough to the rim with plants then feed them with a liquid fertilizer. Within weeks you'll be rewarded with the same colourful and prolific growth. Select your main plant, perhaps a *Cordyline australis* or a yucca, then surround it with spillover plants such as sweet alyssum, convolvulus, lobelia, ivy-leaved pelargoniums or a small-leafed trailing ivy.

Hidden treasure

Treasure flowers, or gazania, are so named because eighteenth century gardeners thought the flower centres were like pearls

sunjewels

Plants that love the summer sun have vibrant colours and can be combined to create a dazzling massed flower effect. The sunny yellows of annual sunflowers or helianthus, marigolds and rudbeckias, the reds and oranges of salvias, portulacas, lampranthus and dahlias, and the lipstick pinks of verbenas and bedding begonias create vibrant splashes of colour in the garden and in containers.

on velvet. But they could well be called treasure flowers after the shining golden flowers or the silver-plated foliage.

Whatever the reason, gazanias are certainly invaluable as summer flowers. They are sturdy plants, easily grown from seed or cuttings and perfect for any inhospitable area such as by the seaside, as a ground cover for the nature strip or for any tub that dries out quickly. Their only enemy is frost and lack of sun, as their flowers close when the sun fades away.

Oops a daisy

Sunny as a daisy, the family Asteraceae boasts some of the world's great plants. Throughout summer and autumn, various daisies come into flower continuously and this makes them unsurpassed as flowering plants. There are daisies for every position and use. Annuals — such as zinnias, sunflowers, cosmos and marigolds — give superb colour for summer. Place them strategically in pots or plant them in pockets around the garden. Perennials normally grown as annuals include *Rudbeckia hirta* varieties which make a superb display throughout summer and into autumn.

The cottage-garden style of planting is increasingly popular and there are many daisy-flowered annuals: old favourites such as marguerites (argyranthemum), China asters (*Callistephus chinensis*), pot marigolds and cornflowers. Sow or plant these liberally among favourite cottage-garden perennials and old roses.

Many daisies, such as sunflowers and zinnias, are long-lasting cut flowers. Some daisy-flowered annuals can be cut and dried for winter floral arrangements, such as the straw flowers, *Bracteantha bracteata* and rhodanthe.

Far left: Schizanthus, tulips, kale and lobelia make a stunning potted display.

Centre: The jewel-like flowers of the gazania.

Above: Sunflower cultivar, *Helianthus* 'Russian Giant'.

Preserving flowers

The range of uses for flowers, beyond having them on display in the garden, is extraordinary. At this time of the year your garden is buzzing with bees as they feast on summer flowers. It seems such a waste to leave the flowers to the insects, especially when an enormous amount of plant material can be preserved, allowing it to retain much of its fresh glowing colour and form. You can re-create summer, perhaps in the shape of a beautiful rose, knowing that it will remain perfect throughout winter.

The types of flowers that can be preserved are virtually endless. There are the tall spires of pink and cream astilbes and even taller delphiniums in all the colours of the sky, as well as cornflowers and love-in-a-mist and an infinite variety of roses.

For fragrance, lavender and yarrow, great spicy lilies and roses will continue to fill the room with their perfumes in dry form. Foliage, such as pressed ferns and mahonia leaves, make striking arrangements, and dried eucalyptus leaves, painted twigs or tortured willow also look great on their own or mixed with flowers. Silvery foliage is also often aromatic.

Plants can be preserved in a number of ways. The most popular is the air-drying method where bunches are hung in the air by their stems to dry out in a dark, well-ventilated place. Some people prefer to use desiccants such as sand and silica gel or borax. Others prefer to press flowers in a press or book. Many kinds of foliage, such as gum and maple leaves, can be preserved with glycerin.

Did you know? Lavender is named after the Latin word *lavare* (to wash), reflecting the ancient Romans' use of it as a bath oil.

Air drying

All plant material should be picked in dry weather, preferably at or after midday when any dew will have evaporated. Flowers should be picked about four days before their prime. In the case of roses, this is when the bud is colourful and on the verge of opening.

Ideally, the material should be air dried by hanging the picked stems in a room that is cool, dry, well-ventilated and dark. If it is damp or humid, the material will rot, especially where the stems or flowers are touching — for example, at the tying point of a hanging bunch.

Before hanging the material, remove all the lower leaves and wipe away any moisture on the stems with a kitchen towel. Tie the stems together into bunches using lengths of raffia or string, or even a plastic bag. Fan out the flowers, seed heads and leaves in each bunch so that there is as little contact between the leaves and petals as possible. Hang bunches on a rail, ensuring that they don't touch each other, otherwise they will decay. Don't be tempted to interfere with the flowers until they have completely dried out or they will droop and disintegrate. The required time for which the material is suspended will vary from three weeks to several months, depending on the plant.

Easily dried flowers include bracteantha, rhodanthe, limonium, delphinium, hydrangea, yarrow, Chinese lantern and dahlias.

AIR DRYING FLOWERS

1 You'll need string, scissors and bunches of suitable flowers. We used roses, limonium (annual and perennial), lavender, banksias and eucalyptus leaves.

2 Strip the leaves from the lower stems and make small bunches.

3 Tie the bunches together with string or raffia.

4 Hang them upside down on a rack, such as this clothes horse.

5 Remember to store the rack in a cool, dry, well-ventilated and dark place, otherwise the plants will rot before they get a chance to dry out.

Pressed fern fronds, pansies, wallflowers, geraniums and columbines.

Pressing

One of the simplest ways of drying flowers and leaves is to press them, either with a flower press or between the pages of a heavy book. Always sandwich the plant material between sheets of absorbent paper, such as blotting paper or newspaper. When pressing flowers with bulky centres, add a layer of dry foam to help supply an even pressure. With large heads of flowers change the absorbent paper regularly, and place extra books on top for more pressure.

Easily pressed flowers and foliage include violas, pansies, primroses and polyanthus, hydrangeas, single roses, sweet peas, any daisy-like flowers, poppies and hellebores, fern fronds, leaves of choisya and lamb's ears, grey-leaved brachyglottis (senecio) and autumn leaves.

Using desiccants

Desiccants draw the moisture out of plants while supporting them, and can result in a replica that is close in colour, size and texture to the original. Drying agents such as silica gel, borax, alum or fine dry sand can be applied to accelerate the process.

First, ensure all the material is in perfect condition. Pick plants in the afternoon when they are completely dry. Place a layer of desiccant on the bottom of an airtight container and gradually trickle the desiccant around the plant material, using a fine brush to ensure that every part of the flower or leaf is fully immersed. Once the plant material is completely covered, replace the lid and seal it with tape. Test the flowers or leaves every couple of days, as they can become too dry and thus too brittle.

wiring **flower stems**

It is a good idea to wire the flower heads upright before drying so they won't become brittle. Using a piece of fine wire about 50 cm long, push one end through the centre of the stem just under the flower. Twist the ends of wire around the stem. For thicker stems, use thicker wire. If wiring for a bouquet or a vase, use green florists' tape to disguise the wire.

Excellent results can be achieved with these: lilies, peonies, roses, freesias, narcissus, ranunculus, alstroemeria, camellias and orchids.

Using glycerin

The process of preserving plant material with glycerin depends on replacing the water in the plant with glycerin, which keeps the plant in a stable condition over a long period. Leaves, rather than flowers, are best suited to preservation with glycerin.

Make up a solution of 60 per cent glycerin and 40 per cent hot water and stir the mixture thoroughly. Cut stems at a sharp angle, and hammer the ends of any woody stems to crush them flat. Place the cut stems in a vase containing about 10 cm of the hot solution so that the stems are firmly supported by the sides of the container. Place the vase in a cool, dark place for at least six days so that absorption can fully take effect. At the stage when little beads start to form on the upper part of the plant material, it has absorbed all it needs. Remove it from the vase immediately and wash it thoroughly.

The leaves of deciduous and evergreen plants and trees can be preserved in glycerin. It is particularly good for beech, eucalyptus, ivy, mahonia, choisya, bells of Ireland, fatsia, pittosporum, aspidistra and holly.

It is important to note that immature plant material cannot be preserved with glycerin, so spring leaves are not suitable for this kind of treatment.

Larger foliage For larger examples of foliage, such as that of beech, maple, ash, plane tree and bamboo, try drying the leaves under a rug, carpet or mattress.

petunias

modern petunias

Petunia breeding is continuous on both sides of the Atlantic and every year we see new varieties being introduced. Among the modern developments are yellow-flowered petunias, of which there are now several varieties available. They create a very sunny effect in containers and beds. But one of the greatest revolutions in breeding has been the development of trailing petunias with tiny bell-shaped flowers. These create a waterfall of colour in hanging baskets, window boxes and patio tubs. Another popular development is the trailing Surfinia® petunias which are grown from cuttings rather than seed. Again they have small flowers, but masses of them, and they are very weather-resistant. All have a long flowering period.

It would be hard to name an annual that has enjoyed more breeding and improvements than the petunia. The wild species were originally purple and white, but 150 years of cultivation has resulted in the sturdier, showier types we are familiar with today. These include doubles, singles, miniatures, perennials and cascading types in every colour except true blue and orange.

Vital statistics

Scientific name: *Petunia* x *hybrida*.
Family: Solanaceae.
Plant/bulb type: Annual.
Height: 25–45 cm (depending on the variety).
Planting time: Late spring and early summer.
Soil: Any free-draining soil.
Position: Full sun with protection from wind.
Planting depth and spacing: 25 cm apart (large growers can be spaced further apart).
Watering: Water regularly until established, then they will tolerate dry conditions.
Fertilizer: Too much fertilizer produces sappy plants that flower poorly.
Flowering: Late spring to early autumn.
After-flowering care: Cut off spent flower heads to encourage repeat flowers.
Comments: Sensational used in mass plantings, hanging baskets and pots.

check list

jobs to do now

- Deadhead petunias, violas, pansies and other bedding plants and feed them for another show.

- Deadhead finished foxgloves, lupins and campanulas.

- Prune lavender, stake dahlias and deadhead agapanthus.

- Stake or loosely tie chrysanthemums to prevent the weight of the buds breaking stems; disbud for single blooms.

- Top dress dianthus and lavenders with a complete fertilizer.

- Lay snail traps around the new shoots of your dahlias.

- Divide and repot late-flowering cymbidiums.

- Pot on all begonias if necessary into larger pots, both flowering and foliage types.

- Deadhead all daisy-flowered annuals for more blooms.

- Trim faded flowers to keep plants tidy and prevent seed from setting.

- Lift and divide bearded iris. Discard old, gnarled rhizomes.

- Cut back all of the old flowered stems of any spring-flowering perennials.

- Keep newly planted bedding plants and annuals watered.

- Prepare sites where you intend to plant spring-flowering bulbs in late summer or autumn. Dig in bulky organic matter, especially if your soil is light and well drained, and include some grit as well as compost if the soil is poorly drained.

- Make sure gladioli are well staked to prevent them toppling over when in flower. A single bamboo cane for each plant is usually sufficient. Keep them well watered in dry weather.

plant now

- Late spring and early summer is the time to plant summer bedding plants. Many hardy and tender annuals can also be sown in early summer for flowering later in the season. All of these make good gap fillers in beds and borders.

- Calendulas, renowned for providing summer colour, have flat daisy-like flowers which cheer up the garden and help control pests like whitefly and aphids. Poor man's orchid, which looks a bit like a bright small orchid, is inexpensive and easy to sow from seed.

- Plant window boxes and hanging baskets with trailing plants such as lobelia, sweet alyssum and petunias.

- Plant out seedlings of zinnias, impatiens, salvia, verbena and petunias.

- You are still able to plant asters, celosia, coleus, dahlias, amaranthus, portulaca, nasturtium, sunflowers and marigolds.

- Begonias make a stunning massed display and are great for brightening up any holes in the garden. They also adapt to sun or shade.

- Artemisias and senecio are wonderful for swathes of grey foliage colour.

- Cottage gardens can be given a lift with fresh displays of phlox, cosmos, gypsophila, cleome, rudbeckia, Swan River daisy (*Brachyscome iberidifolia*), zinnia, verbena and oenothera varieties.

- Hardy, autumn-flowering miniature cyclamen can be planted in late summer.

- Order spring-flowering bulbs from mail-order bulb specialists, or buy from a garden centre, and when received store them in a cool, dry, airy place until planting time in the autumn. Some bulbs can be planted in late summer, including daffodils.

- Seeds of hardy bulbs (species only) can be sown as soon as ripe. Sow them in pots and then stand them in a cool, shady place. They may take time to germinate.

flowering now

- Annuals such as ageratum, amaranthus, asters, begonias, celosia, cosmos, foxglove, gazania, linaria, larkspur, lobelia, marigolds, nasturtiums, petunias, phlox, poor man's orchid, portulaca, rudbeckia, salvias, snapdragons, sweet alyssum, sweet William, and zinnias

- Perennials such as acanthus, achilleas, agapanthus, aquilegia, cannas, daylilies, delphiniums, gerbera, perennial phlox, shasta daisies, kniphofia and sunflowers

- Bulbs such as alliums, crinum, lilies, gladioli and star of Bethlehem (*Ornithogalum umbellatum*).

Perennials

For fuss-free flowers and foliage so you can enjoy idle summer afternoons, fill your garden with carefree plants for stunning colour and attractive foliage.

- A number of perennials are not frost-hardy and will only behave as perennials in mild, frost-free climates. In areas prone to frosts they are grown as annuals, for summer bedding or in containers. Among these are arctotis hybrids or African daisies that come in shades of white, pink, red, yellow, apricot and orange. Marguerite (*Argyranthemum frutescens*) will flower virtually all year round in mild climates or in a heated conservatory.

- Fibrous-rooted or bedding begonias (*Begonia semperflorens*) are excellent for dappled shade and moist soil. Flowers come in shades of pink or red, while some varieties are white, and the leaves are purple- or red-flushed or plain green. If begonias are lifted and potted before autumn frosts in a heated conservatory, they will continue flowering into winter.

- Impatiens, also known as busy Lizzies (correctly *Impatiens walleriana*), have the same uses as bedding begonias. Like begonias, they also love partial shade and moist soil. The stems are succulent and the plants fast growing, with large, flat flowers at least 2.5 cm across. Flower colours include white and shades of pink and red, with newer varieties including orange and salmon shades. Modern varieties are very compact in habit. Keep them well watered during dry spells and feed with liquid fertilizer once plants are established. As with begonias, if plants are lifted in autumn before the frosts commence, potted and taken into a heated conservatory, they will continue flowering into winter.

Opposite, clockwise from bottom left: Impatiens, bedding begonias and marguerites.

Left: Common sage (*Salvia officinalis*) in flower.

Up-and-coming salvias

One of the great plant families for our gardens is the mint family (Lamiaceae). This is a huge group, comprising mints (mentha), salvias, lavenders, rosemary, lamiums, monardas, thymes and catmints.

Most of us have enjoyed great success growing this group, but have stayed clear of the salvias because of their lack of availability. Now salvias are making their presence known, and are proving invaluable for use in cottage and flower gardens, herb gardens and drought-tolerant landscapes.

For diversity of habitat, colour, texture and leaf fragrance, it's hard to go past salvias. Loved by bees and easy to grow in any temperate climate, they add colourful splashes of blues, purples, pinks and reds to the garden from spring through to late summer and autumn.

The best known in this group is common sage, although it is only one among a genus of 900. Some of the deepest blues and truest reds can be found among the flowers of this genus and many have stunning colour contrasting foliage, but the square stems, opposite leaves and scented foliage can identify them all.

To make your selection easier, here's a guide to some of the best salvias.

• Common sage (*S. officinalis*). The grey-green leaves and blue-mauve flower spikes in summer are familiar to any keen cook and herb grower. Said to cure anything from headaches to fever, from greying hair to palsy, sage has long been a popular home remedy. The aromatic leaves are also used for flavouring pork, veal, poultry, stuffings, and cheese and egg dishes. Common sage also comes in a dwarf form, 'Nana', and in coloured-leafed varieties: 'Icterina', green and yellow, 'Purpurascens', reddish purple and 'Tricolor', grey, pink and cream.

Biennial clary (*Salvia sclarea*).

- Annual or scarlet sage (*S. splendens*).
Many may recognize this popular bedding
plant which flowers scarlet throughout
summer and autumn. There are various
cultivars, growing from 15 cm to 60 cm
tall. There are now other colours available
such as pink, salmon, purple and white.
Buy young plants in spring or raise them
from seed. Plants are not frost-tolerant.
- Mealy sage (*S. farinacea*). A perennial
grown as an annual, the mealy sage is very
popular for summer bedding. Growing to
about 60 cm in height, it produces spikes
of flowers on white-mealy stems, light
blue in the species, white or deep blue in
the various varieties. In frosty climates
plants can be kept over winter in frost-free
conditions as they are not frost-tolerant.
- Pineapple-scented sage (*S. elegans*).
This 1.5 m perennial or sub-shrub is a
great variety to grow in your herb garden.
The leaves are fruit-scented and can be
used for flavouring drinks and salads.
Throughout autumn and winter this sage
is crowned with stunning (and edible)
scarlet flowers. It is a frost-tender species.
- Gentian sage (*S. patens*). So named after
the incredible gentian blue flowers, this
perennial is one of the best flowering
sages. Throughout summer it is smothered
with flowers on stems to 1 m, and looks
great planted in masses with the paler blue
form. This plant takes a low of -5°C.
- Bog sage (*S. uliginosa*). This perennial is
hardier in heavy soils, and tolerates shade
and poorly drained soils. It is an excellent
spreading plant for any garden border,
although it can romp if left unchecked.
The flowers, sky blue-lipped with white
markings, smother the shrub over summer
and autumn. Takes a low of -5°C.
- Mexican bush sage (*S. leucantha*). The
most durable species, Mexican sage grows

Lamiaceae: the mint family

This family of mainly
annual or perennial herbs
and the odd shrub is
characterized by aromatic
foliage, square stems and
flowers with a tongue-like
appearance; the 'tongue'
acts as an insect landing
pad (see the catmint
flower above). It
comprises about 200
genera (including *Salvia*,
Thymus and *Lavandula*)
and 3200 species. It is an
economically important
family, as many of these
plants contain essential
oils for cooking, perfumery
and medicines. The mint
family can be found
worldwide: mint in Europe
and Africa; basil in Asia,
the Pacific Islands and the
Middle East; and
Westringia sp. in Australia.

to 1 m with white woolly hairs all over the stems, underside of the foliage and flower buds. This evergreen sub-shrub flowers from winter to spring. The blooms are white, with showy purple calyces. It takes sun or partial shade and is not frost-tolerant.

- Autumn sage (*S. greggii*). This is a small evergreen shrub whose flowers, in summer and autumn, may be red, purple, pink, violet or even yellow. It is best with partial shade and is fairly drought-tolerant. Autumn sage takes a low of -5°C.
- Germander sage (*S. chamaedryiodes*). This has wonderful deep blue flowers and grey down-like foliage that makes a great foliage contrast in the garden. Germander sage takes a low of -5°C.

Growing tips for salvias

- In frost-prone climates salvias that are not frost tolerant may be grown in a cool conservatory, or bedded out for the summer. Most salvias like free-draining soil. Although drought-tolerant, they respond well to watering and flower better if given liquid feeds.
- Prune salvias back hard at the end of winter, then mulch with manure to promote new spring growth.
- Salvias look great as low informal hedges, similar to lavender, among herb borders where their aromatic foliage will make a contribution, in pots and other containers or in the flower garden.
- Salvias look terrific combined with grey-leaved perennials such as artemisias, verbascums and catmints; also with white-flowered perennials and ornamental grasses.

Grow pineapple-scented sage (*S. elegans*) as a flavouring for summer drinks and salads.

Salvias tolerate hard pruning at the end of winter.

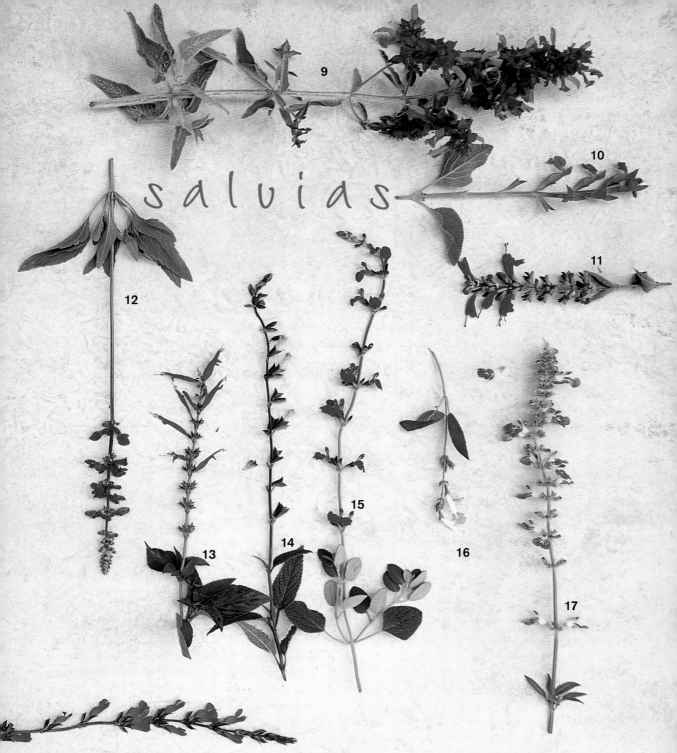

salvias

1 _Salvia farinacea_ (mealy sage). 2 _S._ 'Black Knight'. 3 _S. farinacea_ cultivar. 4 _S. leucantha_ (Mexican bush sage). 5 _S. guaranitica_.
6 _S. sclarea_ (biennial clary). 7 _S. africana-lutea_. 8 _S. chiapensis_ (chiapas sage). 9 _S. canariensis_ (Canary Island sage). 10 _S. greggii_.
11 _S. coccinea_ 'Lady in Red'. 12 _S. farinacea_. 13 _S. elegans_ (pineapple-scented sage). 14 _S._ 'Waverly'. 15 _S._ 'Harmony'. 16 _S. microphylla_
(syn. _S. grahamii_). 17 _S. uliginosa_ (bog sage).

Pelargoniums are great plants. Portable, easy to grow and strike, full of colour — perfect for beginners, children and the elderly.

Pelargoniums

Pelargoniums are classic plants – charming in cottage gardens, fabulous as potted plants on window sills and in conservatories and superb in hanging baskets (trailing kinds). They add a touch of the Mediterranean to courtyards and balconies. Remember, though, that pelargoniums will not tolerate frost, so gardeners in frost-prone climates can grow them out of doors only in the summer and autumn, until the frosts arrive.

They like an open sunny position with good drainage. Humid conditions can cause leaf spots such as rust, which can be treated by removing the affected leaves and spraying with a fungicide. It is best to avoid splashing the leaves when watering, and to water in the morning so foliage can dry completely during the day and spores don't form as easily. This also protects the flowers from spoiling.

A variegated zonal pelargonium.

From left to right: 'Icing Sugar Baby', 'Sugar Baby', 'Pac Penve', 'Pac Julianne', 'Pink Happy Thought' and 'Pac Bergpalais'.

Tip prune your plants from the time they start to make new growth. Take cuttings every few years to ensure an ongoing supply of new plants. Strike the cuttings with a heel.

Pelargoniums have a reputation for being so tough that they don't need any care. While it's true they don't need a lot, they certainly thrive with extra attention, flowering so much more with a little TLC. Regular feeding with a phosphorus-based liquid feed will promote masses of blooms that will continue flush after flush from spring to the end of autumn, especially if you deadhead them as the flowers fade.

Many pelargoniums are popular for both their leaves and their flowers. Some varieties have superb leaf colour and some are perfumed. These fancy leaf and scented leaf types are becoming increasingly popular, with the simpler flowers allowing the attractive markings and delightful fragrances of the leaves to take centre stage.

The down side of pelargoniums is that they can look straggly and woody after a few years. At this stage the best thing is to replace them with fresh plants. Just take cuttings and plant these. They are fast growers – your gaps will fill in no time.

Spicy leaves The 'spice' pelargoniums come in rose (*P. graveolens*), nutmeg (*P. × fragrans*), lemon (*P. crispum*) and many other flavours, and their leaves can be used as liners for baking tins to flavour plain cakes. Some, such as the variety 'Citronella' can even be grown as insect repellents.

Geraniums

Geraniums are popularly known as cranesbills. Most are hardy herbaceous or evergreen perennials that are found growing wild throughout the temperate regions. They form mounds or clumps of lobed leaves, sometimes deeply cut. With some varieties the leaves take on attractive red tints in the autumn, while others have purple or brown markings on the leaves. The foliage of many geraniums is highly aromatic, including that of *Geranium macrorrhizum* and its varieties.

But it is for the flowers that geraniums are primarily grown, for they have an exceedingly long flowering period. Some geraniums start flowering in late spring, most bloom in summer and some continue into autumn. Most geraniums have saucer-shaped flowers and colours are shades of pink, blue, purple and magenta, plus white.

Cranesbills are among the most popular hardy perennials for the garden and there is a huge range of species and varieties, with new varieties being introduced every year. They make particularly good ground cover among shrubs and trees or in a woodland garden, especially the mat-forming and spreading kinds, but can also be grown in groups in ordinary mixed borders. They are an excellent choice for cottage-style gardens and also look good planted among old and modern shrub roses. Smaller species can be grown on rock gardens.

Hardy cranesbills grow in any type of soil provided it is well drained but do best in reasonably fertile conditions. They can be grown in full sun or partial shade. Small kinds grown on rock gardens appreciate soil with very fast drainage.

Keep plants well watered during dry spells and apply a general-purpose fertilizer in the spring each year. A permanent mulch of leaf mould or chipped bark would be appreciated.

Some geraniums are tender and will not take frost, such as *G. maderense*, a native of Madeira. So if you want to grow these kinds and live in a frosty climate, plant them in pots of soil-based potting compost and keep them in a cool conservatory. There they should be provided with light, airy conditions. Water them normally in summer, and liquid feed every three to four weeks, but be very sparing with water in winter when the plants are resting.

To keep geraniums growing and flowering well, regularly remove dead flowers and old, tatty foliage. The best way to increase plants is to divide established clumps in spring. Alternatively propagate by taking basal cuttings in spring as soon as the shoots are about 8 cm high and root them with bottom heat.

Slugs and snails are often a problem outdoors so lay slug pellets around plants as soon as any foliage damage is seen. Mildew may affect the leaves during dry periods and should be controlled by spraying with a suitable fungicide.

A modest garden contains, for those who know how to look and to wait, more instruction than a library.

Henri Frédéric Amiel

1 *Geranium* x *magnificum*. 2 *G. albiflorum*.
3 *G. maderense*. 4 *G. phaeum*. 5 *G. maderense*.
6 *G.* x *cantabrigiense*. 7 *G. phaeum*.
8 *G.* x *magnificum*. 9 *G.* x *cantabrigiense*.

1   2   3   4   5

cranesbills

6

9

10

7

8

11

1 *G. psilostemon*.
2 *G. cinereum* 'Lawrence Flatman'.
3 *G. phaeum*.
4 *G. clarkei* 'Kashmir Purple'.
5 *G. phaeum*.
6 *G. maderense*.
7 *G. aristatum*.
8 *G.* x *magnificum*.
9 *G. phaeum* f. *album*.
10 *G.* x *cantabrigiense* 'Biokovo'.
11 *G. sanguineum*.

Columbines (top and right) and hostas (above) thrive in partial shade.

Shady ladies

A shady refuge on a hot summer's day is one of life's simplest pleasures. Some people associate a shady garden with a dark, dingy, flowerless grotto. Happily, this need not be the case, because many perennials relish some protection from scorching sun.

For flowers in partial shade during the summer consider columbines (aquilegia), various species and varieties of viola, and primulas, especially the candelabra types. For spectacular foliage in light shade try bear's breeches (*Acanthus mollis*), with bold, deeply dissected leaves, which have long been copied in architectural details, and

flowers like oysters on tall spires. These make superb background plants. Harmonize them with hostas, some of the most elegant of plants with their shiny leaves of various colourings — some sea-green, others lime-gold and some cream-striped. The palest of lavender or white flowers, some with a pleasant perfume, appear in summer.

Hostas

Of all the foliage perennials, hostas, or plantain lilies, are one of the most striking.

Popular herbaceous plants for shady glens, they prefer a moist spot and are perfect for growing near water or in bog

Plantain lily (*Hosta* sp.).

gardens. Many hostas are scented too, so it's worth waiting until they are in flower before you choose one.

These handsome plants have been bred and hybridized to produce marbled, white, gold, bluish green and various other foliage variegations. Some, such as *H. plantaginea*, with bright green foliage, have pure white flowers. Some hostas are very large growers, with ultra-large leaves, such as *H. montana*. On the other hand, there are many miniature hybrids available which are ideal where space is limited. New varieties of hosta are appearing every year, being bred intensively on both sides of the Atlantic.

Many are available only from specialist mail-order nurseries.

Unfortunately, hostas succumb easily to slugs and snails, which can destroy their tender young leaves. Make an environmentally friendly slug and snail trap by half burying a partly filled beer bottle in the soil.

Snail alert The sort of cool moist places that these plants favour are also slug and snail havens, so you need to be vigilant to guard against tatty leaves.

daylilies

If you're after a foolproof plant, then this is it. Daylilies are easily grown in a wide range of conditions. As its name suggests, each flower only lasts a day but don't be put off — new flowers open over a long period. The colour range is ideal for a hot summer border, with shades of tangerine, butterscotch, lemon, magenta and purple in both singles and doubles. It's come a long way from the yellow single daylily that was first brought to England during the sixteenth century from eastern Asia, where it grew wild. Daylilies may be herbaceous, evergreen or partially evergreen, and all have strap-shaped or grassy foliage.

Vital statistics

Scientific name: *Hemerocallis* sp.
Family: Hemerocallidaceae
Plant/bulb type: Clump-forming hardy perennials.

Height: 25–95 cm (depending on the variety).
Planting time: Early spring or autumn.
Soil: Any, moist or dry, but enrich with manure or compost before planting.
Position: Full sun or part shade in warm climates.
Planting depth and spacing: Plant with crown at soil level. Space 30 cm apart, or more for large growers.
Fertilizer: For strong healthy growth, top dress with a complete fertilizer in early spring.
Flowering: From late spring through summer.
Watering: Regular watering until established, then the clump becomes drought tolerant. Better blooms expected from plants given a good soak once a week.
After-flowering care: Cut off spent flower heads and remove any dead foliage on herbaceous varieties in late autumn.
Comments: Best used in mass plantings — large clumps or long borders are ideal.

Bulbs

Spring is usually the season associated with bulbs, but that is because most bulbs grown are from cool climates, where bulbs have adapted to cope with extreme cold, and shoot as soon as the weather warms a little.

There are also many bulbs that flower later which have adapted this way to cope with drought and heat. Many good garden centres stock a surprisingly wide range of bulbs for summer flowering; alternatively they can be purchased from mail-order bulb growers. Generally speaking summer-flowering bulbs are planted in the spring.

Summer bulbs

Bulbs are normally associated with springtime, but here is a hidden world of luxurious, exotic bulbs that speak of hot balmy days, colours of the rainbow and intoxicating perfume.

Some commonly grown summer-flowering bulbs include several allium species or ornamental onions, which are becoming increasingly popular, such as *A. giganteum* and *A. sphaerocephalon*. Other popular summer-flowering bulbs include crocosmias (which actually grow from corms), notable for their brilliant red, orange or yellow flowers over a long period, and *Nectaroscordum siculum* which looks like a giant allium.

A tropical bulb which must be grown in a warm conservatory in frost-prone climates is the Amazon lily (*Eucharis* x *grandiflora*). It has clusters of white, fragrant, daffodil-like flowers. The belladonna lily (*Amaryllis belladonna*) comes from South Africa and

The Aztec or Jacobean lily is a tender bulb which should be grown in a temperate conservatory in areas prone to frost.

has fragrant pink flowers in late summer or autumn. It is hardy to -5°C. Other South African bulbs are the crinums. Most commonly grown is the hybrid, *Crinum* x *powellii*, completely hardy and with fragrant, pink, trumpet-shaped flowers in late summer and autumn.

For warm tones and fabulous cut flowers try the Peruvian lily (alstroemeria). For a dash of red in the conservatory in spring or summer, try the stunning Aztec or Jacobean lily (*Sprekelia formosissima*).

Lilium 'Nirvana'.

Lovely lilies

Easy to grow, lilies provide a veritable feast of colour, perfume and floral display from early summer into autumn. Liliums flower for three or four weeks, but the bulbs last for decades in the ground and multiply in the soil, producing even more flowers next year. For a small investment for your first bulb, within five years you'll have perhaps a dozen or more for free.

The Easter lilies are the first to display their elegant, pure white trumpet flowers. As they finish, up pop the very tall regal lilies with trumpet-shaped fragrant flowers in white flushed with purple. A few weeks later the shorter but richly coloured Asiatic lilies spear through the ground and bloom in late summer. Then it's the turn of the oriental lilies to flower into autumn.

Lilies need prepared, well-drained soil enriched with manure, although some varieties can be grown in pots. Most lilies are planted in autumn. Plant them as soon as they are purchased as they do not like being out of the ground.

Glory lily

The glory or climbing lily (*Gloriosa superba* 'Rothschildiana') is a flamboyant tuberous plant for the cool conservatory in frost-prone climates. With their crimson wings and golden hearts, the upturned flowers resemble exotic butterflies in mid-flight, touching down upon glossy green, tendril-tipped leaves.

The tubers are planted in early spring in pots of gritty, soil-based potting compost. Set them about 10 cm deep. Give the plants good light under glass. Liquid feed every two weeks during the growing season once the plants are growing vigorously. The plants die down and rest over the winter, when they should be kept dry. When the tubers become congested in their pots, pot them on into larger pots in late winter. In frost-free climates grow the glory lily out of doors in very well drained, fertile soil in full sun. Avoid cold wet soil which can cause the tubers to rot over the winter.

tuberose

Known for their rich scent, the heavily perfumed flowers of tuberose are used in both floristry and perfumery. The double variety known as 'The Pearl' is the most widely grown.

Vital statistics

Scientific name: *Polianthes tuberosa.*
Family: Agavaceae.
Climate: Grow in a warm conservatory in frost-prone climates.
Culture: The tubers die down and rest over the winter.
Colours: Flowers white with a pinkish tinge at the base.
Height: 90 cm flower spike.
Planting time: Early spring.
Soil: Well-drained, soil-based potting compost.
Position: Provide full light under glass.
Planting depth and spacing: Plant the tubers 5 cm deep and about 10 cm apart.
Fertilizer: Apply a complete plant food every month after the new growth appears.
Pests/diseases: None.
Cutting: Remove spent flowers and continue watering until the foliage dies off.
Propagation: Carefully remove offsets when the tubers are dormant.
Storage: Keep the compost dry over the winter.

summer
grasses, ground covers & climbers

A sweeping expanse of lawn, a wall with spillover plants cascading gently, a lovely ground cover or an arbour draped in fragrant climbers – these elements are charming in their own right, but also help to link buildings to their surrounds and soften hard landscaped features such as paths and retaining walls.

Grasses

Summer is grass-growing season. Every weekend the buzz of a lawn mower can be heard somewhere in the suburbs as it carves its way through another backyard.

Most gardeners yield to the inevitable temptation to lower the mower's blades for a 'close shave', hoping to extend the time between cuts. This is the worst thing you can do. Lift the mower blades in early summer because short grass is stressed grass, more likely to turn into a browned off dust bowl than a bowling green. Be prepared to let your lawn grow a little taller than normal, as this helps stressed grass cope with wear and tear. Cut just a little, more frequently and you'll be rewarded with lush growth.

Make sure you keep your mower blades sharp, as torn grass edges brown quickly in the summer heat.

St Augustine or buffalo grass (*Stenotaphrum secundatum*) is a familiar lawn grass in warm (frost-free) climates such as Mediterranean areas and parts of North America.

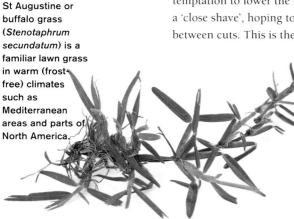

Set the mower blades a bit high for a slightly longer, lush lawn.

Lawn fix

Nothing sets off your garden better than a backdrop of green, healthy lawn. Build up strong roots and fast-repairing, emerald green leaves with a dose of balanced lawn food and your lawn will cope with weekend cricket matches.

Along with summer's high temperatures and, in some areas, high humidity come a set of troublesome lawn problems, pests and diseases.

Various grubs and caterpillars may eat roots or stem bases of grass in summer and autumn, causing dead patches to appear. They are difficult to control as there are no really effective pesticides. If available, use a biological 'insecticide' based on parasitic nematodes. Try watering the lawn heavily and then covering it with a sheet of black plastic for the night. By morning, some grubs may have risen to the surface, when they can be swept up and disposed of.

Earthworms do a great job of aerating the soil but they leave small mounds of sticky soil on the surface of the lawn which, if flattened by feet or mower, will smother and kill the grass. Therefore brush up the mounds before mowing.

When you mow, don't scalp your lawn. Raise the lawn mower blades and leave the grass a little longer for a lush-looking lawn. Scalping weakens the grass, allows weed seeds to germinate and looks ghastly.

Also, beware of applying too much nitrogen during summer, as it can encourage soft leafy growth which only needs more mowing, and it can also burn your turf if applied on a hot or dry day.

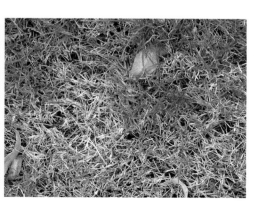

This dead growth of a lawn grass was caused by grubs feeding on the roots and stem bases.

check list

jobs to do now

- Water the lawn once or twice a week, water restrictions permitting.

- Keep the lawn mown, but not too low.

- Apply a wetting agent to the lawn to improve water penetration.

- Check the lawn for early signs of grub damage.

- Watch out for weeds in the lawn and spray with a selective lawn weedkiller.

- Keep the lawn edges trimmed for a neat appearance.

- Remove excess growth on wisteria vines to maintain control of these vigorous climbers.

- Take semi-ripe cuttings of shrubs and climbers and root in pots containing a mix of equal parts peat and coarse sand.

- Give a summer lawn feed if the grass is growing and not suffering from drought.

plant now

- Sow grass seed on any bare patches, provided you can keep them steadily moist.

- Plant some young gazanias to create a stunning ground cover in the sun.

- Tropical annual climbers such as thunbergia can be planted outside for summer display.

flowering now

- Flowering ornamental grasses such as blue fescues, miscanthus, quaking grass, feather or needle grass, ribbon grass and squirrel tail grass, plus various sedges or carex

- Ground covers such as ajuga (early summer), cerastium, convolvulus, erigeron, lambs ears, Australian violet, verbena

- Climbers such as allamanda, bougainvillea, campsis (orange trumpet vine), mandevilla, pandorea (bower vine), passion flowers, thunbergia

Breathless, we flung us on the windy hill.
Laughed in the sun, and kissed the lovely grass.

Rupert Brooke

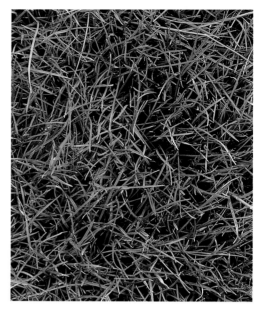

Perennial rye is used in grass-seed mixtures for cool and cold climates but is not drought tolerant.

Drought-tolerant grasses

There are no reliably drought-tolerant lawn grasses for cool and cold climates, but perennial rye grass is one of the toughest, so regular watering in dry periods is the rule, to prevent the lawn turning brown. Gardeners in warm climates do have a choice, though, in St Augustine or buffalo grass which tolerates drought reasonably.

Fairy rings

After rain you might find fairy rings popping up in your lawn. These are small to large circular rings of dead grass, often with mushrooms appearing in a mysterious ring pattern.

The soil under the dead areas is frequently packed with white thread-like fungal growth that causes the grass to die by depriving it of water and nutrients. The fungi start growing at one point, but gradually spread out into a circle so that the rings expand each year. Often the grass in the centre of the ring is green, as it is only where the fungi actively grow that it does any damage.

The fungi causing fairy rings are common in pastures and turfed areas, and can grow for many years unless treated. They are spread via the mushroom-like fruiting bodies, especially in warm and moist conditions.

The main treatment is to ensure adequate water penetration into the areas where the fungus is actively growing. Hollow tyne forking or coring the affected areas as deeply as possible will assist water penetration, as will wetting agents.

Problem patch

Do you have a troublesome patch of lawn where any water applied simply runs off and it's hard to get a good grass surface going? Even well-prepared soil can compact over the years, stopping water or fertilizer from penetrating. This makes the maintenance of even a small patch an endless chore.

To beat the problem, you should aerate the lawn either with a hollow-tine aerator or with a garden fork. Both of these can be used to make a series of holes, about 10 cm deep, over the surface of the lawn. You need to work systematically over the lawn, inserting the fork or aerator at 15 cm intervals. Ideally a hollow-tine aerator should be used in the autumn and the holes then filled with a topdressing mix consisting of sand and peat, with perhaps some good loam added. The organic matter in the mix will encourage earthworms, the best free workers in the garden because they aerate the soil as they tunnel about. However, they do produce unsightly mounds of soil which should be swept up before mowing.

In the summer after aerating apply a soil wetting agent to encourage water to penetrate the soil instead of running off.

feature grass
ribbon grass

Ribbon grass is grown for its admirable green and white striped foliage; some cultivars have a pink tinge to the new growth. It is a rhizomatous grower, so plant it in an area where it can spread and fill or keep it contained by planting it in bottomless pots. It makes an excellent ground cover, and is very striking with darker foliage backdrops and bright flowers.

Vital statistics

Scientific name: *Phalaris arundinacea* var. *picta* 'Picta'.
Family: Poaceae.
Climate: Frost hardy.
Culture: Flowers in summer.
Height: Up to 90 cm when in flower.
Planting time: Plant out divisions in late winter, before the new growth appears.
Soil: Easily grown in any garden soil. Suitable for soil stabilization, seaside plantings and waterside conditions.
Position: Full sun or partial shade.
Watering: Keep moist throughout growing season.
Fertilizer: Use a liquid fertilizer after a summer prune to promote fresh new growth.
Pruning: Cut down dead growth in early spring. Dig out unwanted growth in early spring.

Ground covers

Next time you have to mow your lawn, take the time to consider some alternatives to grass. If your garden has a turfed area that could be transformed by a flowering ground cover, make plans now.

Many ground covers flower over summer, creating a colourful carpet. Bugle (*Ajuga*) in early summer, bindweed (*Convolvulus* sp.), gazanias, lamb's ears and verbena are just a few creating a sea of splendour.

Plant a flowering ground cover

A ground cover can be a clumpy, spreading perennial, a creeping one or even a climber which you allow to sprawl over the ground rather than grow upwards. Basically, ground cover plants are those that cover the ground to give it a soft appearance, smothering weeds and integrating built features with garden areas.

A delightful flowering mass could be achieved in summer by planting maiden pink, *Dianthus deltoides*, some perennial candytuft (*Iberis*) and silver-leafed ground-cover plants such as lamb's ears.

Thrift

Thrift forms a low, cushion-like carpet with flowers that vary from white to crimson, making it an excellent choice for the edge of an herbaceous border.

Lamb's ears

Lamb's ears (*Stachys byzantina*) has thick silvery leaves that are covered in grey felt. During summer it will produce purple flowers on tall spikes. It provides a patch of

Australian violet (*Viola hederacea*).

silvery contrast in a mixed border, and its soft woolly leaves growing in a rosette formation make it an attractive ground cover for a sunny position.

African daisy

Its bright daisy-like flowers, which flower profusely through spring to autumn, distinguish the African daisy (*Arctotis* hybrids) from the rest of the silver leaf plants. This plant flowers in pinks, oranges, reds, whites and yellows but comes in special varieties in lilac and plum shades. All have the characteristic black and gold centres.

African daisies make a great ground cover or a bank planting and are very popular in coastal gardens. The flowers close in the late afternoon and this is when the silvery stems and leaves dominate. This is a great plant but you should treat it as an annual.

In frost-prone areas take semi-ripe stem cuttings in late summer, protect them over winter and plant them out in spring.

Catmint

If you have a cat it will love you for planting catmint (*Nepeta* x *faassenii*). It is a low-growing herbaceous plant that carries attractive lavender-blue flower spikes. The serrated leaves are mainly grey-green. It likes a well-drained soil with full sun to part shade and in the right conditions will layer itself, quickly spreading into a matting ground cover. Ideal for rockeries or against walls, catmint can also be grown as a clumpy dwarf hedge in a border.

Snow-in-summer

Snow-in-summer (*Cerastium tomentosum*) is a carpet-like ground cover with masses of white star-shaped flowers in late spring and summer and silvery grey foliage. It's a rapid-growing ground cover, making it great for rockeries and hanging baskets. Plant it in a well-drained position with full sun and water it well during dry weather. It will grow to around 15 cm tall and spread to about 1 m wide.

dead nettle

Dead nettles are ideal ground cover plants for shady areas under trees. The leaves are very attractive: some have striking silvery white markings, such as *L. maculatum* 'White Nancy'; others have golden variegation or a central white stripe. *Lamium* sp. tend to be a little invasive for small gardens or herbaceous borders, but have striking foliage that looks great when massed as a ground cover.

Vital statistics

Scientific name: *Lamium* sp.

Family: Lamiaceae.

Climate: Very hardy, suitable for cool and cold climates.

Culture: Flowers in summer.

Height: 30 cm or under.

Planting time: Propagate by division in either autumn or spring.

Soil: Will grow in any soil.

Position: Will tolerate sun but prefers shade.

Planting depth and spacing: Plant 30–45 cm apart.

Fertilizer: Feed with a slow-release fertilizer in spring.

Watering: Don't let lamium dry out, as it needs lots of water.

Pruning: Cut it back as it outgrows its position.

Succulents for pots

In the future, gardeners will be forced to look at plants that need less water. With water becoming more expensive, lawns, the biggest guzzlers of water, will be too costly to maintain. Xerophytic, or drought-tolerant, plants that store water in their stems, leaves or roots will be the answer.

This concern about water conservation has started to put succulents in the spotlight. For half a century they have been hidden in the collector's corner, or growing quietly on Grandma's porch, but now they've hit the big time.

Their resurgence in popularity is well founded. They are unquestionably tough, surviving hot summers without water and in 50°C heat, but they can also be breathtakingly beautiful. The symmetrical, statuesque and organic shapes look like an underwater landscape, yet they can survive on a dribble of water.

Bear in mind that most succulent plants are frost tender, including those shown here, so in frost-prone climates grow them in patio containers, or plunge the pots in beds, borders and gravel areas, for summer display, and move them into a frost-free conservatory for the winter.

For information on propagating succulents, see 'Autumn'.

Did you know? The sap of *Agave filifera* is fermented to make a light alcoholic Mexican drink called 'pulque'.

Clockwise from top: Saucer plant (*Aeonium* 'Zwartkop'), *Echeveria elegans*, pig's ear (*Cotyledon orbiculata*) and *Echeveria graptoveria* 'Debbie'.

Climbers

In conservatories and small gardens where space is restricted, climbing plants can be grown on walls, fences and trelliswork. There is a wide range of beautiful tender and tropical climbers that flower in summer.

Above: Glory bower (*Clerodendrum splendens*), an evergreen climber for the warm conservatory.

Right: A miniature pink climbing rose softens the wall of this shed.

Soil preparation Climbing plants are usually left in the same position for many years so it is wise to prepare the soil well before planting.

There are lots of choices for supports for your climbing plants; some of them can be decorative features in their own right, but make sure your support is anchored firmly. A climber in full leaf acts as a sail; any strong wind blowing on it can exert tremendous pressure.

Freestanding trellis panels, pergolas, arches and arbours can all be clothed with climbing plants. To decorate a fence you can attach wires or plastic netting to allow the climber to be fixed into place. Climbing roses can be grown over walls, arbours and archways but they also look good decorating an ornamental pillar.

A few climbers — ivy, for example — cling on with their roots. Ivy will climb walls, fences and tree trunks too if you let it escape. Some plants have tendrils with which they grasp the support. Sweet pea is a good example. Climbers naturally grow upwards to seek the light, so twine them sideways rather than upright for a bushy thick cover.

Two fragrant climbers

Two related climbers that require very little effort and give so much in return are hoya and stephanotis. In frost-prone climates these are grown in cool and warm conservatories respectively. Mostly from tropical Southeast Asia and northern Australia, hoya are slow-growing climbers which can last for thirty years in the same pot, flowering every year. Commonly called wax plant, the usual species grown is *Hoya carnosa* with fragrant white flowers. It will thrive outdoors in very mild climates.

Hoya love to be root bound in the pot, so neglect is perfect. Don't prune them or pick the flowers, as new flowers grow from the same spurs as the old ones. Water them and you'll even get flowers every summer!

There are several varieties of *H. carnosa*, including 'Exotica' whose leaves are variegated with pink and flushed with yellow. Other variegated ones are 'Picta' and 'Variegata', both of which have white-edged leaves. 'Krinkle' has unusual crinkly foliage. They all flower from spring to autumn and are at their most fragrant at night.

One very popular but often ignored climber is stephanotis. They were very popular in bridal bouquets in the 1920s and '30s but are enjoying a big revival again.

Their creamy white and sweetly perfumed flowers are irresistible. You don't need a botanical garden in order to grow stephanotis – just a large warm conservatory or a greenhouse.

Flowers beyond reach are sacred to God.

Indian proverb

Stephanotis floribunda comes from Madagascar so it likes warm conditions. In the greenhouse or conservatory grow it in pots or tubs of soil-based potting compost. Provide good light but shade from very strong sun. During the summer provide plenty of water and liquid feed fortnightly. It will also appreciate being sprayed with plain water daily during the summer to maintain a humid atmosphere. When the plant is resting over winter be less generous with water. If you are able to grow stephanotis out of doors, choose a position in full sun but with some shade during the hottest part of the day. A well-drained, reasonably fertile soil is needed, with added bulky organic matter such as garden compost or well-rotted farmyard manure. Plants should be pruned in early spring: simply trim them to fit the space available and prune out any very old wood.

Above: Stephanotis is easy to train, making it a practical cover for a trellis, balcony or fence.

Pruning a grapevine Unless the grape is a fruiting one, its growth can be kept in check by summer pruning. Remove wayward long tendrils back to the secondary growth or older wood. In this way you'll keep only the water shoots required.

Above: *Passiflora coccinea.*

Above right: Bougainvillea.

Below: *Thunbergia alata.*

Fabulous tropical climbers

Many climbers are native to the warm, temperate climates in the rainforests of the southern hemisphere. The best season for these frost-tender climbers is summer, when their spectacular blooms are at their peak.

Bougainvilleas

Perhaps the most easily grown climber is the bougainvillea. It is ideal for Mediterranean-type climates, or in pots or tubs in a cool conservatory or greenhouse. The papery bracts of bougainvillea are long lasting and showy, and are dazzling from spring through summer. Plants need strong supports, and hard pruning to keep them in check. Prune in early spring by cutting back the previous year's shoots to within a few buds of the permanent 'framework' stems. Plants can be grown as standards in pots, ideal for a conservatory. They could then be stood out of doors for the summer. Most climb using hard, hooked thorns, but modern varieties are thornless, some with double flowers.

Passion flowers

The edible passion fruit is the best known feature of the passion fruit vine, but there is more to this vine than just the fruit. The South American climber requires a warm, frost-free position in order for its fruits to reach maturity, but the flowers themselves are also special.

Missionaries in Central and South America used the flowers to describe Christ's Crucifixion. They are highly intricate, consisting of ten greenish white, pink-tinged petals surrounding rows of thin purple, blue and white filaments, which in turn surround five stamens and three styles. The petals look like the crown of thorns, the three styles represent the three nails in the cross and the fruit is the blessing of Christianity.

The common eating type of passion fruit (*Passiflora edulis*) is not the most spectacular species. The red passion flower (*P. coccinea*) and blue passion flower (*P. caerulea*) are more ornamental, with the latter developing orange-yellow, egg-shaped fruit throughout summer before ripening in autumn. The blue passion flower is the hardiest species and can be grown outdoors in frost-prone climates. It will take a low of -5°C. For perfume, try the giant granadilla (*P. quadrangularis*), with red and purple flowers and large edible fruits.

All passion fruit respond well to generous feeding. Lightly dress with high nitrogen fertilizers, ideally every month.

Thunbergia

The best known of all species of thunbergia is commonly called black-eyed susan (*T. alata*) because of its orange petals and black centres. This restrained annual climber is just right for a hanging basket or post.

The other thunbergias are less well behaved, and can get out of hand. Bengal clock vine or skyflower (*T. grandiflora*) is very vigorous, and will cover a support if not restrained or killed off with a hard frost. It has jacaranda blue flowers in summer.

Another species worth growing is the orange clock vine (*T. gregorii*), which has masses of orange flowers. It is an evergreen perennial but is often grown as an annual, either out of doors in warm climates, or in a conservatory in cooler areas.

Allamanda

Magnificent for an intermediate to warm conservatory or greenhouse, the golden trumpet (*Allamanda cathartica*) bears clusters of golden yellow trumpet flowers in summer and autumn. Prune in early spring by cutting back previous year's shoots to within a few buds of the permanent woody framework stems.

Cruel to be kind Bougainvilleas love neglect, so be careful not to overwater or use nitrogen-based fertilizers that promote leaf growth at the expense of flowers.

coral vine

Coral vine is another tropical delight that is actually native to Mexico. The coral pink, heart-shaped flowers are borne en masse from early summer to mid-autumn.

Vital statistics
Scientific name: *Antigonon leptopus*.
Family: Polygonaceae.
Climate: Frost free. In frost-prone areas grow in a cool conservatory.
Culture: Support on fence, trellis or railing.
Colours: Coral pink.
Height: Up to 12 m.
Planting time: Spring.
Soil: Free draining.
Position: Good light under glass; full sun outdoors.
Fertilizer: Complete fertilizer in spring.
Pests/diseases: Pest and disease free.
Pruning: In early spring prune to fit space available.
Propagation: Semi-ripe cuttings in summer, in warm conditions.

summer
shrubs & trees

Three words describe shrubs and trees in summer: green, cool and lush. But that needn't mean an upper storey devoid of flower: many shrubs and trees, the structural plants of the garden, feature colourful and fragrant flowers at this time of year — some are dainty and pretty while others are striking and vibrant.

Of course you want your garden to look good at this time of the year, but keeping up with the family next door can be a hard slog if your garden isn't planned well with hardy summer plants.

At no other time does the value of trees and shrubs become more important than over summer. Gone are the flowers from spring, and instead the shade of trees and the privacy of shrubs become crucial for enjoying outdoor leisure time.

I never before knew the full value of trees. My house is entirely embosomed in high plane trees, with good grass below, and under them I breakfast, dine, write, read and receive my company.

Thomas Jefferson

Shrubs

Shrubs are the mainstay of a garden. They require little maintenance, form a background to flowering 'fillers' like annuals and cottage plants, and will always look green and healthy if they have been chosen well.

There are many colourful shrubs available for flowering in summer. Popular hardy early summer-flowering shrubs are the mock oranges or philadelphus, with white or creamy flowers and a powerful fragrance. They range from dwarf shrubs to tall specimens, up to 4 m in height.

Some grevilleas are frost hardy and will grow successfully in cool or mild climates, and are valued for their unusual petalless flowers. They come from the Southern Hemisphere, as do the bottlebrushes or callistemons. These also have unusual flowers — in the shape of bottlebrushes, hence the common name. Several species will grow outdoors in cool and mild climates. Or potted, they can be wintered in a conservatory and put outside for summer.

Hardy fuchsias are excellent for partial shade and thrive well in seaside gardens. Most of them have blue and red flowers.

Oleanders are a familiar sight in Mediterranean climates but in colder areas they make good conservatory plants. Potted specimens can be placed out of doors for the summer on a sunny, sheltered patio. All parts of oleander are poisonous so bear this in mind. Ideal for seaside gardens oleanders cope well with heat and dryness.

Hibiscus are exotic-looking shrubs for summer. In a frost-prone climate grow the hardy *Hibiscus syriacus*. There are many varieties available in shades of blue, red, pink or white. For frost-free climates or the warm conservatory there is *H. rosa-sinensis* with large, bright, almost gaudy flowers.

Hebes from new Zealand come in a great range of colours from the softest lilac to deep cherry pinks and purple. Plants vary in size from dwarf to tall and the foliage is

Left to right: Butterfly bush, callistemon and fuchsia.

Opposite: 'Antique Rose'.

angel's trumpet

The perfect night-time shrub for the cool conservatory, *Brugmansia* is a relative of tobacco. The flowers have a dreamy perfume that is most noticeable in the evening. The large flared trumpets hang down in their hundreds — white, yellow, orange and apricot. Train to a single stem and remove suckers.

Above: *Grevillea* sp.

attractive, too, being greyish in some species, purple flushed in others. Most hebes are frost hardy to fully hardy so thrive in cool and cold climates. They are especially suitable for seaside gardens.

Southern Hemisphere shrubs

Southern Hemisphere shrubs are becoming popular in the Northern Hemisphere. Some are hardy enough to be grown outdoors in mild areas, while others make good plants for cool conservatories and greenhouses. Extra to those we have already mentioned, the following are worth considering.

Paperbarks or melaleuca, mainly from Australia, need frost-free climates (they are ideal for Mediterranean climates), but elsewhere they make good shrubs for the cool conservatory. They are evergreen and have botttlebrush-like flowers, being closely related to callistemons, the true bottlebrushes. Some have very thin, papery bark, hence the common name. There are many species of melaleuca, so buy whatever is available in your area. *Melaleuca elliptica* is quite a well-known species with pink or red flowers over a very long period, starting in spring and continuing through summer. Best flowering occurs when summers are long and hot. Under glass grow in pots or tubs of soil-based potting compost, provide good light, and be very sparing with water in the winter. Outdoors they will take quite tough conditions: heat, poor or dry soil, wind and, near the sea, salty air.

The red-flowering gum, *Eucalyptus ficifolia*, from Western Australia, so spectacularly illustrated here, is actually a small tree but like other eucalyptus species it can be grown as a shrub by hard pruning it each year in early spring. Simply cut the previous year's stems back to within a few buds of a permanent low woody

framework. Pruning should start when the plant is still quite small. When grown this way it will not produce its spectacular flowers but is grown instead for its lovely green juvenile foliage. The flowers are red, but may also be pink or white. The red-flowering gum will not stand much frost (it is suitable for a Mediterranean climate) so gardeners in frost-prone areas could grow it in a tub in a cool conservatory and stand the plant outdoors for the summer. Grow it in a sandy, soil-based potting compost and provide good light and ventilation. Water well in summer but reduce considerably during the winter. Liquid feed every three to four weeks in summer. Out of doors this eucalyptus needs well-drained, slightly acid or neutral soil and a sunny position, with shelter from cold winds. It is particularly good for seaside gardens.

The mint bush or prostanthera is becoming more widely grown in the Northern Hemisphere. There are numerous species of these Australian shrubs, all evergreen, and they have strongly aromatic foliage. The hardiest is the alpine mint bush, *P. cuneata*, which will take a temperature down to -5°C, so it can be grown out of doors in cool climates. It flowers freely in the summer, the tubular blooms being white, marked with yellow and purple in the throat. A small shrub, it reaches about 90 cm in height. There are numerous other species but they are not so hardy and need to be grown in a cool conservatory in frosty climates. Out of doors prostantheras need very well drained soil and a sunny position. In the conservatory grow in pots of soil-based potting compost, provide good light and be very sparing with water in winter.

Top: *Melaleuca fulgens*, a species of paperbark.

Bottom: *Prostanthera rotundifolia*, a shrub with strongly aromatic foliage.

Main picture: Red-flowering gum (*Eucalyptus ficifolia*).

Cut flowers Cut flowers last longer if you put them into water containing a little sugar solution. Add citric acid to the water to prolong the life of flowers that tend to live only a few days, such as grevillea.

This summer create your own Mediterranean garden with a wall of potted pelargoniums (above) as well as some oleanders (right) and silver plants like this silver bush (*Convolvulus cneorum*) (far right).

Mediterranean paradise

Blue skies, warm seas and balmy nights scented with orange blossom...dreaming of another place? It's the Mediterranean and you can create your own.

- Lime-washed walls, lots of terracotta pots, ceramic tiles and colonnades will give you an authentic start.
- Add a water feature — a simple wall fountain will do.
- Build your garden with plants. The Italian cypress is lovely. Plant formal hedges of box, lavender or rosemary, then fill in with colourful pelargoniums and nasturtiums.
- Climbers can soften the effect. Use bougainvillea if you have a suitable climate, or a hardy jasmine in cooler areas. Grapevines, fruiting and ornamental, can shade pergolas.
- Large tubs complete the look...hydrangeas in shady spots, kumquats in the sun and classic terracotta window boxes overflowing with red pelargoniums give that finishing touch to your very own Mediterranean paradise.

Oleanders

Oleanders come from hot dry climates around the Mediterranean. They're tough, long lived, grow in poor soil and thrive on neglect. For a shrub in a windy and sunny exposed location the oleander is perfect. They flower profusely to brighten up dull and boring suburban streets and roadsides like nothing else can. In parts of Italy with narrow streets and no verge, local councils have turned their oleanders into 3 m tall standards. The sight is spectacular.

During summer the flowers put on a magnificent display in a limited range of white, pink and red shades. There is also a variegated leaf form.

Gardeners in frost-prone climates can grow oleanders in tubs in a cool conservatory and place them outside for the summer. These plants may need cutting back in late winter if they become too large.

Silver and grey plants

The majority of grey plants grow naturally in harsh conditions, such as on the shoreline and in desert and alpine areas. Many silver and grey foliage plants originally came from the Mediterranean, and from the Southern Hemisphere, so now we have a rich variety of plants with these soft silvery colours — a great foil for sombre greens in the garden.

The grey and silver appearance of such plants is caused by white hairs on the leaf surface. The hairs reflect the harsh rays of the sun, reducing water loss and retaining moisture close to the surface. Silver and grey plants are perfect for inland and shoreline areas. Most grey plants will thrive where other plants couldn't survive, but they do need sun in order to create the shimmering effect: otherwise they are simply grey.

There is a wide variety of silver and grey perennials, herbs, ground covers, shrubs and trees available. Choose from the silver bush (*Convolvulus cneorum*), *Senecio cineraria* and its varieties, cotton lavender (*Santolina chamaecyparissus*), artemisias, lamb's ears, lavenders, catmints, snow-in-summer, *Elaeagnus angustifolia* (oleaster or Russian olive), and brachyglottis (formerly senecio).

Senecio cineraria

Senecio cineraria is an evergreen which is native to the Mediterranean. The handsome silvery grey leaves provide a pleasing contrast in a predominantly green garden, making it a great feature plant. The deeply indented leaves are about 10–15 cm long and 5–7 cm deep. The yellow flowers can appear intermittently but occur mainly in late spring or summer. It likes a moderately fertile soil and will tolerate a light frost. *S. cineraria* grows up to 60 cm in height, forming an open bush that is 60 cm across.

Lavender has been used for domestic purposes for centuries: it can be used in clothes washing, herbal remedies, soaps, teas, cooking, lavender bags and perfumes. In fact, lavender hedges used to serve as a form of clothesline: washed items were placed on the bushes to dry, becoming impregnated with lavender oil in the process.

Lavender blue

Lavender is universally recognized as a valuable herb and ornamental shrub. With its perfume, flowers and silver foliage, it has something to offer everyone.

Caring for lavender

Lavender will cope with exposed, sunny, open positions. The best-looking plants are usually those growing in the most inhospitable conditions.

Good drainage is essential. The other critical factor in successfully growing lavender is to add lime to your soil if it is acid, to raise the pH, making it alkaline. An acidic soil is a common problem for these plants both in the garden proper and in pots; it will weaken the plant and make it prone to rot and fungal attack. Mulching around the root system will help to maintain even moisture levels in the soil, and will improve the organic content.

Lavender requires annual pruning in early or mid-spring. Using garden shears, trim back all the old flowered shoots to within 2.5 cm of the older wood but do not cut into the latter as it will not produce new shoots. Without such pruning plants become woody and unsightly.

Apply an organic fertilizer, such as blood, fish and bone, straight after pruning.

Types

There are twenty-eight original species of lavender. Basically they can all be classified into four groups.

True or English lavender

Used for oil production in the perfume industry, this is the most popular type for drying and for potpourris. All English lavenders cope with cold and frost, and have narrow, pointed, smooth grey leaves

and long thin spikes of mauve to purple-coloured flowers which appear in summer.

English lavender is *Lavandula angustifolia*, but was once known as *L. spica*. There are many varieties, with flowers ranging from lavender blue to purple, pink and white. The most popular are 'Hidcote', 'Munstead' and 'Twickel Purple'. 'Nana Alba' is a good dwarf white variety and 'Loddon Pink' has light pink flowers.

French lavender

The winged bracts at the top of each short flower spike distinguish this group. Botanically known as *L. stoechas*, it has grey-green leaves and flowers through the summer. There are many varieties, and new ones are appearing all the time. Flower colours include shades of purple, red, blue, pink and white. Height is around 60 cm.

Toothed lavender

Lavandula dentata is easily recognized by the leaves, which have toothed margins. It is not as hardy as some species and in areas with hard winters should be grown in a cool conservatory. The leaves are dark green and the plant flowers in mid- and late summer, the colour of the slightly fragrant blooms being purple-blue. It grows to about 1 m in height. The toothed lavender likes an open, sunny spot in the garden.

Spike lavender

With its broad grey-green leaves and branching flower spikes, *L. latifolia* makes an interesting addition to any garden. It is moderately hardy but in regions with severe winters it would be best grown in a cool conservatory. Blooming in mid- and late summer, the fragrant flowers are pale purplish blue. Height is up to 1 m.

cotton lavender

Cotton lavender (*Santolina chamaecyparissus*), a low shrubby perennial from the Mediterranean which has golden blooms like tiny pompoms in the summer, is grown for its distinctive aromatic foliage. The foliage, which looks rather like a feather duster, grows into a compact bush that is ideal for the front of a border or even as a feature plant on a rock garden.

Many gardeners clip it into a round shape, discouraging flowering. Cotton lavender also looks great woven through a parterre or edging a herb garden.

This plant prefers mild winters, but can take a low of -5°C, and hot dry summers. It particularly relishes light sandy soil and needs a position in full sun.

1

2

3

4

5

6

7

8

9

10

lavender

13

12

11

1 *Lavandula stoechas*
'Lavender Lace'. 2 'Bee
Brilliant. 3 *L. stoechas*
subsp. *pedunculata*
'Avonview'. 4 *L. stoechas*
'Helmsdale'. 5 *L. stoechas*
'Tickled Pink'. 6 *L. stoechas*
'Fairy Wings'. 7 *L. stoechas*
'Willow Bridge White'.
8 *L. stoechas.* 9 *L. stoechas*
'Kew Red'. 10 'Bee Pretty'.
11 *Lavandula* 'Sidonie'.
12 *L. dentata.* 13 *L.* x *allardii.*

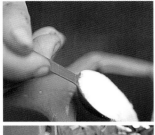

Above: *Hydrangea paniculata* 'Grandiflora'. The species originates from China and Japan. Prune this deciduous shrub back hard in early spring for larger flower heads.

Caring for hydrangeas

Hydrangea literally means 'water loving', which makes them ideal for the shady, moist parts of the garden where most shrubs won't flower. They do cope with sun, provided they receive an adequate amount of water. Try combining water-storing crystals with your soil, and add some rich compost and leaf mould to help keep the roots cool.

The magic surrounding the colour-changing ability of hydrangea flowers all comes down to pH. The lower the pH, or the more acid the soil, the bluer the flower, while the higher the pH, or the more alkaline the soil, the redder the bloom becomes.

To change the colour of your hydrangeas, start feeding in autumn with either lime, for pink flowers, or aluminium sulphate, also called bluing tonic, to produce purple and blue flowers. Keep this up until the buds have formed in early summer.

If you're wondering how to change your hydrangea to white, you can't. White hydrangeas are unaffected by pH differences.

Hydrangeas

When it comes to summer flowers, it's hard to ignore the appeal of hydrangeas. Their clusters of flowers in red, pink, purple, blue and white are perfect for classic bunches of flowers in vases, for brightening the shady side of the house, or in pots. They also have a traditional feel about them, which makes them appropriate for plantings around older-style homes.

These bushy, generally deciduous shrubs originated in China, Japan and North America. Growing up to 4 m tall, they are long lived and extremely versatile.

Pruning

Some people make a fuss about how tricky it is to prune hydrangeas, but the truth is it's a simple task, providing you understand hydrangeas a little.

If you like large, showy blooms, cut the plants back by about one third each winter, until you find a pair of fat double buds. Trim them neatly here. To have masses of smaller blooms, just trim off the old flower heads at the end of autumn, lightly shaping the plant.

Don't hard prune the entire bush, or the following season you'll have lots of healthy green growth, but not many flowers.

Varieties to choose from

The common or mop-head hydrangea (*Hydrangea macrophylla* Hortensia Group), with its large showy heads, is the most popular, but there are many other types which are popular with both collectors and keen gardeners.

Ruffled edges

- **Lacecaps.** These delicate blooms look like lace doilies, with the centre buds made up of tiny fertile flowers, and the surrounding blooms the larger infertile flowers which form the basis of the common hydrangea. Lacecaps, comprising a group of *H. macrophylla*, come in white, blue and pink, and also a variegated leaf form that is useful for lightening up dull corners of the garden.
- **Japanese forms.** These are a variation on the common type, but have tightly curled florets that look more like rose buds.

- *H. paniculata* 'Grandiflora'. This has upright, 25 cm long conical heads of creamy white bracts which turn pink with age. Grows to 2 m.
- *H. aspera* Villosa Group. This Chinese hydrangea flowers later in summer than the traditional type. Pink-white infertile flowers surround the scattered deep blue bracts of fertile flowers. Grows to 3 m.
- *H. quercifolia*. Known as the oak-leaf hydrangea, it has clusters of white fertile and infertile flowers in summer. The deeply lobed leaves colour red and burnt orange in autumn before falling.
- *H. anomala* subsp. *petiolaris*. This climbing hydrangea from the Far East is a vigorous grower once it is established. The flat heads of white flowers smother the plant throughout summer, making it ideal for decorating shady fences and walls. It climbs by using adventitious roots (like ivy), which means it self-clings.

New ways for old favourites

- Standards. Hydrangeas can be trained as standards to make fabulous summer specimen plants. Simply trim off all side shoots till the desired height is reached, staking the plant firmly as you go. Nip the top from the leader when it's the right height and trim to a round ball.
- Pots. Hydrangeas make classic container plants. Used extensively in Italy for decorating outdoor living areas, they can also be brought inside for a lasting flower display. Place a saucer under each pot to keep up the water in hot, dry weather.
- Drying. Hydrangea flowers can be either dried on the bush naturally and picked in autumn once they've greened, or cut fresh and placed in glycerin solution so that they keep their colour.

Hydrangea, the quintessential summer flower, shown here in just a few of its many forms.

Above: *Syzygium wilsonii* showing its colourful new foliage.

stand frost so grow the plant under glass in cool and cold climates. If dwarf, compact varieties are available, these are best for containers. Grow in soil-based potting compost, provide good light but shade from the strongest sun, and carry out moderate watering in summer with even less in winter. Liquid feeds about once a month in summer ensure good growth. In some areas plants are prone to sapsucking insects which cause leaf curl (psyllid). Spray with an insecticide such as a horticultural oil.

Summer azalea care

To keep azaleas bushy and producing the maximum quantity of flowering branches, lightly trim your azalea bushes now. Remove any tall, irregular sucker-like growths as these will make your plants look misshapen and encourage them to become leggy.

Mulching with peat, leaf mould or chipped bark will protect the shallow roots during warm summer weather and prevent the soil from drying out. Do not use fertilizers on azaleas.

By autumn you may notice silvery grey leaves on your azaleas and rhododendrons, but by the time the damage is visible it's too late — the insect has gone. Now is the time to control lace bug, the pest that causes the

Brush cherry

Here's something unusual for the warm conservatory — syzygiums. In the myrtle family, these are aromatic trees and shrubs from the tropics, often with copper- or bronze-flushed new leaves. The most freely available is S. *paniculatum*, the brush cherry from Australia, with white 'shaving-brush' flowers in summer, followed by red, pink or purple fruits. Like all the species it won't

TREATING A PSYLLID INFESTATION

1 A syzygium which has been badly damaged by an infestation of psyllid.

2 Trim any psyllid-infested growth. Place the prunings in a plastic bag before throwing them out.

3 Spray with horticultural oil to prevent reinfestation.

silvering. Look on the reverse of the leaves: black blotches and small winged insects mean lace bugs. It won't be long before they start sucking the sap from the foliage and, if left unchecked, will seriously reduce the health and vigour of your plants.

To control lace bug, hose down the underside of the foliage before applying a suitable insecticide such as an insecticidal soap, again to the underside of the leaves. Several applications may be needed. Even more effective would be a systemic insecticide. Discoloured leaves will not regain their green colour and may remain on the plants for some time.

Hibiscus

One of the most rewarding shrubs to grow is the tropical hibiscus. In frost-prone climates it is grown in a warm conservatory, but where frosts are not a problem hibiscus is a great shrub for a sunny spot outdoors.

Although they are commonly known as Hawaiian hibiscus, they are actually native to China. The Latin name *Hibiscus rosa-sinensis* means Rose of China. There are many varieties with flowers in shades of red, pink, orange and yellow, plus white.

To get the most out of hibiscus, see that they get plenty of sunshine. Give them

Above: An Hawaiian hibiscus cultivar (*Hibiscus rosa-sinensis*).

blood, fish and bone, cow manure and a sprinkle of the pelletized fertilizers, all with extra water throughout the growing seasons of spring, summer and autumn.

Prune hibiscus heavily every year after frosts in late spring because they flower on new season's branches. If you don't, you will get fewer and fewer flowers. Cut them back hard in late spring, feed and water them, then stand back and and admire the display.

TREATING LACE BUG

1 Prune affected foliage.

2 Spray with an insecticide.

pollution

As house blocks and gardens get smaller and our suburbs become choked with noisy traffic, privacy and pollution are becoming greater problems.

While solid fences and walls block out the view of traffic, they can also create an air vacuum behind the wall and suck in the sound. On the other hand, a combination of trees and shrubs of varying heights and leaf textures improves the view, increases privacy and filters pollution and traffic noise.

Add some more pleasant noises, such as the sound of splashing water in a small fountain, and you'll be amazed by how much traffic noise is reduced.

Right: This tall bay hedge draws the eye to the garden bench at the end of the gravel path.

Far right: Escallonias are fast growers and suitable for an informal hedge.

Hedge your bets

Hedges are back! A garden hedge is more than just a boundary to a property, keeping out unwanted animals and people, and providing privacy. A hedge can also be used as the 'skeleton' of your landscape, helping to create garden rooms for you to decorate, conceal utility areas and unsightly views, and act as a windbreak.

Privacy is an important aspect in a garden, but that doesn't mean you have to build a 1.8 m brick wall around your home. A hedge creates a sense of seclusion without making you feel trapped in the backyard.

Clever use of boundaries can lift a garden out of the ordinary to create an environment that seems remote from the outside world. In fact, they should be a positive feature in any garden design, providing a framework and background to the life within. Living boundaries increase the value of your property and extend your outdoor living area.

Small hedges form borders along driveways and paths. Tall hedges provide windbreaks and shelter from salt spray and hot, drying, dust-laden winds. Hedges offer more protection than a solid wall because plants slow down the wind, filtering the air in the process. Solid walls, on the other hand, provide a barrier, increasing the turbulence in your garden.

Formal or informal, flowers or foliage, there are hedges suitable for all areas of the garden. The traditional garden hedge is close-clipped and neat, usually screening the front garden from the street and masking traffic noise, but there is a huge number of attractive shrubs that will form low-maintenance, informal hedges.

All shapes and sizes

Before planting your hedge, consider the eventual height, purpose and time span which you've allowed for growth. Fast growers may screen quickly but their vigour will mean more maintenance later on to keep them in bounds.

• Conifers (for example, Leyland cypress) form a fast-growing hedge which, being

evergreen, is a perfect windbreak or screen. Many reach enormous heights.

- Native trees and shrubs, particularly berrying or fruiting kinds, used as hedges and screens will attract wildlife such as birds to the garden.
- Try yew, box, *Lonicera nitida* (box honeysuckle) or *Euonymus japonicus* (evergreen euonymus) for formal low hedges.
- Taller flowering hedges of escallonia, photinia, *Viburnum tinus* (laurustinus) and *Berberis* x *stenophylla* can look great.

Keeping trim

Hedges require regular trimming to keep them looking good. Start trimming from the bottom so that the clippings fall clear. A hedge should be wider at the base than the top. This allows vital light to reach all parts. Hedge trimmers and shears give more control, especially if you want a particular shape. Don't use a mechanical pruner on large-leafed plants as it damages the leaves.

If your hedge has grown out of control, check that your particular type of shrub will reshoot after pruning. Most of the conifers will not. Start by cutting the top of the hedge first, then one side. Wait until that side has greened up before you prune the other side.

Remember to feed your hedge and mulch it to keep it looking good for years to come.

How to plant a hedge in five easy steps

1 For a really straight hedge, mark out the run with a string line. Dig a trench at least 60 cm wide and 45 cm deep.

2 Incorporate lots of well-rotted manure or compost. Fill the trench back in, which will create a small mound.

3 Using a measuring stick, space out all the plants. Dig a hole for each plant, add some slow-release fertilizer, and plant, ensuring that the soil has not built up around the trunks.

4 Tip prune all new shoots to encourage branching. Do this for the first few seasons so that a well-branched, thick-to-the-base hedge is developed.

5 Trim to shape. Secateurs allow precise cutting and are suitable for pruning conifers and all informal hedges. They are ideal for the initial shaping of young plants. For larger plants in an informal hedge, use shears: they produce the best shape and leave the foliage unmarked. They can also be used on formal hedges for a perfect, but time-consuming cut, or you can use electric hedge trimmers in slow even cuts.

Walls have tongues, and hedges ears.

Jonathan Swift

PRUNING A HEDGE

1 Measure the height you want your hedge to be.

2 Tie the string to the hedge at one end.

3 Run the string along the hedge and then tie it at the other end.

4 Cut the top of the hedge first with a hedge trimmer or shears.

Old-fashioned roses have a charm like no other. Their perfume is a joy. 'Troilus' (above) is a David Austin rose bred in more recent times but still capturing the beauty of heritage roses.

Roses

Summer is the time when your rose bushes will be laden with blooms. Don't be afraid to pick bunches of them for the house and for friends — the more you pick vase-length stems, the more you encourage further flowering. For blooms that will last indoors a week or more, pick flowers first thing in the morning and plunge the stems immediately into a bucket of water.

Worldwide, countless millions of roses are sold each year, a fact that makes the rose one of the most popular garden plants. This is a plant that commands respect, and it is almost sacrilege not to have at least one rose in your garden. The trick is to ascertain what rose is right for your garden, and how to make the most of your selection.

Sweet spring, full of sweet days and roses,
A box where sweets compacted lie.

George Herbert

Planning and planting

Roses are prickly creatures, and care needs to be taken when finding a home for them. For example, don't plant roses beside a path where the thorns could be dangerous. Find a spot that provides the rose with plenty of room to spread, lots of air circulation to minimize fungal disease and preferably eight hours of sunshine a day.

The rose is a hardy and forgiving plant. It can tolerate some neglect but the more care you give the better it will respond. Growing gorgeous roses is quite simple if you start with tough, robust varieties and keep the plants well watered and well fed. For best results, pay careful attention to pest control, pruning and general care.

You must plant roses in well-prepared soil. That means digging in compost or another soil conditioner prior to planting. Roses can be planted in autumn as bare-rooted specimens or any time of the year if

Above: Rose beds can be mulched with straw.

they have been grown in pots. Autumn is an ideal time for planting container specimens as the plants still have flowers to select from, while the soil is still warm to encourage rapid establishment. Dig in plenty of rotted animal manure, incorporate water-storing granules and add some fresh soil if you are planting in a spot where roses have grown previously.

Grafted onto hardy disease-resistant understock, roses will grow anywhere as long as there is lots of sunshine. When planting be careful not to bury the graft union below soil level. Determine which shoots grow from above the graft (desirable water shoots) and which shoots grow from below the graft, and must be removed (undesirable suckers).

Feeding and mulching

Don't feed roses until they are established. Wait six weeks from the time of planting and then feed during the growing season — spring and summer. Use a proprietary rose fertilizer or a more general flower garden fertilizer. Roses are heavy feeders and require two or three feeds during the growing season. Apply the first in spring before the leaves are fully open and then again in early and midsummer, following the recommended dosage on the packet.

Do not feed roses in early autumn, because the plants should be hardening for winter at that time and should not produce soft new growth that is cold-sensitive.

Mulch roses with bulky organic matter such as garden compost, well-rotted animal manure, chipped or shredded bark, or even straw. Roses love a mulch. A 5-7 cm layer stops weeds from growing and the evaporation of water, and helps to keep the roots cool in summer. Apply it in the spring and top up annually if necessary.

> ### Planting spacing for various rose types
>
> Traditional and shrub roses: 75–90 cm
>
> Cluster roses: 75 cm
>
> Hedge roses: 60 cm
>
> Climbing roses: 1.2–1.5 m
>
> David Austin English roses: 90 cm
>
> Ground cover roses: 1.2 m

roses

1 'Peace'. 2 'Just Joey'. 3 'Altissimo'. 4 'Iceberg'. 5 'Blueberry Hill'.
6 'Blushing Pink Iceberg'. 7 'Regency'. 8 'Pink Iceberg'. 9 'Suffolk'. 10 'Sussex'.
11 'Oxfordshire'. 12 'Kent'. 13 'Yellow Simplicity'. 14 'Red Simplicity'. 15 'Simplicity
(This is a representative selection of modern roses and not all are necessarily
available in all areas.)

'Madame Grégoire Staechelin', 'Constance Spry' and 'Complicata'.

The basics of rose care

- Keep roses moist at all times but never allow the roots to sit in water.
- Feed your plants generously and frequently.
- Keep pests to a minimum (this is usually not a problem if you start with a strong variety and keep it well watered and fed).
- Prune hard back in late winter or early spring, depending on your climate. (See the 'Spring' guide to 'Rose pruning', page 86)
- Keep the area weed-free and ensure 6–8 hours of sun per day during summer.

Watering

Roses are drought tolerant but they will not thrive in very dry conditions. Keep the soil moist at all times: a few centimetres into the soil, the deeper soil should still be slightly moist. Ideally, you should water by slowly soaking the bed quite thoroughly to 10–15 cm deep. Sprinklers are acceptable if the top 15 cm of soil receives enough water and if the foliage has enough time to dry before nightfall. If the foliage remains wet overnight (especially in the cooler weather of spring and autumn) the plants will be much more susceptible to diseases.

Pruning

There is a lot of rigmarole peddled about rose pruning. True, it can be done incorrectly, but even a bad trim is better than no pruning at all. There is no need to waste the cuttings: a 15 cm pruning can be planted into three parts sand and one part peat and kept moist until the new growth appears. (If you see a rose you like, ask for a cutting — roses strike at almost any time of the year.) In mild climates most roses can be pruned in late winter, but in colder areas early spring is the favoured time. Rambler roses are pruned after flowering in early autumn.

Types of roses

Roses come in the form of shrubs, pillars, climbers and ramblers, ground covers and smaller varieties suitable for containers. There are old-fashioned roses and modern bush roses which include hybrid teas and floribundas (or cluster-flowered roses). Many varieties are delightfully fragrant and these should be planted in a position where their perfume can be readily enjoyed. For varieties that will cope with less sun check in specialist rose catalogues.

- Modern bush roses such as the hybrid teas and floribundas are among the best flowering. They grow in warm, cool and cold climates in any reasonable garden soil. They develop several stems at ground level and grow into a shrub that should be pruned hard in late winter or early spring. Plant them in a flower border.
- Climbing roses can be trained up walls and fences. They produce masses of blooms and give a fine flower display. Plant climbing roses to disguise an unsightly outhouse, shed or garage.
- Pillar roses are slender climbers; they are not too vigorous, and so are useful for training around a decorative pillar, post or verandah railing. Make sure that the thorns will not be in the way of passersby.
- Rambler roses are vigorous climbers suitable for covering larger structures. Some of the largest growers can be trained into mature trees. Most flower only once in summer and they are pruned after flowering in the autumn.
- Hedge roses are usually shrub roses which need plenty of space. They can be grown as an informal hedge — old-fashioned rugosa roses, for example, have a dense habit which makes them excellent hedging specimens. They are hardy, disease-free and drought-tolerant, and flower for an extensive period. Lightly prune after each flush of flowers.
- Old garden roses are frequently seen these days, no doubt because of their simplicity and perfume. Many types such as bourbons, China, hybrid musks and damask have a fascinating history.
- English roses bred by David Austin are a relatively new type with the charm and scent of old-fashioned roses but with the colours and free-flowering qualities of modern roses. This was achieved by using

old and modern roses in the breeding programme. The breeding continues, and new varieties are launched every year.
- Ground cover roses are a comparatively new group. They do just what the name implies: cover the ground. These roses may be completely prostrate in habit, or form low bushes or long, arching growths. They form dense, impenetrable growth and most flower over a long period in summer, some having one flush of blooms, others several. They need little pruning apart from the removal of very old and dead wood.

ROSE POTPOURRI

Make a rose potpourri with this easy recipe. Combine the following ingredients, then leave in an airtight container for a few weeks to blend the scents.

4 cups dried roses
4 cups dried pelargonium leaves
1 cinammon stick
12 whole cloves
1 teaspoon orris root chips
5 drops rose perlargonium oil
10 drops rose oil

Left to right: *Rosa* sp., 'Julia's Rose' (for cutting), 'Blue Moon' (fragrance), 'Felicia' (hedging), yellow 'Charles Austin' (arches) and 'Tom Thumb', a patio rose.

Rose selection

Not all of these varieties are necessarily available in all areas. Good alternatives where necessary will be found in specialist rose catalogues.

Cutting roses

Why buy a bunch of roses from the florist when you can grow your own? The long-stemmed roses 'Adolph Hortsmann' or 'Catherine McCauley' are beautiful yellows, 'Eiffel Tower' or 'Peter Frankenfeld' superb pinks, 'Mr Lincoln' an intense deep red and 'Pascali' the purest of whites. Though not as strong in colour, 'Just Joey' and 'Julia's Rose' have fabulous bronze tones. To extend their lives as cut flowers, recut the stems under water before placing them in a vase.

Perfumed roses

It is hard to go past old-fashioned roses when it comes to scent. They are also easy to maintain and resistant to disease. Many people consider that among the best are 'Constance Spry', with its huge, clear pink cabbage-like blooms; 'Souvenir de la Malmaison', a blush pink bourbon rose which flowers even in autumn; and the hybrid musk 'Penelope', which has a pink bud opening to cream. Most of the English rose breeder David Austin's selections are also highly perfumed. The best modern cultivars for fragrance include 'Double Delight' (with crimson and ivory blooms) and 'Blue Moon' (pale lilac).

Hedging and ground cover roses

Roses can easily be grown into a bushy, repeat-flowering hedge. For a tall screen try the yellow-apricot 'Buff Beauty', delicate pink 'Celestial' (also known as Céleste), 'Felicia' with its mix of coral and apricot blooms, or soft yellow 'Mountbatten', while pink 'Seduction', white 'Iceberg', pink 'China Doll' and bright scarlet 'Satchmo' make good hedges to around 1 m. Many modern hybrids such as the carpet roses

---

Rosa rubiginosa (syn. *R. eglanteria*)

The 'sweet briar' or 'eglantine rose' made famous by Shakespeare is distinguished by the exquisite apple scent of its foliage, especially noticeable after rain or when the leaves are crushed. The bush grows to around 2 m, is very thorny and makes a great hedge plant if clipped into shape. It is very hardy and adaptable. Delicate rose-pink, single-cupped flowers about 2.5 cm across with showy yellow stamens are produced in midsummer. These are followed by glistening red hips which last for months and have a high vitamin C content.

have been bred with the intention of creating a ground-smothering mass. These respond well to being pinned down along the ground, which can be done with bobby-pin-like hooks made from old coat hangers. Indeed, this will force side branching which tends to increase flowers.

Roses for containers

Any rose can be grown in a pot, as long as it has adequate fertilizer, water and a rich soil, but some roses have been bred with dwarf root systems, making them ideal for containers. Look for these patio roses at your local nursery.

Miniature roses are easily grown in tubs and many new varieties are introduced each year. Some particularly good varieties are 'Orange Sunblaze', 'Starina', 'Magic Carousel' and 'Rise 'n' Shine'.

Roses for arbours and arches

Roses can be breathtaking when they are grown to sprawl over arbours, trained flat on a sunny wall, grown in rose cradles or as pillars. If you have space for a pergola, you can smother it with roses. Masonry columns and timber rafters are the basic

elements of a pergola — plant a climbing rose at the base of each column and in no time it will be onto the rafters. You can place a piece of garden art (such as an urn or a statue) as a focal point at the end of the pergola with a background of dark green foliage behind it, against which both the chosen ornament and the rose blooms will stand out.

To cover garden structures, try growing the climbing roses 'Monsieur Tillier', which has a coppery purple lustre; 'Blackboy', which has velvety red blooms; 'Altissimo', with its single blood red but scentless blooms; and 'Crépuscule', an apricot rose which never stops flowering.

A stunning and well-known climber is 'Pink Perpétué' with double, very fragrant, old-fashioned looking pink flowers over a very long period in summer and autumn.

…the nodding violet grows
Quite over-canopied with luscious woodbine,
With sweet musk-roses, and with eglantine…

William Shakespeare

Rose care tips

- Avoid picking flowers in the first year.
- Never take more than one third of the flower stem; this helps to keep the rose bush productive and in shape.
- Use a sharp blade and always cut to an outward facing bud.
- Cut roses early in the morning when the plant's moisture and sugar levels are high.
- Remove the thorns and leaves that will be below water level in the vase.
- Immerse the stems in warm water and cut them again under water. Add a floral preservative to the vase water to prolong the life of the blooms.
- For larger, prize-winning blooms, 'disbud' the rose bush by removing all the side buds while they are still small. This will allow the plant to concentrate on the top bud. The end result is fewer, but larger, blooms.

Rose **problems** and **treatment**

Problem	Solution
Aphids Prevalent in summer, these very small green or black insects are usually found on the underside of leaves and on new growth.	Thoroughly hose aphids off the foliage. You can also apply insecticidal soaps in spray form to control aphids. Ensure you apply these sprays to both the upper and lower surfaces of the foliage.
Black spot Leaves develop black spots and eventually fall off. This is a problem mainly in summer.	Pick off isolated leaves; control with a combined rose spray or systemic fungicide. Provide good air circulation and allow foliage to dry out (refrain from overhead watering) before nightfall.
Caterpillars and leaf miners The foliage becomes badly damaged and filled with holes, before the leaves are rolled up by the insects (which pupate inside the rolled-up leaves). Prevalent in summer.	Remove all badly damaged leaves by hand if feasible and spray plants with a systemic insecticide.
Chlorosis Leaves pale and can turn yellow in between the veins. Usually not a serious problem, it can be caused by a lack of iron, nitrogen, manganese or magnesium. It might also indicate a salt build-up.	Add chelated iron to the soil, or in severe cases spray iron sulphate on the foliage. Apply a solution of Epsom salts and water (1 tablespoon of Epsom salts to 10 L of water) to the soil every 2–3 weeks in spring and summer.
Dieback Rose stems turn dark brown or black and die off progressively down the stem. Occurs mainly in winter.	Cut out any dead or dying stems back to healthy tissue as soon as noticed. Avoid damaging healthy stems, although pruning cuts are a necessity. Use sharp secateurs to make clean pruning cuts which heal rapidly.
Mildew Leaves are distorted and covered with fine white fungus growth.	Carry out a regular spray program using a combined rose spray or systemic fungicide.
Thrips Flowers and foliage become deformed and mottled. Edges of petals blacken.	Spray with insecticide containing malathion.
Rust A serious disease with orange spots on the undersides of the leaves, eventually turning black. Appears in summer.	Spray plants with a systemic fungicide.
Yellow leaves Leaves turn yellow and may fall off. Could be caused by poor drainage.	Ensure good drainage, if necessary by replanting in a better prepared bed or border. Re-firm plants if loosened by winds or frost.

Troubleshooting

Strong rose varieties that are well cared for are generally trouble-free. 'Clever' watering will also help your roses to stay healthy.

Ideally, water roses at their base rather than from overhead so that the foliage does not remain wet, which is conducive to disease. If you are using a sprinkler, ensure you water early enough to allow the foliage to dry before nightfall. This is especially important during spring and autumn, when cool nights and wet foliage encourage foliar diseases. Dry climates with cool nights can encourage mildew. Coastal and warm areas inevitably succumb to black spot each summer. To combat this, try to keep low-growing shrubs away from your roses to increase air circulation, and prune rose bushes into an open vase shape.

There are a number of fungicides and insecticides available for controlling diseases and pests of roses, but you may find it convenient to use a proprietary combined rose spray, specially formulated for rose problems, which contains both. There are also systemic fungicides and insecticides available which enter the sap stream of the plant and so are not washed off by rain. If used early on in an attack systemic pesticides prevent the problem increasing. It is certainly best to spray roses before diseases appear as they are difficult to control once they become established.

The chart on the opposite page lists rose problems that may arise. However, the choice of whether or not to apply a solution is yours. You may choose to ignore the problem and accept that some of the blooms will not be pristine. You will also find that many of these pests and diseases will come and go along with changes in the weather.

Left: Dieback, a fungal disease, varies in severity acording to the variety of rose. When susceptible varieties are infected, the stem progressively dies back to the base.

Centre: A less severe infection of dieback.

Right: Small pink rings are symptoms of grey mould infection on roses.

Clockwise from above: 'The Fairy', 'Frühlingsmorgen', 'Dainty Bess' and a crimson David Austin rose.

Rose care Summer prune and fertilize repeat flowering roses, removing all twiggy growth. For proper hardening of canes for winter in frost-prone areas, do not fertilize after late summer.

Summer roses
Oldies but goodies!

Heritage roses are really in fashion. They are easy care and disease resistant, and their stunning perfume makes them a charming addition to the garden. 'Lady Hillingdon' is a lovely coppery pink with purple and bronze foliage; 'Crépuscule' has masses of semidouble, apricot-gold flowers virtually all year; 'Mutabilis' has flowers that start out pink and fade to a coppery yellow; and 'New Dawn' has delicate, sweetly smelling shell pink flowers perfect for making jellies, jams and sorbets.

Not every rose is a flouncy mass of petals. Some of the most charming are single roses. Look for 'Dainty Bess', 'Wedding Day', 'Frühlingsmorgen', 'Canary Bird' and 'Altissimo'.

Bored with the same old bushes?

An increasingly popular way of growing roses is the standard rose. Standard roses are grafted on top of a long stem and can range in height from 60 cm to 2 m tall. They are great as features, with the added bonus that the flowers are raised up to eye height.

Check the ties each winter to make sure that the tie is secure, and that borers aren't attacking underneath the tie. Stretchy ties like budding tape, Velcro or even strips of old stockings work best.

Now growers are making standards even more interesting by grafting more than one variety of rose on to each stem, sometimes at staggered heights to create poodle-like features in an array of colours.

The thornless rose

The first thornless rose appeared in a Californian garden during trials designed to create disease-resistant roses. It became apparent that some stronger new seedlings had no thorns and fewer diseases. These characteristics were then enhanced and passed on to more new rose varieties and now, after much trialling, there is a small number of thornless varieties available. Which varieties are available depends on country so the best advice on how to find them is to look through the catalogues of mail-order rose growers. Some varieties are prefaced by 'smooth', such as Smooth Lady and Smooth Prince, both hybrid teas.

project
plant **training**

Standards are simply plants grown into a 'ball on a stick' shape. You can either buy them ready made, which costs more but could be worth the time saved, or train your own young plant into a standard by cutting off lower branches and lifting the crown till you reach the desired height, then trimming the top into a ball. This is quite a simple process provided you choose a seedling with a single trunk.

Continue to keep your standard in shape by trimming off side branches and tip pruning the main ball to keep it thick and lush.

1 *Duranta erecta* 'Geisha Girl', a suitable shrub for training as a standard.

2 Prune the lower branches.

3 Pinch off any growth from the stem, leaving the growth at the top.

4 Make sure you remove all growth from the stem.

5 Cut the leader, or main shoot, from the crown.

6 Lightly trim the growth at the top.

7 Keep the top trimmed into a ball shape and within a few years your shrub will grow into a lush 'ball on a stick'.

gardenia

Vital statistics

Scientific name: *Gardenia jasminoides*.

Family: Rubiaceae.

Climate: Frost free. A favourite shrub for the warm conservatory in cool and cold climates.

Culture: A common problem is yellowing of lower leaves – keep them watered and fed and treat yellowing with Epsom salts.

Colours: White and creamy yellow.

Height: 45 cm to 2.5 m.

Planting time: Plant or pot in spring.

Soil: Rich, lime-free, soil-based potting compost under glass.

Position: Ensure bright light under glass but shade from strong sun.

Planting depth and spacing: Grow in large pot or tub.

Fertilizer: Liquid feed once a month in summer with a balanced fertilizer.

Pests/diseases: Scale, mealybug, whitefly, grey mould (botrytis). Treat with appropriate insecticide or fungicide.

Cutting: Lightly trim plants after flowering.

Propagation: Take semihardwood cuttings in summer.

Storage: The flowers keep in a vase, but be careful not to handle blooms as they do bruise easily.

Native to the subtropical south of China, this is a shrub that wins many hearts. The white flowers appear in summer and autumn, and they always have a lavish perfume that refreshes, even on the hottest days.

There are numerous varieties of gardenia but they may not be available everywhere. The varieties differ from the species in respect of overall size of plant and size of flowers. Some varieties also flower much more freely and over a much longer period than the species. Most of them have double flowers but some bear single blooms.

Close relatives of the gardenia include coffee and bouvardia, although the plant known as tree gardenia is actually not a gardenia but a rothmannia (see below).

Tree gardenia

Gardenias are favourite conservatory shrubs because of their perfume and lush glossy foliage. Apart from the common gardenia described above, *G. thunbergii*, a small tree or large shrub, is also worth growing. It has a very upright habit and produces tubular, single, white or cream flowers, again with a powerful fragrance, in winter and spring, backed by deep green, shiny foliage. It is grown in the same way as *G. jasminoides*.

The other tree gardenia, *Rothmannia globosa*, is a spreading small tree or large shrub with bell-shaped, scented, creamy white flowers in summer. It will thrive in an intermediate conservatory, otherwise it is grown in the same way as gardenias.

Trees

The value of trees becomes very clear in summer. Their cooling green canopy is a great relief on a hot summer's day, but many people don't realize that trees have more than leaves to offer in summer.

There are numerous hardy ornamental trees that look good in summer. If you want to give your garden the Midas touch, try *Robinia pseudoacacia* 'Frisia' with rich yellow foliage which gradually turns yellow-green, or *Gleditsia triacanthos* 'Sunburst', also with golden yellow leaves, greening as they age. The variegated box elder, *Acer negundo* 'Variegatum', is a very popular small tree with white and green variegated foliage. Another good box elder is *A. negundo* var. *violaceum* with green leaves, conspicuous blue-grey shoots, and pendulous tassels of purple-violet flowers in spring.

The ornamental pear, *Pyrus salicifolia* 'Pendula', is an attractive small deciduous tree of weeping habit with willow-like, silvery grey leaves. A great favourite for larger gardens is the silver or European white birch, *Betula pendula*, with lacy green foliage, and white bark on the trunk and main branches.

Clockwise from top: Golden robinia, a white-barked trunk of *Betula pendula* and *Pyrus salicifolia*.

Ideas for a tranquil garden

If your block is bare, your home and garden exposed to the full glare of the sun, you need shade! A living canopy creates an atmosphere of total serenity, so cast a peaceful and cool spell with shade trees.

Choosing a shade tree

Whether summer heatwaves are frequent or rare, it is good to have a shade tree in the garden for when they do occur. Trees create . a cool microclimate that can drop the temperature up to 10°C, and they add value to your home. So, how should you go about choosing the dominant plants in your garden, and what should you look out for?

The critical consideration is the root zone. Direction and division are the key things: make sure that the roots are oriented outwards, with no circling, and that they branch uniformly right out to the fine hairs.

Other indicators of a good tree include its ability to support its own weight, and having an even taper from the trunk collar to the tip. Disease-free foliage is a clue to the tree's vigour.

Many people forget to water trees, especially during warm dry spells. Watering is essential when the soil starts drying out, at least for the first year after planting. Bulky

a few do's and don'ts

Don't plant your tree closer than 5 m to your house. It could damage foundations and block drains.

Don't pave close to your tree. Allow space for the trunk to develop and for air and water to penetrate down to the roots.

Don't prune your tree at the wrong time. Autumn is the best time for pruning as the sap flow slows down at this time of year.

Don't expect grass to grow beneath your tree once it's mature.

Do find out how big your tree will grow; make sure it will fit your garden without the need for constant pruning.

Do feed your tree to encourage new growth and stake it for the first year only.

Water your tree as necessary until it is well established.

organic matter in the soil will help because it holds moisture during dry periods.

Feed in early spring each year with slow-release fertilizer. Keep the grass, or other ground covers, away from the trunk right out to the drip line, as these can compete for food and moisture and slow the growth of your tree.

Plant a tree on the birth date of each child born. It will be a joy for that child to watch it grow.

Tropical foliage

The gardening world is currently indulging in a passion for tropical plants. This is nothing new as the Victorians grew them in their glasshouses and used them outdoors for summer display. Outdoors they practised 'plunge bedding', whereby potted foliage plants were plunged into beds for the summer to create exotic schemes. Today, we call it tropical or subtropical bedding.

Tropical or subtropical plants with large and/or coloured leaves are mainly used, such as bananas (particularly *Musa basjoo*), angels' trumpets (brugmansias), dracaenas, cordylines, palms, acalyphas, ginger lilies (hedychiums), philodendrons and cannas. Among these can be planted smaller exotics, such as solenostemon (coleus) and the annual amaranthus or Joseph's coat with their multicoloured leaves, and variegated spider plants (chlorophytums).

Choose a sunny, really sheltered spot for your exotic bedding, as winds can damage the leaves of some plants. The pots are plunged up to their rims and the surface of the compost lightly covered with soil, so that they are not visible. Obviously you must remember to water the pots regularly as they can still dry out, albeit more slowly.

Clockwise from left: Bismarckia palm, philodendron and cordyline.

cannas

Cannas are the great all-rounder. They cope with anything, look great for nine months of the year, and have stunning foliage and flowers, which range in colour from the common yellows, reds and oranges to pink, cream and apricot. They also work in with a variety of gardening styles, from Victorian to tropical Thai or the modern perennial border. There are hundreds of varieties available. Cannas love a warm, frost-free climate but if you live in a cool area, mulch generously: this will protect the rhizomes from the cold. In areas with hard frosts lift and store the rhizomes under glass for the winter.

check list

jobs to do now

- Mulch camellias, rhododendrons and azaleas with leaf mould, chipped bark or peat.

- Prune back spring- and early summer-flowering shrubs like philadephus, weigela and spiraea when their display is finished.

- Prune back azaleas now for compact, disease-free growth. Carefully watch for lace bug on fresh foliage. A few early sprays under the leaves with a suitable insecticide can reduce the infestation.

- Keep roses well watered and remove spent blooms to promote further flowering. Your roses will flower well if you trim the hips off.

- High humidity can be a problem for rose lovers. Pick off and destroy any leaves affected by black spot and mildew, and spray with a specific fungicide.

- Fertilize roses to prepare them for the autumn flush.

- Keep an eye on your trees and shrubs, especially shoot tips, for possible pests such as aphids and other sapsuckers which are prevalent at this time of year and spray accordingly.

- Snip off dead flowers of all shrubs and trees if possible.

- Water all recently planted trees and shrubs as necessary.

plant now

- Provided they are in containers, trees can be planted in summer.

- Plant a hedge, using container-grown shrubs and trees. Try laurustinus (*Viburnum tinus*), photinia or escallonia for an informal hedge, and yew or box for a very formal hedge.

- Semi-ripe cuttings of many plants, including fuchsias and camellias, can be taken now.

- Plunge some exotic foliage plants in beds to create a subtropical or tropical bedding scheme.

flowering now

- Shrubs such as abutilon, brugmansias, buddleja, callistemons, fuchsias, gardenias, grevilleas, hebes, hibiscus, hydrangeas, lavenders, melaleuca, oleanders, philadelphus and prostantheras

- Trees like tree of heaven (*Ailanthus altissima*) and Indian bean tree (*Catalpa bignonioides*). Trees with attractive foliage are *Gleditsia triacanthos* 'Sunburst', golden robinia (*Robinia pseudoacacia* 'Frisia') and variegated box elder (*Acer negundo* 'Variegatum').

Classic combinations

Some plants are good by themselves, but even better in combination with a contrasting plant that flowers concurrently. A classic mix, such as climbing or rambler roses and clematis scrambling over a pergola or an arbour together, is one such example.

It's easy to overlook the tree canopy when creating perfect pairings, but that's often where the most impact is made.

The delicate tracery of silver birch contrasts with the darker greens of surrounding shrubs.

Obviously one can only have attractive tree combinations in larger gardens, as they take up quite a lot of space. Glean ideas from local parks or gardens open to the public.

Go for contrasts in shape, colour and texture. Attractive combinations include a golden-leaved tree, such as *Robinia pseudoacacia* 'Frisia', with a background of a dark-leaved conifer. Birches, producing dappled shade, also look good with conifers, such as pines or a Lawson cypress variety.

Fungicide Make your own fungicide to spray on roses with black spot. Just mix 1 part of milk with 10 parts of water and spray on any affected foliage.

jacaranda

Flowering in late spring and early summer, the jacaranda is a beautiful deciduous tree with graceful and fine fern-like leaves. It is frost tender and only suited to Mediterranean and warmer climates. In frost-prone regions it makes a fine pot or tub plant for the cool conservatory. Under glass it is grown mainly for its foliage although larger plants may produce flowers.

Vital statistics

Scientific name: *Jacaranda mimosifolia*.
Family: Bignoniaceae.
Planting time: Any time from pot, but planting during flowering allows you to select the right shade of blue.

Climate: Mediterranean or warmer, or cool conservatory.
Height: 9–12 m.
Width: 9–12 m.
Aspect: Full light under glass, full sun and sheltered position out of doors.
Soil: Free draining.
Watering: Under glass water liberally in summer, but much less in winter.
Fertilizing: Tree pellets in spring until established.
Flowering: Late spring to early summer.
Comments: Jacarandas can be reluctant to flower, especially in very windy situations such as by the sea, or if there is insufficient warmth.

summer
herbs, fruit & vegetables

If there is a season for the edible garden, then surely this is it. Your spring plantings have come to fruition, and now there's a glut you can share with friends. Extend harvest time to late autumn with repeat planting.

Guavas are used for making jams, jellies and juice.

Peas in pods.

Sowe Carrets in your gardens, and humbly praise God for them, as for a singular and great blessing.

Richard Gardiner

Fragrant basil with ripe tomatoes, or sweet melons and passionfruit, epitomize summer. But as summer vegies finish, think about planting vegetables for the new season. Prepare the soil with a good soil conditioner. Home-made compost is the best. A light dusting of lime is good too.

At the end of the season you can sow seeds of overwintering vegetables, but there is a quiet revolution taking place in the vegetable garden. Asian herbs and vegetables with new and exciting flavours are changing the way we think about food. Most of them are available in seed packets now. Choose from tender pak choi (Chinese cabbage), the Japanese greens tatsoi and senposai, and lemongrass which is a perennial lemon-scented grass.

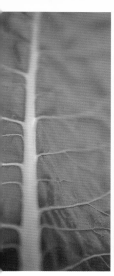

Herbs

Summer produces a glut of all the best herbs. Basil, lemon grass, various mints, and parsley (curly and flat-leaved French), are all ready for harvesting.

Keep these herbs well trimmed by consuming them regularly or by picking bunches and drying them, as they will bolt into flower and lose their flavour if you neglect them.

Basil

There are several types of basil, all with a different flavour. Genoa or sweet basil, the best known and most common, has a spicy smell and is used extensively in Italian cooking. Some varieties have purple leaves, Greek basil has smaller leaves and a pungent flavour, and Thai or holy basil complements Thai and Southeast Asian dishes.

Basil should be torn, not chopped, and added to hot food at the last moment to preserve the flavour. It doesn't dry well.

Sweet basil.

UNDERPLANTING TOMATOES WITH BASIL

1 Clear a small space for the seedling, being careful not to disturb the roots.

2 Remove seedlings from the pot. Divide into bunches of two or three plants.

3 Plant around your tomato plants and replace mulch.

Pest-repelling plants

Planting a garden to help deter pests is so
much nicer than using chemicals. Five
favourites are described below.

Tansy

This pretty and hardy perennial, with its
tiny button-like flowers, was once grown in
monastery herb gardens to repel pests.
When planted near fruit and nut trees,
vegetables and berry fruits, it discourages
fruit fly, ants, beetles and aphids. Near
cabbages tansy will repel cabbage moth and
cabbage white butterfly. Dried tansy flowers
can be sprinkled on pantry shelves to
discourage flies.

Coriander

Also known as Chinese parsley, this pretty
aromatic herb has a strong pungent scent
that discourages aphids. Bees and other
beneficial insects are attracted to the umbels
of tiny white flowers.

Rue

A sturdy evergreen herb with blue metallic,
feathery leaves, rue is useful as a disinfectant
and as an insecticide. Plant it by doors and
windows to repel mosquitoes, flies and
other insects, in the garden to discourage
beetles and slugs, and rub it over pets to
help reduce fleas.

Wormwood

This is one of the most bitter herbs known,
and for centuries it has been used to repel
insects, including fleas, flies and moths. It
was once used as an ingredient in ink to stop
mice eating old letters. Strangely, it is also a
major ingredient in apéritifs and herb wines,
such as absinthe and vermouth. Legend has
it that as the serpent slithered out of Eden,

Plant wormwood and tansy
(above) to deter pests.

wormwood sprang up in the impressions left
by its tail on the ground, and it has been
used ever since to keep away evil spirits.

Pick wormwood leaves for drying in
summer, and mix them with dried mint and
lavender in sachets to keep your clothes
fresh and free of moth holes. (See 'Tarragon
and wormwood' in the 'Winter' section.)

Mint

There are many species of mint, including
apple mint, spearmint, eau de cologne mint,
pineapple mint and pennyroyal. Mint repels
most pests, especially fleas and beetles
which dislike the smell. Dried mint sachets
in the wardrobe will freshen clothes and
keep moths at bay. Fresh mint in the pantry
will deter ants.

Rub fresh mint leaves on your hands,
neck and face to protect your skin from
mosquitoes. Plant mints around a dog
kennel or strew near animal cages to repel

flies. Rub fresh mint around the eyes and mouths of horses or cows to discourage pesky flies. Mint is the perfect companion plant for cabbages and tomatoes because it repels cabbage white butterfly, aphids and whiteflies — all insects which can ruin your crop.

Plant a mint garden

Mints have long been grown for their oil-rich leaves, which flavour teas, condiments and salads. The menthol improves digestion and has antiseptic and decongestant properties. However, mint can easily escape so take steps to control it: plant mint in a container, leaving a small ridge above soil level. In early spring split established clumps into pieces of rhizome and replant these immediately. For fresh leaves out of season, some rhizomes can be potted in autumn and forced in a greenhouse or on a warm windowsill indoors.

PLANTING A MINT GARDEN

1 Place the mint in a pot and add potting mix.

2 Dig a hole and insert the pot of mint. The lip of the pot should protrude so that the runners won't easily spread into the surrounding soil.

3 All kinds of mint can be grown in this way, including the popular spearmint shown here. Mulch the pot and surrounding soil and keep well watered.

Make your own insecticide

You can make an all-purpose insecticide by combining equal quantities of mint, chopped onion, garlic, and lavender tops and stems in enough water to cover. Leave the mixture for twenty-four hours, then strain it. Use the liquid for spraying any plants plagued by caterpillars, aphids or flea beetles. Or make your own chive tea for treating mildew (see the step by step instructions below) and chilli and soap spray (see page 239).

Gardens are not made by sitting in the shade.

Rudyard Kipling

Tropical herbs

When it comes to herbs and spices, Asian influences are particularly strong in the garden. The popularity of laksa, curries and noodle dishes have turned some plants into household names. Lemongrass (*Cymbopogon citratus*), cardamom (*Elettaria cardamomum*), ginger (*Zingiber officinale*) and turmeric (*Curcuma longa*) are just as easy to grow as traditional herbs if you can give them a warm greenhouse or conservatory (or you live a warm climate).

The white, bulbous base of lemongrass is used to flavour curries, while the leaves can be dried and made into tea. Cardamom is the world's second most expensive spice (after saffron). The whole seed pod or individual seeds are ground with a mortar and pestle and are used for flavouring curries, pickles and custards. With ginger and turmeric the rhizome is either finely chopped or ground into powder for use in many Eastern dishes.

CHIVE TEA FOR TREATING MILDEW

1 Harvest a generous bunch of chives from your vegetable garden, or buy some.

2 Roughly chop the chives.

3 Add the chives to a watering can.

4 Cover with boiling water and steep for at least one hour before using.

galangal

turmeric

cardamom seeds

ginger

Tropical herbs and spices need to be grown in a warm conservatory or warm climate.

check list

jobs to do now

- Cut back and tidy herbs, so that they don't go to seed.

- After fruiting, summer prune any fan-trained stone fruits such as cherries, peaches, plums and apricots.

- Ensure all fruit is mulched with garden compost or well-rotted manure.

- Keep all fruit, especially soft fruits, well watered during dry spells.

- Thin out any excess fruits on trained fruit trees such as peaches and nectarines while they are still small.

- Stake tomato plants and remove side shoots.

- Water tomatoes frequently.

- Pick globe artichokes before the scales open.

- Celery, one of the easiest and most attractive vegies to grow in the home garden, produces an appealing, green clump of vertical stems topped with a cluster of leaves. Celery can be harvested over a long period and used in a range of dishes, both hot and cold.

- Control aphids and whitefly with a horticultural soap insecticide spray.

- Feed vegetables with a liquid fertilizer to prevent bitterness.

- Potatoes that were planted in the spring are growing well now and should be earthed up (mounded up around the stems with soil) and watered during dry periods. They will also benefit from being fed with a balanced organic liquid fertilizer.

plant now

- Annual herbs like basil, parsley and dill can be sown in early summer.

- Most fruits, particularly tree fruits, can be planted in summer. Keep them well watered during their first year.

- Plant or sow lettuce, radish, Swiss chard, beetroot, cabbage, carrot, cucumber, spinach, squash, beans, cauliflower, sweet corn, pumpkin, courgette (zucchini) and melon. Others to plant, as early in summer as possible, are eggplant or aubergine, tomato and peppers (capsicum) - sweet, chilli and hot.

flowering now

- Herbs such as basil (prune the flowers), coriander (keep the flowers for the seeds), lavender, rosemary, sage

- Fruit such as berry fruits, melons, olives, various tropical fruits

- Vegetables such as eggplant, tomatoes, courgette (zucchini), sweet corn

coriander

Today used as frequently as parsley, coriander or Chinese parsley was actually a popular herb in England until Tudor times, and has been cultivated for over 3000 years. It is a tender annual used fresh or as dry seeds.

Vital statistics

Scientific name: *Coriandrum sativum*.
Family: Apiaceae.
Climate: Enjoys a dry atmosphere and is difficult in damp or humid areas. Plant after frosts have finished.
Culture: Can be grown in the ground or in containers. Has a short season and needs reseeding constantly.
Colours: White flowers.
Height: 70 cm.
Planting time: Mid- to late spring in frosty areas and through summer.
Soil: Light, well drained.
Position: Sunny position.
Planting depth and spacing: 20 cm apart.
Fertilizer: Liquid feed every few weeks.
Pests/diseases: None.
Propagation: Seed.
Storage: Seeds can be stored.

The Apiaceae family

The Apiaceae family contains about 200 genera, distinguished by aromatic foliage and umbels of many small flowers. The family is important economically for products used for food, condiments and as ornamentals.

Carrots, parsnip, celery, parsley, chervil, fennel, lovage, angelica, sea holly (*Eryngium*) and Queen Anne's lace are all popular members of this family. But not all members are edible: hemlock and fool's parsley are both poisonous.

Planting Apiaceae genera in the garden will help attract hoverflies and other beneficial insects.

Cooking with coriander

Probably the most popular herb for Asian cooking is coriander. You can use the leaves, stem and root, and each has its own purpose. Use the roots in curry pastes, the stems when a strong coriander flavour is needed, and add the leaves to a dish at the end of cooking, both as a flavouring and an attractive garnish.

Fruit

It's hardly surprising that most of us consume more fruit over summer. Delicious tropical fruit, mouth-watering stone fruit and succulent berries are all part of summer's fruit palette.

Blackberries – delicious!

Tropical delights

Nothing evokes the feeling of summer quite like succulent juicy fruit. Although few of us are able to grow tropical fruits, a wide range can be bought from supermarkets these days, such is the demand for exotic produce.

Tropical fruits need to be grown in a warm greenhouse or conservatory in cool and cold climates and few people have sufficiently large structures for such plants. Some gardeners, though, like to grow various tropical fruits as small foliage plants under glass and some are very attractive grown in this way. Bananas are often grown in tubs and placed outdoors for the summer. Pineapples are easily accommodated in a small conservatory but without a lot of heat and humidity are unlikely to fruit.

Top ten

Here are some favourite tropical fruits that you can enjoy during the summer and at other times of year.

1 Avocado. One of the most nutritious fruits in the world, avocado provides a well balanced supply of protein, carbohydrate, minerals and vitamins. Many people, especially children, like to grow avocados from the stones after they have eaten the fruit, and young plants certainly make attractive pot plants.

2 Banana. In many countries where rice, wheat and potatoes are not known, the banana is the major source of carbohydrate. Although it is referred to as a tree, the banana really is an evergreen perennial, and should be grown in rich fertile soil where it has plenty of space to spread. It makes a good tub plant.

3 Custard apple. The white flesh of the custard apple has a melting, juicy texture which is delicate and sweet but rich. The custard apple is also known as cherimoya and can actually be grown out of doors in Mediterranean climates.

protect your **harvest**

It's very demoralizing to nurture your fruit trees and vines only to watch birds and insects feast off the pick of the crop before harvest time. Keep birds from attacking your ripening harvest with such devices as painted plastic pots, cat cut-out silhouettes, fake hawks, bits of shiny paper strung in trees and netting.

Red bananas (*Musa velutina*).

Left: Pawpaws ripening on the tree.

Centre: The fruit of the red papaya is delicious with the seeds removed and a squeeze of lemon juice added.

Right: The unusual star fruit tastes like an apple and looks like an ornament.

Some tropical fruits (left to right): Ripe persimmon, immature persimmon on the stem, tamarillo, lychees, longans, pomegranate and mangosteen.

4 Lychee. Capable of withstanding cold to −2°C once established, lychees are related to rambutans and longans, and are extremely popular in Asia. The tree reaches 7 m, although it can be a little slow at first. The fruit is pinkish red on the outside and grape-like inside.

5 Macadamia. This is grown commercially in some countries for its sweet-tasting nuts which follow the spidery cream flowers. A high-quality oil is obtained from the kernels, and the substances in the hull are used for tanning leather. The trees are evergreen and round-headed with deep green, leathery foliage.

6 Mango. The mango is a close relative of the cashew nut, and is native to India where it has been cultivated for 4000 years. As well as a delicious fresh fruit, in flavour something like a peach, it is also used for making chutney.

7 Pawpaw. This tree is grown throughout the tropics for its delicious fruits. To produce fruit, male and female trees are needed. Pawpaw makes a very attractive pot plant with its large, deeply lobed leaves.

8 Passion fruit. These are very vigorous climbers and would take up a lot of room in a conservatory. The hardiest is

P. caerulea, with edible fruits, which can be grown out of doors in cool climates.

9 Pineapple. A bromeliad, the pineapple needs high temperatures and humidity to fruit. But it is an attractive pot plant in a cooler conservatory. Plants can be raised by removing and rooting the tuft of leaves at the top of the fruit.

10 Star fruit or carambola. This is a small tree (about 6 m high) with ridged sides and a fruit with a crisp, apple-like flavour.

Stone fruits

The hardy stone fruits are comparatively easy to grow in cool climates. Peaches, nectarines (which are actually hairless peaches), apricots, cherries (both sweet and sour) and plums can all be grown as fans, trained flat to a wall or fence. Therefore they take up little space and are ideal for small gardens. They should be grown in a warm, sheltered, south-facing aspect for best results. Peaches and nectarines can also be grown on the back wall of an unheated conservatory to protect the flowers from frost, at which time a little heat could be introduced. Choose low-chill types if you live in a frost-free area.

stone fruit

Stone fruits at their peak: peaches, nectarines, cherries, apricots, plums.

fig

Ripe figs Figs must be allowed to ripen on the tree. They are ready for picking when the flesh yields to gentle pressure from being squeezed between finger and thumb.

Made world famous by Adam and Eve's modesty, the fig is a quick-growing deciduous tree that has been cultivated for thousands of years. The fruits can be eaten fresh or dried, and are often used for making jams.

Vital statistics

Scientific name: *Ficus carica*.

Family: Moraceae.

Climate: Warm dry climate best; takes a low of -15°C.

Culture: Require little pruning and are generally free of disease, but watch for fruit fly.

Colours: Skin is either green, brown or black, and the flesh can be pink, white or red-brown.

Height: Between 3 m and 10 m in ideal conditions.

Planting time: Winter, when dormant.

Soil: Plenty of soil moisture, especially in summer.

Position: Inland rather than coastal as fruit can split from excess humidity.

Fertilizer: Apply a complete fertilizer in late winter

Pests/diseases: Fruit fly in some countries or areas.

Propagation: Hardwood cuttings about 20 cm long in winter, under glass in cold areas.

Storage: For fresh fruit, pick when mature; for dried figs, leave longer on the tree to develop fully.

Vegetables

Summer is a rather crazy time in the garden. Almost anything you plant now will grow.

Salad greens

Leafy salad crops, such as non-hearting or loose-leaf lettuce which provides leaves over a long period, are great in summer. The young leaves grow quickly and will be sweet and tender for summer salads.

One big advantage that gardeners have over non-gardeners is their ability to produce salad vegetables. By growing your own, you can guarantee that your salad will be fresh. Take advantage of the huge range of varieties that are available in seed packets. Salad vegetables need fertile soil with plenty of well-rotted organic material incorporated in it. Most salad vegetables need a sunny, open spot to achieve their best.

They are quick growing and need lots of water. Healthy plants make it difficult for pests and diseases to gain hold, so keep your garden free of weeds as they attract diseases.

The popular non-hearting or loose-leaf lettuce comes in a range of varieties: most have deeply cut or crinkled leaves and some are red or purplish in colour while others are the normal green colour. You can either remove a few leaves at a time as required, or cut off the whole plant 2.5 cm above the soil and leave the stem to produce new leaves. Watch out for rocket, which has a spicy flavour. It is an annual that can be sown throughout summer.

Feed lettuces Lettuces will 'bolt' into flower if they are not fed enough or if the weather is too hot. Giving the plants light side dressings of nitrogen fertilizer or liquid feeds every 10–14 days helps.

For a spicier salad mix, try nasturtium (above) or rocket leaves (below). Nasturtium flowers are also edible and add a decorative touch.

Left to right: Tomato flowers; developing fruit; pinching out laterals; and a staked tomato plant.

Tomatoes

Summertime and as usual there's a glut of tomatoes. Tomatoes give a higher yield for space occupied than any other vegetable. An average is 2–5 kg per plant.

Tomatoes are frost tender and need a season of about three months to fruit, so in climates with cool or short summers they are invariably grown under glass. Buy healthy young plants and avoid any that look yellow or starved or are flowering prematurely. Don't rush into buying too early in spring — wait until the weather begins to warm up, especially in cool districts.

There are more varieties of tomato than any other vegetable crop, but for real tomato flavour, pick when red-ripe on the vine and choose a flavoursome cultivar. Yellow tomatoes are usually very tasty.

Tomatoes are quite easy to grow from seeds sown during the spring under glass. They need a temperature of about 21°C to germinate. Grow on the seedlings in small pots and give them plenty of heat.

With so much fruit there are bound to be pests eager to munch away the crop. Watch out for whitefly, a real pest for tomatoes. You shouldn't spray just as you are about to harvest them, so paint a piece of board bright yellow, coat it with grease and place it among your tomatoes. The

tree tomatoes The tamarillo (*Cyphomandra betacea*) or tree tomato is a small, soft-wooded evergreen shrub from the sub-tropical areas of South America. Red or orange-red in colour and the size of a hen's egg, the fruit ripens in autumn. Inside there are many seeds surrounded by edible flesh. The fruits are best eaten only when fully ripe. Appearing in spring and summer, the somewhat star-shaped flowers are white or light buff-pink. In frost-prone climates grow the tree tomato in an intermediate conservatory.

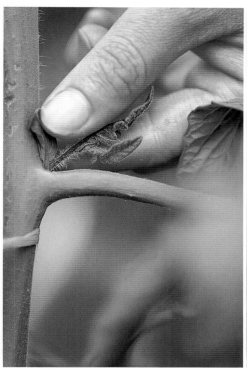

plant a Greek salad

Sweet peppers (capsicums) are closely related to tomatoes and can be grown in the same way. Plant seedlings out in the warmth of spring, and harvest fruit when the skins have developed a rich colour. If the skins have started to wrinkle, the flesh will be coarse and tough. For the perfect Greek salad, just add feta cheese, cucumber, tomatoes, red onions and black olives!

whiteflies are attracted to the yellow board where they get stuck in the grease. Planting French marigolds between tomatoes will deter whitefly. Under glass you could use biological control (a parasitic wasp) to control this pest. Slugs may eat holes in the fruits but these are easily controlled by placing slug pellets around the plants.

Excess tomatoes

At the end of tomato time, you may wish to dispose of your remaining crop. You can enjoy the delicious flavour of homegrown tomatoes throughout winter by trying some of these preserving ideas.

Apart from pickling and making chutneys and relishes, you could try sun-drying or semi-drying your tomatoes. Core

and slice them lengthways and place them on a rack cut side up. Sprinkle with sea salt and bake for up to eight hours in a slow oven (75°C) until the excess moisture has evaporated. The tomatoes should be completely dry and almost leathery, but not crisp. Cool and store them in sterilized jars in the fridge for up to six months. To sterilize jars, rinse them in hot soapy water and dry them in the oven for ten minutes along with the tomatoes.

Or store whole, unblemished tomatoes in a jar. Just cover the ripe fruit with olive oil and keep them in the fridge.

Tomato relish is an excellent substitute for shop-bought tomato sauce.

Did you know? When tomatoes first arrived in Europe they were gold, not red.

tomatoes

1 Vine-ripened tomatoes. 2 Purple tomato*. 3 Cherry tomatoes. 4 Black plum tomato*. 5 Orange tomato*.
6 Yellow egg-shaped tomato.* 7 Green-striped tomato.* 8 Yellow lemon-shaped tomatoes. 9 A 'black' tomato.
10 'Roma', a small fruited, almost seedless variety. 11 Yellow pear tomatoes. 12 A 'meaty', large-fruited tomato.
13 Red pear tomatoes. 14 A large-fruited yellow tomato. 15 A large red tomato with good colour throughout.

* Heritage varieties.

8

10

9

11

12

13

14

15

Sprouting seeds

Microvegies or sprouts have become very fashionable with nutritionists and gardeners alike. They are probably the easiest vegetable to grow, especially for children, who are impatient gardeners. Sprouts contain lots of antioxidants and are readily available in supermarkets and greengrocers.

Cress and mustard seeds have always been harvested for their young leaves, but the value of sprouts wasn't appreciated until the advent of alfalfa. Principally grown as a garnish, alfalfa used to be the only sprout available, but now there are bean, broccoli, mung, daikon, radish, sugar or snow peas and onion sprouts. They all begin life as seeds, and may be in the form of grain or dried legume. Once they are soaked in water and drained, germination starts and their nutritional value rockets. Harvest them between two days and two weeks.

How to grow sprouts

1 Buy certified edible seeds from a supermarket, health food shop or mail-order seed company.
2 Soak the seeds for 4–6 hours or overnight, then drain.
3 Place the seeds in a jar and cover with a fine gauze material such as a clean stocking, muslin or cheesecloth.
4 Leave in a cool spot.
5 Rinse with fresh water daily and drain.

Sprouts of sugar or snow peas (an edible-podded type).

Crazy about cucurbits

The warm season vine crops, often referred to as cucurbits, are a fabulous addition to the summer garden. They all need frost-free conditions, with seeds sown immediately after the last frost, or indoors until the weather is more dependable. To help flowers and fruits form, prepare the richest soil you can manage, keep the water up to plants and add a side dressing of blood, fish and bone.

Melons

The sweet, delectable flavour of today's melons is a testament to plant breeding. Melons are, in fact, a relative of courgettes (zucchini), cucumbers, pumpkins and marrows, and have been turned into such delicious fruit through hundreds of years of selection and hybridization. Like their relatives, they are vine crops, needing a fair bit of space to sprawl over the ground, or a strong trelliswork if you are training smaller melons vertically. In temperate climates with cool summers melons are grown in a greenhouse or cold frame, or under cloches.

Sweet melons are the most popular, especially the cantaloupe and musk (including honeydew) types. Watermelons require a long, very warm growing season to succeed and are not so popular with home

Left to right: A pumpkin flower; ripe watermelon; and courgettes (zucchini) with flowers.

gardeners. A sweet melon is ready to pick when the stem pulls easily from the fruit, while a watermelon is ready when the side lying on the ground turns yellow and the fruit sounds hollow when you tap it.

Cucumbers

Cucumbers too have come a long way since they were first cultivated in South Asia over 3000 years ago. Now they are green, yellow, white or spotted. The shapes vary even more — from round to globe-shaped, long and short, large and small — and the flavour has also changed from sweet to tangy to low acid; a quarter are even burpless.

The method of growing cucumbers has also changed because the plants no longer roam all over the garden: they too have become more compact. Some new varieties are small bushes and don't require any support or trellising, unlike the old types. Plant breeding caters to generally smaller gardens today. There are varieties for growing out of doors and in the greenhouse.

Cucumbers are very easy to grow and there is still time in warm areas to grow one more crop before autumn comes around.

You can harvest them early for pickling or let them grow to pick fresh from the patch for summer salads. Cucumbers are 96 per cent water so don't let your plants dry out.

Courgettes

Courgettes (also known as zucchini) are marrows or summer squashes, picked when immature, about 15 cm long, to encourage continuous cropping. They are quick and easy to grow, and their flowers, lightly battered then cooked in olive oil, are especially delicious.

Some Asian melons.

Growing tips Plant seeds in groups of 4–5 and thin out to the best two. The first few flowers will be male, and therefore won't set fruit. When three fruits have set on any one runner, pinch out the tip of that runner.

1 Burpless cucumber. 2 Mini white cucumber*. 3 Scalloped marrows or summer squashes. 4 An unusual heritage cucumber*. 5 Courgettes (zucchini). 6 Lemon cucumber*. 7 A green courgette (zucchini). 8 A golden courgette (zucchini). 9 A greenhouse cucumber. 10 Chinese sweet and striped cucumber*. 11 Seychelles cucumber*. 12 Lebanese cucumber. 13 Armenian cucumber*.

* Heritage varieties.

The red hot chilli peppers

Do chillies come from Chile? Well, sort of. The origin of the chilli is thought to be South America, where it was a staple diet of Incas and Aztecs. Chillies are now grown throughout the world, and are used extensively in Thai, Mexican, Cajun, Asian, Hungarian and Portuguese cuisine.

The rest of the world was introduced to them when Columbus sailed to the West Indies in 1492. He believed the various fiery varieties of capsicums used by the locals were pepper. As a result, the name pepper has stuck (even though true peppercorns grow on a vine) and 500 years later we still call them chilli peppers.

Peppers are so versatile and there are many different types. Some varieties add pep to savoury food, some can be used in desserts and some are simply ornamental.

Spring is the season for sowing peppers. There are at least ten different species of *Capsicum*, although only three main types are commonly grown in home gardens.

1 Ornamental chilli. This is a non-edible variety with much smaller fruits that change with maturity from green or purple to yellow, orange and scarlet. The fruits or berries are extremely hot, so take care.

2 Edible hot peppers. There are two types of edible hot pepper. Chilli peppers have long pointed fruits that may be used green (immature) or red (ripe). The riper the fruits the hotter they become. They can be used fresh, pickled or dried. Hot peppers, also known as cayenne peppers, have small, slim, red, orange or yellow fruits that are extremely hot and pungent and used for flavouring and sauces or ground for cayenne pepper and paprika.

3 Sweet peppers. The large fruited, non-hot sweet peppers (also called bell peppers and capsicums), can be eaten unripe (green) or ripe (red, yellow, orange or purple) in salads, cooked in sauces, char-grilled for antipasto, or used as a stuffed, cooked vegetable.

Hot stuff

All hot peppers should be handled with care, as they are known to cause inflammation on contact with broken skin, eyes and mucous membranes. If you have sensitive skin, wear rubber gloves, wash your hands thoroughly after handling them and be careful not to rub your eyes as this can cause severe burning. To reduce the intensity of the heat, consume milk, yoghurt or other dairy products. Capsaicin (the hot compound) is in its most concentrated form in the seeds, so remove these if you are worried about the intensity of your chillies. Apart from their value as cooking ingredients, chillies are effective in a spray for deterring rabbits and sapsucking insects such as aphids. (See the recipe for 'Chilli water' opposite.)

There are many varieties of chilli and hot peppers available and the range will vary from one country to another. Some are universally grown however, including 'Cayenne Long Slim' and 'Long Red Cayenne', both of which are often used for drying; 'Hungarian Yellow Wax Hot' whose name describes the fruit; 'Habanero' and 'Anaheim' (the latter is mildly hot). There is a very wide range of varieties of sweet peppers and again these will vary from one place to another. Some

CHILLI AND SOAP SPRAY

1 Gather the ingredients and materials you'll need: chillies, soap, grater, sharp knife and chopping board. You'll also need a spray bottle and some water.

2 Grate soap (or use pure soap flakes instead).

3 Add soap flakes to a spray bottle that is nearly full of water.

4 Chop about eight chillies.

5 Add the chillies to the bottle and screw the lid back on.

6 Shake the contents vigorously and spray your home-made insecticide onto any plant.

are well-known universally though, such as 'California Wonder' and 'Yolo Wonder'. The catalogues of mail-order seed companies generally list good ranges of both hot and sweet peppers which are well illustrated and described. It is best not to save your own seed from one year to another as the resulting young plants may be disappointing or different from their parents.

Chilli water

For a spicy, environmentally friendly insecticide, use a food blender to purée twenty or so chillies to form a paste. Mix the paste with water, then leave it to stand so the pulp can settle. Use the strained 'tea' on a still day so that it won't blow into your eyes.

Alternatively, make a chilli and soap spray (described above).

How to grow peppers

Peppers are frost susceptible, so the best sowing time is spring to early summer. They need a warm, sunny position with shelter from strong winds, or grow them in a greenhouse. Peppers prefer fertile soil with added organic matter and a mixed fertilizer. Water regularly and mulch in dry weather.

Once the small white flowers have appeared, feed with liquid fertilizer every two to three weeks to encourage prolific fruiting.

How to use peppers

The benefit of using peppers in cooking is both the sweet, fruity flavour and the stimulating 'bite' of heat. When chilli and hot peppers are dried the sugars are caramelized, which is why they taste so different from fresh. Normally fresh peppers are used in quick-cooking Asian dishes, while slow soups, stews and curries use dried peppers.

Pure soap insecticide If you use detergent instead of pure soap, the spray will break down the waxy coating on the leaves. In the old days, when pure soap was used in households, the used washing water was thrown over citrus trees and vegie patches to deter pests.

peppers

1 'Desi Teekh'. 2 'Fiesta'. 3 'Thai'. 4 'Thai' (new cultivar). 5 Green bird's eye chilli. 6 F220. 7 F118. 8 'Hungarian Wax' (mature form). 9 'Thai' (new cultivar). 10 Red bird's eye chilli. 11 'Hungarian Wax' (immature form). 12 Flowers of 'Thai' chilli. 13 'Cyklon'. 14 'Yellow Gypsy'. 15 'Hungarian Sweet' (green stage). 16 'Black Hungarian'. 17 'Californian Wonder' (green stage). 18 'California Wonder' (red stage). 19 'Cayenne'. 20 'Hungarian Sweet' (red stage). 21 'Chocolate'. (Bear in mind that not all of these may be available everywhere.)

Plant a root crop, such as turnip (above) or carrot, after a leaf crop and your vegie garden will flourish.

Crop rotation

Long before science and technology took an interest in gardening after World War II, farmers and home gardeners practised a very complex rotation of vegetable crops each season. Phases of the moon were taken into account and the whole method took on almost mystical qualities.

In the garden vegetable patch it is very wise to break the crop relationship cycle. Plant a root crop such as turnip, beetroot or carrots where you've just had a leaf crop such as lettuce. Plant onions prior to a crop of tomatoes, and peas and beans after cabbages and Swiss chard. And avoid planting anything in the same family season after season in the same bed — for example, do not plant tomatoes after potatoes or cabbage after broccoli.

It was Charles 'Turnip' Townsend who introduced the turnip, a root crop, to England from Europe in the early 1700s and advocated its use in crop rotation. The turnip is from a different family to the potato, the most popular root vegetable, so farmers could alternate their root vegetable crops and still practise crop rotation successfully. This basic rotation of crops stops any soil-borne insects and disease from remaining in the same garden bed year after year, and avoids the depletion of certain soil nutrients that results from planting similar vegetables in the same plot.

The idea was taken to various countries by colonial farmers but was discredited in the twentieth century by modern agriculture; however, the introduction of a legume crop such as peas or lupins every few years provides free nitrogen fertilizer and organic matter to the soil.

Living stake Climbing beans are sometimes planted next to corn which acts as a living stake.

beans

Scarlet runner beans and French beans (snap beans) are very popular summer vegetables for the home garden. There are climbing and dwarf varieties of both and special varieties of French beans for dried seeds.

Vital statistics

Botanical name: *Phaseolus coccineus* (scarlet runner beans), *Phaseolus vulgaris* (French beans).

Family: Papilionaceae.

Climate: They grow best in a temperature of 15–30°C so are cultivated in spring and summer in temperate climates. Neither are frost tolerant.

Culture: At flowering, beans need humid conditions, and you may need to water with a sprinkler. Take care not to disturb the shallow roots when weeding.

Colours: Flowers may be scarlet, pink or white. The pods of French beans may be yellow or purple, or green streaked with purple, as well as the normal green.

Height: Grow to 30 cm to 2.5 m, depending on variety.

Planting time: Sow seeds directly into the soil in spring after all cold snaps have finished.

Soil: Free-draining (not too sandy) with added organic matter, although they can grow in heavier clay soils than peas. Mulch with grass clippings or compost.

Position: Full sun for half of the day is plenty, and will help guard against heat stress. Shelter from prevailing winds and excess heat.

Planting depth and spacing: Space dwarf and climbing beans about 10 cm apart. Plant dwarf types in 60 cm rows, climbing varieties in 1 m rows.

Fertilizer: Add a balanced granular fertilizer to the soil before sowing.

Pests/diseases: Slugs, aphids and whitefly. Place slug pellets around young plants, and spray for aphids or whitefly as soon as noticed.

Harvest: Always pick when young and tender, usually twice a week before the pods go lumpy. If drying, wait till the pod has ripened completely and dried on the vine, and then shell and store for winter.

Propagation: Grow from seed.

Storage: Beans can be frozen (blanch a few minutes then freeze), or seeds of certain varieties can be dried.

Brisk walks. Long shadows across the lawn. Warm days, cool crisp nights. Crunchy leaves, clippings and compost. Golden hues. Harvest and finale.

autumn

Dried leaves, the essence of autumn, are the basis of any good garden compost.

autumn

overview of the season

Autumn brings its own special pleasures and ambience. Sure, it's a time when flowers are fading, but this signifies the beginning of something that is just as exciting — the harvest.

You see, plants flower first before setting fruit, and it's this completion of nature's purpose which is surely as much cause for celebration as the blossom itself.

There is a sense of fulfilment and maturity in autumn that no other season evokes. Gone are the floral tributes of summer, and in their place we have plenty — ripening fruit, delicate seeds, the last of the season's flowers, bright berries and, loveliest of all, colouring leaves.

To really make the most of this season, plant a selection of foliage, fruit and flowering plants. Deciduous trees, chrysanthemums, dahlias and the rich and subdued colours of Michaelmas daisies all combine to promote a feeling of warmth and harmony.

Let misty autumn be our part!
The twilight of the year is sweet;...

Ernest Dawson

For inspiration, visit some of the many magnificent gardens open for inspection at this time.

If you don't have space for a tree, but still want some foliage contrast, there are plenty of smaller plants that develop autumn colour. Dwarf nandina, berberis and some viburnum species will give a really good show. The smokebush (*Cotinus* sp.) also colours well: it has pretty plum-coloured leaves, and in late summer, flowers that look like plumes of smoke before the leaves turn orange-bronze in autumn.

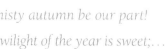

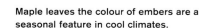

Maple leaves the colour of embers are a seasonal feature in cool climates.

The many moods of autumn — blazing trees, long shadows and small details such as bracket fungi and lichens.

Harvest

Gathering berries, collecting seeds, storing nuts and squirrelling away treasures are all part of autumn. As the weather becomes colder, remove crops such as tomatoes, aubergines, squash and melons. Gorge on the last of their fruits, or bottle, dry or marinate in oil for later use. Store hard-skinned pumpkins in a dry place, and dig up old potatoes. When your larder is full and the cupboards are bursting, autumn is drawing to a close.

Hard work

As far as the climate is concerned, autumn is one of the most pleasant times for gardening. This is fortunate, as there is much to do. Your secateurs get a real workout tidying many perennials, pruning shrubs and taking cuttings.

Few plants need feeding in autumn as their growth is slowing down. However, any late crops that are still productive such as tomatoes, peppers and dahlias can be fed with a high-potash fertilizer. Lawns can also be fed, using an autumn lawn fertilizer to toughen up the grass for the winter.

Frost-tender plants will need protecting for the winter, perhaps by moving them under glass if they are in pots or tubs.

Planting

Don't underestimate the benefits of autumn planting. Although most of us are tempted to buy plants when they're in flower over spring and summer, the cool night temperatures and warm autumn soils make this a better time for root growth, which means quicker establishment and fewer losses than at other times.

Select deciduous shrubs and trees for coloured foliage during their autumn display and your plants will perform exactly as you'd hoped. Transplanting existing specimens can also be done now to lessen the shock of the move.

weatherwatch
Never work when the earth is sodden. Wait until it is damp and crumbly before planting out.

A 'green' backyard

Most of us think gardening is an environmentally friendly occupation, but how green is your backyard? Wood and garden materials make up around 21 per cent of all household waste. We all pay for collecting and dumping this waste in landfills, where it produces greenhouse gases and polluting leachates. And of course we pay again when we buy in soil conditioners, fertilizers, manures, composts and mulches.

In addition, fertilizer, excess water and toxic runoff regularly wash into our waterways, polluting streams, causing algae blooms and a decline in marine life.

Hosing down paths and watering the lawn and garden drain our summer water supply. Waste water from the kitchen sink and from washing the car literally goes down the drain, adding to the pollutants in the waterways.

You can turn the equation around, and really have a 'green' garden. Learn the three Rs — re-use, reduce and recycle. Re-use grey water from the laundry wherever possible (it's great for controlling scale on citrus plants). Reduce the numbers of high-maintenance plants in your garden and recycle garden scraps into compost. With huge quantities of grass clippings, spent annuals, perennials and vegetables, there is no better time to start a composting system. Recycle all this waste vegetative matter and turn it into free fertilizer.

Benefits to you

- Save time. Use low-maintenance plants and you won't have to work so hard in your garden.
- Save water. To reduce water use in the garden cut down on the size of your lawn, or in small gardens replace the lawn altogether, for example with gravel. Keep beds and borders permanently mulched with bulky organic matter to help prevent the soil from drying out.
- Save money and effort. Make your own mulches, composts and fertilizers out of recycled organic matter. Reuse water to cut down on demand and make your water bills up to 25 per cent lower.
- Increase your property's value. An easily maintained, 'green' oasis will attract more buyers when you decide to sell.

Liquid fertilizer Make your own liquid fertilizer from blood, fish and bone, chicken manure pellets or seaweed. Steep any of the above in hot water, letting it sit for a few weeks. Then use a cup of the liquid in 10 L (a watering can) of water.

You can use plastic garbage bins to store compost and kitchen scraps.

Worms

Worms are often accused of killing grass and of eating the roots of pot plants and vegetables. The truth is worms in the garden help to aerate the soil, improving drainage and soil structure. They consume organic waste materials and convert them into humus. That's what those small mounds of worm castings are on your lawn. So worms don't damage grass or plant roots. Overusing fertilizers and insecticides discourages worms, but by adding organic matter, such as compost, you encourage these beneficial friends of the garden.

God Almighty first planted a garden; and, indeed, it is the purest of human pleasures.

Francis Bacon

Benefits to the environment

- Less waste to landfill. The more you compost, the less is buried.
- Less pollution runoff. Organic gardening and permaculture techniques reduce your dependence on chemicals for sustaining your garden.
- Better habitat for insects, birds and animals. A garden is not just a place for plants, it's also a place to be shared with other forms of life that exist in a garden — birds, small mammals, frogs, toads and beneficial insects. Give them food, water and shelter and you will have hours of enjoyment watching their antics. Provide them with nesting sites and they will take up residence, protecting many plants by keeping insect numbers under control.

Protect native animals Be careful to keep cats and dogs inside at night, as they prey on birds and other creatures. Make sure they have working bells tied to their collars.

Earthworms

Earthworms are indicators of good soil structure and fertility. The 'earthworking' worm species has been shown to improve soil structure and fertility; these worms increase water penetration into the soil and reduce both water runoff and the subsequent loss of topsoil through erosion. Soils with increased earthworm activity display increased crop yields.

Composting worms, bought for compost heaps, are of no direct value to the soil but are very effective in reducing organic waste such as lawn clippings and kitchen scraps into valuable garden nutrients. Your compost heap can then be dug back into your garden soil.

Trench composting

Composting doesn't have to be difficult or messy. Trench composting is an effective way of improving the soil over the cooler seasons of autumn or winter in preparation for new trees, shrubs, vegetables or flowers.

Step 1

Mark out the area to be dug over in a series of trenches and mark the lines of the first two parallel trenches.

Step 2

Dig out a single trench about 30 cm wide and 30 cm deep, and move the soil from the trench to the end of the plot, which will be the very last section to be trenched.

Step 3

As they become available, gradually fill the trench with plant debris, vegetable scraps and kitchen waste.

Step 4

Dig out a second trench in a similar way to the first one. Cover each layer of material in the first trench with the soil that has been dug from the second parallel trench.

Step 5

Start filling the second trench with garden and kitchen waste as it becomes available and then fill this trench with soil from the third. Each completed trench will gradually settle over a month or two as the plant material decomposes.

Step 6

Shred any woody material, such as prunings or cabbage stems, before you bury it so it will decay more quickly.

Repotting

After a few years in the same pot most plants need repotting. Telltale signs include roots circling on the surface or growing out through the drainage holes, and plants wilting quickly despite frequent watering.

Carry out repotting when plants become dormant; for example, when deciduous shrubs or trees have dropped their leaves. Either graduate to a larger container, or root prune, then replace back into the same size container with fresh mix. A handy way of combining both techniques is to take out 'cores' each year. Cut down into the root ball with a sharp knife and remove no more than 30 per cent of the feeder roots, replacing them with fresh mix.

Plants in pots need special care. Don't scrimp on the quality of potting mix as your plants depend on this for survival. Use controlled-release fertilizer and just a few water-absorbing granules to prevent plants drying out.

Moving pots

Moving a heavy pot is difficult. Make the task easier by placing 30 cm lengths of timber dowel under the pot so you can roll the pot to wherever you want. Alternatively, buy pot stands with wheels.

Where pots are too large to move, rejuvenate the potting compost by replacing some with fresh compost. The surface can be mulched with a layer of shingle. Once the pots are repositioned, keep them raised off concrete so the plants can drain freely.

CORING

1 First, cut the surface roots with a sharp knife.

2 Lift out this clump of matted roots and soil.

3 Then cut the exposed feeder roots with secateurs.

4 Fill the hole with fresh potting mix. Repeat the process (steps 1 to 4) twice more so that you remove approximately 30 per cent of the feeder roots.

5 Water thoroughly.

Dandelion, a broad-leaved perennial with a tap root.

Weeds

If weeds are the only thing looking healthy in your garden at the moment, we have some helpful tips for you. The trick is, don't wait any longer to attack them.

Spray perennial weeds now before the weather gets too cold and their growth starts slowing down. A weedkiller containing glyphosate is still effective at this time of year. Broad-leaved perennial weeds such as dandelions in your lawn are easily removed by digging them up with a narrow, forked hand tool known as a daisy grubber. Remove all of the root otherwise the weed will grow again. Remember that weeds like

dandelions have long tap roots so dig down deeply. Lawn weedkillers are best used in spring and summer, especially if the lawn is badly infested with weeds. Annual weeds in beds and borders can be hoed out before they set seed, choosing a warm, dry day when the surface of the soil is dry.

The best method of weed control in beds and borders is to plant more and decrease the available space in which weeds can take hold. For example, dense, low-growing ground cover can be planted between larger subjects such as shrubs. Also keep the soil surface well mulched with bulky organic matter to prevent the growth of annual weeds.

What is a weed? A plant whose virtues have not been discovered.

Ralph Waldo Emerson

WEED FERTILIZER

Replace nitrogen in the garden by making liquid fertilizer out of weeds.

1 Almost fill a plastic garbage bin with weeds.

2 Cover the weeds with water and replace the lid.

3 In warm weather it will take a few weeks for the weeds to break down. Dilute the fertilizer 10:1 with water and pour it onto the garden.

knee **pad**

Every gardener needs something to protect their knees from stony or damp ground. You can buy a ready-made product, such as a pair of strap-on knee pads, but why not make your own?

1 On top of a piece of scrap timber (we used some timber laminate) fold some cotton wadding several times until you achieve a thick pad the same size as the timber piece.

2 Place the cotton padding and the timber on top of a piece of waterproof material, leaving about 10 cm extra on each side. You could use oilskin but that is rather expensive. We used some cheerful floral plastic, thick enough to be stapled without tearing.

3 Holding the plastic down firmly, staple one side. Staple the opposite side before doing the remaining pair.

4 Tuck the corners in as you go.

5 Your custom-made knee pad should last for years.

autumn
annuals, perennials & bulbs

Imaginative planting makes the most of any season. There is plenty to brighten the void and extend the summer flurry.

Annuals

Autumn can be a difficult time for annuals, as many of them die or at least start shutting down in preparation for cold weather.

Make use of long-lasting summer annuals such as dwarf and tall snapdragons, amaranthus, salvia and begonias, which have more than one flush of flowers. Don't be too quick to pull out sweet alyssum and lobelia either, as these will continue flowering until the frosts commence.

The hot bed

Although it's a quiet time for most flowers, there are still some that can warm up your garden in shades of red, tangerine and gold. Sparks seem to fly when these colours are concentrated together in the garden. Their vitality and strength can actually cheer you up and brighten the greyest of days!

The marigold that goes to bed with the sun, And with him rises weeping.

William Shakespeare

Dahlias are a bold and cheerful staple of the autumn cutting garden.

The gloriosa daisy or black-eyed Susan (*Rudbeckia hirta*) makes a vivid summer and autumn display. Great for cutting, this showy annual has yellow daisy-like flowers with a brown, cone-shaped centre. Varieties are normally grown, such as the popular 'Marmalade' with rich golden orange flowers. 'Goldilocks' is also recommended, with its double or semi-double, rich golden orange flowers. 'Irish Eyes' is unusual in that the yellow flowers have a green centre.

Each flower has its own charm. Children love snapdragons because the flowers will snap open and shut when squeezed at the sides. Marigolds are terrific companion plants, keeping nasties like root nematodes at bay. Feverfew, also said to keep pests at bay, has white, gold-centred daisy flowers throughout summer and into autumn and aromatic, soft ferny foliage in fresh green or golden yellow.

Not so pleasant smelling but just as showy are French marigolds. In cheerful colours, singles and doubles, they establish easily, often flowering right into winter.

Celosias or cockscombs are still flowering, including the plume varieties and crested kinds. The former are often bedded out while the latter are usually grown as greenhouse pot plants.

Technicolour dream

If zany colour and wild foliage appeal to you, try amaranthus, including Joseph's coat (*Amaranthus tricolor*) and love-lies-bleeding (*A. caudatus*). These half-hardy annuals can create a truly tropical effect in summer and autumn bedding schemes and are often used in outdoor subtropical and tropical displays in frost-prone climates.

Joseph's coat, also known as Chinese spinach and tampala, is grown for its multicoloured foliage. The colour can be green, purple or red shades, flushed with other colours. The flowers are not at all showy. Some well-known varieties include 'Flaming Fountains' with narrow leaves in shades of red and bronze and 'Molten Fire' with scarlet and yellow leaves.

Love-lies-bleeding, or tassel flower, has long, dangling, tassel-like flowers. They are generally deep red, although there is a variety called 'Viridis' with bright green tassels that turn to cream. There are some varieties with red- or purple-flushed leaves.

In the same family is the globe amaranth (*Gomphrena globosa*) with egg-shaped, purple, pink or white flowers during summer and autumn. The flowers are cut and dried for winter arrangements. It is half-hardy and will not stand frosts.

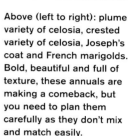

Above (left to right): plume variety of celosia, crested variety of celosia, Joseph's coat and French marigolds. Bold, beautiful and full of texture, these annuals are making a comeback, but you need to plan them carefully as they don't mix and match easily.

Spot flowering Although autumn can be a quiet time in terms of flower colour, there are some plants that 'spot' flower. That is, outside the main flowering flush, they have a smaller show as an added autumn bonus. Such plants include the bottlebrushes (callistemon) shown here, some of which can take outdoor cultivation in frost-prone climates. Other spot flowerers are campanulas or bellflowers and roses.

check list

jobs to do now

- Prune any diseased or dead growth from perennials, such as pelargoniums, cannas and salvias.

- Prepare the garden bed where sweet peas will be grown next year. Dig in plenty of well-rotted manure or garden compost. If the soil is acid, give an application of lime.

- Remove old annuals and think about some of the new releases for autumn.

- When your dahlias are blackened by frost cut them down and lift and store the tubers.

- Feed chrysanthemums regularly with liquid fertilizer, and disbud if extra-large blooms are required.

- Don't prune spent perennials if they are self-seeders which you want to encourage.

- Water windflowers to prolong their season.

- Feed Christmas cacti (schlumbergera) with a fertilizer that is high in potash and phosphorus and low in nitrogen to encourage flowering.

- Take off any older, tattered leaves from your gerberas and divide them if required. Watch out for pests such as aphids and whitefly and spray with insecticidal soap.

- Under glass make sure cymbidiums receive full light in autumn and winter.

- Enjoy the last few days of your perennials — such as shasta daisies, stokesia, Michaelmas daisies and perennial phlox — but be ready to pick the last bunches for the house before dividing and replanting the others. Artemisia, delphiniums, perennial phlox, physostegia, agapanthus, anemone, campanula and rudbeckia are just some of the many perennials that can be lifted and divided once they have become dormant.

- Prepare your garden beds with lots of organic material in readiness for planting spring bulbs.

- Lift any gladiolus while they still have some leaves and allow them to dry off. After the stems have completely withered, dust them in derris and store them in plastic bags.

- Lilies can be lifted, separated and replanted once they are dormant.

- This is also the best time to lift any congested clumps of spring-flowering bulbs such as daffodils, tulips and alliums. Separate the bulbs and replant them.

- Tidy bearded iris and make way for new growth by cutting back dead foliage. The more sun the rhizomes get, the more flowers you'll have.

plant now

- Plant annuals and biennials for spring colour such as winter-flowering pansies, violas, polyanthus, wallflowers and forget-me-nots.

- Sweet pea seeds can be sown now, in flowering positions in mild areas, in a cold frame in hard-winter areas.

- Certain hardy annuals can be sown outdoors in early autumn in their flowering positions to bloom next spring, such as pot marigolds (calendulas), love-in-a-mist (nigella) and cornflowers (centaurea).

- Plant out some biennials for cutting such as Canterbury bells, foxgloves and sweet Williams.

- Autumn is the best time for planting lily bulbs to flower next summer. Lilies like their roots shaded by other plants, and their heads in the sun, so choose positions carefully.

- Plant spring-flowering crocuses in gaps of crazy paving.

flowering now

- Annuals such as salvia, amaranthus, China asters, snapdragons, California poppies, celosia, globe amaranth, candytuft, French marigold, nasturtium, verbena, mallow, sweet alyssum, zinnia, floss flower, petunias

- Perennials such as dahlias, gerberas, daisies (including Michaelmas daisies), gaillardias, salvias, coneflowers, Stokes' aster, coreopsis, obedient plant or false dragonhead, chrysanthemums, golden rod, black-eyed Susan, kaffir lily (schizostylis), windflower, convolvulus, carnation, monkshood, *Aster* sp., helianthus, geraniums, penstemon, phlox

- Bulbs flowering in autumn include nerines, belladonna lily (*Amaryllis belladonna*), autumn-flowering crocus such as *C. speciosus* and *C. sativus*, colchicums, *Zephyranthes candida* and *Sternbergia lutea*.

Flowers for spring

Now the weather has cooled, it's time to plant the flowers that bloom in spring. In sunny spots you can plant virtually anything. Probably best are pansies and violas. They grow into carpets of colour and are good value as they flower for several months.

In positions with partial shade plant primulas for spring or early summer colour. There is a huge range to choose from. Polyanthus primulas are very popular for spring bedding schemes and patio containers. Most primulas like moist soil. Honesty can be planted in autumn, also in partial shade.

Various annuals can be grown as cutting flowers. It is best to have a special bed in full sunshine for this purpose. Many people have a cutting bed on the vegetable plot.

Sweet peas are among the best annuals for cutting. They are very hardy and in mild areas can be sown where they are to flower, but in colder regions are best sown in a cold frame and planted out in spring. Other annuals that can be sown in flowering positions in autumn especially for cutting include pot marigolds (calendulas), cornflowers (centaurea), love-in-a-mist (nigella) and larkspur (consolida). In regions with hard frosts protect young plants with cloches over the winter.

Top: Heartsease or Johnny-jump-up (*Viola tricolor*) is an easily grown spring-flowering annual or biennial that self seeds freely. Above: Polyanthus are favourite spring bedding plants that should be planted now.

Seed-saving principles Summer and autumn are the seasons for collecting seeds of a wide range of garden plants, from annuals to a whole range of hardy perennials. This way you can perpetuate your garden from one season to the next. Therefore do not be in too much of a hurry to pull up annuals and cut down perennials – let them set seeds first. Some plants sow themselves (such as honesty, shown here) so you always have new plants coming along.

Most seeds are sown in spring and so need to be stored for the winter. First they will need to be dried, so lay the seed pods and capsules on sheets of newspaper on the greenhouse bench or warm windowsill for a few days. When dry, remove the seeds and packet them up into paper envelopes. Make sure you label each packet with the name of the plant. Then store the packets in a cool dry airy place indoors until sowing time in the spring.

Sweet peas

Sweet pea seeds can be sown in the autumn, direct in flowering positions in mild areas, or in pots in a cold frame in areas with severe frosts. Sweet peas need plenty of sunshine and a sturdy tall trellis in order to grow well (although you can grow dwarf varieties in pots). A wall of these sweet-smelling blooms will provide you with cut flowers for many weeks in summer.

A fence in full sun is perfect. Just attach some chicken wire to support the climbing tendrils. To prepare the soil, add some well-rotted animal manure or compost and cultivate deeply. Apply a liberal dressing of complete fertilizer (about half a cup per square metre) and a handful of lime per square metre (unless your soil is alkaline). Lightly cultivate this fertilizer into the top 15 cm of soil and water well.

Allow a week for the soil to settle before sowing your sweet pea seeds. Failure to germinate is usually due to overwatering or rainy conditions. Once the seeds are sown just damp down the soil. Do not water again until the seedlings appear. Always plant two seeds in each hole, just to be sure.

Perennial pea

The sweet pea family contains many other species but the annual one is the most popular. The perennial pea, *Lathyrus grandiflorus*, is a semi-climbing perennial suited to temperate climates. It has rosy red flowers in seemingly endless supply in summer. Cut it right down in autumn. Another species, also known as the perennial or everlasting pea, is *L. latifolius*. This herbaceous, perennial climber has pink or purple flowers throughout summer and early autumn.

If replanting sweet peas (above) each year sounds too hard, try one of the perennial peas such as *Lathyrus latifolius* (left).

poor man's **orchid**

The poor man's orchid, or butterfly flower, is a stunning annual which creates a beautiful display when planted en masse in pots. The ruffled flowers look like ornate trumpets and come in regal purple and magenta shades.

Vital statistics

Scientific name: *Schizanthus pinnatus*.
Family: Solanaceae.
Climate: In frost-prone areas, grow as a cool-conservatory pot plant or as a half-hardy summer annual outdoors.
Culture: Pinch out growing tips to promote bushy growth.
Colours: Purple, magenta, red, pink and white.
Height: 30–45 cm.
Planting time: For summer and autumn flowering sow seeds in mid-spring. For winter flowering in conservatories sow in late summer or early autumn.
Soil: Soil-based potting compost for pot plants. Outdoors any well-drained fertile soil.
Position: In conservatories provide shade during hot sunny periods. Full sun outdoors.
Planting spacing: 20 cm.
Fertilizer: Use a liquid fertilizer monthly.
Pests/disease: Generally none.
Cutting: Long-lasting as a cut flower.
Propagation: From seed.

The Papilionaceae family

The pea family is characterized by a distinctive type of flower with five petals: a large upright petal known as the standard, two side 'wings', and two lower petals that are partly joined together, known as the keel and containing the sexual organs. Lathyrus (sweet peas and perennial peas) are well-known examples in this family, but others include lupins, edible peas and beans and various woody plants including brooms (cytisus and genistas).

Despite their showy blooms, what makes the pea family so interesting are the roots. The roots of peas and their relations have nitrogen-fixing nodules which take nitrogen from the air and convert it into an available form for the plants to use as food.

Because of this nitrogen-fixing ability, various members of the pea family are used as green manures to enrich soils, typical examples being lupins, lucerne or alfalfa and clover. These are dug into the soil before they set seeds.

project
bamboo **trellis**

If you don't have a sunny wall, you can create your own support for sweet peas, making light bamboo trelliswork. Pinch sweet peas as they reach about 15 cm high to create three or four laterals which can be trained upwards.

1 First, assemble the materials you'll need: ten 1.5 m bamboo stakes, twine, potting mix, two terracotta pots, secateurs and sweet pea seedlings.

2 Choose a sunny spot in the garden. The more sun sweet peas get, the more they flower, so all day is best. Insert the first bamboo stake at an angle of about 60 degrees, making sure that the stake is firmly embedded in the ground.

3 Insert four more stakes parallel to the first, keeping them about 200 mm apart.

4 Push in the other five stakes, this time working at the same angle but in the opposite direction. This should form a diamond-shaped lattice.

5 Secure each junction neatly with twine, cutting off any loose ends (see above also).

6 Place two pots, each filled with potting mix, in front of the trellis. Make sure they're evenly spaced, then plant out the sweet pea seedlings.

7 The completed bamboo trellis.

8 As the seedlings grow, feed them weekly with diluted liquid fertilizer. Pick lots of flowers once they start to bloom — the more you pick, the more they will flower.

7

8

PLANTING SEEDLINGS

1 For each seedling, dig a hole large enough to accommodate the roots.

2 To release the seedlings, gently squeeze the bottom of each cell in the punnet.

3 Plant a seedling in the hole and backfill.

4 Add some mulch around each plant.

5 Sprinkle snail bait.

6 Cyclamen seedlings in leaf litter.

Seedling care

Planting in autumn gives seedlings the maximum time in which to grow before flowering so that they develop into big, healthy plants during the cool weather. When growing annuals, remember to pinch prune them in their early stages. This simply means removing the first few centimetres of growth, which causes branching lower down. The overall effect is a bushier plant with more flower buds in the long term.

Some soils are low in nutrients and while this is acceptable for many annuals, which often flower better in poor soils, it is nevertheless advisable to ensure the soil is not too poor, otherwise the plants may well show deficiency symptoms such as yellowing or reddish foliage and stunted growth.

Before you sow or plant it is always a good idea to dig well-rotted manure or garden compost into the soil and then apply a complete fertilizer. This will ensure deficiencies don't affect your display. If you've been caught out, feed with a liquid fertilizer throughout the growing season, and then switch to a potassium-rich fertilizer when they start to bud. Your annuals will look great, and you won't have wasted all that money on seedlings!

Look for pests like aphids, although these hibernate for winter. But if any are seen spray plants with an insecticidal soap. To grow cinerarias in the conservatory for winter and spring flowering, watch out for leaf miner. This grub causes pale scribbly trails on the leaves. You will need to use a systemic insecticide to control this pest.

So you're not disappointed, remember to counteract snails — young seedlings are too delicious for these pests to resist.

slugs and snails

Slugs and snails can be quite a problem in wet autumn weather. New seedlings and the emerging shoots of spring-flowering bulbs are particularly vulnerable. Protect these new shoots with snail pellets, but if you're concerned for dogs or children hide these pellets in a piece of open pipe or inside an old broken terracotta pot. Snails love these places. Or try beer bait. Place some beer in a bottle and half-submerge it in the soil so that the snails can get inside, but can't escape.

The array of flower shapes, colours and styles in chrysanthemums is seemingly endless — from button size to blowzy, from subtle to show-off.

Perennials

Although it is a quiet season for flowers, there are some rich autumn-toned perennials that you can weave through your garden beds. Most popular of all are the chrysanthemums, with their array of scarlet, gold, bronze, dusky pink and white flowers.

Continue the warm colour theme with Michaelmas daisies and other kinds of aster, gaillardias, rudbeckias, helianthus and, for shaded parts of the garden, Japanese anemones. The flat-headed sedums are in full bloom in autumn including varieties of *Sedum spectabile* and *S. telephium*.

Chrysanthemums

Chrysanthemums are the very essence of autumn and no garden is complete without them. The Japanese improved them over thousands of years, and the chrysanthemum is their national flower as well as the flower of the Imperial Royal Family. These popular and showy perennials are still being hybridized and crossed, which makes it almost impossible to track down their origins.

Chrysanthemums are essentially plants for cool climates and as the days shorten they reach their peak of flowering. They prefer a rich, well-drained soil in full sun. Unlike dwarf varieties, taller varieties need staking. Colours include many shades of yellow, pink, red and amber, plus white.

Potted chrysanthemums are more compact than the old garden varieties, making them ideal for indoor display. These are sold all year round and are manipulated into flower by artificially lengthening the hours of darkness. The flowers last well and buds continue to open for several weeks.

Chrysanthemums can be grown from seed sown in spring or from soft basal cuttings. Feed with liquid fertilizer in autumn and remove excess buds for larger blooms.

Black aphids

Unfortunately chrysanthemums have more than their fair share of pests and diseases and you should watch out for aphids, earwigs, leaf miners, whitefly, grey mould (botrytis) and mildew, among others, and take remedial action as soon as noticed by spraying with an appropriate pesticide.

Above: A large-flowered hybrid.

Dahlias

The longest-flowering perennials for the warm season garden are those bright and blowzy dahlias, flowering from mid-summer right to the end of autumn. There are many different flower shapes and sizes — some are like cactus, others spidery, some with simple single petals. Some strike as cut blooms, others as bedding plants or foliage contrast.

Magnificent purple-foliage varieties are becoming popular and they are suitable for bedding as well as for borders. They include 'Redskin' which is seed raised and ideal for summer bedding; the old favourite 'Bishop of Llandaff' with single, brilliant red flowers; and 'Moonfire' whose single flowers are yellow with a red centre.

Growing tips

Dahlias can survive with little care, but respond to good cultivation, blooming over a long period. In late autumn, after the plants die down, cut off the stems 15 cm above ground level. Dig up clumps, remove surplus soil and store in a cool dry place in sawdust or bark chips.

Ideally, tubers should be planted in spring, about 7 cm deep and into enriched soil. If the site is windy, or a particular variety needs support, insert stakes now about 7 cm away from the tuber.

When the leader reaches about 50 cm, pinch out the central shoot to encourage side shoots. Fertilize as buds appear, and disbud if you want to encourage fewer but larger blooms.

Below: Double-flowered hybrids.

Tree dahlia This magnificent plant (*Dahlia imperialis*) towers over most perennials, easily reaching about 2 m. The large trusses of bell-like blooms (above) hang on throughout mid- and late autumn. Flowers may be lilac, yellow tipped with red, or white. Support your plants with sturdy stakes or grow them near a fence, as the hollow stems are quite brittle and don't stand up to windy weather very well. Pieces strike easily from 30 cm sections.

Did you know? Dahlias were originally imported into Europe as a food source because the tubers, like potatoes, are edible.

Perfect pastels

Mauve, soft blues, pale pinks and white are easy colours to use. This palette can be carried into autumn with well-known flowers such as asters, phlox and Japanese windflowers but some lesser-known additions will add great charm.

If you find gardening tricky, try obedient plant (*Physostegia*). It is easy to grow and tolerates dry conditions, but flowers better with moisture. The willow-like stems bear spikes of bell flowers.

Vanilla-scented heliotrope is a useful plant for summer and autumn bedding (it's not frost tolerant so winter in the conservatory in frost-prone climates). The flowers are used to scent herbal bouquets and potpourri. There are numerous varieties including 'Iowa' with dark purple blooms.

Plectranthus is a genus of plants often overlooked. From various subtropical areas, they are grown for their foliage or mauve-blue flowers in autumn. Some species have soft grey felted leaves, others have maroon undersides, and resemble fresh fern fronds. Plectranthus will not stand frost so in frost-prone climates use them for summer and autumn bedding, or in patio containers, and winter the plants under glass.

The medicinal echinacea or purple coneflower is native to the great prairies of North America and is said to increase the body's resistance to infection. Whether or not this is true, echinacea does flower into autumn with a display of handsome plum-coloured blooms that feature a black eye, very similar to those on rudbeckias.

Also used as a herbal remedy is the pincushion flower (*Scabiosa* sp.). Blooming from spring to autumn, the papery shells left by the flower heads are decorative in dried arrangements.

Pale colours look their best in the soft light of morning and evening.

Above: *Anemone hupehensis.*

Right: *A. x hybrida.*

Far right: *Stokesia laevis.*

Windflowers

One of the prettiest perennials in the autumn garden is the Japanese windflower, or *Anemone × hybrida*. It has dainty white or pink flowers, in double, semidouble and single forms, which are borne over many weeks. Their long stems make them ideal as a cut flower, and give rise to their common name 'windflower', because they gently wave in the breeze.

The foliage is present for most of the year, and forms a clump that spreads widely from fleshy rhizomes that are easily divided and propagated on. The leaves are broad and handsome, so the foliage is a feature in its own right.

The great thing about windflowers is their adaptability. Related to buttercups, and just as easily grown, they grow in full sun to semishade, and need little or no attention. Just dig in a little leaf mould and they're ready to go.

If you haven't tried them, you are missing out on one of the easiest and most rewarding of shade growers. They are invaluable in gardens, flowering from mid- to late summer and well into autumn, and they combine well with most other autumn-flowering perennials. They look great with ornamental grasses such as miscanthus.

The autumn asters

Many perennial daisies come into their best bloom in autumn. Asters or Michaelmas daisies are rewarding and easy to grow in a sunny position. They are simple to care for: the formula is to water in dry weather, stake tall flower stems, cut back the clump to the base after flowering and then finally divide in spring. Colours include shades of purple, blue, violet, red and pink, plus white. There are dwarf varieties which are suitable for the front of borders, and intermediate and tall varieties.

The early days of [autumn] bring with them the best bloom of the Michaelmas Daisies, the many beautiful garden kinds of the perennial Asters…and in glad spring-like profusion, when all else is on the verge of death and decay, gives an impression of satisfying refreshment that is hardly to be equalled throughout the year.

Gertrude Jekyll

peruvian **lily**

The Peruvian lily or alstroemeria, a tuberous perennial, is most often offered as Ligtu Hybrids. They flower in summer but other hybrids may continue till frosts in early autumn. For blooms next year plant in the autumn.

Vital statistics

Scientific name: *Alstroemeria* sp.

Family: Alstroemeriaceae.

Climate: Frost tolerant and suitable for temperate climates.

Culture: Clumps best left undisturbed for a few years.

Colours: Cream, yellow, orange, red and pink, with spots or streaks of contrasting colours.

Height: 30–75 cm tall.

Planting time: Autumn.

Soil: Very adaptable.

Position: Full sun to semishade.

Planting depth and spacing: Plant 20 cm deep, 30 cm apart.

Fertilizer: Don't overfertilize as it produces too many leaves at the expense of flowers. Slow-release granular fertilizer in spring is more than sufficient.

Pests/disease: Prone to slug damage.

Cutting: Lasts brilliantly as a cut flower, and even longer if stems are scalded before arranging.

Propagation: Seed or division in autumn.

If you love cornflowers you'll adore Stokes' aster, the summer version, which also flowers into autumn. Plants flower for months if deadheaded regularly, and last well in a vase. The flowers are lavender blue, white, rose pink and lilac.

Golden rod (solidago) has tiny daisy-like yellow flowers in flattened heads and grows easily in sun or part shade. Some species can be too vigorous so select specially bred garden types.

The blue daisy or blue marguerite (*Felicia amelloides*) produces daisy flowers, in various shades of blue, through summer and into autumn. It will not tolerate frost, so flowering stops only when frosts start. In frost-free gardens it continues flowering into winter. Hence in frost-prone climates it is often grown as an annual for summer and autumn bedding schemes. The blue daisy is also a good container plant and can be grown in patio tubs or hanging baskets. It likes a very sunny spot and well-drained, not too rich a soil and should be watered regularly in dry spells. Trim plants after the first flush of flowers. Propagate from stem-tip cuttings in late summer, and winter the young plants in a cool greenhouse.

Left: Snowflake bulb.

Below left: Snowflake (*Leucojum aestivum*).

Right: Beautiful white tulips add a dramatic touch to the garden.

Bulbs

Now that autumn is here it's time to think about planting spring-flowering bulbs. Lying within each inert-looking package is a little bit of sunshine, just waiting to burst into bloom.

Every bulb contains what is necessary for its journey to flowering, with food, protection and blossom wrapped up inside a rather dull-looking exterior.

Nature's hidden treasures

Most bulbs need a sunny well-drained spot to flower well. Some soil preparation helps bulbs settle in and flower for years. Before planting, add compost or soil conditioner to improve soil texture and drainage.

For extra colour in the ground, cover planted bulbs so that once the leaves have yellowed and died down, bare summer soil

There is an endearing self-sufficiency about bulbs. Each is a masterpiece of packaging, complete with food storage and protection for the next year's precious plant in miniature.

Jane Edmanson

is avoided. Plant hardy perennials such as catmint, which flowers during summer when most spring-flowering bulbs are over. Other spreading ground covers include varieties of dead nettle (*Lamium maculatum*) with pink or white flowers, and snow-in-summer (*Cerastium tomentosum*), which is good in hot, dry areas. Bugle

(*Ajuga* sp.) is better in moist, shaded areas planted over bluebells and grape hyacinths.

Picture drifts of bulbs in flower in your garden. If it sounds too expensive, try raising some from seed. Sow in pots as soon as ripe and plant out the bulbs when large enough, but you will have to wait for three to four years for most bulbs to flower.

Balcony and courtyard gardeners can plant bulbs in pots. Top off the display with spring-bedding plants such as polyanthus, coloured primroses, forget-me-nots, wallflowers, pansies and violas or double English daisies. Once the bulbs have finished flowering maintain watering and carry out liquid feeding until the leaves have died down. Then lift and store the bulbs. If you need the containers for summer-flowering plants, lift the bulbs before they have died down, heel them in on a spare piece of ground and again keep them watered and fed.

Left: Anemone bulbs.

Right: Dutch iris bulbs.

As bulbs can remain in the ground for many years, add some bulb food to the soil each year as the new shoots come through the soil.

Bulb tips

- Daffodils are probably the most popular bulbs, available now in pink, white and cream as well as yellow. Like all bulbs, they look best planted in informal clumps or drifts.
- Some bulbs have perfume. Jonquilla and Tazetta narcissus (daffodils) and hyacinths are particularly noted for their scent.
- Ranunculus grow from tiny tubers. One tiny ranunculus tuber can produce up to thirty blooms, ideal for cutting. Make sure you don't overwater as they are susceptible to rotting in wet soils.
- Daffodils no longer flowering? Divide them every three years or so by removing the offsets and replanting them separately into freshly dug over, improved soil.

- If lifting your bulbs and replanting them sounds daunting, select old-fashioned favourites that look after themselves. Plant them in bold drifts among plants such as shrubs, or plant them in grass. This technique is called naturalizing. Try crocuses, including autumn-flowering species such as colchicums and bluebells.
- While most bulbs like a full sun position, some tolerate more shade. If you have a shadier garden, plant bluebells, grape hyacinths, snowdrops, erythroniums and daffodils.
- Because bulbs have evolved to withstand cold winter temperatures, it's important to wait till the heat of summer has completely gone before planting. Early autumn is probably best, although tulips should be planted in late autumn once the soil temperature has dropped.
- The flowers of many bulbs, such as daffodils, tulips and lilies, are ideal for cutting and arranging indoors. However, remember to plant tall kinds rather than dwarf or miniature varieties for this purpose as they have much longer stems. They could be planted in rows in the vegetable garden specially for cutting.
- When growing bulbs in containers use a good-quality potting compost, ideally a well-drained, soil-based type. Place drainage material in the bottom of the container before adding compost.

Above: Seeds of some of the easier hardy bulbs, such as bluebells, can be sown direct in the soil where they are to grow (above left and right) but you will have greater control over them if they are sown in pots and the seedlings planted out when large enough.

Tiny tots Miniature varieties of spring-flowering bulbs are ideal for pots. There are many small varieties of daffodils, as well as species like *Narcissus bulbocodium* and *N. cyclamineus. Ipheion uniflorum* and varieties (shown) are also recommended.

Cool storage Tulips and hyacinths, like most other spring-flowering bulbs, should be stored cool and dry in the summer prior to planting in autumn. Tulips (left) are best planted late in the autumn. They like deep planting, to a depth of 10-15 cm. Hyacinths (right) are planted about 10 cm deep, ideally in the early weeks of autumn.

PLANTING BULBS IN THE GARDEN

1 Bring your bulbs out of cool storage, ready for planting.

2 Dig a hole for a bulb to up to three times the height of the bulb. Daffodils like deep planting and large bulbs could go into holes 15 cm in depth.

3 Place each bulb in its hole so that the growth point (the narrow end) faces upwards.

4 Once the bulb is in the hole, backfill with soil.

5 Insert a marker in the soil.

Plant a hyacinth bowl

Many bulbs look charming when used as a one-off indoor flowering display. Hyacinths, paper-white narcissus and colchicums are all ideal candidates because of their sturdy stems and delightful fragrances.

You can either plant bulbs in gravel and water (see instructions at right) or, if you prefer, plant bulbs into free-draining potting compost, then oversow with grass seed once you have brought them out into the light. The grass makes an attractive carpet by the time the bulbs come into flower.

Step 1

Fill a ceramic bowl with gravel and place the bulbs on the gravel.

Step 2

Fill the bowl with water just to the base of the bulbs. Keep the water level topped up to this point until the roots start to appear. This will take about two weeks.

Step 3

Freshen the water every week until the flowers finish, then throw the exhausted bulbs away.

bulb varieties

1 Grape hyacinth. 2 Ranunculus. 3 Cape cowslip (*Lachenalia aloides*). 4 *Gladiolus* x *colvillei* 'The Bride'.

5 Anemone. 6 Ixia. 7 Bluebell. 8 Freesia. 9 Dutch iris. 10 Watsonia. 11 Hyacinth. 12 Tulip. 13 Snowflake. 14 Daffodil.

ginger lily

Although they're commonly associated with the tropics because of their fragrant and showy flowers and lush foliage, ginger lilies are also tolerant of temperate climates. The most popular species is *Hedychium gardnerianum* (shown here), a species from the Himalayas which has perfumed pale yellow and red flowers from late summer into autumn.

Vital statistics

Scientific name: *Hedychium* sp.

Family: Zingiberaceae.

Climate: Frost free. Winter plants in a cool conservatory in frost-prone areas and place outdoors for the summer.

Plant/bulb type: Not a true bulb but grows from a thick, fleshy rhizome.

Colours: White or yellow.

Height: 2 m.

Planting time: Lift and divide clumps in spring.

Soil: Water-retaining and enriched with organic matter.

Position: Full sun or partial shade.

Planting depth and spacing: Plant rhizomes 10–15 cm deep and 23–30 cm apart.

Watering: Water regularly in spring, summer and autumn.

Fertilizer: Generally not needed.

Flowering: Late summer and autumn.

After-flowering care: Cut the whole plant to the ground once flowers finish. New stems will flower the next year.

Comments: In frosty climates grow it in a tub to make it easy to move under glass for the winter.

Flowering gingers

There are many other flowering gingers. Although not in the ginger family, the so-called blue ginger (*Dichorisandra thyrsiflora*) has deep violet flowers in autumn. But surely the most sensational of all is the torch ginger (*Etlingera elatior*) which has a stunning red bloom on top of a 1.5 m stem.

Other plants include the beehive ginger (*Zingiber spectabile*). The *Curcuma* species have stunning perfumed flowers that grow between large bracts. Best known is turmeric (*Curcuma domestica*). All make super indoor floral arrangements. The edible ginger is a *Zingiber* species (see 'Tropical herbs' in 'Summer'). All of these need a warm conservatory in frost-prone climates.

Bulbs that flower in autumn

If you enjoy your spring bulbs, why not think about mixing in some summer- and autumn-flowering bulbs like liliums, naked lady (amaryllis), mini hippeastrum, spider lily (*Nerine* sp.) and crocus.

Autumn crocuses

For a touch of spring in autumn, look no further than autumn crocuses. Not all are true crocuses, but there are several species of crocus that produce their blooms in the autumn, such as the saffron crocus (*Crocus sativus*), *C. speciosus* and *C. nudiflorus*. The first is the world's most expensive spice.

Colchicums are also called autumn crocuses and indeed they do have crocus-like flowers. Another popular name is naked ladies. The best known species is the pink-flowered *Colchicum autumnale* or meadow saffron. With all colchicums, the flowers emerge before leaves. Popular with fully double pink flowers is *C.* 'Waterlily'.

Sternbergias have yellow crocus-like flowers in autumn, *S. lutea* being the best-known. Plant them in natural drifts in a warm, well-drained position and leave undisturbed to grow into large clumps.

The flower of zephyranthes, rain flowers or zephyr flowers, are somewhat crocus like and appear in summer and early autumn. Best-known is *Zephyranthes candida* with white flowers, produced after rain in the wild.

All of these bulbs are hardy and suitable for temperate climates.

Hippeastrum

The huge flowers make the hippeastrum a sensational potted houseplant. Plant the bulb while dormant in autumn. It will bloom in winter. Liquid feed every two weeks when bulbs are growing.

Create an autumn display with bulbs. Clockwise from above left: rain or zephyr flower, *Amaryllis belladonna*, nerine and *Sternbergia lutea*.

PLANTING A HIPPEASTRUM
Keep the neck of the bulb (about a quarter) above the soil level. Plant into good quality, free-draining mix. Water once, then not again until buds appear, then weekly. It should flower annually if you cut the flower stalks close to the point of origin after fading.

autumn
grasses, ground covers & climbers

Autumn is a good time to repair elements that have become neglected or worn. The weather is fine generally, although cold nights mean that plant growth has slowed to a 'catch-up' pace. The seasonal slow-down affects the whole garden.

Grasses

The seasonal slow-down can also mean a lack of colour, with the lawn's lush green fading and demanding extra care.

Now is a great time to feed your lawn, using an autumn lawn fertilizer, to encourage a strong, healthy grass cover for the next six months. A vigorous lawn will be weed and drought resistant with a deeper root system and more coverage. Autumn is the right time to fix problems so weeds don't take a hold over winter.

Try this method. Thoroughly water the lawn, apply an autumn lawn food, then water again. Avoid using sulphate of ammonia as it really only softens the grass and turns it green temporarily. Balanced lawn fertilizers will encourage a strong root

Below left: A vigorous and luscious winter lawn requires work in autumn.
Below right: After raking, apply an autumn lawn fertilizer according to the maker's instructions.

OVERSOWING LAWN SEED

1 Using either existing soil or some topsoil, rake up a fine tilth.

2 Sow bare patches of turf with lawn seed. Here a spreader is used to distribute seeds evenly. You can mix together the lawn seed and starter fertilizer and apply them at the same time.

3 Tamp down with a rake.

4 Water in.

system, more stems and lots more leaves. Thick, healthy grass leaves no room for weeds. Light fertilizing in autumn encourages thick growth before winter, but don't overdo it, or the residue will wash into our waterways.

Dethatch your lawn by raking vigorously with a steel-tined rake to remove old leaves. Even better would be a special spring-tine lawn rake.

If your lawn has become uneven and worn in patches you can sow grass seed now in warm areas. Choose a seed mixture to match the existing grass in your lawn. For example, if it is a perennial ryegrass lawn, then use a mix consisting mainly of

this particular grass. The seeds will germinate rapidly and fill in the bare patches, keeping your lawn looking green and lush throughout winter.

After a full season's growth, you may find that your lawn has developed a thick thatch. To deal with a thatch build-up, scarify your lawn, which simply means raking the lawn with a steel-tined rake. When combined with an autumn feed, scarifying will rejuvenate your lawn and green it up in time for the winter chill. Scarifying should be carried out before applying fertilizer.

Scarifying or dethatching removes the mat of old leaves and decaying plant matter. If you neglect to do this, the thatch can form a waterproof barrier and stop added nutrients and rain penetrating to the roots where they are needed. Removing this layer will help activate a new flush of growth.

Dandelion, with globe of down,
The schoolboy's clock in every town...

AERATING THE LAWN

An effective way to rejuvenate your lawn is to improve the drainage. For a small garden, use a garden fork or, for larger areas, either strap on a pair of aerating shoes and walk all over the lawn or use a roller with tines.

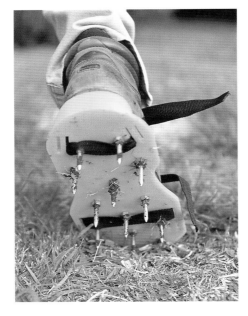

Longer grass When the lawn is left just that little bit longer, the roots go deeper and the grass develops a stronger, thicker cover. Your children and the pets will love its softer, friendlier surface. Longer grass is more drought resistant and more resilient to wear, and weeds don't get a foothold in the thick luxuriant lawn. Don't ever cut more than one third of the blade of grass at one time, or your grass will suffer stress.

Aerating

Improving drainage always helps your lawn to stay healthy. Grass roots need air. Your turf will start to suffer if air can't work its way down into the soil. The two main ways of achieving this are through scarifying with a rake to remove any thatch (see the previous page), and also aerating, where spikes penetrate this layer with tiny holes and allow air to travel downwards. You can either leave the hole open or top-dress with a free-draining mixture, such as coarse river sand.

To aerate your lawn, simply push an ordinary garden fork about 5–8 cm into the turf and lever it backwards slightly. Do this about ten times a square metre. For larger areas it is more efficient to use specialized equipment, such as hollow-tined forks and tined rollers, which you can purchase or hire from most equipment centres, hardware stores and nurseries. Alternatively, put on some aerating shoes (they look like strap-on thongs with spikes) and walk all over the grass.

Aerating your lawn is of particular benefit to heavy soils with a high clay content, as these tend to compact easily with traffic. Aerating the lawn under trees is also important as they can suffer if the ground is compacted. Like grass, trees also need a good supply of air and efficient moisture penetration. Aerate the lawn under trees in the ways described earlier.

Liming and feeding the lawn

All plants need feeding and watering, but grass seems to be greedier and needs more regular attention. Mowing removes nutrients in the growing tips, which means that you have to return these on a regular basis in spring, summer and autumn by applying an appropriate lawn fertilizer.

You should vary the amount of nitrogen in feeds, according to the time of year. Late summer and autumn feeds should contain less nitrogen than spring feeds. A slower-acting fertilizer that contains a lower proportion of nitrogen and higher ones of both phosphate and potassium will help promote strong root growth and repair through autumn.

Very occasionally it may be necessary to apply lime to a lawn, but having said that, bear in mind that liming is rarely needed and applying it too often can cause the lawn to deteriorate and the fine grasses to die out. Lawn grasses grow best in moderately acid to neutral soil. If you know there is a serious shortage of lime, indicated by sparse grass, an over-abundance of moss and the prolific growth of acid-loving weeds such as woodrush, carry out a soil pH test using a simple test kit. If the pH is below 5.5 (indicating very acid soil) you can give one light application of lime in autumn. Apply ground limestone at 56 g per square metre (do not use any other form of lime).

LIMING THE LAWN

Use a pH test kit to check the acidity of the soil, or observe signs of acidity in your garden such as blue hydrangea. If your soil is very acid, apply ground limestone at 56 g per square metre. Water it in thoroughly as soon as it is applied.

Raising the level of your garden bed with brick, stone or timber retainers not only defines the edge but can also improve drainage.

Get the edge

Is grass getting into your garden beds? This happens often, especially if the grasses are vigorous and spread rapidly by means of stolons. This is more common with warm-season grasses than with cool-season types.

However, there are ways to prevent this happening. Solid garden edging which is concreted below the surface provides a physical barrier and prevents stolons from growing into beds and borders.

Putting in an edging may also provide a means of raising beds and borders to improve drainage. This is useful if you have a heavy clay soil which remains very wet in winter. Many plants overwinter better if the soil is well drained, particularly the many Mediterranean, grey-leaved and similar plants that are now being grown more and more in our gardens.

All kinds of solid materials can be used to provide an edging to beds and borders. However, it is sensible to choose something that suits the style of your garden. For example, in a country garden some kind of rustic or natural edging would be a good choice, while in a contemporary city garden a more modern material providing a 'clean' line might be more appropriate.

When adding edging, consider maintenance and accessibility. Although a rock edge may look natural, remember that grass runners may work through non-mortared joints and necessitate hand clipping when you mow. Choose an edge that can be trimmed with a grass trimmer, run over with an edger, or mown easily.

Edging helps separate sections of the garden. It keeps lawn out of garden beds and accentuates the beds. The range of styles is growing constantly. Timber strips of ply are traditionally used but plastic edging, which can be sunk into the ground with the

TRIMMING GRASS EDGES

1 Trim grass edges with a sharp spade.

2 Make sure you remove runners, both surface and underground.

top edge flush with turf, is also available now (see picture, top right). Both are great as mowing strips, and don't draw attention away from the bed. More decorative edging, such as Victorian terracotta tiles, bricks, stone, pavers, logs and concrete sections can be used above ground to both form a barrier and add ornamentation. A sharp, clean cut through lawn areas with a spade can also look effective as a free, although shorter-lived, edging option.

check list

jobs to do now

- Autumn feeding will rejuvenate your lawn and green it up in time for the winter chill. Edge your lawn and define garden beds.

- Check for the presence of any fly or beetle grubs or larvae in the lawn which feed on grass roots. Dead patches are signs of an attack.

- Cut flower heads from ornamental grasses if self-seeding is a problem.

- Deadhead ground-cover plants like gazanias for more flowers.

- Divide and replant perennial ground covers if necessary when they become dormant.

- Trim climbers, such as jasmine and potato vine, which can run wild.

plant now

- Sow grass seed in any bare patches in the lawn.

- Plant ground covers such as ajuga, nepeta, stachys and santolina.

- Choose deciduous vines when in leaf colour.

flowering now

- Many grasses, such as fountain grass and the stately miscanthus species and varieties and pampas grass

- Ground covers such as ivy-leaved pelargoniums used for temporary display, and some campanula species like *C. poscharskyana*

- Climbing plants for the conservatory such as allamanda, Rangoon creeper, Azores jasmine, coral vine (antigonon), Chilean jasmine (mandevilla), glory bower or bleeding heart

PLANTING A NEW GARDEN BED

1 Arrange a length of rope or hose until you're satisfied with the shape of the bed, then sprinkle sand over the hose to mark the edges.

2 Or mark the new garden bed with turf paint. Then use a spade to dig an edge.

3 Position the plants.

4 Dig a hole for each plant.

5 Water the hole.

6 Sprinkle fertilizer in the hole.

7 Plant, backfill and water.

Reshaping your lawn

Autumn is a good time of year to think about lawn edging. Perhaps your garden beds need reshaping because there are areas where grass is no longer thriving, or perhaps shrubs have outgrown their bed and need more room.

If you need to reshape your lawn, do it now so it grows back before winter. Experiment with new shapes with a hose or length of rope, a sprinkle of sand, or turf spray paint.

Once you've settled on a new shape, create a well-defined edge with a sharp spade. If you need to remove large areas of turf, consider hiring a turf cutter.

A word of warning, however. Although replacing or installing edging is a suitable garden job for the cooler weather, be careful not to do this after long periods of rain: the ground may have become soggy and the edging may shift as it dries out. In addition, turf will not tolerate wear and tear well when it is very wet.

fountain **grass**

Many ornamental grasses look their best in late summer and autumn when most other perennials have started to lose their appeal. Fountain grass has wonderful plume-like flowers at this time and some species have the added advantage of attractive evergreen foliage. There are various species: the tallest is the Australian fountain grass (*Pennisetum alopecuroides*) with its silvery brown panicles, and the shortest is oriental fountain grass (*P. orientale*), similar to the Australian species although the flowers are purplish and bloom earlier. The crimson fountain grass (*P. setaceum*) has slightly pink flowers but can become a weed in mild climates. All are great in perennial borders as soft, swaying accent plants, and they last well as cut flowers.

Vital statistics

Scientific name: *Pennisetum* sp.
Family: Poaceae.
Climate: Almost anywhere except the very coldest areas.
Culture: Divide the clump every 5–6 years to encourage flowering.
Colours: Silvery brown to purple-pinks.
Height: 60 cm to 1.2 m.
Planting time: Any.
Soil: Any.
Position: Full sun.
Planting spacing: 50 cm apart.
Fertiliser: Not needed.
Pests/diseases: None specific.
Cutting: If desired, cut back to 15 cm above base when leaves look tatty. Remove flowers if using any self-seeding types in your garden.
Propagation: Seed or division.

Above (left to right): Some representatives of the great range of sedum plants — rosette type (*Sedum adolphii*), jellybean type (*S. rubrotinctum*) and horsetail type (*S. morganianum*). These are hardy, except for *S. morganianum* which should be grown in a cool conservatory. It makes a particularly good hanging-basket plant.

Ground covers

Good ground cover plants should have value and interest as ornamentals throughout the year, not just be a means of smothering weeds and covering bare soil.

Coloured leaves, such as those of silver ground-hugging forms of artemisia and snow-in-summer, provide the perfect foil for larger background plantings and flowers.

Autumn-flowering ground covers are also very useful. These include temporary plants for summer and autumn display, such as ivy-leaved pelargoniums, fanflowers and gazanias, all of which will be stopped by frosts. Hardy perennial ground covers for summer and autumn flowering include some campanula species such as *C. poscharskyana* and certain geraniums.

Succulents

Many succulents grow effectively as ground covers. The variety of foliage colour and their adaptability makes them ideal for a wide range of positions and their dramatic forms make them ideal as potted plants.

Sensational sedum

Known as 'stonecrop', this diverse group of plants varies in appearance and form, from that of jellybeans to rosettes and upright growers that fit perfectly into a perennial flower garden.

Cutting bunches of *Sedum* 'Autumn Joy'.

Here a variety of stonecrops has been planted into an old clamshell. Drainage is adequate because of the shallowness of the container and its sinuous sides. The shell accentuates the 'seascape' feel of the different forms and textures of this succulent.

As with most succulents, you can grow sedum virtually anywhere that drains freely. Pots, edging, rockeries, or tucked into notches between rocks are ideal spots. However, make sure you use only the hardy species in the garden.

Some good hardy ground-cover sedums include S. adolphii which has attractive yellowish green leaves with red-flushed edges. S. rubrotinctum also has red-flushed leaves which make very attractive ground cover. Probably the best-known species for ground cover is S. spathulifolium which has a very vigorous, spreading habit. The leaves are usually silvery in colour and flushed with purple. There are several varieties with even more attractive foliage including 'Cape Blanco' whose leaves are covered in white powder, and 'Purpureum' with grey leaves that are heavily flushed with rich purple.

Taller sedums are the autumn-flowering S. spectabile and its varieties, with flat heads of flowers, and the similar 'Autumn Joy'.

These are excellent plants for the front of borders and although tallish they still make quite good ground cover with their large, succulent leaves.

Propagating succulents

When potting or planting succulents such as sedums you will find that no matter how careful you are, leaves will break off from the mother plant. Don't throw them out. Many succulents readily propagate themselves from these leaf cuttings. Simply let them dry out for a week or so, during which time the wound will callus over, preventing the cuttings from rotting off. Then plant these shallowly into 100 mm tubes. The new plants will grow from the calluses, supporting themselves on the stored energy inside the discarded fleshy leaves. Once they are well rooted and of adequate size they can either be potted for the conservatory, planted out in the garden or given away to friends.

PROPAGATING SEDUM

1 Propagating sedum from leaf cuttings.

2 A new rosette forming from a leaf cutting of *Sedum* sp.

fan**flower**

The fanflower is a wonderfully adaptable Australian ground cover which has undergone some clever plant breeding lately. Now the larger flowers come in many colours and are as showy as ivy-leaved pelargoniums.

Vital statistics

Scientific name: *Scaevola aemula*.
Family: Goodeniaceae.
Climate: Frost free. Grow outdoors for summer and autumn display only in frost-prone climates.
Culture: They make a great basket specimen, pot plant or spillover.
Colours: Colours include mauve, blue and white. Some good varieties include 'Blue Wonder' and 'Purple Fanfare'.
Height: 50 cm.
Planting time: Spring, when frosts are over.
Soil: Any.
Position: Sun or partial shade.
Planting spacing: 50 cm apart.
Fertilizer: Not needed.
Pests/diseases: None specific.
Cutting: Trim back old flowers when they look tatty.
Propagation: Seed or softwood cuttings.

What is a ground cover?

A ground cover is defined as a plant that quickly smothers weeds and covers bare earth, usually requiring little maintenance, especially when planted on sloping sites.

Ideal ground covers are plants that divide and propagate themselves by clumping, carpeting (using runners or spreading with underground stolons or rhizomes), or simply by sprawling or creeping low to the ground over a good distance. These characteristics help them bind the soil, combat erosion and reduce the amount of space available to those opportunistic weeds.

Autumn division

Autumn is a good time of the year for propagating many ground covers by division. This can be done in one of the following three ways:

1 Simply pull off a rooted portion of a plant and replant it where required.
2 With a spade or knife cut large chunks from a large established plant.
3 With herbaceous perennial clumps that often die in the centre and need breaking up to refresh them, insert two forks back to back in the centre of the clump and use them to lever it into smaller pieces that can then be broken up and planted.

Climbers

A pergola makes an ideal support for climbing plants. In hot weather it can also provide you with welcome shade once it is well clothed with foliage. A pergola can also help to create an outdoor room, especially when it is positioned over or partly over a patio.

The ornamental vine *Vitis coignetiae* is one of the best for autumn leaf colour. It is vigorous and can attain 15 m in height.

This outdoor room adds an extra dimension to your lifestyle. A deciduous vine trained over the pergola is often the best choice for a living screen because it loses its leaves in winter to admit the sunshine and has the added bonus of autumn colour and edible or ornamental fruits.

Choice climbers

Probably the best climber for a pergola is wisteria. In spring its sweetly scented flowers hang in huge panicles which provide decoration and shade. A word of warning though. Wisteria can be an extremely strong and vigorous climber, so make sure the support is stable, or plant it on its own post and allow it to fall over your pergola. (For a feature on wisteria, see 'Spring' on page 72.)

Another great choice is the grapevine (*Vitis vinifera*), either an ornamental or a fruiting variety, one of the showiest deciduous vines, whose leaves take on autumnal tints before they fall. Be wary of creepers such as common ivy and Virginia creeper that adhere to your walls like glue and need a blow torch to be dislodged. Only use them on stable surfaces where their roots can't damage mortar joints and where you won't need to paint.

Screening for privacy is an important priority for urban living. Evergreen twiners

Above: Ornamental grape-vine under deciduous trees.

Above right: Blue butterfly bush gets its name from its butterfly-shaped flowers.

Below: Bleeding heart or glory bower.

are useful for decorating lattice panels, wire and boundary paling fences. For a quick effect the Chilean potato tree, *Solanum cristum* 'Glasnevin', is great, but it can easily outgrow its allotted space unless you cut it back in early spring each year. The purplish blue flowers of this frost-hardy climber are produced in summer and autumn.

There are numerous climbers that provide colour in the intermediate to warm conservatory. Try the Rangoon creeper (*Quisqualis indica*). The scented flowers look like pink shooting stars and have a delicious perfume that lies heavy in the air during evening and early morning. Many of the tropical climbers, such as mandevilla and allamanda, flower well into autumn.

Bougainvillea provides great colour too, having its final flowering flush before the onset of winter, but it can be too vigorous for some conservatories. In this case why not try growing it as a standard, like a small tree, in a pot or tub?

Bleeding hearts

Native mainly to the tropics and subtropics, the genus *Clerodendrum* contains about 400 species of trees, shrubs and climbers,

known by various names such as glory bower, pagoda flower, butterfly bush and bleeding heart.

Bleeding heart or glory bower (*Clerodendrum thomsoniae*) is so named because of the unusual appearance of the flower. The large, showy white calyx has a crimson corolla shooting out from its centre, almost like a drop of blood. There is a hybrid (*C. thomsoniae* × *splendens*) which has a dull red calyx, and another species which produces intense scarlet flowers (*C. splendens*).

Other charming clerodendrums include the blue butterfly bush or blue glory bower (*C. ugandense*) (see the 'Shrubs' section) and the pagoda flower (*C. paniculatum*) which is a loose, trailing shrub to 1.5 m with similar flowers to its namesake.

In the conservatory clerodendrums can be grown in large pots or tubs of well-drained, soil-based potting compost, or in a soil bed or border. They need maximum light but shade from strong sun. Provide airy conditions in summer. When the plants are growing water well and liquid feed every three to four weeks. Reduce watering considerably in winter.

chilean bellflower

Named after a great patron of gardening, the Empress Josephine of France (née Tascher de la Pagerie), the bellflower is the national flower of Chile, where it grows in the mountains' forests. The silken sheen on the crimson-flowering bells makes this one of the most attractive temperate climate creepers. The Chilean bellflower can be grown in a cool conservatory in frost-prone climates or outdoors in very mild areas.

Vital statistics

Scientific name: *Lapageria rosea*.
Family: Philesiaceae.
Climate: Mild, frost free, but will tolerate a slight frost.
Culture: Can be grown in a large container.
Colours: Red, pink or white.
Height: 5 m.
Planting time: Autumn or early spring.
Soil: Lime free.
Position: Dappled shade outdoors; shade from sun under glass.
Planting spacing: 1 m.
Fertilizer: Mulch outdoors; feed under glass in summer.
Pests/diseases: It dislikes sun on its leaves and is fussy about position.
Pruning: May trim after flowering but best not pruned.

Other Chilean beauties

Another stunning plant, also native to Chile, is the sacred flower of the Incas (*Cantua buxifolia*).

This semi-climbing shrub flowers profusely in spring. It has trumpet-shaped blooms, the long tube being pink or purple and the lobes red. Although it will not tolerate frost it is ideal for the cool conservatory. Grow it in a tub of soil-based potting compost.

The Chilean jasmine, *Mandevilla laxa*, actually comes from Argentina and Bolivia, and needs the same conditions as cantua.

Mandevilla laxa has clusters of deliciously scented white trumpet flowers in summer and autumn. It is quite vigorous in habit and will twine to a height of around 3–5 m, but it can be pruned in early spring to keep it within bounds by cutting back the side shoots to three or four buds of the main framework stems.

autumn
shrubs & trees

Autumn can be a particularly colourful time if you plan it well. Many plants are still flowering, while others produce displays of a different nature. Berrying plants are extremely ornamental features throughout autumn and the range of colours is also a seasonal delight.

For many gardeners, a falling maple leaf captures the essence of autumn.

Shrubs

Various shrubs will still be flowering in autumn, including fuchsias, deciduous ceanothus, ceratostigmas, heathers (calluna), hibiscus and potentillas. Many roses will produce a further flush of blooms. Some shrubs start flowering in autumn including *Camellia sasanqua*. Like all camellias, it can only be grown in acid or lime-free soil, but will also make an excellent patio tub plant.

In the intermediate or warm conservatory the tropical hibiscus continue to produce flowers, as do other shrubs such as ixora and tibouchinas.

Plumbago or Cape leadwort will still be flowering prolifically in autumn. This shrub will not stand frost, but it makes an excellent tub plant for the cool conservatory and can be moved onto the patio for the summer. Gardeners in frost-free climates can use it as cover on banks, to screen a wall or fence or as a hedge. Easily grown in virtually any soil, it tolerates drought. Under glass grow in soil-based potting compost and provide light, airy conditions.

Many deciduous trees and shrubs produce autumn colour, the leaves taking

on brilliant, fiery tints before they fall. Others also produce colourful fruits and berries, which often persist into winter. Every garden should have at least a few such plants to reflect this season. But you need to choose carefully, for some plants produce better autumn colour than others.

However, much of the autumn garden's beauty does lie beyond flowers. Foliage,

fabulous coloured leaves all year, and these can work particularly well in a shrub border that contains autumn-turning leaves of berberis, smoke bush and viburnum. Even evergreens can colour at certain times of the year. Mahonias display a range of tints in late autumn and early winter, and bergenia and heuchera can colour brilliantly as the weather cools.

The warm tones of autumn leaves can be mimicked in the conservatory by the orange or red flowers of *Ixora coccinia* (left). *Abelia* x *grandiflora* (centre). Many roses (right) have a lovely flush of blooms in the autumn.

Season of mists and mellow fruitfulness,
Close bosom-friend of the maturing sun;
Conspiring with him how to load and bless
With fruit the vines that round the thatch-eaves run;...

John Keats

both deciduous and evergreen, can be a highlight in its own right or act in a 'supporting role' to the flowers in season.

Many shrubs — such as the purple tones of cannas, flax and coleus (see 'Foliage plants' in 'Winter') — have

Seeds and berries too are quite often a splendid feature of this season, adding colour and, sometimes, interesting shapes. Just as flowers are the beginning of the cycle of growth, berries signal its fruition and symbolize completeness and wholeness.

A glimpse of oak leaves in autumn colour.

Fabulous fuchsias

In the botanical world, fuchsias lend a touch of whimsy: they dance from bending boughs like ballerinas in tutus, making them a charming plant for any shaded spot.

Fuchsias were 'discovered' by Europeans in South America during the late fifteenth century and named for Dr Fuchs. They found their way to the northern hemisphere during the great plant-trading era of the late eighteenth century.

Their popularity has waxed and waned over the years, but now fuchsias are a mainstay of the hanging basket and conservatory growing cultures throughout the world.

There are more than 8000 varieties of fuchsia, so it pays to narrow your choice down to the less troublesome. They flower continuously in summer and well into autumn.

Growing conditions

Fuchsias need a protected spot in a reasonably shaded area that receives enough light that you can take a photograph without using a flash. Plants in baskets are liable to dry out rapidly and be damaged by strong winds, so place them in a position where they can be watered easily.

Problem areas

Although fuchsias can tolerate temperatures up to 40°C, a reduction in night-time temperature is crucial for their survival. Most fuchsias are frost tender so in frost-prone areas these should be wintered in a cool greenhouse and used outdoors for summer and autumn display. Some are hardy enough to be grown as permanent garden plants in the milder areas.

Pruning

In early spring prune back hard to a permanent framework of woody stems, or cut back to base if stems have been killed by frost. Remove dead flowers regularly.

Feeding and watering

In the growing period, feed fuchsias with liquid fertilizer fortnightly after watering. Water a potted fuchsia by immersing it in a bucket of water. Air bubbles will rise when the soil is thoroughly watered and the plant is ready to be removed for draining.

Fuchsia types

Basket fuchsias

To fully appreciate the basket varieties' cascading habit of growth and exquisite blooms, hang these at eye level. Basket fuchsias tend to be easy varieties and there are a great number available. Buy whatever is available from your local garden centre.

Small shrubs

Smaller upright growers are excellent as border or bedding plants. Grow them in a row to create a dramatic display, or dot them about the garden in groups of three. Also known as bush fuchsias, there are countless varieties, mostly frost tender but a few will tolerate moderate frosts.

Tall shrubs

The taller rambling varieties are the tough stalwarts of old gardens. They will trail over garden walls, grow against a wall and thread their way through latticework. *Fuchsia magellanica* is well known together with its variety *gracilis*. *F.* 'Riccartonii' is a large shrub. Both are hardy.

Standards

Growing fuchsias as standards is a lovely way to set off their 'teardrop' blooms. 'Peppermint Stick', 'Harbour Bridge', 'Voodoo' and 'Swingtime' all make successful standards. To grow a fuchsia as a standard, choose a young plant and tie in the main or leading shoot to a cane as it grows, and at the same time remove any side shoots but retain the leaves on the stem. When the stem reaches the desired height, say 90–120 cm, pinch out the tip. This will encourage branches to grow at the top and will present a cascading effect. For step-by-step instructions, see 'Plant training' in 'Summer'.

There are thousands of hybrid fuchsias, some old, some new. They may have fully double flowers or single blooms, some large and blowsy, others small and petite, but all more or less bell shaped. There are varieties suitable for pots, hanging baskets and garden display.

check list

jobs to do now

- Give mature hedges a final trim of the year, particularly evergreen hedges.

- Deadhead all plants that have just finished a flush of flowers. Sometimes this encourages more flowers to follow.

- Top up mulches around shrubs and trees, using leaf mould or chipped bark.

- As many plants are now starting to become dormant for the winter, feeding should cease in the autumn, apart from any plants that are coming into flower under glass. Fertilizer applied at this time of year will not be used by most plants.

- Start thinking about transplanting and remodelling your established shrubs. Autumn is a great time for moving plants about, as the air temperatures have cooled sufficiently to ease the 'sunburn' but the soil temperatures still encourage root growth.

- Potentillas that have finished flowering can have a light trim.

- Prune any diseased or twiggy growth from abelia, hydrangea, buddleja, hypericum and any other summer-flowering shrubs.

- Buddleja or butterfly bush looks beautiful at this time of year. Take time to smell the flowers. They attract butterflies and come in lots of colours – pink, white, purple, near black, yellow and white. Water buddlejas when in flower to help make the flowers last.

plant now

- Plant camellias, deciduous plants and transplanted specimens.

- You'll start to see roses appear in nurseries, so order some from your local garden centre. At this time of year you can order roses that are bare rooted, or wrapped in bags. It is not essential to buy roses like this (potted roses can be bought at any time) but it does give them an excellent start, and is much cheaper.

- Autumn is the best time of year for planting deciduous and evergreen trees and shrubs.

flowering now

- Shrubs such as fuchsias, *Camellia sasanqua*, oleanders, buddlejas, hibiscus, bouvardia, osmanthus (some species), justicia, ceratostigma, ixora, plumbago, roses, caryopteris, ceanothus (some species), tamarix (some species), hebes, potentillas, hydrangeas (some species), tibouchina, correas and croweas

Conservatory shrubs

Numerous shrubs from the Southern Hemisphere are becoming popular conservatory plants with gardeners in frosty climates. One such genus is *Correa*, popularly known as Australian fuchsia. These small evergreen shrubs have a long flowering period, generally starting in autumn and going on through winter. The pendulous blooms are tubular or bell shaped and come in red, pink or white. Grow in a cool conservatory in pots or tubs of lime-free potting compost. Provide good light and airy conditions. Be sparing with water in winter. Trim lightly after flowering. Watch out for scale insects.

Croweas are also small evergreen shrubs and have star-shaped pink or white flowers over a very long period, generally starting in spring or summer and going on through autumn. Grow in a cool conservatory as for correas but in pots of soil-based potting compost. Trim back all old flowered stems immediately after flowering. Again scale insects may be a problem.

Above: The pretty flowers of *Crowea saligna*.

buddlejas

Buddlejas have spikes of fragrant flowers laden with nectar that attracts butterflies and bees. They flower mainly in summer but some continue into autumn, particularly varieties of *B. davidii*, the most popular.

Vital statistics

Scientific name: *Buddleia* sp.

Family: Buddlejaceae.

Climate: Cool and cold climates are suitable for many species including *B. davidii*.

Culture: Many species are short lived, but their rapid growth makes them perfect for new gardens or as instant filler shrubs.

Colours: White, mauve, rose, dark blue to purple-black.

Height: Most species reach around 3 m in a few years, but can grow taller with age.

Planting time: Autumn and spring.

Soil: Will grow in any soil.

Position: Prefer a sunny position.

Planting spacing: 2 m.

Fertilizer: Flourish with extra manure.

Pests/diseases: None usually.

Cutting: In early spring prune back last year's growth to within a few buds of a permanent low, woody framework.

Propagation: Hardwood cuttings in winter.

Banksias

Banksias are also native to the Southern Hemisphere and are gradually becoming better known with gardeners in northern climes. They are evergreen shrubs and trees in the protea family and in frost-prone climates need to be grown in a cool conservatory. Many species are flowering in autumn and all are notable for their large, cone-shaped flower heads which last for a long period. Their pinnate foliage is also an attractive feature.

Grow banksias in light, airy conditions in pots of acid soil-based potting compost with extra grit and peat added. Feed in summer with a liquid fertilizer that does not contain phosphorus. Be very sparing with water in winter. Quite a few species are available, but you have to search for them, and perhaps the best known is *Banksia integrifolia*, the coast banksia, with light yellow 'cones' in late summer and autumn. *B. ericifolia* (shown here) is also available.

Above: A tibouchina species in all its glory.

Glory bushes

Commonly called glory bush, tibouchinas are spectacular shrubs for the cool to intermediate conservatory, producing their five-petalled flowers, mainly in rich purple, in summer and autumn.

Glory bush originally came from Brazil where they grow in semi-rainforest conditions with regular rainfall and warm weather. Grow them in good light but shade from strong sun to prevent scorching of the foliage. They make good container plants and should be grown in soil-based potting compost.

The late Australian plant breeder Ken Dunstan made great progress with the development of these plants. A visit to the northern rivers region of New South Wales will reveal the impact of his work. In Alstonville, streets lined with tibouchinas have given rise to the Tibouchina Festival. The cultivar 'Alstonville' was named after the town. Other famous hybrids — 'Jules', 'Noelene' and 'Kathleen' — he named after members of his family.

These new cultivars are a huge improvement on the old-fashioned tibouchinas. They have large panicles of flowers, varying in shades from purple and pink to white and magenta, often almost concealing the foliage with their abundance.

Unfortunately most varieties raised in the Southern Hemisphere have not yet arrived in the Northern Hemisphere, but no doubt with time we shall see more of them. *Tibouchina* 'Jules' is certainly available though, and is worth looking out for. It is a dwarf variety and grows to only about 1 m tall. In the meantime, northern gardeners will have to be content with the species *T. urvilleana* with its sumptuous red-purple flowers. It has several varieties including 'Edwardsii' and one with variegated leaves.

Tibouchinas will need pruning to restrict their size under glass, unless you are

Spanish shawl
(*Heterocentron elegans*)

The magenta flowers of Spanish shawl are reminiscent of tibouchina. It is a frost-tender carpeting evergreen sub-shrub for the cool to intermediate conservatory and looks pretty in hanging baskets.

growing a dwarf variety. This is best done in
late winter by cutting back last year's shoots
by about one-third to half their length.

Prune lightly after flowering and you'll
keep them looking thick and bushy.

A fragrant few

For those who appreciate perfume, three of
the best flower in autumn. Bouvardia,
luculia and osmanthus are essential shrubs
for the conservatory. Bouvardias have a
reputation for being perfumed but only one
species — *B. longiflora* — actually is. This
has beautiful white star-shaped flowers.

In frost-prone climates bouvardias are
ideal shrubs for the cool conservatory. Grow
them in large pots or tubs of soil-based
potting compost. Provide shade from hot
sun. Water the plants well in summer and
give them a liquid feed every three to four
weeks. Be sparing with water in winter.

Bouvardias need trimming as soon as
flowering is over to keep them neat and
compact. They will look untidy unless
regularly trimmed each year. Cut back the
flowered shoots close to the older woody
stems, to within about 2.5 cm.

Another heavily perfumed shrub is
Luculia gratissima. Grow in a cool to
intermediate conservatory if you live in a
frosty climate. It will thrive in a tub of soil-
based potting compost if given good light
and, in summer, a humid atmosphere.
Water well in summer but keep only
barely moist in winter. Prune back lightly
after flowering.

The half-hardy *Osmanthus fragrans* will
scent out the cool conservatory. To be frank,
the flowers on sweet olive, as this plant is
sometimes known, are uninspiring — they
are off-white, tiny and held close to the
leaves where they are difficult to see.
However, nature has given it a rich apricot
nectar scent to attract pollinators. A single
plant will produce an intoxicating, rich,
apricot nectar fragrance. This species can be
grown outside in mild areas provided they
are frost free.

*The best way to get real enjoyment out of the garden is to put
on a wide straw hat, hold a little trowel in one hand and a cool
drink in the other, and tell the man where to dig.*

Charles Barr

Above (left and right): Holly,
Ilex aquifolium.

Below: Sprig of another
Ilex sp.

Berried treasures

With most of us directing our energies to choosing flowers, we can easily overlook ornamental berries that add colour throughout autumn and into winter. Ornamental fruiting plants have many advantages, often giving a twice yearly display — spring flowers followed by autumn berries. They also have the advantage of holding their display much longer than most plants hold their flowers, with fruits lasting months at a time.

As an alternative to cotoneaster, try pyracantha or firethorn. It has bright orange or ruby red berries, which look terrific espaliered across a wall. This spectacular shrub is known for its fiery berries throughout autumn and into winter. Similar to cotoneaster, it can be distinguished by its thorns.

Holly is the most famous berrying plant, renowned for its shiny red fruit and toothed spiky foliage. As it bears fruit in winter, coinciding with the festive season, it is

Shiny clusters of jewel-like fruit hang as if placed like autumn decorations.

Cotoneaster are among the finest and most versatile of the berry-bearing shrubs. Some species grow as ground covers and can be grafted on to standards to show off their cascading habit. These make fabulous weeping focal points. Others can be shaped into small trees or grown as hedges. They flower in spring, producing masses of creamy white cup-shaped flowers that are followed by a profusion of red berries.

As they need no special conditions for growing well, coping with climatic extremes and even sunless positions, they have long been a favourite in gardens and today there are many species and varieties to choose from.

popular for Christmas decorations. There are many variegated foliage forms that vary in colour from silver-white to gold, which will effectively break up an all-green background. The prickly foliage gives way to smooth-edged leaves as the plant matures.

For something really unusual, try the striking callicarpa. Known as 'beauty berry', this shrub will grow in all but the coldest areas to about 3 m, in any soil, and has a spectacular display of violet, iridescent berries that hold well in winter. These berry clusters form up and down the length of its stems. Being deciduous, the bare stems really show the berries off to their best

advantage. Callicarpa has small pink-purple flowers in spring. Duranta is another great plant, which has sky blue or white flowers in summer, and is followed by golden chains of fruit in autumn. Grow it in a warm conservatory.

Several other conservatory plants are grown for their berries. There are many types of *Syzygium* (warm conservatory) and *Acmena* (cool conservatory) species, all of which are noted for their glossy green foliage, attractive new growth, fluffy white spring flowers and a profusion of coloured fruit in autumn. Depending on the type you choose, the berries will be white, pink or purple. They may be reluctant to flower and fruit under glass until well established.

A lovely Australian rainforest tree or large shrub that produces attractive fruits is *Pittosporum rhombifolium*, popularly known as the Queensland pittosporum or diamond-leaved laurel. Unfortunately it is half hardy and will not take frost, or at best only a very light frost, so in frost-prone areas grow it in a tub and winter it in the cool conservatory. It can be stood outside for the summer. It has perfumed white flowers followed by pumpkin-coloured clusters of berries that hold on till the next flush of blooms appears in late spring or summer.

Ardisia crispa is a great choice for the intermediate conservatory and can also be grown as a houseplant. It is an evergreen shrub with leathery, deep green leaves. The rich red berries cluster around each stem like tiers on a Christmas tree. Ardisia reaches 1 m and has fragrant white or pink flowers in spring, then holds its berries right through winter.

Other berrying ornamentals (all hardy) include aucuba, crataegus (these are mainly trees), roses that produce colourful hips, euonymus, berberis, hypericum, viburnum and strawberry tree or *Arbutus unedo* (a spreading, somewhat shrubby tree).

After the weather has really turned cold, you're tucked away inside, and all the flowers seem to have finished for the year, consider some of the berries that you could bring inside to brighten the place up. Fruit and berries look great mixed with leaves, flowers or on their own, and will bring some warmth into the coldest of nights. For a sense of harvest, satisfaction and plenty, nothing beats them.

Footnote Unfortunately the berries of some garden shrubs and trees are favourite foods of birds and in some areas they can be quickly stripped from the plants even before they are properly ripe and have fully coloured up. Holly berries are particular favourites as are cotoneaster and crataegus berries. There is little that can be done about this and the only consolation is that we are feeding our feathered friends. A garden should help to attract and conserve wildlife.

1 Sacred bamboo (*Nandina domestica*). 2 Pepper tree (*Schinus molle*). 3 Red cotoneaster (*Cotoneaster* sp.). 4 *Syzygium* sp.
5 Narrow-leafed firethorn (*Pyracantha angustifolia*). 6 and 7 St John's wort (*Hypericum pseudohenryi*).

berries

8 Japanese beauty berry (*Callicarpa japonica*). 9 Golden dewdrop (*Duranta erecta*). 10 Lilly-pilly (*Acmena smithii* 'Minipilly').
11 Red firethorn (*Pyracantha crenatoserrata*). 12 Strawberry tree (*Arbutus unedo*). 13 Ivy (*Hedera canariensis*).

Autumn rose care Roses should be making good growth ready for their autumn flush of flowers. Keep them thriving with deep watering if the soil starts to become dry but don't wet the foliage as this encourages black spot fungus, prevalent in areas with high humidity. If your roses are infected (yellow leaves with black spots), you can use a combined rose spray every ten days.

And watch out for aphids – tiny insects that breed quickly and smother the new growth, sucking the sap and spoiling the blooms. Remove them by hand with a damp tissue or use a combined rose spray.

Roses need a handful of pelletized manure each month in their growing season, until late summer. Mulch them well with garden compost or animal manure to enrich the soil, keep the roots cool and stop weeds.

A luscious, voluptuous bloom – 'The Prince', a David Austin rose.

Roses

Although the main display of roses is in summer, many (the repeat-flowering varieties) continue flowering into autumn, or produce a second flush in this season. If you deadheaded your roses in summer you should have some lovely blooms now. It is well worth visiting the many gardens that are open for inspection at this time to see the roses and perennials in full flower, or you could visit rose nurseries to select and smell rose varieties while they are in full flower. Choosing a rose is a task that should not be undertaken lightly, so perhaps visit a rose show at a nursery. It's not like buying a punnet of poppies...a rose can live for sixty years or more!

Designing with roses

As roses are deciduous plants, towards the end of autumn gardens devoted to roses only can start to look a little tired. The Victorian habit of separating plants out into collections can be charming, but there is no golden rule that says roses must be in a bed by themselves.

The trend these days is to plant roses among other plants in the garden, rather than isolate them in their own bed. Like any other shrub, roses have evolved with many other plants around them, and can be grown with great success in the same way.

This planting method disguises their bare branches over winter, and also provides a smokescreen for insects which might be after their delicious new growth. An underplanting of pest-deterring plants may also help keep aphids, mites and scale under control. Try nasturtium, garlic, parsley, spearmint and southernwood to help keep pests away.

Before you start planning your rose garden, however, consider these tips: the other plants you choose shouldn't be so greedy as to eat up all the available food, or so vigorous — a lawn, for example — that they choke the roses.

Suitable ground covers include lamb's ear, fleabane (*Erigeron*), scabiosa, sedges, snow-in-summer, thrift and thyme. Many perennials look great planted with roses. Achillea, aster, coneflower, dahlia, gaillardia, gaura, rudbeckia, *Salvia chamaedyroides* and *S. greggii*, sedum, shasta daisies and trachelium all do well, and contrasting foliage from the strap leaves of bearded iris, dwarf agapanthus, angel's fishing rod (*Dierama pulcherrimum*), kniphofia and fountain grass can also work.

Shrubs that go with roses include the smaller plants such as heliotrope, cistus, *Convolvulus cneorum*, curry plant (*Helichrysum italicum*), dwarf myrtle, English lavender, pelargonium, penstemon, Russian sage (perovskia), cotton lavender and the larger ones, such as buddleja, escallonia, echium, French lavender, choisya, purple cotinus and silver-leaved elaeagnus.

If you still prefer to plant roses in their own garden bed, maximize their impact by planting three or four of each colour, rather than one of every variety.

Rose hip The seed pods that develop from the finished rose flower, hips have traditionally been made into rose hip jelly. Some roses set hips well, while others do not. *Rosa rugosa* (shown here) sets lovely hips that are bright red and orange in autumn. A few other roses that produce hips include *R. brunonii* (long, pale orange-apricot hips), *R. giraldii* (clusters of small hips), *R. longicuspis* (small dark red hips), *R. moyesii* (red bottle-shaped hips) and *R. glauca* (mahogany red hips).

Gather therefore the rose, whilst yet is prime,
For soon comes age, that will her pride deflower:
Gather the rose of love, whilst yet is time,
Whilst loving thou mayst lovèd be with equal crime.

Edmund Spenser

Trees

Trees, the 'roof' of a garden, add a sense of human scale to buildings and can provide privacy, add colour and attract wildlife.

Autumn is not only the season of blazing leaf colour, but some trees, mainly tender kinds, are flowering at this time of year. Gardeners in frost-free climates can consider these for their gardens, but those of us in colder areas would have to grow them in tubs in a conservatory or enjoy them in botanical gardens.

Coppice or pollard

Coppice (prune back to ground level) or pollard (prune back to a stump-like framework) foliage gums for year-round bunches of cut leaves. Silver dollar gum grows particularly well like this and looks sensational as a backdrop to annual displays.

The flowering gums

Eucalyptus flower mainly in the summer in the Northern Hemisphere but some continue into autumn, including the spectacular red-flowering gum from Western Australia, *Eucalyptus ficifolia* (also known as *Corymbia ficifolia*). This is not frost hardy so in frost-prone climates would have to be grown as a shrub in a tub (see coppice or pollard, left) and wintered in a cool conservatory. Thus grown it will not flower but makes an attractive foliage plant.

This autumn-flowering gum tree is probably the most spectacular of all gums. It has huge fluffy flowers, varying in colour from near white through to salmon, vermilion and pink. Unfortunately, this colour variation has always been a problem, in that seed-raised plants cannot be guaranteed as one colour or another.

The West Australian flowering gum is a smallish tree, growing to about 10 m with a broad-domed crown shape. The foliage is

No man manages his affairs as well as a tree does.

George Bernard Shaw

thick and leathery, with a nice sheen when healthy. Plant this gum in a well-drained, full sun position. Or under glass grow in a tub of well drained, soil-based potting compost and provide light, airy conditions.

The firewheel tree

A native of Australia and a very showy tree, the firewheel tree (*Stenocarpus sinuatus*) is sometimes grown outdoors in relatively frost-free Mediterranean climates, but elsewhere needs to be grown in a tub in an intermediate conservatory. However, in the latter instance it will not flower but makes a very attractive foliage plant.

It forms masses of spoke-like flowers, which can be produced at any time of year, although summer and autumn are the main flowering seasons. The glossy green, wavy leaves make this a handsome tree.

It grows very slowly and outdoors needs a warm, sheltered spot with moist soil, but under glass it can be grown in a tub of soil-based potting compost. Provide good light but shade from strong sun.

The firewheel tree
(*Stenocarpus sinuatus*).

tropical **gardens**

In northern climes many gardeners have the urge to create a tropical or subtropical 'paradise' out of doors. This is possible, albeit of a temporary nature for the summer and autumn, until the frosts arrive. This is nothing new as Victorian gardeners also created tropical displays out of doors during the summer.

The way to do it is to grow plants in tubs or large pots and to keep them in a conservatory for the winter, placing them outside when there is no risk of frost, in late spring or early summer. The best spot for them is on a sunny patio with shelter from winds.

There are many suitable subjects for this, including eucalyptus that can be grown as a foliage shrub by coppicing it in early spring each year. Bougainvilleas could be grown as standards in tubs. Strelitzias or bird of paradise (shown here), and bananas are excellent plants for tubs. Brugmansias or angels' trumpets, with huge trumpet-shaped flowers in summer and autumn can also be recommended.

gums

1 *Eucalyptus plenissima*. 2 *E. caesia* 'Silver Princess'. 3 *E. macrocarpa* (mottlecah or Rose-of-the-West). 4 *E. haemastoma*. 5 *E. ropantha*. 6 *E. torquata* (coral gum). 7 *E. gunni* (alpine cider gum). 8 *E. hypochlamydea*.

1 *E. macrocarpa* (small-leaved mottlecah). 2 *E. tetragona* (tallerack).
3 *E. cinerea* (Argyle apple). 4 *E. youngianna*. 5 *E. gillii*. 6 *E. stoatei*
(scarlet pear gum). 7 *E. ficifolia* (syn. *Corymbia ficifolia*).
8 *E. transcontinentalis* (redwood).

Above: A superb planting of claret and golden ash lights up an avenue in autumn.

Above right: A tranquil place to sit and ponder the miracles of nature.

Create a rich tapestry

Deciduous trees come into their own each autumn. Canopies of coloured leaves create a marvellous rooftop for the garden below.

Autumn's sunset brilliance is governed by many factors. When temperatures drop at this time of the year, the leaves of deciduous plants change colour and fall. This change is due to the green pigment chlorophyll disappearing from leaves, allowing the natural colours of carotene and other pigments to shine through.

In general, the cooler the climate, the more pronounced the process and the better the autumn colour. The cool and cold regions of Northern Europe and North America are noted for their fine displays of autumn leaf colour.

Colour in autumn ranges from buttery yellows to fiery oranges and russet reds. For a rich gold, try a golden robinia or an ash such as *Fraxinus angustifolia*, which look like balls of gold and are very tough and drought tolerant.

The golden full-moon maple (*Acer shirasawanum* 'Aureum') is among the most dramatic. It rarely reaches more than 6 m and is even more stunning than the more commonly planted Japanese or full-moon maple (*A. japonicum*).

For the sheer delight of its buttercup yellow leaves, the maidenhair tree (*Ginkgo*

Autumn in felted slipper shuffles on, Muted yet fiery,— Autumn's character.

Vita Sackville-West

foliage. Its scientific name means 'water nymph', and the whole genus is great for damp and poorly drained soil.

In cool areas the Japanese maples make superb courtyard specimen trees. Some of the finely dissected varieties will need to grow in semishade so that the sun does not burn the tender leaves. Most of these maples prefer rich moist soils. Some have pretty red leaves in spring and others colour gold, bronze and russet in autumn. Others worth investigating include the trident maple (*Acer buergerianum*), which is more upright and colours well, even in warm temperate areas.

Also useful for smaller gardens are dogwoods, loved for their pretty spring flowers and very deep, shining red leaves in autumn. For average-sized gardens, claret ash (*Fraxinus angustifolia* 'Raywood') named for its rich burgundy autumn colour, is one of the best autumn foliage trees.

The Chinese tallow tree has one of the prettiest, heart-shaped leaf shapes and turns bright red, then a lovely deep claret colour. It grows to a height of approximately 10 m and develops a rounded crown, making it a good choice as a courtyard or street tree. It is only suitable for the mildest gardens with slight frosts, or Mediterranean climates.

Some deciduous oaks give superb autumn leaf colour but are suitable only for large gardens. The leaves of the pin oak (*Quercus palustris*) change from yellow and red shades to russet brown before they fall. The red oak (*Q. rubra*) turns deep red, reddish brown or orange in autumn. The scarlet oak (*Q. coccinea*) colours brilliant scarlet in cool or frosty autumns.

Top to bottom: *Acer palmatum* var. *dissectum*, *A. palmatum* (Japanese maple), flowers of *Cornus florida* (dogwood) and *Sapium sebiferum* (Chinese tallow tree).

biloba) is unsurpassed. Fastigiate or columnar in shape, this lovely tree has leaves shaped like maidenhair fern fronds which change from green to clear yellow at this time before they fall to make a lovely carpet beneath the tree. Ginkgo makes an excellent lawn specimen and is very tolerant of a polluted atmosphere. It eventually grows to around 30 m in height.

The classic fiery and red shades are best achieved with the American sweet gum (*Liquidambar styraciflua*) or one of its varieties. The American tupelo (*Nyssa sylvatica*) is also a great choice. This spreading tree has impressive tabletops of

Deciduous trees Unless you live in a very cold area, this is the best time to plant these trees: the soils are still warm and the roots can settle in before winter. Most autumn trees are suitable for planting but some colour better than others, depending on the climate and whether they've been grown from seed or not. Select them from your nursery now while they are still showing their colourful display. Flower colour can also be in short supply at this time, so it makes sense to plant for this foliage colour. Add the dimension of time, with the passing of seasons, to your garden.

TRANSPLANTING

1 Use a sharp spade to cut through the roots in a circle about 40 cm away from the trunk. Dig a trench out from this circle so you can get under the roots and lift the tree (in this case a yew tree was transplanted).

2 Slide the spade under the roots and lift the tree onto some hessian, trying to keep as much soil as possible on the roots.

3 Carefully wrap the root ball in the hessian.

Transplanting

Gardeners are prone to both overenthusiasm and overplanting, underestimating the mature size of a plant or simply mixing up a combination. Trees and shrubs that might be in the way of home extensions or pool constructions may also need relocating. So take stock now and make a few moves in the garden.

When to transplant

Autumn is a good time for transplanting evergreens as they quickly become re-established in the still warm soil. Transplant deciduous trees and shrubs as soon as they become dormant. Only dig up plants you can physically manage. Two or three people should be able to easily handle a plant that is 1–2 m high.

If you want to transplant hardy palms do not move these until the summer as they like warm weather to help settle them in. Note that deciduous trees and shrubs can also be transplanted during the winter, provided the ground is not wet or frozen.

The main reason transplants die is water stress. Following these simple steps will increase the likelihood of a smooth, trauma-free transition.

Preparation

Before you lift your tree or shrub, dig a large hole in the new spot and improve the removed soil by adding well-rotted manure and compost. Then add just a sprinkle of slow-release fertilizer and use this improved soil for backfilling.

Step 1

Using a sharp spade (see the tools listed in 'The garden shed' section in 'Winter'), cut through the roots in a circle at least 40 cm

Planning is everything If possible, plan ahead and cut the surface roots a few weeks ahead. This lessens the shock on the day.

away from the trunk (or ten times the width of the trunk). You'll need to widen this trench in order to get under the roots.

Step 2

Slide the spade under the roots and lift the tree onto some hessian or an old sheet, trying to keep as much soil on the roots as you can.

Step 3

Wrap the root ball in the hessian or sheet. This method is called 'ball and burlap'.

Step 4

Use the wrap to slide or lift the plant into its new position.

Step 5

Place the plant in the prepared hole, backfill with the improved soil, then water in well using a watering can with a little soluble seaweed solution added to the water. Spray your plant with an anti-transpirant to reduce stress. Prune off any unnecessary growth, and cover it with an old sheet or shade cloth to protect it from the sun. Keep the soil evenly moist, especially if the weather turns warm or windy. It will take up to six weeks for the plant to re-establish itself in its new home.

Step 6

Insert a stake if your transplant seems top-heavy and unstable, or if you are in an exposed position, but be careful not to damage the root ball. Use three stakes if necessary and attach them with flexible ties — such as proprietary tree ties, old stockings or hessian webbing — in a figure eight. This allows the trunk to bend with the breeze and still remain stable.

4 Gently lift the tree into its new position.

5 Backfill the hole with improved soil.

6 Insert a stake.

Positioning As plants grow, they have a definite front and back side. Try to position them in their new home with their best side facing correctly. Failing this, orient them in their original aspect so that they don't become sunburnt as easily.

crape myrtle

The crape myrtle is a tree for all seasons. The smooth mottled bark makes it a feature in winter, it flowers spectacularly in late summer and early autumn, and the butter yellow, turning to scarlet, leaves make it a feature in late autumn.

Vital statistics

Scientific name: *Lagerstroemia indica*.

Family: Lythraceae.

Climate: Grows in frosty climates (down to -5°C) but needs long hot summers to flower well and ripen wood.

Culture: Dwarf types suitable for containers, others best in the ground. A perfect tree for small gardens.

Colours: Silvery white to purple, carmine, rose, lavender and pink.

Height: 1–8 m.

Planting time: All year.

Soil: Adaptable, although well drained with added compost is best.

Position: Full sun, shelter from cold wind. Best against south-facing wall.

Planting spacing: 1–5 m.

Fertilizer: Not needed.

Pests/diseases: Powdery mildew in humid climates, although new varieties are bred to be resistant.

Pruning: Little needed. Only cut out any awkwardly placed branches in early spring.

Propagation: Semi-ripe cuttings in summer, in heated propagating case.

Falling leaves

Everywhere you look in autumn, people are busy raking up leaves. Never put them in the garbage or, worse still, burn them. Decayed leaves are very good for enriching your garden soil.

- Pile them in some hidden corner and allow them to decompose, then spread them on the garden. This leaf mould is particularly good for acid-loving plants such as camellias, rhododendrons (including azaleas), pieris and kalmias. Add them slowly to the compost heap.
- Some leaves decompose more quickly than others so beware of putting all freshly fallen leaves on your garden, as any waxy coating will act as a barrier to water penetration. Running the mower over them to shred them helps.
- If you have a surplus, fill some garbage bags with lightly moistened leaves and poke a few holes in the bag. Leave them out in the sun for a fast breakdown into compost or in the shade for rich mulch later on in the year.
- To speed up your compost pile, add some handfuls of blood, fish and bone (about 2 cups to each wheelbarrow load) and the kitchen scraps, and keep it moist and turned.

Spades take up leaves
No better than spoons,
And bags full of leaves
Are light as balloons.

Robert Frost

herbs, fruit & vegetables

Autumn is a time of ripening fruits and nuts, and storing away for the winter. It is as if mother nature had planned for this, creating long-lasting harvests such as pumpkins, apples, cabbages and root vegetables to tide us over till spring.

Top left: *Aloe vera*.

Above left: *Piper nigrum* (pepper).

Herbs

Autumn is a time for harvesting and preserving herbs for use in winter, for pruning hedges of evergreen herbs, such as rosemary and lavender, and for collecting seeds and dressing beds with manure.

Unusual herbs and spices

Plants make our lives easier in many ways. Fruit and vegetables supply us with essential vitamins and minerals, trees clean the air and herbs have aided us medicinally for thousands of years. Some are just there to spice up our lives.

The first aid plant, *Aloe vera*, is a succulent that contains a thick gel famous for its healing properties when applied to human skin, and horehound leaves (*Marrubium vulgare*) can be used to give a bitter flavour to homebrew beer. The stems and leaves of angelica can be crystallized and eaten as sweets.

Pepper comes from the berries of an Indian vine (*Piper nigrum*). Black pepper is made from unripe berries that turn black as they are dried in the sun, while white pepper is the white seed inside the fruit. Green peppercorns are pickled unripe berries and pink peppercorns come from peppercorn trees.

Sesame seeds are harvested from the fruit pods of a small herb that looks like a foxglove. They're grown commercially for the edible oil. Liquorice sticks are the solidified juices extracted from the roots of a subtropical herb. The spice cinnamon comes from the ground bark of a tall Sri Lankan tree that is closely related to the weedy camphor laurel, and nutmeg is the dried seed kernel of a tree from the West Indies.

dried chrysanthemum
flowers

sage

thyme

rosemary

rose hip

mint

Vanilla extract

Vanilla is a spice produced from the seed
pods of a climbing tropical orchid from
South America. Pure vanilla extract is easy
to make at home. Simply split two vanilla
beans and put them in a sterilized glass jar
or bottle with 1 cup of unflavoured vodka.
Cap and store in a cool dark place, shaking
gently every few weeks. It's ready in two
months but lasts for ages.

Tea please

Herb teas have been consumed since
ancient times. A small handful of fresh or
dried herbs can be made into tea by either
pouring boiling water over sprigs (herb tea)
or simmering herbs and water in a pan for a
few minutes before straining (herb brew).
Try the flowers of German chamomile,
lavender and bergamot, and the leaves of
mints, lemon balm, lemongrass or verbena,
hyssop, oregano, parsley and rosemary,
various thymes and sages. Pick young
tender leaves before the flowers open and
before the heat of the day.

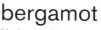

orange blossom

bergamot

Native to North America, bergamot (*Monarda*
sp.) replaced Indian tea in many American
households following the Boston Tea Party of
1773. The common name, bergamot, comes
from an Italian word because the crushed leaf
resembles the small bitter Italian orange that is
used in aromatherapy, perfumes and cosmetics.
Native Americans used it for colds.

Did you know? A spice is any part of a plant, other than its leaves, that is used to flavour food.

check list

jobs to do now

- Lift and divide horseradish and comfrey.

- Dust derris or diatomaceous earth on your vegies to control thrips.

- Watch out for caterpillars, slugs and snails that may still be active while the weather is mild.

- Fungal diseases are all prolific at the moment, so be vigilant.

- Check ripening grapes. Cover fruit with netting if birds are a problem.

- Prepare strawberry beds by adding blood and bone.

- Remove mummified stone and pome fruit clinging on to fruit trees as they carry brown rot.

- Cut asparagus stems down to the ground when the foliage yellows and then weed the beds.

- Harvest herbs — there are only a few more weeks in which to dry basil, coriander, dill and other annual herbs before the cold gets them.

plant now

- Plant chives. Sow mustard and cress indoors on a windowsill.

- Autumn is a good time to plant new fruit trees such as apples, pears, plums, cherries, peaches, apricots and figs.

- Plant rhubarb crowns into deep, well-drained soil. Incorporate large quantities of animal manure, and choose sturdy crowns.

- Bulb and spring onions can be sown in late summer or early autumn for overwintering. Also, onion and shallot sets can be planted now.

- Some vegetables can be sown in the autumn to overwinter, resulting in earlier crops the following year, including peas, broad (fava) beans, hardy spinach, spring cabbage, calabrese, leaf beets and Swiss chard. Hardy overwintering lettuce can be sown in a cold greenhouse or under cloches.

- Lift and store self-blanching celery before frosts start. Other celery can be protected from frost with a thick covering of straw.

- Pak choi can be sown in autumn, choosing a cold-resistant variety that can take a certain amount of frost. Chinese cabbage can be sown in late summer/early autumn.

flowering now

- Bergamot is flowering now.

Edible flowers

There was a time when the line between vegetables and flowers wasn't as clear. A plant had to be useful to justify its space in a garden.

Flowers are our forgotten harvest. Some edible flowers commonly found in the garden are calendula, roses and carnations (the white heel or base of pinks must be removed, as this is very bitter), orange and lemon flowers, cornflowers, fuchsias, salvia, violets and pelargoniums.

A dish or drink graced by flowers should be a celebration of a distinctive and lovely scent. Try them. Some are sweet, and make an elegant dessert decoration when dipped in egg white, rolled in caster sugar and dried. Others such as chive and nasturtium flowers have nutty or peppery flavours and really add colour when tossed fresh from the garden into salads.

Citrus flowers can be added to water for a delicious summer drink or, for the ultimate in relaxation, try a Pimms, dry ginger ale and borage blossom — it reinvigorates the spirits! Mexicans are partial to a drink infused with Jamaica flowers (*Hibiscus* sp.), while Europeans flavour wine, fruit compotes and jams by stirring sprays of elderflowers into them.

Cloves (*Syzygium aromaticum*), from the Moluccas, and capers (*Capparis spinosa*) are flower buds. Clinging to walls throughout Italy, the caper bush appears to scorn soil and water and love heat.

The peoples of the Mediterranean and Middle East probably have the longest tradition of cooking with flowers. Draw some inspiration from those cuisines and experiment with flowers from your garden.

Like herbs, essential oils are stronger in flavour than floral waters, and fresh petals impart more subtle flavours than dried.

lavender ice cream

In a saucepan put 8 washed and dried stems of English lavender with 600 mL thick cream and 1 small piece lemon rind. Heat until almost boiling, then stir in 160 g sugar until dissolved.

Strain through a fine sieve, then gradually pour onto 4 egg yolks, lightly whisked in a bowl. Return to the pan and stir over low heat until thick enough to coat the back of a spoon – do not boil. Pour into a chilled metal tray to cool. Freeze until frozen around the edge, but not in the centre.

In a food processor or bowl, beat until smooth. Freeze again and repeat this process twice more. Cover with greaseproof paper and freeze. Serves 6–8.

Edible flowers (left to right): Pelargonium, French lavender, salvia, pineapple sage.

rose**mary**

There's rosemary, that's for remembrance.

William Shakespeare

Highly ornamental, with long-lasting fragrant flowers that attract bees, rosemary has strongly aromatic, leathery leaves that are dark green above, white and felted beneath. Some plants have an upright bushy growth, making them perfect for hedging and topiary, other types are sprawling and useful on rock walls and sunny banks.

Traditionally, rosemary was thought to bring good fortune and fertility; Henry VIII's fourth wife, Anne of Cleves, wore a rosemary wreath at her wedding. She didn't bear him children but she survived the marriage!

Rosemary is an evergreen Mediterranean herb that flourishes in a warm, sunny position. Harvest the leaves at any time of year. It is easily propagated from semi-ripe cuttings in summer and these are best wintered under glass and planted out in spring. Hedges can be trimmed when flowering is over. Trim other plants in early spring.

Vital statistics

Scientific name: *Rosmarinus officinalis*.

Family: Lamiaceae.

Climate: Dislikes cold wet winters, but can withstand temperatures down to −10°C if the site is well drained.

Culture: Replace every five or six years.

Colours: Either white, blue, dark blue or pink.

Height: To 2 m.

Planting time: Spring is best, or early autumn.

Soil: Well-drained neutral to alkaline soil that is not too rich in nitrogen.

Position: Full sun with shelter from cold winds.

Planting spacing: 45 cm.

Fertilizer: Feeding is not needed.

Pests/diseases: Rots, mainly if soil doesn't drain; no pests due to aromatic foliage.

Cutting: Harvest for culinary use; use either fresh or dried.

Propagation: Seeds sown in spring, or semi-ripe cuttings in summer.

Storage: Dried leaves and flowers, essential oils and herb vinegar.

Fruit

Autumn's selection is based on nuts and the firmer fleshed fruit such as apples and pears, which store well. There are also some late harvests from exotics available in temperate climates: these will add interest to the fruit bowl and delight your taste buds.

Pome fruit

Pome fruit are all members of the rose family and include apples, pears, quinces, medlars and loquats. If growing fruit yourself sounds appealing, but you don't have the space for a whole orchard, consider espalier (see 'Winter') or a potted collection.

Many trees have dwarf varieties that are suitable for containers. Apples and pears can also be bought on totem-like plants, which produce virtually all their fruit on an upright pole, making them perfect for narrow, sunny verandahs. The beauty of this is that you not only have small, manageable-sized crops, but also one crop followed by another.

Walnuts and pears you plant for your heirs.

Old proverb

Apples and pears grow best in temperate and cold temperate regions, and are seldom damaged by frosts. They are some of the hardiest and longest lived of all fruit trees.

The modern apple varieties have been developed from crab apples (*Malus* sp.). There is now a great range of varieties available. Choose from 'Cox's Orange Pippin', good for cold areas; 'Golden Delicious', which stores well and has good yield; 'Granny Smith', the most popular culinary variety, suited to any climate; and 'Jonathan', which is popular commercially.

Apples make excellent home garden trees because they do not need considerable attention and have excellent keeping properties. At planting time, prune the leading shoots back to three buds. They do need cross-pollination, and should either be multigrafted or planted 10 m or closer to another suitable apple.

Pears (*Pyrus communis*) withstand more frost than stone or other fruits. Most varieties require cross-pollination so check with your local garden centre. The flavour varies greatly according to the variety. 'Beurre Bosc' is a good dessert pear, a regular and heavy cropper. 'Doyenne du Comice' is a favourite large-fruited desert pear with beautiful flavour and texture. 'Winter Nelis' is a late-maturing dessert variety of fine flavour and it keeps well. There are many other varieties of pear so buy locally, or consult a mail-order catalogue.

Loquats (*Eriobotrya japonica*) are widely cultivated in Asia, but are less popular elsewhere. The fruits are yellow to orange and can be eaten fresh, stewed or preserved. Loquats are frost hardy but should be grown against a warm wall in full sun. They flower in autumn and the fruits develop over winter and ripen in spring.

Quinces (*Cydonia oblonga*) grow on a deciduous tree that reaches around 4 m. The fruit tastes delicious once cooked, when it miraculously transforms into a pink-fleshed, sweet-tasting sensation, perfect for jam, jellies and stews.

From top to bottom: 'Conference' pears, 'Granny Smith' apples, 'Jonathan' apples and quince.

pome fruit

Quinces, apples and pears produce a bountiful autumn harvest and are available in many varieties.

The entrance hole of codling moth larvae; eventually secondary fungi will develop in the damaged tissue and foul the fruit.

Pest patrol: codling moth

The codling moth is a small brown moth approximately 1 cm long. It can cause a significant amount of damage to apples, pears, crab apples, quinces, stone fruit and walnuts.

The moth lays eggs on or near the fruit. Once hatched, the larva chews its way into the fruit core, where it feeds and produces webbing and droppings.

Once the larva is fully fed (having ruined your fruit), it chews a tunnel out and moves down the branches and trunk searching for a suitable place to pupate. There may be up to three generations during the warm weather.

At this time of the year, codling moth are pupating for their final cycle before winter. You can trap them now by tying a piece of hessian around the tree trunk, then checking this at regular intervals and destroying the 1 cm long pupae.

Another method of control, a really up to date one, is to hang pheromone traps in the trees during late spring and summer to attract and trap male moths, so reducing mating with females. This should result in smaller populations of codling moth.

The pineapple guava

The pineapple guava (*Acca sellowiana*, formerly *Feijoa sellowiana*), is a beautiful tree, not only because of the delicious fruit but also because of its handsome foliage, which has a silver underside, and its marble-patterned trunk. The green-skinned oval fruits are about the size of a passion fruit and can be eaten fresh, juiced or cooked. Although the

pineapple guava is frost hardy, it needs a warm climate to fruit, so in cool temperate regions it must be grown in a heated greenhouse or conservatory to encourage the production of fruits.

Grow it in a tub of soil-based potting compost and provide good light. In summer water freely and liquid feed monthly and be sparing with water in winter.

The pomegranate

Although the pomegranate (*Punica granatum*) is frost hardy, fruits are only produced after a long, hot summer. In cool climates more success may be achieved in a warm greenhouse (maintain 15°C in autumn). Otherwise grow as for pineapple guava. It is an attractive shrub or tree with showy, bright red flowers.

persimmon

The persimmon is a handsome tree, with its picturesque trunk, glossy green leaves which change colour to burnt orange and scarlet as the cold weather approaches, and a delightful, pendulous habit to many of the named cultivars. The orange-skinned fruit has a unique texture and flavour, but male and female plants are needed for its production. The plant is frost hardy but long hot summers are required for fruit production; in cool temperate climates grow it in a heated greenhouse.

Vital statistics

Scientific name: *Diospyros kaki*.
Family: Ebenaceae.
Climate: Subtropics to cool temperate zones.
Culture: Trees have a fragile root system, which should not be allowed to dry out during planting.

Colours: The flowers are small, greenish yellow and rather insignificant.
Height: Up to 13 m, normally half this in gardens.
Planting time: Autumn.
Soil: Will tolerate moist conditions and heavy clay.
Position: Full sun for maximum leaf colour and cropping.
Planting spacing: 6 m apart from other trees.
Fertilizer: Outdoors apply a general-purpose fertilizer in early spring.
Pests/diseases: Birds love the fruit. Fruit fly can damage the skin.
Propagation: Varieties are grafted onto rootstocks of *D. kaki* in winter. Seed when ripe.
Storage: Ripen fruit indoors once the skin has coloured, but the flesh is still firm. There are astringent (eat when mushy) and non-astringent (can be eaten like an apple) varieties, so choose to suit your taste.

In a nutshell

Nuts evoke some of the magic of autumn. Images of squirrelling away reserves of food for winter come to mind, as do open fires, roasted chestnuts and hearty conversation. Hardy nuts for cool temperate and cold climates include the hazel (*Corylus avellana*), a large, easily grown shrub with round, well-flavoured and popular nuts. The filbert (*C. maxima*) is similar with roundish or oblong nuts. Squirrels love hazels and filberts and may strip the nuts before you have a chance to harvest them.

Sweet or Spanish chestnuts are also very popular but they are produced by a huge forest-type tree (*Castanea sativa*), suitable only for the largest gardens. It has magnificent, long, toothed leaves and the nuts are enclosed in spiny husks.

Almonds (*Prunus dulcis*) are also grown in cool temperate climates and while they produce nuts they crop better in warm temperate regions. Spring frosts may kill flowers and therefore nut production is reduced. However, it is an attractive flowering tree, producing pink or white blossoms in early spring.

Some pines have edible nuts, the most noteworthy being the stone pine (*Pinus pinea*), the source of pine nuts. This hardy pine comes from the Mediterranean. The macadamia nut from Australia is subtropical. The nuts have round, white kernels that are sweet and soft. It is an extremely popular nut that most people have to buy rather than grow.

Who will eat the kernel of the nut must break the shell.

Proverb

Above left: The casings left by sweet chestnuts.

Above: A bountiful harvest.

Try feeding your cabbages with beer, said to be an effective plant food.

Vegetables

Nutritionists tell us that when it comes to vegetables, fresh is best. Well, nothing could be fresher than home grown.

Select the best varieties and you can harvest vegetables at their peak of natural flavour. Choose a sunny spot and improve the soil. Some vegetables can be sown in early autumn including bulb and spring onions, peas, broad (fava) beans, hardy spinach, spring cabbage, calabrese, pak choi, Chinese cabbage, leaf beets and Swiss chard.

The Brassica family

Brussels sprouts, cabbages, cauliflower and broccoli are among the most notable members of the Brassica family, which also contains other plants such as mustards, pak choi, calabrese, kale, kohlrabi and cress — all basically cool weather crops.

Cabbages tend to be overlooked by those who remember childhood meals with boiled cabbage, but the Chinese and eastern Europeans have utilized them extensively. They are strong growers, not fussy about climate, and store well, fresh and pickled. The many varieties are all suited to different climates and seasons, making them available year round. The leaves are bluish, red or green with smooth or crinkled textures.

Broccoli, like cauliflower, is actually a head of flowers that are eaten green, before the yellow petals show. Like Brussels sprouts, the central head can be picked, which forces side shoots that will also crop.

Broccoli Before eating, soak broccoli heads in cold salted water to kill hidden caterpillars.

beetroot

This colourful root vegetable, once highly valued by the ancient Greeks and Romans, is considered a caretaker of the immune system. Both the leaves and roots are edible and packed with goodness, such as vitamins, minerals and readily absorbed fruit sugar (fructose).

Vital statistics

Scientific name: *Beta vulgaris.*
Family: Chenopodiaceae.
Climate: Almost anywhere except the very hottest areas where roots can become woody.
Culture: Doesn't like weed competition, so mulch well.
Colours: Red, yellow or white tapered or rounded roots.
Planting time: Late summer to autumn.
Soil: Loose soils which allow the root to grow freely. High in organic matter, well limed and with good drainage.
Position: Sun or partial shade.
Planting depth and spacing: Sow seed 1 cm deep, in rows 30 cm apart. Thin seedlings to about 10 cm apart.
Fertilizer: Do not overfertilize.
Pests/diseases: Seldom.
Harvest: Leaves can be used fresh in salads; beets mature 3–4 months after sowing, before setting seed. Maincrop beetroots are harvested in autumn.
Propagation: Seed.
Storage: Pickling. Maincrop beetroots can be wintered in the ground in mild areas, or lifted before hard frosts.

Gone underground

Much of what we eat has been grown underground. Potatoes are the most widely eaten vegetables in the Western world. Potatoes are tubers, a root modified as a starch storage vessel. They can be propagated from the 'eyes' of seed potatoes (see 'Winter'), normally purchased in your local nursery as certified disease-free. For a similar flavour, try Jerusalem artichokes.

Although readily available in shops, home-grown spuds can be harvested early, to eat as 'chats', which are sweet baby potatoes. Other interesting potatoes include 'Desiree', which has pink skin; 'Purple Congo' which has purple or bluish skin; and sweet potatoes.

You can grow other root vegetables from seed directly into your patch of earth. These include carrots, beetroot, parsnips, celeriac, turnips and radishes, white or red, all of which are deliciously sweet eaten fresh.

Some root vegetables are actually bulbs rather than tubers. These edible bulbs include garlic, spring onions, chives, onions, leeks and shallots. As a cultivated vegetable, the onion goes back so long that its origins are now uncertain, although the Romans probably introduced it to Europe.

For centuries garlic has been renowned as a remedy and preventative of infections. Its sulphur content acts as a strong disinfectant. In the Middle Ages it was hung outside the door to ward off the plague and the juice has been used to heal gunshot wounds: sphagnum moss soaked in garlic juice was used in World War I as a wound dressing. Roman soldiers ate garlic to keep their strength up. Garlic is also said to prevent leaf curl in peaches and ward off black spot on roses. The longer garlic is cooked, the milder the flavour. Reduce 'garlic breath' by eating parsley, basil, mint or thyme, or do as the Chinese do and chew cardamom pods.

Other vegetables are covered with earth, but it's the stems and leaves that are eaten, not the roots. With asparagus, celery and witloof or Belgian chicory, you can really surpass shop-bought specimens with some care. The taste of these vegetables can be improved enormously by a technique called 'earthing up': mound the soil around the plants as shoots emerge and the stalks will become elongated, white and tender. Asparagus, though, does not need earthing up as it is planted quite deeply.

Rogue pumpkins have a habit of coming up in the garden, courtesy of the compost heap. 'Queensland Blue' and 'Butternut' are both oldies but reliable fruiters. If buying plants select the bushy varieties with fewer leaves and they won't take over the garden. These include 'Golden Nugget', which are common in the shops, 'Baby Blue' and 'Butterbush'. They can even be grown in a large pot, or over an arch, a great idea for a balcony or courtyard garden. Let the plants die completely before harvesting your crop at the end of the season. Gourds are extremely ornamental versions: some are worth eating, others simply decorative.

pumpkins and gourds

1 'Delicata'. 2 and 3 'Queensland Blue'. 4 and 5 'Pompeon'. 6 'Butternut'. 7 Gourd. 8 'Golden Nugget'.
9 and 10 Gourds. 11 'Japanese'.

Quiet. Chilly days, skeletal leaves and bare branches. Cold noses, rosy cheeks, chapped lips. Cardigans and coats. Big plans. Winter in the garden.

winter

winter
overview of the season

These cooler months can be the best time of the year in the garden. There is time for pause and contemplation, drawing together events from the gardening year and making plans for the one to come.

Winter also gives you a chance to warm up with hard physical work; after all, there's plenty to do in the garden, and no excuse for hibernating. Tidy up, fix fences, and service machinery and tools, ready for the more demanding seasons which follow.

What winter lacks in colour it certainly makes up for with fragrance. Many of the finest perfumed plants – such as daphnes, viburnums, wintersweet (chimonanthus) and winter honeysuckle (*Lonicera fragrantissima*) – give scented atmospheres.

Temperatures are low enough to consider doing some serious work. It's a great opportunity to move plants that need rearranging, get control of the weeds and put any of those grand plans into action.

Major projects — such as putting in ponds, gazebos, garden lighting and paving — can all be done with a minimal effect on anything that has to be shifted.

Mulching now will help contain the warmth which has built up in the soil over summer and autumn. It will also keep weeds at bay and save watering throughout summer. A thick blanket layer of leaf litter will return all those lost nutrients to the soil where they will benefit your garden. Either use old leaves as mulch or compost them into nutritious leaf mould. Old mulch may be harbouring fungal spores so replace any around roses and other disease-prone plants now. In regions with severe winters protect roses from frost by mounding soil around

That time of year thou mayst in me behold
When yellow leaves, or none, or few, do hang
Upon those boughs which shake against the cold,
Bare ruin'd choirs, where late the sweet birds sang.

William Shakespeare

The golden flowers of *Kerria japonica* lie waiting to emerge in spring.

the base of stems, and when the mound is frozen, cover with straw.

There is often a bit of wind around in winter so check plant ties and make sure they are secure but not cutting into trunks or branches. Cold drying winds during winter can damage vulnerable plants by scorching the foliage. Therefore erect windbreak netting on the windward side to protect them, or surround with a cylinder of netting.

Old houses often have old terracotta pipes full of hairline fractures that are vulnerable to attack by tree roots. PVC pipes are much safer around trees, as root hairs can't penetrate unless there are existing cracks. There is a belief that some trees 'search' for water and will crack pipes. Few trees do this, although obviously the larger the tree, the more extensive a root system it needs to support itself. Remember that all above-ground parts will be mirrored below the ground and slightly beyond. Avoid willows, poplars, oaks, chestnuts, elms, alders, forest-type maples and limes unless you have a very large garden or estate to accommodate their roots. Some trees can act as enormous soaks: a mature oak, for example, can take up 450 litres of water on a hot day.

In cold zones

If you live in a cold climate, where snow and heavy frosts occur throughout winter, you may need to take extra precautions during late autumn and winter. Frost-tender plants such as pelargoniums, dahlias, gladioli and other tender perennials used for summer display should be stored over winter in a cool but frost-free greenhouse.

Even ponds may need some work. Store or keep floating aquatics in a frost-free spot, and remove, clean and dry pumps so that ice doesn't damage them. You may need to cover delicate new seedlings with a cloche or some other covering. In areas with heavy snowfall, bind conifers with twine to stop branches breaking and disfiguring formal shapes after heavy falls.

Did you know? **Judas allegedly hanged himself from a *Cercis*.**

weatherwatch
If your plants die off suddenly in rainy weather, you may have drainage problems. Address wet spots and other issues with drains. These can either be subsurface, such as agricultural pipe, or surface drains such as gravel trenches (known as French drains).

Garden design and detail

During these cold, gloomy days, take the time to consider your garden's design. Perhaps your garden lacks a focal point or needs some interest, especially in winter. It's fun to add your own stamp and personality with detailing.

Whether it's a piece of sculpture, a fountain or a seat for relaxation after a hard day's work, there are many non-essential but attractive features that can be added to the basic framework of your garden. Whatever feature you choose, remember to ensure it fits into its surroundings and requires minimum maintenance. Combine sympathetic materials, such as timber or stone, or pick up on the theme or style of your garden.

Garden furniture

A garden seat is a pleasurable thing. From your garden seat you can relax, plan your next endeavour, note the combinations of texture and colour that work well and keep a garden diary with notes and ideas for next year.

Well chosen garden furniture can provide an extra dimension to a small garden. In tight spaces it is unlikely that you'll have room for more than one seat, so siting that chair or bench is worth some careful consideration.

Decide whether you want to sit in the sun or in the shade then use your seating as accent points — tucked into a corner, set against a wall or hedge or sheltering under an arbour where you'll have some cover. Try and anchor furniture with background shrubbery and pots of trailing plants around their base.

What lies beneath your seating can be just as important but is often forgotten. Try to position your garden furniture on a solid level surface of pavers, bricks or compacted gravel. Grass might look idyllic, but the charm will soon wear off after you've spent a few weekends lugging a heavy bench out of the mower's path, or have to remedy a muddy patch in front of it.

Select furniture that matches the style of your garden as well as your lifestyle. For example, wicker furniture might look great, but if you don't have a verandah for weather protection, it won't last. One of the most durable of materials is stone or reconstituted stone. Its classic look is rarely out of place, it will never date and it lasts forever in all weathers.

Timber has long been popular, with the classic teak bench remaining the 'benchmark' by which others are measured. Not all timbers weather as well, and will probably need sanding back and oiling at least every few years. If your garden has a rustic, cottage feel to it, furniture made from rough-hewn logs would complement it well.

Iron and iron/timber combinations, such as the classic railway bench, last well, although the iron may need repainting every few years to keep it free from rust. Iron and glass furniture has become very popular, but if you're considering this option, ensure the glass is double-laminated and positioned in a sheltered part of the garden, such as a courtyard.

Garden furniture can be made from just about anything. In the right spot even a couple of planks of wood placed on brick bases can work, so use your imagination.

Whether you have a courtyard or a large block, good design will ensure that your garden has something interesting to offer all year round. A well placed seat or piece of sculpture and the right paving and hedging can all state your personal style.

Sculpture and garden ornaments should be in proportion to their surroundings. The birdbath (at right) is beautifully offset by the hedging and provides a striking focal point at the end of the path.

Sculpture and garden ornaments

Browse around any garden centre and you'll find figures of every size and description, ranging from gnomes painted in football team colours to stalking cats. The selection of statuary and ornaments varies so much it is worth shopping around: look in galleries as well as in shops specializing in garden artistry. Sometimes a good piece is hard to find, and you might have to wait until it finds you, or even make it yourself!

Whatever your choice, try and site it in a logical place — for example, at the end of a narrow path or nestled beside a tree. A focal point should draw your eye and entice you through the garden, personalizing it. Be sure to secure garden features properly and plant around them so that they become part of the garden.

Origins

In the earliest gardens, ornamental features fulfilled a useful domestic role: sundials indicated the time of day; dovecotes housed pigeons which were eaten when fresh meat was in short supply; wellheads supplied drinking or bathing water; and urns held funerary ashes.

Fine detail Adding small finishing touches such as tap tops, wall plaques and plant stands can really make a garden, so keep your eye out for those small details that complete the picture.

Their sculptural forms make succulents popular pot plant specimens (far left). Oriental sculptures (left) and potted urns (above) can bring a feeling of history, calm and contemplation to the garden.

Today, the function of such garden features has changed: they often serve merely as a design element or focal point but of course there is nothing to stop you from using them.

Adaptions

Objects of garden history, old agricultural equipment and even architectural details can all enjoy second lives as garden sculpture. Forcing pots for rhubarb, old ploughs, barrows and even chimney pots can add character and interest.

Make your own ornament

Creating your own garden art is easy. Stack pebbles on top of each other to form a tower, or make your own birdbath using terracotta pots and a large saucer or dish: just stack two or three pots of different sizes by inverting them on top of each other so that the largest is on the bottom. Top the stack off with the terracotta saucer or dish, but make sure you waterproof it with a silicon-based waterproofing agent before you fill it with water.

Installation art is very popular now, and can look great in the garden. It is simply a short-lived display, so it's perfect for adding

The air is cold above the woods;
All silent is the earth and sky,
Except with his own lonely moods
The blackbird holds a colloquy.

Richard Henry Thorne

a bit of seasonal whimsy or fun. Hang strings of fake hibiscus on fishing line from a tree or plant pink flamingoes.

Lighting creates mood cheaply and simply. Extend your outdoor living into the evening with the soft glow of candles and lanterns.

After hours

You have probably concentrated all your efforts on making the garden look great from the outside and you're ready to withdraw to the comfort of your home, but look around you. Have you remembered to link your outdoor rooms with your interior views? Examine your garden again. This time, look out the kitchen window, or through the dining room's French doors. Can you see inviting glimpses of nature from your lounge or family room?

If not, jot down a few ideas on how to create views, frame windows, or let the winter sun in. You may need to prune branches or remove excess plants. Winter is still a good time for moving many shrubs, or for planning a major transplantation of any large deciduous plants (see 'Transplanting' in 'Autumn'). Don't be nervous about moving things around. A garden should always change and be adaptable to the needs of its owners.

Another way to enjoy the best of the garden from inside your home is to install some exterior lighting and transform your garden from a black hole after dark to an extension of your indoor rooms. Diffuse outdoor lighting will allow you to enjoy the patio or the whole garden area at night — in the warmer months for outdoor living, and in winter as illuminated views. So use this dormant time in the garden to lay wiring.

Lighting can either be decorative, such as uplighting in trees or wash lighting in a pond, or functional, lighting up driveways and paths, or perhaps making your home more secure. Carefully placed lights will highlight any features in your garden, such as stone work, a statue or a wall plaque. Sometimes picking out small details can make all the difference.

The advent of low voltage garden lighting in recent years has made the job safe and a lot of fun. First, select the areas that must be lit, such as paths and accessways, and then add some imaginative touches. Some light here for effect, a pool of colour there for impact, but don't overdo it. Less lighting always works better. Finally, always employ a qualified electrician to install an all-weather power point outdoors.

Starting from scratch

Taking the time to plan your garden carefully will pay off in the long term.

If you're gardening on a new site, don't try to landscape the entire area in one year. Rushed gardens seldom last.

Instead, sow grass seed to green up the area and prevent mud and dirt being tracked into your new home. Grass seed is cheap and lawns can be removed later as the garden takes shape.

The next step is to make a plan of the site on graph paper. Plot the essentials first: the clothes line, paved area for entertaining and barbecue, a playground, vegetable patch, compost area and garden shed. Plot the open lawns, pathways and garden beds. Look through magazines, books on garden design and open gardens for inspiration and create a 'source' book of ideas.

If you have the space, plan for a small to medium-sized deciduous tree to provide shade in hot weather, or perhaps a pergola over or partly over a paved area for the same purpose, to be covered by a grapevine or ornamental climber. Then tackle one small area at a time. This way you won't break your back or your budget.

To green a bare look, plant fast growers to fill areas quickly. Annuals are ideal. Sown in spring, they will flower during the summer. Annuals can be sown between fast-growing shrubs such as brooms (cytisus), butterfly bushes (buddlejas), Spanish broom (*Spartium junceum*), lavenders, potentillas, mock orange (philadelphus) and weigelas. Most hardy herbaceous perennials give a quick effect and bulbs are worth planting for spring colour. All of these subjects like sunny positions. Plant slow-growing, longer-lived shrubs that can eventually take over from the fast growers, such as magnolias, camellias and rhododendrons (both for acid soils) and viburnums.

This bay tree garden gets its interest from the shape of each plant rather than from the variety of plant material. Standards, low hedging and spire-shaped conifers are the only contrast required.

Pruning

Late winter is a particularly busy time for pruning, so sharpen those tools. Roses, fruit trees, grapevines and many shrubs can be pruned once any severe weather is over. In very cold regions it is better to wait until early spring before wielding the secateurs or pruning saw.

The object of pruning is to encourage growth — to create a bushy, vigorous, well-shaped plant. Pruning stimulates growth because the 'terminal bud' — the first shoot or leader — contains a chemical which inhibits growth below it. Light pruning removes this chemical control mechanism, resulting in bushier growth.

Flowering and/or fruiting can also improve as a result of pruning. The removal of unproductive wood and letting in more sun encourages fruit set and flower.

But don't make the mistake of pruning back the entire garden. You should wait until after flowering before pruning

winter- and spring-flowering shrubs (if they need it), otherwise you will remove the flower buds. It is important to understand the degree to which plants produce new growth, and also the age of flower-bearing wood. Once you have this knowledge, you can decide whether to prune, and when to prune.

Some pruning is clumsy, unnecessary and often ruinous. Magnolias and hamamelis, for instance, should never be cut back as pruning destroys their wonderful, natural shape and results in stress growth at awkward angles and a framework that can never be regained.

A pear tree has been trained as an informal espalier to camouflage this large wall.

Timing

Be careful not to start winter pruning too early or stems may be killed back by frost. In mild regions prune in late winter. In hard-winter regions wait until early spring before pruning. If in doubt, prune later rather than earlier.

Pruning tender evergreens too early encourages frost-prone new growth. With these, wait until the last chance of frost has gone, otherwise you may cause more harm than good. If a frost-hardy tree or shrub has grown too big for its location you can prune it now, as the sap flow has slowed. Roses are particularly vulnerable to hard frosts, so wait until the severe weather is over before pruning. In many areas this is early spring. Rambler roses are pruned at a different time to others: in early autumn, after flowering.

Some rules for pruning

- Removing up to a third of the growth is generally quite safe, but some plants can take considerably harsher treatment. The golden rule is to prune after the flowers have finished, but there are exceptions — as with some deciduous shrubs, or shrubs that are grown for fruit as well as flowers.
- Have clean sharp tools. Make sure the cut is a clean one as tearing or bruising stems can result in infection, and slows down the callusing process.
- To protect against the spread of disease, wipe the blades with a cloth moistened in bleach or disinfectant before pruning the next plant.
- If you are going to use a wound dressing, make sure you apply it immediately after cutting. Also, use a quality product

The hand that clutches the secateurs has snippers itch. Tommy Garnet

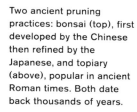

Two ancient pruning practices: bonsai (top), first developed by the Chinese then refined by the Japanese, and topiary (above), popular in ancient Roman times. Both date back thousands of years.

Above right: *Camellia sasanqua* trained as an espalier effectively covers this wall.

rather than a tar concoction or a homemade brew.

- With shrubs, cut immediately above a bud – do not leave a length of stem above, or it will die back. Make an angled cut, slanting away from the bud, or a flat cut where there are two opposite buds.
- If you are trying to encourage bushy growth, you should tip prune, which means trimming back by 10 cm or so, just enough to remove old flower heads and encourage branching.
- To rejuvenate an entire plant which has grown woody, you can cut it back hard, say to within 30–60 cm of the ground. This will encourage new shoots to be produced from near ground level. Plants that respond to this treatment include rhododendrons, yew, hollies and buddlejas. However, not all shrubs will tolerate this. It will kill brooms, so check which shrubs will respond successfully.

Other pruning techniques

Some plants are trained into shapes through pruning techniques such as topiary, bonsai, coppicing, pollarding and pleaching, or trained as espaliers and standards.

Pruning tip   When pruning shrubs and trees, always cut back as close as possible to a bud or another shoot. Do not leave a 'stub' or length of stem above, as this will die back and could result in the plant becoming infected by disease.

- Coppicing. This technique was developed in order to give a constant and renewable supply of wood for cane work and firewood. Basically, plants are cut back regularly to near ground level, which encourages a mass of new growth. This new growth is often more striking than older wood, and therefore has ornamental value. Typical candidates for this sort of pruning are cornus and willows.
- Pollarding. This is similar to coppicing, but growth is cut back to a permanent framework. Plants that can be pollarded include eucalyptus, willows (salix), limes (tilia) and elders (sambucus).
- Topiary. Pruning plants into shapes — such as balls, cones, spirals and animals — is a popular pruning technique. Suitable species include box (buxus), box honeysuckle (*Lonicera nitida*) and yew

(taxus). Training a plant as a standard is a popular form of topiary. Climbers as well as shrubs can be grown up on a single stem, then shaped on top into a ball, or series of balls, or a weeping plant.
- Bonsai. This is the art of dwarfing plants by regular pruning and cramping root growth. Theoretically, any plant can be treated this way.
- Espalier training. This involves growing trees and shrubs flat against a wall or framework. Commonly used for fruit trees, camellias and pyracantha. (See 'Espaliered fruit trees' on page 412.)
- Pleaching. Popular in the sixteenth and seventeenth centuries, pleaching creates a hedge on stilts. The branches may be interwoven or plaited. Suitable subjects include limes or linden (tilia) and hornbeam (carpinus).

PLEACHING

In this example coffee trees are used but the technique applies equally to hardy trees such as hornbeam and lime (linden).

1 Create a standard by removing the bottom two thirds of the side shoots until the desired height is reached.

2 Shorten lateral growth to encourage bushiness.

3 When the plant is tall enough, remove the top shoot or leader.

4 Prune until 'standards' emerge, then shear back as for a traditional hedge, removing low side shoots as they appear. In traditional pleaching, branches of adjacent plants are woven or plaited together.

STORING HAND TOOLS IN OIL AND SAND

1 In a small bucket, add oil to dry sand.

2 Thoroughly mix the sand and oil together.

3 Use the bucket for storing your hand tools.

The garden shed

If you're serious about gardening, get serious about your tools, and they'll repay you with a lifetime's service. Now is the ideal time to sharpen your spade and secateurs as well as restore any cracked or splintery handles.

Buy the best quality tools you can afford, which doesn't necessarily mean the most expensive. Look for high-carbon steel with solid, well balanced wooden handles. Stainless steel, which is alloyed with chromium and nickel, is an expensive but good rust-resistant option for those who occasionally leave tools out in the garden!

Store each tool neatly by tying a string loop through a hole in the handle and hanging it on a tool rack. You can either buy one especially or make your own by mounting an old rake head on the shed wall. Alternatively, keep sharp hand tools clean and oiled in a bucket of sand mixed with oil.

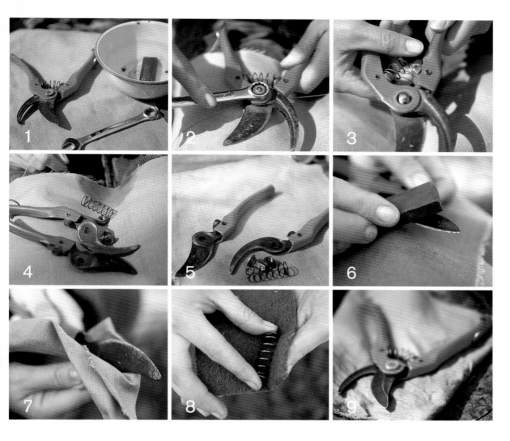

SHARPENING AND CLEANING SECATEURS

1 Assemble what you need for sharpening and cleaning your secateurs: secateurs, spanner, bowl of mineral turpentine and an oilstone.

2 Loosen the bolt using a spanner.

3 Remove the spring.

4 Take the secateurs apart.

5 Spray the parts with lubricant.

6 Sharpen the cutting or bevelled side of the blade on an oilstone. Make sure you hold the blade away from you.

7 Clean the cutting blade with an old rag.

8 Soak the spring and the nut and bolt in the bowl of turpentine. Rub the spring with an abrasive pad.

9 The secateurs, sharpened and cleaned.

RESTORING HANDLES

1 First, assemble the materials you'll need for the job: steel wool, rag, mixture of linseed oil and turpentine in an old jar, sanding block, fine and medium grade abrasive paper and the handle that needs restoring.

2 Sand back the spade handle with medium grade abrasive paper and then clean it.

3 Dip the rag into the linseed oil and turpentine mix. Rub the handle with the soaked rag, then leave it to dry overnight.

4 Lightly sand with fine grade abrasive paper. Repeat the process if necessary.

5 Finish by rubbing the handle with some steel wool.

6 The restored spade handle.

Essential tools

- Round-nosed shovel. This long-handled tool is ideal for moving garden materials and lifting.
- Secateurs. These should always be parrot-beaked. This allows one blade to hold the stem while the other cuts cleanly. The cutting blade should face the plant so that a clean cut, not a bruised branch, is left behind.
- Spade. When it comes to digging, the traditional spade has no equal.
- Hand trowel. The indispensable planting tool.
- Flat-head soil rake. The hard tines of this rake are useful for scarifying lawn and breaking up clods of earth, while the flat reverse is good for levelling the planting surface.
- Leaf rake. These flexible tines can be made from metal, plastic or bamboo and are great for cleaning the lawn and gravel.
- Cultivator. A hand tool for weeding and cultivating small areas.
- Mattock. Terrific for breaking up heavy ground as the weight of the head does most of the work.
- Fork. The best tool for breaking up soil, especially in the bottom of trenches when digging. Use also for aerating a lawn.

A bad workman quarrels with his tools.

English proverb

Top (left to right): Garden fork, mattock and spade.

Bottom (left to right): Round-nosed shovel, leaf rake and flat-head soil rake.

Did you know? The wheelbarrow was invented by the Chinese about 200 AD. It was a fulcrum with two levers.

Construction tools

There are a number of basic tools required for any construction project in the garden, whether it is a simple edge or a retaining wall. Add these to your list of essentials:

- Measuring tape
- Spirit level
- String line
- Claw hammer
- Lump hammer
- Bolster
- Handsaw
- Steel float
- Wooden float

- Hedge shears. These shears will certainly save your wrists if you have lots of pruning to do, but note that they will leave a brown line on a cut leaf.
- Barrow. The single-wheel barrow was first developed as a gardening tool in the fourteenth century, and has been invaluable ever since.
- Knife. Great for trimming roots when repotting, opening bags and all sorts of odd jobs.
- Pruning saw. Don't ruin secateurs and loppers by using them to cut through oversized branches. This is the tool you should use.
- Telescopic-handled loppers. Great for high-up branches that need trimming.
- Hand rake. Good for clearing small areas for seed sowing and bulb planting.

Top (clockwise from bottom left): Weeder, three-pronged cultivator, double-sided cultivator, secateurs and trowel.

Bottom (left to right): Long-handled loppers, pruning saw and hedging shears.

winter
annuals, perennials & bulbs

Although this is a quiet time for colour in the flower garden, there are some exceptional beauties that can brighten winter beds. These include wallflowers, spurges, early bulbs, hellebores and primulas. But perhaps the best part about winter is planning for the warmer seasons ahead.

A hippeastrum bulb, a surprise package.

Annuals

Don't suffer grey days and winter whiteouts each year. Instead, make the most of your cool conservatory by growing some annuals as winter-flowering pot plants.

Annuals such as cinerarias, primulas, stocks and schizanthus are sown in the previous summer. As soon as seeds have germinated the seedlings are transplanted individually into small pots and grown on steadily. During the summer they could be put into a well-ventilated cold frame as they like cool growing conditions. Pinch out the growing tips of plants like schizanthus to encourage bushy growth. Pot on the young plants until they are in final 15 cm pots. Well-drained soilless potting compost can be used for all potting. Liquid feed when established in final pots.

If you sing all summer, you'll weep in winter.

Bulgarian proverb

Favourite winter-flowering annuals

Annuals are rewarding to grow in conservatories as they give a great show of colour for comparatively little effort.

Cinerarias

These colourful daisy-like flowers (correctly *Pericallis* x *hybrida*) have flowers in shades of blue, red, pink, magenta and white. Some varieties have bicoloured flowers, while others have flower heads in single colours. Seeds are sown in mid-summer for winter flowering. They like cool growing conditions and shade from hot sun. Most varieties are of dwarf and bushy habit.

Stocks

For perfume in the cool conservatory, stocks are without peer. Despite being related to Brussels sprouts, stocks have a delicious clove-like scent and are great picking flowers with shades of pink, red, blue, purple, mauve and violet, plus white. Various kinds can be grown under glass including Column, East Lothian and Brompton stocks. Stocks grown as pot plants generally bloom in late winter and spring when sown in mid- to late summer. They must be grown in cool airy conditions and provided with really good light.

Primulas

There are several primulas for winter and spring flowering in the cool conservatory. *Primula malacoides*, the fairy primrose, has dainty whorls of fragrant flowers in pink or purplish shades, plus white. *P. obconica* bears heads of pink, blue, red or white flowers. *P.* x *kewensis* is somewhat different with its fragrant, yellow flowers. *P. sinensis* has whorls of pink, red, blue or white flowers. Primulas are sown in spring and grown very cool, shaded from strong sun. (See also 'The primula family' on page 352.)

Pansies and violas

Not just pretty faces, winter-flowering pansies and violas are extremely versatile and are grown outdoors as bedding plants

Leaf miner The only problem with growing cinerarias is the leaf miner, a tiny caterpillar which tunnels in the leaves and causes deterioration of the plants. You need a systemic insecticide to control this pest. However, if you keep your plants growing vigorously they will tolerate an infestation.

Annuals flowering in winter: above, *Browallia* sp., and right, poor man's orchid (*Schizanthus* sp.).

in areas where winters are not too severe. They will flower throughout winter and spring, in a wide range of colours, and are great in window boxes. Plants are raised from seed sown outdoors in early summer, grown on in a nursery bed and planted in autumn. (See 'Violets and violas' on page 380.)

Poor man's orchid

Schizanthus are popular pot plants for cool to intermediate conservatories and if sown in late summer should flower in late winter and into spring. They have masses of tiny orchid-like flowers in a wide range of colours, usually in beautiful combinations. There are many varieties available and they are generally short, compact, bushy plants. Pinching out the tips of young plants will promote this bushy habit.

Grow the young plants in a well-ventilated cold frame until autumn. Airy conditions are needed always.

Amethyst flower

Correctly known as browallias, these plants deserve to be better known as they make a good show in the winter. They are very free flowering, low-growing plants with blue or white flowers in the *B. speciosa* cultivars, of which there are many to choose from. The blooms are violet-blue in the species *B. viscosa*, and *B. americana* has blue, violet or white flowers. Best results are obtained in a slightly warmer conservatory, say with a minimum of 13°C. Sow seed in late summer for winter flowering. Grow plants in good light but shaded from strong sun. Pinch out the tips of young plants to encourage a bushy habit.

Jerusalem cherry

This small evergreen shrub (*Solanum pseudocapsicum*) is grown as an annual, not for its flowers but for the striking red or yellow fruits in winter (these are not edible). Several varieties are available. Ideal for the cool to intermediate conservatory, sow seeds in spring. Stand young plants out of doors until the autumn and pinch out the growing tip plus the resultant side shoots. Spraying the plants with water when in flower aids fruit set. The winter cherry (*Solanum capsicastrum*) is similar.

All the colours of the rainbow

Now is the time to plan for summer colour in the garden. Historically, the most successful garden designers have used colour in the same way as artists, selecting from their palettes and blending each colour to create a harmony which results in a certain mood or effect. The result may be restful or flamboyant.

The three primary colours — red, blue and yellow — are the building blocks of all other colours. The three secondary colours — green, violet and orange — are mixtures of these. Together, the primary and secondary colours make up the colours of a rainbow. Shades or hues vary depending on the strength and intensity of each primary colour, while tone is a measure of the black and white component in each colour. Black, white and grey are inert colours: they don't change the colour, only the brightness.

The colour wheel can be divided into halves: the 'cool' colours of green, grey, blue and mauve, and the 'warm' colours such as yellow, red, orange and hot pink. Colours next to each other on the colour wheel, or near by, are called harmonious colours, while colours opposite each other are called contrasting colours.

check list

jobs to do now

- Make sure any impatiens and begonias you want to keep are in a frost-free greenhouse for the winter.

- Lift and store the best dahlias of any not yet lifted. Discard inferior plants.

- If the weather is still clement and the soil not wet or frozen, hardy herbaceous perennials can be divided, including asters, astilbes, achilleas and shasta daisies. Pull the clump apart, or cut with a sharp knife.

- Towards the end of winter you can make a start cutting down the dead stems of hardy herbaceous perennials and grasses.

- If the ground is not frozen or wet, you can start planting hardy perennials towards the end of winter, such as astilbes and hostas, plus any that bloom in spring including pulmonarias, primulas, symphytum and ajugas.

- Hardy outdoor chrysanthemums can have their stems cut down in early winter. In hard winter areas the plants should be lifted and wintered as dormant 'stools' under glass.

- Bulbs planted in bowls for early flowering should be removed from the dark as soon as shoots are 3–5 cm tall.

plant now

- Towards winter's end, start sowing summer bedding plants under glass, primarily those needing a long period to develop. These include bedding pelargoniums, ageratum, antirrhinums, fibrous-rooted begonias (*Begonia semperflorens*), bedding dahlias, lobelia, scarlet salvias and verbenas.

- Gerbera makes a good pot plant under glass. It can be raised from seed, which is sown towards the end of winter or in early spring.

- The rhizomes of tuberose can be planted in pots in late winter or early spring for flowering in the warm conservatory.

- Pot hippeastrum bulbs by start of winter for conservatory flowering.

flowering now

- Annuals in the conservatory, including cinerarias, stocks, primulas, poor man's orchid, amethyst flower and Jerusalem cherry (fruits). Outdoors, winter-flowering pansies and violas.

- Hardy perennials such as some bergenia species, *Helleborus* x *hybridus* cultivars and Christmas rose (*Helleborus niger*). Some orchids and clivias will be in bloom under glass.

- Bulbs such as snowdrops, the earliest crocuses, *Cyclamen coum*, tender cyclamen under glass, *Iris reticulata*, *Iris danfordiae*, freesias under glass.

Colour creates a mood, which can vary from season to season, year after year, to suit the fashion or feeling of the day.

Use this knowledge as a tool in garden design. For example, for a vibrant garden full of vitality, use contrasting colours from opposite sides of the wheel — red and green, purple and yellow, blue and orange. Start with a cool colour as a base and add the hot colour as a highlight to intensify the effect of both colours. Alternatively, hues next to each other on the colour wheel harmonize. If you're trying to create a tranquil haven, then select complementary colours — for example, pink and mauve — on the same side of the wheel.

All gardening is landscape painting.

Alexander Pope

Some tips for using colour

1 Colour outside should be used to back up the function and mood of the garden, the flower colour adding to the effect of the foliage, form and texture of shrubs, trees and ground covers.

2 Colour has a big effect on mood. Use bright colours in lively environments, and softer, subtle tones in restful areas.

3 Locate the strongest colours in the foreground, and allow the colours to become paler with distance. Too much strong colour at a distance foreshortens the space.

4 Work with any surrounding colour schemes, including the house as well as the boundary and distant views.

5 Grey foliage 'cools down' bright colours, and white flowers help contrasting colours to blend effectively.

6 Colour changes, depending on the time of day and the intensity of sunlight. Pale colours look soft and gentle in the morning and evening light, yet can appear bleached and washed out during the day. Conversely, colours that work in the heat of the day can appear garish in softer light. Also remember that seasonal changes affect the strength of light.

7 Colour attracts the viewer's attention. Thus, when you want something to stand out and be noticed, a loud splash of colour nearby will hold the eye.

8 Select a range of colours that suits your home and personality, but try deviating from this range to allow contrast into your garden.

9 Try working with foliage colour as the backbone of your garden and it will have interest all year round. Darker foliage makes colours more pronounced.

10 Large flowers are harder to blend successfully than smaller ones.

plant your own **colour** scheme

Colour	Plant	Mood
	Scarlet salvias, nemesia, pansies, polyanthus, poppies, snapdragons, strawflower, violas, wallflower	**Red** Passion; makes time seem longer; excellent for the creation of ideas
	Calendula, French marigolds, pansies, poppies, snapdragons, strawflower, violas	**Orange** Drama
	Calendula, linaria, pansies, polyanthus, poppies, snapdragons, calceolarias, strawflower, violas, wallflower	**Yellow** Happiness
	Bells of Ireland, mignonette, *Zinnia elegans* 'Envy'	**Green** Reduces nerves and facilitates concentration
	Cineraria, delphinium, forget-me-not, lobelia, love-in-a-mist, lupins, nemesia, pansies, statice, violas	**Blue** Cooling; makes weight seem lighter and time even shorter
	Alyssum, cineraria, lobelia, love-in-a-mist, pansies, polyanthus, primula, stock	**Purple** Intrigue, mystery, power
	Alyssum, Canterbury bells, cinerarias, lobelia, pansies, polyanthus, poppies, primula, snapdragons, stocks	**Pink** Romance
	Candytuft, cineraria, gypsophila, lobelia, nemesia, pansies, primula, snapdragons, stock, violas	**White** Simplicity, peace, coolness
	Aquilegia, pansies, polyanthus, violas	**Black** Sombre, mournful mood

Did you know? According to American superstition, it is unlucky to plant on Fridays.

The dainty flowers of the primula family in their various forms (clockwise from bottom left): *Primula obconica*, *P. vulgaris*, *P. obconica*, *P. pulverulenta* and *P. malacoides*.

The primula family

The primula family starts flowering in winter, mainly under glass, peaks in spring and continues into summer. The family comes in many guises, known variously as primroses, cowslip, auricula, primula and polyanthus. They all form rosettes of lush leafy clumps, with tubular flowers that are flattened and face-like, or held on candelabra-like whorls. They like a moist, humus-rich soil. A spot under a deciduous tree is perfect: the spring sunshine promotes flowering and the canopy gives needed summer shade and coolness.

For the earliest flowers in frost-prone climates it is necessary to grow annual primulas as pot plants in the cool conservatory. Among the most popular for this purpose are the fairy primrose (*Primula malacoides*), *P. obconica*, *P.* x *kewensis* and the Chinese primrose (*P. sinensis*). (For further details see 'Primulas' on page 347.)

Cowslip is the name given to a few perennial species: *P. veris*, spring flowering, *P. florindae* (giant cowslip), summer flowering, and *P. sikkimensis*, late spring and early summer flowering. All have yellow

...pale primroses,

That die unmarried, ere they can behold

Bright Phoebus in his strength,— a malady

Most incident to maids....

William Shakespeare

Polyanthus have been cultivated since the seventeenth century and they make terrific container plants.

flowers. Perennial candelabra primulas such as *P. aurantiaca*, *P. beesiana*, *P. bulleyana* and *P. japonica* produce tiers of flowers up to 1 m high and look superb around pools.

Strictly speaking, primroses (derived from *P. vulgaris*) have short flower stems. Polyanthus are a cross between primroses and cowslips, and traditionally have flower heads borne on a single stem clear of the leaves. As these plants have been subject to intensive breeding, this distinction has been lost and the two fade into each other. They make a great spring-flowering perennial.

Their buttercup yellow, red, white, blue, lavender and terracotta flowers look terrific in pots, or when planted in masses in the garden they give the effect of a colourful modernist painting. Normally five-petalled, occasionally the odd flower will have six petals. Once it was believed that such flowers brought you luck, and if you were in love, they were a certain sign that your love was returned.

The soft petals, cheerful faces and wonderful colours of the primula family make them an asset in any garden.

Did you know? The irritating hairs on *Primula obonica* can cause an allergy. Sometimes other species also cause skin rashes. Just in case, always wear gloves when handling them.

Wallflowers

Wallflowers earned their name by growing in cracks in walls or stone work. Both annual and perennial types tend to be extremely hardy plants, surviving in difficult positions and flowering at a time when little else is showing colour. They originally belonged to two genera, *Cheiranthus* and *Erysimum*, but now belong only to *Erysimum*. All like to be in well drained positions and benefit from regular trimming to promote new compact growth and flowers.

The season starts in late winter when the perennial *E.* x *kewense* begins to bloom. It is a bushy evergreen with yellow-orange flowers that change to pale purple. It continues flowering into early summer.

The plant that everyone knows as the wallflower is *E. cheiri*. Although a short-lived evergreen perennial, it is grown as a biennial for spring bedding. In the mildest areas it often starts flowering in late winter. The flowers are fragrant and come in a wide colour range, from strong to pastel shades.

Throughout spring the Siberian wallflower (*E. allionii*) makes a stunning display of apricot or brilliant orange-scented flowers. The variegated wallflower (*E. mutabile* 'Variegatum'), with its pinkish brown flowers in spring, has cream-striped leaves, which make it useful for edges and contrast.

For paler tones, try coast wallflower (*E. capitatum*), which has pale yellow flowers that fade to cream, and the fairy wallflower (*E. linifolium*) with its grey-green leaves and purple or violet flowers in spring.

All wallflowers make great cut flowers ('Cheiranthus' means hand flower). They add scent and colour to the garden for most of the year and last well in a vase if the water is changed regularly.

Top: Variegated wallflower. Bottom: Varieties of *Erysimum cheiri*.

mignonette

Mention mignonette and one thinks of summer. So why include it in winter? It can be grown as a pot plant in a cool to intermediate conservatory where it will bloom in late winter and spring, and where its sweetly scented flowers can be easily enjoyed, a trick used by Victorian and Edwardian gardeners.

Vital statistics

Scientific name: *Reseda odorata*.

Family: Resedaceae.

Climate: Suitable for growing in warm or cold climates.

Culture: Widely used as a cut flower.

Colour: Green, inconspicuous pink, coppery red and various blends.

Height: Plants grow 20–30 cm high.

Planting time: For late winter and spring flowers under glass sow in late summer.

Soil: Grow in pots of well-drained potting compost.

Position: Provide good light and airy conditions.

Planting depth and spacing: : Sow thinly in a 13 cm pot and thin seedlings to 2.5 cm apart.

Watering: Take care that the soil does not become too wet or soggy.

Fertilizer: Additional feeding is not needed.

Pests/diseases: None.

Flowering time: Flowers winter to spring.

Pruning: Pinch out tips to promote branching. Remove plants once flowering has finished.

Propagation: From seed.

Closely related are stocks (*Matthiola* sp.) which have spicy clove-scented blooms. Although they generally need to be replaced each year, they are worth the effort for their array of colours: from white to apple blossom, peach, pink, lilac, lavender and lemon tones. (See 'Favourite winter-flowering annuals'.) They last well as a cut flower if the water is changed often.

See how the flowers, as at parade,

Under their colours stand displayed:

Each regiment in order grows,

That of tulip, pink and rose.

Andrew Marvell

Above (left to right): pink
hellebores, *Bergenia
cordifolia*, and
Iris unguicularis.

Perennials

Although winter is a quiet time in the herbaceous border, some plants are
braving the elements and flowering their heads off.

There is no need for the garden to be devoid
of colour in the winter as there are several
hardy perennials that are at their best at this
time of year. They may be in flower, or
displaying attractive foliage. Make the most
of them by planting generous groups among
shrubs, particularly winter-flowering shrubs
such as witch hazels (hamamelis), as
well as viburnums and wintersweet
(chimonanthus). And do not forget to mix
some winter- or spring-flowering bulbs
among these perennials, such as snowdrops.

Hellebores

Many species of hellebore (helleborus) are
flowering in the winter. Not only the
Christmas rose (see feature perennial on

facing page), but also Lenten roses
(*Helleborus* x *hybridus*). These may be
herbaceous or evergreen and saucer-shaped
flowers are produced in winter and spring
There are many varieties, with flowers from
white to pink, purple, yellow and green,
often heavily spotted with a contrasting
colour. *H. torquatus* and its varieties are
similar. If you want a hellebore with really
deep purple flowers, try *H. atrorubens*
which has saucer-shaped blooms.

The stinking hellebore (*H. foetidus*) is
so named because the leaves have an
unpleasant smell when bruised. The bell-
shaped flowers are green, with purple edges
to the petals. The Corsican hellebore
(*H. argutifolius*) also has green flowers.

Did you know? *Helleborus niger* is so named because of its black tap root. The flowers are actually white.
The black-flowered helleborus is a cultivar called 'Queen of the Night'.

christmas **rose**

The Christmas rose is liable to flower at any time in winter, not necessarily in time for the festive season. It is a dwarf perennial with large saucer-shaped white flowers and looks good mass planted around deciduous or evergreen shrubs. Best for climates where winters are cool or cold.

Vital statistics

Scientific name: *Helleborus niger*.
Family: Ranunculaceae.
Climate: Cool and cold.
Culture: Best not to move plants once planted.
Colours: White.
Height: Plants grow 30 cm high.
Planting time: Plant in autumn, or in spring when flowering is over.
Soil: Soil should be heavy, alkaline to neutral and moisture retentive. Dig in leaf mould or garden compost before planting.
Position: Dappled shade, with shelter from cold, drying winds.
Planting spacing: Plant in bold groups, setting the plants 45 cm apart each way.
Watering: Keep moist at all times.
Fertilizer: No need to apply fertilizer but mulch in autumn with bulky organic matter.
Flowering time: Winter and early spring.
Pruning: Remove dead leaves and flowers.

All of these are ideal for dappled shade and moist, alkaline to neutral soil. Plant them under and around deciduous trees.

Colourful leaves

Although bergenias flower in spring, many are valuable in the winter garden with their large, rounded leaves. In some species and varieties these take on red or purple tints in winter. Best for this are *Bergenia cordifolia* whose leaves are tinted with purple during the cold months; *B. crassifolia* whose leaves take on red tints; and *B. purpurascens* which turns rich purple-red.

Grow bergenias with hellebores, as they like the same conditions and make a good contrast. They also make excellent ground cover and look good all the year round.

It may surprise gardeners to learn that there is an iris that flowers in winter. The winter iris (*Iris unguicularis*) produces fragrant, lavender-blue flowers among its contrasting, grassy, deep green foliage.

Cymbidium orchids.

Orchids

Winter and into spring is the main orchid season. The cymbidiums look great, and the moth orchids (phalaenopsis), slipper orchids (paphiopedilums) and some dendrobiums also start to flower. Orchids are so beautiful when in flower that most people think they must be tricky to grow, but the truth is they are some of the toughest plants around, and actually thrive on adversity.

All of these easily grown orchids can be cultivated in an intermediate conservatory, but many people will prefer to grow them on windowsills in a warm room indoors. All the popular orchids make surprisingly good house plants. The cymbidiums are among the most widely grown orchids. Their blooms vary in colour from the purest white through to pinks, chocolate, yellows, lime green and bicolours. Many even have a rich perfume, so sample the perfume before you make your choice!

When not in flower, cymbidiums are a mass of strappy green leaves that cope well with neglect. However, like all orchids, they will repay you well given tender loving care. In summer give them good light but shade from strong sun, and airy conditions. Feed with an orchid fertilizer at every third watering in summer. During winter ease up on watering and provide maximum light.

Dendrobiums, mainly spring flowering, are easily grown and are good windowsill plants. They are best grown in slatted orchid baskets but will also thrive in clay pots. In spring and summer provide partial shade, humid conditions (mist foliage twice a day) and feed at every third watering. Provide maximum light in autumn and winter and keep the compost almost dry.

Moth orchids (*Phalaenopsis* sp.) produce elegant, butterfly-shaped flowers in white, pink or lilac which bloom all the way up their long elegant stems — perfect for a glazed ceramic pot on a coffee table or mantelpiece. These are easy to grow. Other orchids, like the spectacular vandas, need to be brought into a heated, well lit room over winter, or left for tropical climates.

Growing tips

1. Orchids don't grow in ordinary soil, as they prefer a specially formulated orchid mix that caters for their particular needs.
2. When an orchid has filled its pot to the brim, take the clump out and chop it into smaller pieces (see 'Repotting orchids' opposite).
3. Discard any dead or dry-looking bits and replant your smaller pieces, each still with its leaves and roots, into fresh orchid mix.
4. Don't bury the bulb, which should be sitting above the surface. You can repot at any time, but spring and early summer are best.
5. There are plenty of orchid foods available on the market. Try selecting one that comes as a two-part preparation: one for flowering time, the other for foliage growth.
6. Water plants regularly in hot months, but allow your orchids to virtually dry out between waterings in cooler weather.

REPOTTING ORCHIDS

Repot an orchid after flowering or, for a non-flowering plant, in early to mid-spring. Grow in half shade. During the growing season, feed frequently with a proprietary orchid fertilizer (follow the maker's instructions closely).

1 The roots of an orchid which has spent about ten years in the same pot.

2 Divide the plant.

3 Remove old back or pseudobulbs (these will be leafless), old growth, dead stalks and pottery shards.

4 Trim the roots clean.

5 A baby shoot.

6 Trim dead or damaged leaves.

7 Place enough coarse grade orchid compost in the bottom of the pot to allow for root growth. Crocking is not necessary because of the open texture of the compost.

8 Carefully position the plants in the pot so that the pseudobulbs are proud of the potting mix.

9 Top up with orchid compost so that the mixture is almost overflowing the pot.

10 Again, trim any dead or damaged leaves.

11 Water in and allow to drain.

12 Keep the plant moist, not wet, and don't allow it to dry out.

Clockwise from bottom left: *Freesia alba*, tulip, daffodil, iris and *Hippeastrum* 'Apple Blossom'.

As winter ends, some early spring bulbs, such as certain crocuses and daffodils, rub shoulders with the winter-flowering snowdrops, especially if the weather is mild.

Buy summer-flowering bulbs

Although it is too late to plant spring-flowering bulbs, winter is the time to buy many summer-flowering bulbs for spring planting, like gladioli, gloriosa, pineapple flower (eucomis) and tuberous begonias.

Hippeastrums

The large trumpet-shaped flowers of hippeastrums are seen in many warm conservatories. These tender bulbs are also at home on windowsills in warm rooms. The large bulbs are planted in pots in autumn and flower during winter and spring. Hippeastrums are currently popular and their popularity has been steadily growing as more colours — from white to soft apple blossom, stripes and rich reds — have become available.

Bulbs

Bulbs, no matter what time of the year they flower, add a touch of surprise and magic to a garden. Their ephemeral nature makes them special and unique, so it's worth planting them even if it's only for a few weeks or months of their company.

Hippeastrum The neck of the hippeastrum bulb should protrude 15 cm or so above the soil level to help with heat exposure. Water after planting, then leave it alone until leaves appear. Snails can eat these, so keep an eye out.

Keep them in bright light but shade from direct sun. When in full growth, water regularly, keeping the compost steadily moist, and feed with a balanced liquid fertilizer once a fortnight. When flowering is over and the leaves start dying down, gradually reduce water and keep the compost dry while the bulbs are dormant in the summer. Growth resumes in autumn when you should start watering again.

Cyclamen

Cyclamen are looking their best over winter. Their elegant tulip-like blooms come in a range of colours, from pure white through to cherry, lilac, fuchsia pink, musk, wine red and scarlet, both pure and bicoloured. The foliage is also a feature, with interesting markings of dark green, verdigris and silver.

The florist's cyclamen (*Cyclamen persicum*) is the one grown as a conservatory pot plant and has many varieties. Also flowering now is the hardy miniature *C. coum*, ideal for massing around shrubs and under deciduous trees. This is followed in autumn by the similar *C. hederifolium* (syn. *C. neapolitanum*).

Growing tips

1 Water the soil, not the flowers or foliage. Do this carefully with a small can or, alternatively, place the plant in a saucer for a few hours each week and let it soak the water up from the base. Never keep the saucer filled permanently.

2 Get into the habit of taking your cyclamen out at night as they are prone to disease (especially botrytis) if they stay inside heated rooms.

3 Remove any old flowers or yellow leaves, right at the base, with your fingers.

4 To prolong flowering right up until late spring, feed with liquid fertilizer every two or three weeks.

5 A sunny light room is the best environment for *C. persicum*.

Buying tip Catalogues of specialist bulb growers are bursting with summer-flowering bulbs, which can be ordered and bought now ready for spring planting. Garden centres should also be starting to stock up with these bulbs once the festive season is over. Remember to keep dormant bulbs in a cool, dry, airy place until planting time.

Above (left to right):
Chinese evergreen
(*Aglaonema* 'Silver King'),
Dracaena deremensis and
arrowhead (*Syngonium
podophyllum*). If you
manage to kill this
selection, buy yourself
some good fakes!

Indoor plants

Air inside the home and workplace is
polluted by fumes given off by electricals —
such as computers, TVs, microwaves — and
by chemically treated surfaces, paints and
plastics. Apart from producing oxygen,
plants absorb poisonous gases, especially
those produced by plastic furniture and
synthetic carpets.

The best thing you can do for your
indoor environment is to bring a little of
the outdoors in. 'Plantscaping' your home
need not be boring. There are many
imaginative ways to decorate with plants.

How to choose an indoor plant

First, consider what function you want your
indoor plant to perform. Ask yourself the
following questions:

1 Should it feature flowers or foliage?
2 Should it stay small, grow tall, wide or
   narrow? For example, choose small
   plants for a kitchen windowsill and tall
   ones with striking foliage for a large
   living area.
3 Should it be mobile? Sometimes smaller
   plants that can be spelled outdoors in the
   shade for half the time make ideal table
   setting decorations.

Position

Few plants grow in the dark so don't expect
your house plants to perform miracles. Give
them a little sunlight and as much daylight
as possible. Avoid draughts, as nothing dries
out a pot faster than a windy corridor or
foyer. Finally, indoor plants often have the
odd flower when you first buy them, but
remember that the nursery has grown the
plants in perfect conditions, so be satisfied if
you have happy, healthy leaves; flowers are
a bonus.

Growing conditions

Will your plant have to endure heating in
winter, poor light or air-conditioning?

Because there is no such thing as a
naturally occurring indoor plant, we have to
mimic outdoor conditions. Most indoor
plants grow best in bright positions.
However, if you have a full sun position
inside, try to keep your plants away from
the glass. This can really heat up and will
actually cause sunburn (dead, brown
patches on leaves) or bleaching (whole leaf
turns yellow or white). Cacti, succulents,
croton, mother-in-law's tongue and ixora
should be content in this spot, provided
they are given regular drinks.

Tougher and hardier plants, such as peace lily (spathiphyllum), kentia palms, cissus, aspidistra, fatsia, ivies and philodendrons, will tolerate low levels of light, provided you don't let them get too wet. If the spot you have is really terrible, try rotating your plants every 2–3 weeks. Take them outside into a shady area, or let them stand in the rain.

Tips for growing indoor plants
Hygiene
To keep your indoor plants thriving, wipe over the leaves with proprietary house plant leafshine or a tissue moistened with water to remove the dust and grime that clog up the breathing pores.

Repotting
The best time to repot is when the plant will recover quickly. This is usually just after flowering, or at the beginning of spring. Vigorous plants will need repotting every year, while slower plants such as rhapis palms will last for 3–4 years.

If the leaves on your indoor plant are getting smaller, appear to wilt soon after watering, or if roots appear on the surface, then your plant needs to be in a bigger pot.

Quality potting mixes contain slow-release fertilizer and water crystals and will save you maintenance time. If using a cheaper mix, don't forget the plants are totally dependent on you for food, so give them some nine-month slow-release granular fertilizer.

Feeding
Plants need feeding if their leaves yellow, start to show chlorosis (yellowing between the veins) or have different leaf sizes. For optimum health, vigour and flowering, try a two-pronged approach to feeding. First use a slow-release fertilizer designed specifically for indoor plants. For maximum benefit in the warmer weather, apply this in late winter. Second, apply a diluted liquid fertilizer every fortnight during the growing season. Good organic fertilizers can be applied to the soil and used as a foliage spray. Use foliar feeding at half strength, and apply it more frequently than you otherwise would.

Watering
Indoor plants need regular watering, especially during warm weather, or when you are applying liquid fertilizer. Although

DIVIDING PEACE LILY

1 Remove the plant from the pot and divide the plant into sections.

2 If the roots are damaged or tangled, trim them.

3 Place the plant in a suitably sized pot and fill with good-quality potting compost. A soilless type is particularly suitable.

4 The repotted peace lily.

project
plant a **terrarium**

For planting a terrarium, choose miniature plants, such as small parlour palms, African violets and plants with attractive foliage such as hypoestes, selaginellas, nerve plant (fittonia) and peperomias.

1 Select a suitable vessel. Anything with a sealable top can be used, although the larger the better. You can purchase terrarium glass jars from your nursery, or use your imagination — cookie jars make ideal containers. You will also need some peat-based compost or some African violet potting compost, some charcoal, paper towel and sphagnum moss.

2 Place a layer of charcoal on the bottom of the jar. This helps absorb wastes and cleanses the sealed environment.

3 Fit a cloth, such as some paper towel, to stop the potting compost from working its way into the charcoal layer.

4 Add a small amount of peat-based mix or African violet potting compost.

5 Gently plant your chosen greenery, firmly tamping down around the roots.

6 Decorate the top with a layer or two of coloured pebbles or sphagnum moss.

7 Water in gently, washing down any dirty leaves. Replace the lid.

8 The finished terrarium.

Foggy glass Although the terrarium is a closed environment and will regulate its own watering needs, you may need to help establish the right moisture balance for a while by removing the lid if the sides of the glass become foggy.

water is important, don't make the mistake of sitting plants in saucers. This may rot the roots, and should only be done if absolutely necessary, such as with African violets or ferns. Sit the pots on pebbles or stands to keep the roots free draining.

It is also better to water house plants thoroughly once a week than to sprinkle them daily. They can even be taken outside for a hose down. And, most importantly, appoint someone in your house or workplace to do the watering. More indoor plants die from overwatering than from all the other causes combined.

In winter, when plants are not growing, don't water until the surface becomes dry. If hot, dry air from heaters is a problem, try misting the leaves rather than watering the soil. An atomizer can also be handy in air-conditioned rooms throughout summer. The best way to tell if your indoor plants are dry is to use your finger. If the soil is dry at the second knuckle, then you need to water. Try not to let them wilt between waterings, as this will put them under stress and make them prone to disease attack.

Problem pests

The most common indoor plant pest is mealy bug. Almost anything is a suitable meal for this fuzzy cotton wool-like pest. The best method of control is to keep leaves clean, and spray or soak the root ball in a pesticide solution.

The other problem is scale. These look like small raised lumps, and can be white or dark brown. Scale particularly affects palms, and can be treated with horticultural soap.

Sometimes indoor plants can get red spider (two-spotted mite), a particularly difficult pest to control. Mites thrive in dry, dusty conditions, so regular spells outside and a good hosing will help prevent attack.

never-say-die
indoor plant

Most indoor plants suffer the most horrendous treatment. Often housed in dark rooms with air-conditioning, poor ventilation and no natural light, they may be watered only by cups of cold tea.

If this is a description of your workplace, but you'd still prefer the real thing over an artificial plant, try a Chinese evergreen (*Aglaonema* sp.). It has interesting mottled foliage and copes with just about anything. Or for flowers indoors, it's hard to go past the peace lily (*Spathiphyllum* sp.), which has white spoon-shaped blooms, while dragon trees (*Dracaena* sp.) make interesting indoor sculptural elements. Garden centres sell several varieties of syngonium, which are tough plants with attractive foliage. Although they rarely flower indoors, they are semi-climbing in habit and will also cascade from a hanging basket.

WICK WATERING

1 Wrap a cotton wick around the root ball so that a length of wick is left at the bottom of the plant. Feed this end through one of the draining holes in the plastic pot and place the plant in the pot.

2 Put the plant and pot in a decorative container, then place the end of the wick in a small container of water.

African violets

African violets (*Saintpaulia* sp.) are probably the world's most popular house plant, but they can be very stubborn and sometimes refuse to flower.

A windowsill with winter morning sunshine is ideal, as African violets need lots of light in order to flower well plus year-round feeding to keep them healthy. Stand each plant in a saucer of water, or better still, on a container filled with water to which some drops of special violet fertilizer have been added. Make a hole in the lid of the container and pass a cotton wick (Venetian blind cord is good) from the pot, out through the drainage hole and into the water container beneath. This way the solution is soaked up into the plant as it is needed, and it's impossible to overwater as most people do! Alternatively, just run the wick between the plant and a small container of water.

Each year African violets need repotting into special potting mix. Don't be tempted to plant them in large pots as they tend to get waterlogged and die.

Propagation

African violets are easily propagated and using leaf cuttings is the simplest method. Place the leaf stalk (petiole) into a peaty mix and keep it moist. New leaves will grow from the stalk, feeding off the original leaf until they develop roots. Once this happens, pot them into small pots and place them on a sunny windowsill. You'll soon have flowering-sized plants.

PROPAGATING AFRICAN VIOLETS

1 Dampen some peat.

2 Spread the peat in a seedling tray.

3 Pluck some leaves from an African violet and plant the petiole in the peat moss.

4 Keep moist till roots appear, then pot up into small pots.

snow**drop**

These bulbs, especially the common snowdrop (*Galanthus nivalis*), are among the first to flower, producing pendent, bell-shaped flowers in winter, often through the snow. The flowers are white but the inner petals are tipped with green. Snowdrops are very pretty mass planted around shrubs or under deciduous trees.

Vital statistics

Scientific name: *Galanthus* sp.
Family: Amaryllidaceae.
Plant/bulb type: They are true bulbs.
Climate: Cool and cold.
Culture: Great bulbs for partial shade, needing little attention once planted.
Height: Depending on species, 10–20 cm.
Planting time: Immediately after flowering. Alternatively as dormant bulbs in autumn.
Soil: Moist, well drained, containing plenty of humus.
Position: Grow in partial shade.
Planting depth and spacing: Plant bulbs 8 cm deep and 8 cm apart.
Watering: Do not allow soil to dry out in summer.
Fertilizer: Feeding not necessary, but mulch with leafmould, chipped bark or well-rotted garden compost.
Flowering time: Autumn, winter, spring, depending on species.
Pests/diseases: Grey mould or botrytis.
After-flowering care: Immediately after flowering is the time to lift and divide congested clumps, replanting them immediately.

Did you know? Tennyson described the snowdrop as the 'February fairmaid'.

winter

grasses, ground covers & climbers

Although winter is a fairly tranquil period for these cover-ups, ornamental grasses can be beautiful in their own right, with spent flower heads and winter silhouettes adding interest and form. The more traditional turf grass has virtually stopped growing and almost all climbers have slipped into a sleep now.

Grasses

The cool or cold weather slows or stops the growth of lawn grasses. This means that mowing is not necessary, or if the occasional cut is needed, raise the height of the mower blades. Feeding is not required until the spring.

While the grass growth has slowed down or stopped, weeds may continue to grow, particularly dandelions and other broad-leaved kinds. These can removed by hand, using a special two-pronged tool

Annual meadow grass or annual bluegrass often continues growing and seeding in winter.

known as a 'daisy grubber'. Annual meadow grass or annual bluegrass (*Poa annua*) may also continue growing and it is best to prevent it from seeding by mowing off the flowers. It is not advisable to spray for weeds at this time of year: you should wait until the grass is growing strongly in the spring before applying a proprietary lawn weedkiller.

Clockwise from above: *Hedera canariensis*, *Bellis perennis* or English daisy and *Oxalis* sp.

If you are doing any remodelling of your garden over winter, remember that lawn is slow to recover from heavy traffic at this time of year, and may need extra care to prepare it for spring growth.

Aerate compacted areas by inserting a garden fork at 15 cm intervals to a depth of about 15 cm. If possible, rope off the lawn area to stop people walking on it. This is especially recommended if the lawn becomes very wet in winter.

If these remedies fail, remember that in spring you can sow grass seed or lay new turf over any bare patches.

Lawn flowers

Weeds aren't the only things that thrive in lawns, coping with repeated mowing and spreading easily. Lawn flowers — including bird's foot trefoil, white clover, oxalis and lawn daisies — do too.

Bird's foot trefoil (*Lotus corniculatus*) and lawn daisy (*Bellis perennis*), the original ancestor of the modern double form of English daisy, can both be bought as seed and sown over turf to create a romantic, whimsical effect. The single white flowers of the lawn daisy show during the cooler months before lawn mowing starts.

Some oxalis species make excellent ground cover through lawns, as they may flower during mild spells in winter when the turf has all but stopped growing. The foliage consists of leaflets and somewhat resembles clover. Flowers may be white, pink or yellow. Some oxalis are pernicious

It is not spring 'til you can plant your foot upon twelve daisies.

weeds and spread like wildfire, so be careful what you choose. The wood sorrel, *Oxalis acetosella*, establishes well in a moist lawn, particularly in shady areas. It has attractive white flowers and light green foliage. There is also a variety with rose-pink flowers.

The common clover can also be too easily dismissed as a weed, but don't forget it is great for improving soil fertility (see 'The Papilionaceae family' on page 259), as it helps fix nitrogen into the soil and can look pretty and lush. Just remember not to run through it in bare feet, as bee stings could be a problem.

check list

jobs to do now

- Remove any broad-leaved lawn weeds, such as dandelions, by hand.

- Trim lawn edges and re-mark garden beds where appropriate.

- Keep an eye on moss in the lawn and if it is building up over winter apply a lawn moss killer in spring.

- If ferns have become shabby, give them a haircut quite close to the crown at the end of winter, just as the new growth is about to start. Feed them with liquid fertilizer and you'll have a fresh crop of fronds in no time.

- Prune ornamental grape back to its main branches.

- Prune wisteria back almost to the main framework stems, leaving two or three buds on each stem that is cut back.

plant now

- In late winter sow seeds of carpeting pinks and carnations (*Dianthus* sp.) in a heated greenhouse.

- Divide ground-smothering perennials such as windflowers, erigeron and shasta daisy.

- Plant deciduous vines such as wisteria and ornamental grape.

flowering now

- No ornamental grasses or sedges will be flowering in winter, but the bleached dead flowers and foliage of many of the former look very attractive though this season.

- The sweet violet (*Viola odorata*) produces sweetly scented flowers.

- In late winter, some bergenias are useful perennials for ground cover.

- The periwinkle (*Vinca difformis*) has light blue flowers in late winter.

- In an intermediate to warm conservatory, the flame vine (*Pyrostegia venusta*) will be flowering.

- Climbers that are useful as ground cover and look lush and green over winter include varieties of English ivy (*Hedera helix*), varieties of Canary Island or Algerian ivy (*H. canariensis*) and star jasmine (*Trachelospermum jasminoides*).

Mosses and fungi

The cool weather encourages moss to grow in the grass, lichens to cover flagging and fungi to emerge from rotting timbers. There are two ways of dealing with nature's fight-back: either celebrate it as a seasonal treasure or combat it with chemicals.

Moss gardening has become a cultural practice in its own right. Mosses can be used as a lawn substitute, particularly in damp, shady areas under trees and on moist, shady banks.

Many people have come to like moss so much that they go to any lengths to get it to grow on pots and statuary. To speed up the softening effect of mosses and lichen on stonework or terracotta, smear on yoghurt or paint over with sour milk. You'll soon have a lovely culture of moss and mould. Use this method to make composite concrete look like stone.

If you are despairing over paths slippery with moss, apply a bit of bleach with a stiff brush; this method will remove the moss without giving your paving the 'brand new' look you'll get with water blasting.

We are only just beginning to realize the importance of symbiotic relationships. Symbiotic fungi are becoming available to add to the soil when planting trees and shrubs to help them establish and thrive.

This damp mossy stone wall is ideal for these begonias which have probably self-seeded.

project
moss in a box

Winter is perfect weather for moss, which thrives in cooler temperatures. If you love the look of moss, plant a container with some ground cover and alpine plants that masquerade as moss — try scleranthus, sagina, pratia, mazus, thrift, fescue and pinks.

Any low container will do. Old boxes, fruit crates, limestone sinks and shallow troughs are ideal. Equip your container with adequate drainage and fill it with coarse, gritty potting compost for aeration and extra peat for moisture retention.

REPLACING CORD ON A POWER GRASS TRIMMER

1 A power grass trimmer with a short cutting cord needing replacement.

2 Cut a new length of cord.

3 Open the cartridge and take out the reel. Remove any remaining cord.

4 Thread the new length of cord through the loop on the reel.

5 Pull the cord through the loop until you have two equal lengths. Wind the two lengths around the reel until you have loose ends about 25 cm long.

6 Pull one end of the cord through a notch on the base of the reel. Pull the other end through another notch on the opposite side of the reel.

7 Thread one cord end through a hole in the side of the cartridge.

8 With the other end inserted through the hole in the other side of the cartridge, insert the reel in the cartridge.

9 Snap the reel and the cartridge back together.

Machinery maintenance

Winter is a handy time to do some basic maintenance on your machinery as well as on your tools (see 'The garden shed').

Strip down and clean your mower, giving it fresh oil and a new air filter and spark plugs (see right). If you're not confident about this, take it to the garden machinery shop for an overhaul and get the cutting blade sharpened at the same time.

Also, you can easily replace the cord on a power grass trimmer. Just follow the step-by-step instructions on the opposite page.

You should regularly clean your garden shredder, changing the air filter and topping up the oil at the same time. And remember to clean and sharpen the blades on your hedge shears.

Every blade of grass has its angel that bends over it and whispers, 'Grow, grow.'

The Talmud

The benefits

Clean sharp blades on grass-cutting equipment stop the spread of weeds and diseases. Uneven, jagged cuts left by unsharpened blades create a scorch line which is unattractive as well as stressful for your lawn. An annual overhaul of your machinery really does make a difference.

Safety tips Don't store the grass catcher with clippings in it; instead, empty them onto the compost heap.

Take care with flammable or poisonous materials. Always store them out of reach of children and pets.

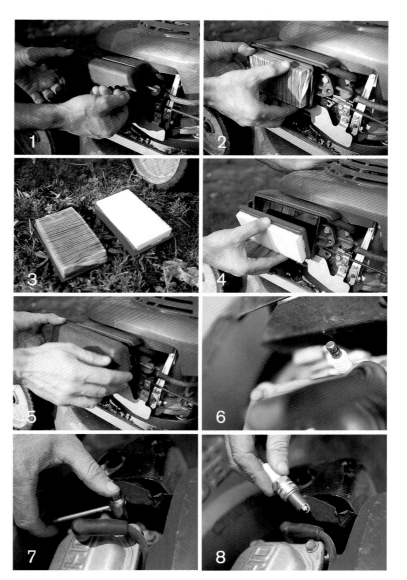

LAWN MOWER MAINTENANCE

1 Remove the cover on the air filter.

2 Take out the old air filter.

3 Once an air filter is clogged with dirt, it inhibits the air flow and your mower will simply stop.

4 Insert the new air filter by pushing it into place.

5 Replace the cover on the air filter.

6 Remove the spark plug cover.

7 Using a spark plug socket, remove the spark plug.

8 Check the spark plug. If the point is dirty, rub it with some abrasive paper.

lily**turf**

Although not a true grass, it does have grass-like foliage, of particular value in winter. This hardy perennial is a close relation of ophiopogon (see below) and does well in most areas with dappled sunlight. Lilyturf can be used to create stunning foliage effects. Some varieties have white or yellow variegated leaves. All do well in urns. The flowers, produced in autumn, are similar to grape hyacinths and show up well if the foliage is dark green.

Vital statistics

Scientific name: *Liriope muscari.*
Family: Convallariaceae.
Climate: Cool or warm areas.
Colours: Purple/violet flower spike.
Height: Grows to 30 cm.
Planting time: Any.
Soil: Well drained and enriched with rotted manure or compost.
Position: Dappled or complete shade.
Fertilizer: Complete plant food in spring.
Propagation: Divide clumps in spring and plant about 45 cm apart each way.

Mondo grass

The genus *Ophiopogon* is similar to liriope and is also called lilyturf, but *O. japonicus* is popularly known as mondo grass. This is not a true grass but has grassy foliage.

It is fantastic en masse and can be used effectively as a lawn substitute in the shade, especially the dwarf varieties, or as a border between beds and pathways. Lawns are not intended for use, only as ornamental features. White variegated varieties are especially attractive. A very popular lilyturf is *O. planiscapus* 'Nigrescens' with black leaves. Mondo grass lawns can be expensive to put in, so try and buy the smallest pots you can as the plants clump up quickly.

If we had keen vision and feeling of all ordinary human life,

it would be like hearing the grass grow and the squirrel's heart beat...

George Eliot

Ground covers

As winter brings out the worst in traditional grass, take time to study nature's many alternatives.

After World War II, turf grass became the most dominant element of the home garden and alternative ground covers were ignored. Although most are not as resistant to wear and tear, ground covers do provide flowers, fragrant foliage and textural contrast.

Ferns

Ferns are one of the most ancient of plant groups, reproducing themselves not by flower and seed production but by spore. They love cool, moist areas and thrive in the shade. The detail in fern fronds lifts these areas by introducing rich texture. There is a great variation in colour and pattern in fern fronds. Some leaves have superb silver markings, bronze new growth or lime young leaves, while others glisten and shimmer.

Ferns can be evergreen or herbaceous, dying back in winter, but whatever the type, most can become shabby at this time and need a close prune back to the crown so

that they can regenerate themselves with fresh spring growth. This is also the time to divide up large clumps. There are many hardy ferns available for frost-prone climates. The lady fern (*Athyrium filix-femina*) is popular together with the male fern (*Dryopteris filix-mas*). The ostrich fern (*Matteuccia struthiopteris*) has a shuttlecock-like arrangement of fronds (leaves). The soft shield fern (*Polystichum setiferum*) has lacy fronds and common polypody (*Polypodium vulgare*) is drought tolerant.

All make good ground cover, but include tree ferns among them. The hardiest is the Tasmanian or soft tree fern (*Dicksonia antarctica*).

There are many good ferns for the conservatory. The asparagus fern (*Asparagus densiflorus* 'Myersii') is not a true fern but has very ferny, bright green foliage. The bird's nest fern (*Asplenium nidus*) with undivided fronds, is a popular houseplant.

Clockwise from above: silver elkhorn fern (*Platycerium veitchii*), tree ferns and asparagus fern (*Asparagus densiflorus* 'Myersii').

A garden is a lovesome thing, God wot! Rose plot, Fringed pool, Fern'd grot.

T. E. Brown

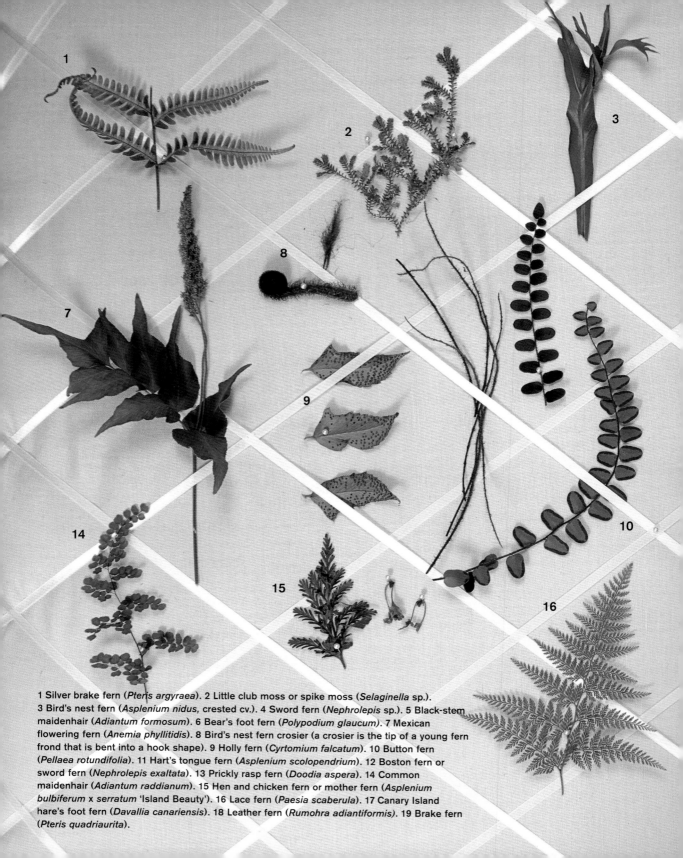

1 Silver brake fern (*Pteris argyraea*). 2 Little club moss or spike moss (*Selaginella* sp.).
3 Bird's nest fern (*Asplenium nidus*, crested cv.). 4 Sword fern (*Nephrolepis* sp.). 5 Black-stem
maidenhair (*Adiantum formosum*). 6 Bear's foot fern (*Polypodium glaucum*). 7 Mexican
flowering fern (*Anemia phyllitidis*). 8 Bird's nest fern crosier (a crosier is the tip of a young fern
frond that is bent into a hook shape). 9 Holly fern (*Cyrtomium falcatum*). 10 Button fern
(*Pellaea rotundifolia*). 11 Hart's tongue fern (*Asplenium scolopendrium*). 12 Boston fern or
sword fern (*Nephrolepis exaltata*). 13 Prickly rasp fern (*Doodia aspera*). 14 Common
maidenhair (*Adiantum raddianum*). 15 Hen and chicken fern or mother fern (*Asplenium
bulbiferum* x *serratum* 'Island Beauty'). 16 Lace fern (*Paesia scaberula*). 17 Canary Island
hare's foot fern (*Davallia canariensis*). 18 Leather fern (*Rumohra adiantiformis*). 19 Brake fern
(*Pteris quadriaurita*).

ferns

PROPAGATING THE CHRISTMAS CACTUS

You can increase Christmas cacti from cuttings by simply sticking leaf sections into small pots filled with coarse sand and keeping them moist.

Right (top to bottom): Schlumbergera hybrid, the true Christmas cactus, and a white-flowered hybrid.

Christmas cactus

Starting to flower in early winter, this beautiful cactus (schlumbergera) makes a terrific flowering plant for the home or intermediate to warm conservatory. It has bright pinkish red flowers in abundance. Most people grow it in a pot, but it looks superb suspended in a hanging basket. For something different again, try growing this cactus in a strawberry pot. Keep the plants moist, otherwise the flower buds may drop.

Plant a herb carpet

Surround yourself with fragrant flowers and aromatic foliage to give you pleasure all year round. Low-growing, matting plants release their delightful fragrance when crushed underfoot, and provide an unusual cover for many situations. Here are just some ideas:

• a path of pennyroyal
• carpeting patches of thyme between stepping stones
• Corsican mint as a ground cover in a fernery
• a herbal carpet in an area too small for a mower
• a cover of ajuga where lawn will not tolerate shade
• a spectacular carpet of thyme on a sunny bank (there are many sorts to choose from: creeping thyme comes in pink, crimson and white-flowered varieties, and there are also golden, orange-peel scented and variegated leaf types)
• a fragrant chamomile footrest beneath the garden seat

Choose herbs that grow with stolons or runners so that they can cover any bare patches which may develop. The mint family will grow where drainage is poor or there is dappled shade, otherwise most herbs like good drainage and plenty of sun.

The carpeting thymes can be recommended, including *Thymus serpyllum* and its varieties, such as 'Pink Chintz' with grey-green foliage and pale pink flowers. The species itself has purple flowers. Varieties of the lemon thyme (*T.* x *citriodorus*) are good, too: 'Silver Queen' and 'Argenteus' have silver foliage and 'Aureus' has tiny golden yellow leaves. All of these thymes are deliciously fragrant when crushed, although do not be too hard on them.

Five steps to success

Grow a wonderful herb lawn by following these five basic steps to success.

1 To prepare a herb lawn, first remove all weeds from the site, then use a product containing glyphosate to poison any that have bulbs so that they don't reappear.
2 Plant your herb lawn in a well-drained soil that is rich in humus, or dig in plenty of compost or manure.
3 Rake the soil to a level finish and plant herbs 20 cm apart.
4 Water well and refrain from walking on the lawn for about one month or until plants are established.
5 Weed regularly and plant any bare patches with rooted pieces from well grown plants.

PLANTING A HERB CARPET

1 Position your chosen herbs until you are happy with the result.

2 Dig a hole for each herb and plant it.

3 Backfill.

4 Finish with pebble mulch.

5 Water in.

6 Granite setts provide an attractive foil for the herb carpet.

Violets and violas

Violets are enchanting flowers: they evoke thoughts of fairies and elves dancing beneath ancient trees and hiding under giant toadstools. There are many species which are enjoying a revival with enthusiasts. Violets and violas can be had in flower during winter, spring and summer.

Best known is sweet violet (*Viola odorata*), popular in posies because of its heavily scented, short-spurred flowers in winter and spring. This perennial grows to 10 cm from a rosette of heart-shaped leaves.

There are many varieties, ranging from the dusty pink 'Rosea' and apricot-yellow 'Czar' to the deep violet 'Princess of Wales', but the most fragrant are known as Parma violets. These have mixed parentage and have shinier leaves and double flowers of mauve, white or violet. This violet was once used to treat respiratory disorders and is still used in the extraction of essential oil in the perfume industry.

Heartsease (*V. tricolor*) was known in Elizabethan England as love-in-idleness, and medieval herbalists used it in treating heart disease. It is also called Johnny-jump-up, because of its prolific self-seeding habit. It carpets the ground around bulbs or shrubs and is not fussy, growing well in light to medium shade. Heartsease is one of the parents of the common garden pansy and the black and brown pansies known as 'All Black' and 'Irish Molly'.

Did you know? In Shakespeare's play *A Midsummer Night's Dream* the flower that is used to make Queen Titania fall in love with Bottom is love-in-idleness, or heartsease. Also, violets were exchanged by Napoleon and Josephine as a symbol of their love.

Some violets have attractive foliage. The purple-leaved wood violet (*V. riviniana* Purpurea Group) makes a decorative ground cover with leaves that are dark purple above and greyish pink underneath. The deep mauve flowers are born on short stems. There is also a violet with a fern-like leaf, *V. dissecta*, which has the palest violet flowers in spring.

Some violets have speckled surfaces like bird's eggs, such as the American species *V. soraria* 'Freckles', which is deciduous and flowers in spring.

The Australian native species, ivy-leaved violet (*V. hederacea*), makes a superb ground cover for sheltered positions, waterways and pond surrounds as well as a useful lawn substitute in shady areas. It has small, kidney-shaped leaves and white flowers with a mauve eye. It will tolerate some sun, and spreads easily from the runners it produces, making it useful for topiary work as well. It will not tolerate hard winters and produces its flowers in the late summer.

There are several varieties of *V. hederacea* which may be available in some areas, including one with white flowers. These are well worth looking out for.

Violets and violas can be propagated by seed, cuttings or division and as most are short-lived should be propagated regularly.

Yet mark'd I where the bolt of Cupid fell:

It fell upon a little western flower,

Before milk-white, now purple with love's wound,

And maidens call it love-in-idleness.

William Shakepeare

1 *Viola* sp. 2 *Viola* sp. 3 Pansy (*V.* x *wittrockiana* 'Ruffles'). 4 Heartsease (*V. tricolor* 'Black Jack'). 5 *Viola* 'White'. 6 *Viola* 'Yellow'.
7 Heartsease (*V. tricolor*). 8 Heartsease (*V. tricolor* 'Prince John'). 9 *V. tricolor* cv. 10 Heartsease (*V. tricolor* 'Tinkerbelle Cream').
11 Heartsease (*V. tricolor* 'Tinkerbelle Yellow'). 12 Pansy (*V.* x *wittrockiana* 'Universal Orange'). 13 Heartsease (*V. tricolor* 'Yesterday, Today and Tomorrow'). 14 Pansy. 15 Pansy 'Clear Crystal Yellow'.

violas

1 Australian ivy-leafed violet (*V. hederacea* 'Baby Blue'). 2 Australian ivy-leafed violet (*V. hederacea*). 3 Purple-leafed wood violet
(*V. riviniana* 'Purpurea'). 4 *V. septentrionalis*. 5 Sweet violet (*V. odorata*). 6 Sweet violet (*V. odorata* 'Princess of Wales'). 7 Parma violet
(*V.* 'Neapolitan'). 8 Parma violet (*V.* 'Compte de Brazza'). 9 *V. reichenbachiana*.

For impossible locations the versatility of succulents is hard to beat. They cope with dry conditions superbly, both in extreme heat and shade, surviving the harshest of conditions. Despite this toughness, some are surprisingly beautiful. For rosettes as attractive as any rose, try growing echeveria, a succulent with a stunning array of colours, from grey to pink, blue, deep purple and green. Without a doubt they are the plant of the future. As water becomes scarcer for garden usage, these toughies will excel. Gardeners in frost-prone climates will have to grow echeverias in an intermediate (temperate) conservatory, or plant them outdoors for the summer.

Vital statistics

Scientific name: *Echeveria* sp.
Family: Crassulaceae.
Climate: Frost free.
Culture: Pot or landscape use.
Colours: Foliage in grey, blue, purple, pink and green.
Height: Up to 30 cm.
Planting time: Any.
Soil: Free draining.
Position: Maximum light, full sun outdoors.
Planting spacing: 50 cm.
Fertilizer: Not needed.
Pests/diseases: Rotting if too wet, especially over winter.
Propagation: Stem or leaf cuttings in spring or summer.

Climbers

Winter is a quiet time for flowering climbers. In the conservatory or frost-free climates, some flower in late winter, including Carolina jasmine and purple coral pea (hardenbergia). The flame vine or golden shower will also be in bloom.

This makes winter an especially good time to take control of some of the more unruly specimens which may have crept up into your eaves or swamped the neighbour's trees.

Climbers such as wisteria and grape are much easier to tackle after they have lost their leaves, but you need to pay special attention when pruning back wisteria. Leave flowering spurs, characterized by smaller lengths between buds, and remove unwanted leaf-producing growth which will quickly get out of hand once the leaves and more tendrils arrive.

Removing non-flowering growth on a wisteria vine.

Here freesias offset the profusion of purple flowers on purple coral pea.

Purple coral pea

This Australian climber (*Hardenbergia violacea*) flowers from late winter and continues through spring to summer. It needs a cool conservatory in frost-prone climates. The profusion of delicate chains of purple pea-like flowers against emerald green leaves are a sight to behold. There are several varieties including 'Happy Wanderer' which is very vigorous and has pink-purple flowers, the pink-flowered form *rosea* and the white-flowered *alba* 'White Crystal'. Provide full light under glass (but shade from strong sun) or full sun/partial shade outdoors. Acid to neutral soil is required. Out of doors in frost-free climates hardenbergia can also be used as ground cover. Prune lightly after flowering to keep the plant in its allocated space.

winter jasmine

The winter-flowering *Jasminum nudiflorum* is a tall slender shrub that can be grown against a wall as a climber. Bright yellow flowers are produced over a long period. It is a plant for cool climates and is fully hardy. Grow in full sun or partial shade. Prune after flowering by cutting back old flowered shoots.

Clothed walls

Sometimes it's not possible to erect trellis or wiring to help climbers attach themselves. This is when plants with adventitious roots (that is, roots that grow from the stem) come into their own. For an easy cover over brickwork, consider the ivy species and varieties (hederas), while Virginia creeper (*Parthenocissus quinquifolia*) and Boston ivy (*Parthenocissus tricuspidata*) are hard to beat for their autumn display and lushness over summer. Campsis will also develop roots along the stems if given help to climb and the stunning summer flowers will make the extra work worthwhile. Some shrubs will also react this way when grown against a wall, *Euonymus fortunei* cultivars being among the easiest and hardiest. There is a wide range of cultivars available, many with attractive silver or gold variegated foliage. *Ficus pumila* is a tender root-clinging climber for an intermediate conservatory.

Blowing your trumpet

The family Bignoniaceae contains many plants with showy, trumpet-shaped blooms. The flame vine or golden shower (opposite) is one, but it also contains other beautiful plants including yellow bells, yellow trumpet flower or yellow elder (*Tecoma stans*), a large evergreen shrub or even a small tree for mild or frost-free climates or intermediate conservatory. The funnel-shaped, bright yellow blooms appear from summer to winter. Under glass it needs pruning and the oldest stems should be thinned out, after flowering, in spring.

There are also some stunning trees that belong in this group. The trumpet tree (*Tabebuia* sp.), from the tropical Americas, has bell-shaped flowers in yellow, white, lilac and pink, and the famous jacaranda from South America flowers profusely in spring with purple flowers like foxgloves. (See the feature tree in 'Summer'.)

Clockwise from above: Ivy pruned to tall stems; *Ficus pumila*; *Parthenocissus tricuspidata* in autumn colour complements this unusual mosaic.

flame **vine**

This evergreen tendril climber from tropical South America has spectacular clusters of tubular, orange flowers and is ideal for providing winter colour in a warm conservatory. The deep green leaves are divided into leaflets and make a good background for the flowers. It is a fast grower to 10 m so grow it up the back wall of the conservatory and into the roof.

Vital statistics

Scientific name: *Pyrostegia venusta*.
Family: Bignoniaceae.
Climate: Warm and frost free.
Culture: Needs to be grown in a warm conservatory in frost-prone climates.

Height: Up to 10 m.
Planting time: Autumn.
Soil: Grow in soil-based potting compost or well-drained soil border
Position: Under glass provide maximum light.
Planting spacing: 3–4 m.
Watering: Keep moist at all times.
Fertilizer: Apply a complete fertilizer after pruning.
Flowering time: Autumn and winter.
Pests/diseases: Red spider mite and scale.
Pruning: Cut back after flowering in early spring to within a few nodes of the previous season's growth. Regrowth will be next season's flowers.
Propagation: Semi-ripe cuttings in summer.

winter
shrubs & trees

Winter is the ideal planting time for almost all deciduous trees and shrubs. Their dormancy allows you to plant them with minimum disturbance. It also means you can save money by buying plants as bare-rooted stock, or move existing deciduous plants about the garden.

The importance of evergreens, whether as hedging or privacy screens, becomes much more apparent in winter when many plants are bare. The tracery of unadorned branches creates a delightful cobweb against the sky, but looks much better against a solid green framework that screens your garden from the neighbour's windows.

Even when flowers are in short supply in the garden, remember the value of variegated leaves, attractive berries and interesting seedpods.

For coloured foliage, try the yellow tones of gold dust plant (*Aucuba japonica*) or euonymus, or the red tips of photinia. The shiny green leaves of *Camellia japonica* and holly are also great 'fillers', and the velvet-brown underside of Bull Bay magnolia (*Magnolia grandiflora*) are very popular with florists.

For unusually shaped leaves, don't forget palm fronds. One of the hardiest palms is the Chusan or windmill palm (*Trachycarpus fortunei*). Strap- or sword-shaped leaves also come into their own in winter, especially those of New Zealand flax (phormiums). These plants are great for creating an exotic touch in frost-prone gardens. Some have cream-striped leaves while others may be purple, or striped with red, pink or bronze. There is increasing interest in phormiums and consequently an ever-greater range of varieties to choose from, some being dwarf plants, others up to 2 m tall.

Shrubs

There is no need for the garden to appear 'dead' at this time as there's a surprisingly large number of shrubs in flower during the winter, especially if you include tender kinds that provide colour in the conservatory.

There is a certain peace about winter blooms, such as camellia, magnolia and daphne. Simple detail in leaves, twigs and even bark, such as this crape myrtle's, is also worth noting.

Many have red or yellow flowers, ideal for adding warmth and welcome to cold days. In the warm conservatory a popular source of winter colour are the poinsettias, which light up the scene with their fiery red bracts. They also make good house plants and are popular around the festive season.

Meanwhile out of doors the flowering quinces (chaenomeles) may be showing colour during the winter and continue their display into spring. The most popular are the cultivars of *C*. x *superba*, popularly called japonica. The flowers are produced on the bare stems and range from crimson or scarlet to shades of red and pink. These spiny shrubs are often grown against a wall or fence and can be trained flat against the support if desired.

If the winter is mild, forsythia may start its spectacular display, continuing into spring, its normal season. The cheerful flowers come in all shades of yellow,

depending on the variety. The varieties of *F*. x *intermedia* are the most popular. Also with yellow flowers is the wintersweet (*Chimonanthus praecox*), with sweetly scented flowers.

Euphorbia species

From the family Euphorbiaceae, these plants may be trees, shrubs, subshrubs, succulents, perennials and even annuals. Many are tender and suitable only for the conservatory in frost-prone climates, while others are fully hardy and can be grown outdoors. This entire family has a highly poisonous white milky sap, a skin irritant. The best known are poinsettias.

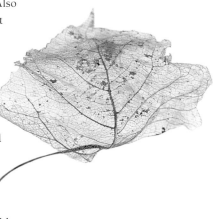

With their bright red bracts, poinsettias (*Euphorbia pulcherrima*) make a showy winter display in the home or warm conservatory; the true flowers are held at the centre of each cluster and are actually

small and yellowish green. Poinsettias are grown in bulk for their Christmas colour.

If left to grow naturally, poinsettias develop into rounded shrubs with many ascending branches. They are evergreen or partially deciduous. When they are grown in the home or conservatory most people treat them as annuals and dispose of the plants once flowering is over, buying new plants each year, as it is difficult to get plants to flower again the following year. Apart from the traditional scarlet, varieties are now available with pink, salmon, cream or marbled bracts.

To improve the life of cut poinsettias, cut the stems at night, after dark, and immediately plunge the lower part into a bucket of very hot water. Hold them up for a few minutes. The sap is comparatively sluggish at that time of evening, and the heat seals off the cut to some degree.

Some euphorbias have adapted to climatic extremes by developing succulent stems. The crown of thorns (*E. milii*) is one such with partially succulent stems and red flowers in spring or summer. This is a small, bushy and very spiny evergreen shrub, popularly grown as a house plant and ideal for warm rooms with a dry atmosphere. Medusa's head (*E. caput-medusae*) has white-fringed flowers upon its grotesque branches in spring or early summer. This is another good house plant.

Green-flowering varieties, known as spurge or milkweed (*E. characias* and *E. amygdaloides*), are popular in cottage gardens. They are drought tolerant and thrive in a well drained, sunny position in any soil. Two cultivars, *E. amygdaloides* 'Purpurea' and *E. characias* subsp. *wulfenii* are great garden specimens.

Clockwise from top: From the showy double red poinsettia 'Henrietta Ecke' to mythical Medusa's head and surreal green *E. characias* and *E. amygdaloides*, euphorbia has many faces.

check list

jobs to do now

- Encourage new blooms on bird of paradise by removing old flowers as they finish.

- Tip prune luculias after their autumn/winter flush.

- Make sure tender fuchsias and pelargoniums are well protected from frost.

- Remove about one third of the oldest shoots on flowering quince to make way for new canes immediately after flowering, otherwise the internals may become very congested.

- In late winter or early spring lightly prune back plumbago to maintain a shapely plant.

- Pot-grown azaleas are popular winter-flowering house or conservatory plants but it is important to keep an eye on watering as the compost must not be allowed to dry out. Use 'soft' or lime-free water.

- Remove any dead flowers from camellias regularly.

- Make sure poinsettias are in good light and free from draughts. Water regularly.

- In late winter or early spring, depending on climate, prune hydrangeas by cutting back old flowering heads to the second pair of buds. Don't go too low as this can encourage leaf growth at the expense of flowers.

- If you want to manipulate the colour of your hydrangea flowers, start now by adding either bluing tonic for blue flowers or lime for pink flowers until late spring.

- Prune, transplant and plant roses into well prepared soil.

- If any plants under glass are infected with scale insects, spray with appropriate insecticide.

- In mild areas roses can be pruned in late winter.

- Prune dead wood from trees and shrubs.

- Take hardwood cuttings from trees and shrubs. Choose healthy growth about the length and thickness of a pencil. Plants that can be treated this way include: berberis, buddleja, dogwood, forsythia, mock orange, plane tree, poplar, currant and willow.

- Replace mulch under roses. This not only replenishes nutrients but also removes any fungal spores.

plant now

- Deciduous shrubs — including viburnum, mock orange, berberis, weigela, hydrangea and lilac — will do well if planted before spring growth appears.

- Deciduous trees noted for autumn leaf colour can be planted in winter. These include acers, oaks, liquidambar and some prunus species.

- Although not much is in flower, winter is a good time to select magnolias and other early flowering deciduous trees such as the Judas tree (*Cercis siliquastrum*), ornamental peach, cherry, pear and apple blossoms.

- A showier, larger tree is the magnificent yulan (*Magnolia denudata*). Its lemon-scented, goblet-shaped flowers are pure white and at their best in spring. After this, lettuce green leaves appear, creating a light canopy of shade.

flowering now

- Some euphorbias, particularly the poinsettia (*Euphorbia pulcherrima*) and some heaths (ericas)

- Flowering deciduous shrubs such as flowering quince, *Jasminum nudiflorum* (winter jasmine), *Chimonanthus praecox* (wintersweet), *Hamamelis mollis* (Chinese witch hazel), *Lonicera fragrantissima* (winter honeysuckle), kerria and forsythia

- Early blossom trees such as peach and Taiwan cherry

- Evergreen shrubs such as winter daphne and the early viburnums (e.g. *V. × bodnantense*, *V. farreri*, *V. tinus*), mahonias, *Garrya elliptica* (silktassel)

- Not flowering in winter, but with bright berries (birds permitting) are hollies (ilex), pyracantha and *Gaultheria mucronata* (syn. *Pernettya mucronata*).

- The earliest magnolias, like the star magnolia (*M. stellata*) start flowering in late winter.

- Some pieris start flowering in late winter and are excellent companions for rhododendrons and camellias.

- Some cultivars of *Camellia japonica* start flowering in winter, particularly in milder regions.

- Australian natives such as wattles and many early boronias, bottlebrush and gums flower in winter.

Flowers in winter: in the foreground, the white flowers of *Erica lusitanica* with the pink flowers of *E.* x *darleyensis* behind.

Heaths and heathers

Heaths and heathers (ericas and callunas) can provide good colour in the garden from flowers and foliage during the winter. They are very hardy and often flower through snow. All need an open, sunny position.

Among the most widely grown for winter flowers are varieties of *Erica carnea*, the winter heath. These low-growing, ground-cover shrubs with heads of tiny bell-shaped flowers look most effective when mass planted. Unlike most ericas they can be grown in alkaline soil. In regions of hot summers the winter heath will tolerate partial shade. Popular varieties include 'Springwood Pink' with pink blooms; the white-flowered 'Springwood White'; 'Vivellii' with purple-pink blooms and bronze foliage; and the very early flowering 'King George' with dark pink blooms.

Similar, and requiring the same conditions, is *E.* x *darleyensis*, sometimes called Darley Dale heath. It stands more heat than *E. carnea*. Popular varieties are 'Darley Dale' with pale pink flowers; 'George Rendall' whose flowers are purple; and 'Silberschmelze' (or 'Molten Silver'), a vigorous plant with masses of white flowers.

Calluna vulgaris varieties (heather, ling or Scotch heather) flower in the summer and autumn but some really come into their own in winter when their foliage becomes tinted with gold or flame shades. These low-growing shrubs also make great ground cover in open, sunny places and they can only be grown in acid or lime-free soil.

Among the best callunas for winter foliage are 'Aurea', which turns from gold to reddish gold; 'Blazeaway', gold, turning fiery red; 'Cuprea', which takes on coppery tints; 'Golden Feather', with gold foliage changing to reddish orange; and 'Robert Chapman', with gold foliage turning to red.

TAKING HARDWOOD CUTTINGS

1 Collect the materials needed for taking hardwood cuttings: wooden box, bucket of peat, secateurs and hardwood cuttings (these were taken from a willow in winter).

2 Spread an even layer of peat in the wooden box.

3 Cut pencil-sized lengths of willow to use as hardwood cuttings.

4 Use the cutting blade of the secateurs to expose the cambium layer in the base of each hardwood cutting.

5 A bundle of hardwood cuttings all ready for planting.

6 Place the hardwood cuttings in the box of peat for callousing.

7 Backfill with peat.

8 Plant out when shoots appear.

Striking Many hardwood cuttings, such as those of the willow, root so easily that they can even be struck in water.

Winter in the perfumed garden

One of the most popular perfumed plants is daphne, a beloved shrub all over the world and a must for the fragrant garden. From winter to early spring the pink or white flowers emit a scent that wafts far and wide.

Daphne has a reputation for being difficult to grow, but this can be overcome by providing adequate drainage and thick organic mulch each spring. It grows to about waist height and will flourish in a shaded corner.

Two of the best daphnes for winter are the deciduous *D. mezereum* with red-purple or white flowers, and evergreen *D. odora*, popularly known as the winter daphne, with purple-pink flowers. Its variety 'Aureomarginata' has yellow-edged leaves.

Boronias start flowering in late winter but in frost-prone climates must be grown in a cool conservatory, in pots of lime-free soilless potting compost, which must be well drained as they are prone to root rot and can die suddenly. The brown boronia (*B. megastigma*) and Australian native rose (*B. serrulata*) have fragrant flowers.

If these two plants sound too tricky, try the hardy mahonias. *M. japonica* and its variety 'Bealei' have yellow flowers which smell like lily-of-the-valley. Winter honeysuckle (*Lonicera fragrantissima*) is near impossible to kill and has a delightful scent. It grows into a rambling shrub and needs to be kept pruned annually of old canes to keep it from overtaking the garden.

Some of the deciduous viburnums have a delicious fragrance. One of the best for winter is *V. x bodnantense* with rose-red to light pink flowers from autumn to spring.

Did you know? The fragrance of flowers is thought to attract insects, birds and animals to pollinate the flowers. The fragrance is an essential oil that is released at different levels throughout the day or night, depending on the plant. Fragrance is more noticeable in a protected position because wind doesn't disperse the oil.

There are several varieties including 'Dawn' with deep pink flowers that turn to white.

Two other deciduous plants are known for their winter perfume. Wintersweet (*Chimonanthus praecox*) has tiny yellow flowers with a very strong fragrance in winter. It's easy to grow and flowers best in a sunny position. Chinese witch hazel (*Hamamelis mollis*) also has yellow flowers with an equally powerful fragrance.

Wintersweet should have place of honour among plants that will flower out of doors during winter months.

Vita Sackville-West

Lily-of-the-valley look-alikes

If you love lily-of-the-valley (*Convallaria majalis*), then you should try some shrubs with similar flowers. Zenobia, clethra and pieris are all known by the same common name, and have similarly lovely flowers.

Clethra arborea, or lily-of-the-valley tree, produces lovely, white, scented flowers in late summer and grows in a similar way to the Irish strawberry tree (*Arbutus unedo*).

Lily-of-the-valley shrub, or *Pieris japonica*, is closely related to azaleas and enjoys a light friable soil with an acid pH and plenty of leaf humus. Many pieris also have sensational red, pink or bronze young foliage, for example, *P. formosa* var. *forrestii* and its varieties. Best planted in a protected position, all have sprays of white flowers in late winter and spring.

An elegant lily-of-the-valley look-alike which rarely exceeds 1 m, *Zenobia pulverulenta* produces lightly aniseed-scented, white bell-shaped flowers at the ends of arching canes in early summer.

Clockwise from left: Lily-of-the-valley, wintersweet, *Daphne odora, D. odora* **'Aureomarginata' and** *Boronia megastigma* **'Arch Chandler's Red'.**

From left: Wormwood (*Artemisia arborescens*), lamb's ears (*Stachys byzantina*), coleus, water fern (*Blechnum* sp.) and Indian shot plants (*Canna* sp.).

Foliage plants

Creating a garden involves so much more than coaxing plants to survive. A truly successful garden is like painting a living picture, where seasons, shapes and forms all play a part in creating drama and ambience. Unlike flowers, foliage plants provide the garden with seasonal interest all year round, and this is especially important in winter when most flowers have long since faded.

Silver foliage

As the colour of silver is elusive, it is often used as a background for other, more brilliant colours. Many silver plants have a sheen that is dazzling in the sunlight or visible at night, while others have rich textures that create a tapestry among the other plants in the garden.

Silver and grey plants are interesting because their neutral colour provides the imaginative gardener with many creative possibilities. They are a wonderful buffer between colours, holding together a diverse palette (even hot tones) with their neutrality, or adding to the harmonious feel of a pastel garden. When silver and grey plants are planted in the border they create a sense of extended perspective.

Wonderful in a thematic garden or when they are used as accent plants, silver foliage plants will highlight any dull corners in your garden, add light to a predominantly dark green garden bed and provide a feeling of freshness to well established areas in your garden.

Variegated plants

The ornamental value of leaves, as distinct from the more obvious attraction of flowers, has long been recognized. Often neglected as a tool in creating tonal interest year round, variegated foliage can lighten up dull corners, break up a solid mass of green foliage and even be a striking focal point.

Brush box (*Lophostemon confertus* 'Variegata').

Nerium oleander 'Variegatum.'

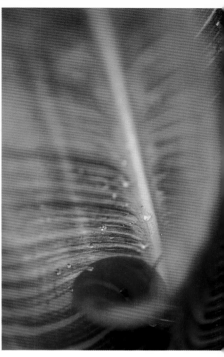

The palette of variegated foliage ranges from the clear hues of smoky grey-greens through to acid yellows and milky whites and creams. There are also plants with purple, pink, orange and red markings. Leaves can have lighter coloured edges, which highlight the leaf shape, or the reverse, which make them look lacy.

The variety of variegated plants is increasing all the time as breeders respond to the demand for combining foliage effects in garden design. Try not to place all your variegated plants together, or the special effect will be lost. Instead, use variegated foliage to highlight areas of importance.

Choose variegated plants with care. If you place a sun lover in too much shade, the foliage will tend to revert to green, whereas shade dwellers in full sun are easily scorched. Some plants will still throw back to their parentage, so simply trim these 'rogue' portions out as you spot them.

Purple foliage

Be adventurous and add some delicious plum and burgundy shades to your garden. Use purple foliage to gently warm silver-leaved plants and add lushness to greens. Muted purple can intensify reds and warm cool tones, and works well with bagged finishes. Wine tones have a wonderful ability to harmonize with anything; they even work well with gold, lime and yellows.

green is a colour too!

It's easy to overlook the value of green leaves in the garden. Some plants have fantastic foliage: try the leatherleaf viburnum (*V. rhytidophyllum*), Bull Bay magnolia (*Magnolia grandiflora*), *Camellia japonica* varieties, and English or cherry laurel varieties (*Prunus lauro-cerasus*). Their foliage is very handsome.

Tropaeolum majus 'Alaska', a pretty variegated nasturtium.

Hedera helix, some variegated ivy leaves.

corkscrew **hazel**

The small genus *Corylus* contains some interesting plants. Some have attractive catkins, while others produce edible nuts (such as hazelnuts). There are also species that feature coloured leaves or extraordinary branches, some of which are used for making walking sticks. The corkscrew hazel or Harry Lauder's walking stick, featured here, has curiously twisted branches, not unlike the twisted Hankow or corkscrew willow. The leaves colour golden yellow in autumn before they fall and the bare stems really come into their own in winter.

Vital statistics

Scientific name: *Corylus avellana* 'Contorta'.
Family: Corylaceae.
Climate: Cool and cold climates.
Colours: Yellow catkins in late winter and early spring.
Height: 3 m.
Planting time: Autumn and winter.
Soil: Well drained and enriched with rotted manure or compost.
Position: Full sun or partial shade.
Fertilizer: Complete plant food in spring.
Propagation: Propagate by layering, suckers or hardwood cuttings in winter.

Did you know? Witch hazel gets its name from the Old English word *wic*, meaning 'bend'.

Trees

Trees make up the 'roof' of gardens, and become the dominant element of all landscapes, both in private gardens and public spaces.

They vary greatly from one climate to another, yet all have winter seasonality with something special to offer.

The outline of bare branches against a grey sky is one of the season's pleasures. The evergreen conifers also come into their own in winter, as does the bark of many trees. Equally delightful in frost-free climates or conservatory is the golden haze from early wattles or acacias.

Trees for paved areas

With the popularity of outdoor living and our increased awareness of sun damage these days, the demand for small, obedient trees that behave well in confined spaces has become greater.

Small deciduous trees that suit this situation include varieties of Japanese maple (*Acer palmatum*) and fullmoon maple (*Acer japonicum*), the silk tree (*Albizia julibrissin*), various ornamental prunus such as flowering cherries and plums, and crape myrtle (*Lagerstroemia indica*). Small evergreen trees that also fit the bill include the strawberry tree (*Arbutus unedo*).

With age, some shrubs can also work as small trees. For example, try the autumn-flowering *Camellia sasanqua* and its varieties. For the double benefit of fruit and foliage try stone fruits such as cherries or, in a Mediterranean climate, citrus fruits.

Top right: Taiwan flowering cherry (*Prunus campanulata*).

Right: The silk tree (*Albizia julibrissin*).

Wyalong wattle, or *Acacia cardiophylla*, is a fast grower.

Wattles

The wattles or acacias flower mainly during the winter and spring and in frost-prone climates are ideal for the cool conservatory. In Mediterranean or frost-free climates they are superb garden plants for borders and for growing as specimens. There are around 1200 species of wattle, all different in habit. They are widespread across the Southern Hemisphere with some endemic to Africa, although most of those have thorns and are commonly known as mimosas.

None are as lovely as the Australian species that burst into glowing masses of golden blossom in winter and spring. It would be impossible to list all the species in this book, but here are some of the most ornamental for gardens. Under glass they should be grown in tubs of well-drained, soil-based potting compost, or in soil borders, and provided with maximum light and airy conditions. Outdoors they need a sheltered spot in full sun and slightly acid to neutral soil.

Proclaimed as Australia's National Floral Emblem in 1988, the golden wattle (*Acacia pycnantha*) represents the spirit and soul of Australians. The wattle has its own day, 1 September, to celebrate its beauty. Found in every state, the golden wattle is actually indigenous to the dry inland districts, where it grows in shallow sandy soils and helps bind the top soil. The large, fragrant, ball-shaped, golden flowers are a magnificent sight in spring there.

The pearl acacia or Queensland silver wattle (*A. podalyriifolia*) has beautiful grey rounded leaves which make it a feature regardless of the season. It is quick growing, to 6 m, and suitable for dry conditions with little or no topsoil. The ball-shaped,

The Bush was grey
A week today
(Olive-green and brown and grey)
But now the spring has come my way
With blossom for the wattle.

It seems to be
A Fairy tree.
It dances to a melody,
And sings a little song to me
(The graceful, swaying wattle).

Veronica Mason

perfumed gold flowers appear in late winter, making it one of the first wattles in the season to flower.

Probably the best known of all wattles, the Cootamundra wattle or Bailey acacia (*A. baileyana*) has ferny grey foliage which is sometimes tipped purple (var. 'Purpurea') and grows to about 5 m, although there is a prostrate variety which only grows to about 0.5 m. The spectacular golden yellow flowers appear in winter. It thrives in most soils but does best in areas other than the tropics and subtropics.

Oven's wattle (*A. pravissima*) is one of the best-known species in the Northern Hemisphere. It grows into a large shrub or small tree and has somewhat weeping branches. The scented, bright yellow flowers are carried in great profusion in late winter and spring. Out of doors it will take some frost.

The Sydney golden wattle (*A. longifolia*) grows to about 4.5 m in height and spread and has golden yellow flowers in late winter and early spring. The foliage is bright green. It is a fast grower and out of doors is a good coastal species, suitable for binding loose sandy soil.

Wattles have long been regarded as great nursery plants. This is due to their ability to come back quickly after bush fire; they also have nitrogen-fixing nodules on their roots which help build up the soil fertility, allowing other species to germinate.

In brand new gardens, wattles grow quickly to stabilize the soil and give protection and screening while other, slower species of plants are growing. Of course, many of these quick growers are short lived, lasting only five years, but long enough to do their job.

Look for the 'babies' of the wattle family. There are now many ground cover wattles and dwarf varieties which may fit more easily into the scale of a home garden or conservatory.

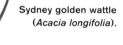

Sydney golden wattle (*Acacia longifolia*).

Wattle stem disfigured by a wasp gall.

Sunshine wattle (*Acacia terminalis*).

what's in a name?

It is said that acacia became known as wattle because the thin branches were used to form the walls of the earliest colonial houses in Australia: they were woven together and then sealed with clay or mud. This form of construction was known in Europe as wattle and daub. Strangely, the plant often used in this wickerwork is called blackwattle, actually not an acacia at all but a callicoma. Another theory is that the name 'wattle' came from the Aboriginal name for the plant – *wattah*.

Whatever the background, there are lots of famous Australian aliases for wattles, including mulga, gidgee, blackwood and mimosa.

wattles

Wattle sprigs (opposite page): 1 Green wattle (*Acacia decurrens*). 2 Sydney golden wattle (*A. longifolia*). 3 White sallow wattle (*A. floribunda*). 4 Fringed wattle (*A. fimbriata*). 5 Sunshine wattle (*A. terminalis*). 6 Cootamundra wattle (*A. baileyana*). 7 *A. cognata* 'Green Mist'. 8 *A. iteaphylla*. 9 *A. longifolia* subsp. *sophorae*. 10 Zig zag wattle or blue-leaf wattle (*A. macradena*).

Care and maintenance

Pruning

Prune back after flowering to maintain a pleasing shape and to control size under glass.

Planning

Repeat planting so that as one wattle reaches the end of its lifetime, there is another well on the way.

Feeding and watering

Under glass, water well during active growth but reduce considerably in winter. During the growing season feed the plants every four weeks with a balanced liquid fertilizer. Out of doors, feed plants annually after flowering with a balanced slow-release fertilizer. Water in dry periods and keep plants mulched with bulky organic matter to conserve soil moisture.

Pests

The main pests of wattles in the conservatory are red spider mites. These are best kept in check by using biological control (a predatory mite). Watch out also for scale insects and if seen, wash these off with water and a stiff brush. Otherwise few pests seem to attack these plants.

Did you know? During World War I, sprigs of wattle were sold by the Red Cross to raise funds for the war effort. Depots were set up in Sydney, Australia, to receive wattle sent in from country areas. After the massacre at Gallipoli, the Wattle League arranged for the planting of wattle trees near the graves of the Anzacs.

feature tree
gordonia

Even without flowers, the gordonia is a handsome tree. The smooth limbs have streaks of colour and the foliage is grass green and shiny, making it good value all year round. It has beautiful flowers too, like enormous poached eggs — pure white petals with fluffy yellow stamens at the centre. Few flowering trees have such a long season, from winter to spring. They can be grown outdoors in mild-winter areas, and elsewhere in a cool conservatory.

Vital statistics

Botanical name: *Gordonia axillaris*.
Family: Theaceae.
Climate: Warm climates suit it best. Will tolerate only light frosts.
Culture: Perfect for paved areas and small gardens.
Colours: White with prominent golden yellow stamens.
Height: 8 m.
Planting time: Autumn or spring.
Soil: Under glass grow in acid soilless potting compost.
Position: Full sun or part shade, shelter from cold wind.
Planting spacing: 10 m.
Fertilizer: Under glass liquid feed every four weeks in summer.
Pests/diseases: Not usually.
Pruning: Can be pruned to keep as a shrub.
Propagation: Layering or semi-ripe cuttings.

1 *Cupressus sempervirens* 'Stricta'. 2 *Chamaecyparis obtusa* 'Crippsii'. 3 *Cedrus atlantica* 'Glauca'.
4 *Afrocarpus falcatus*. 5 *Cupressus sempervirens* 'Stricta'. 6 *Araucaria heterophylla*. 7 *Cedrus atlantica* 'Aurea'. 8 *Cupressus macrocarpa* 'Greenstead Magnificent'. 9 *Juniperus chinensis* 'Aurea'.
10 *Picea pungens*. 11 X *Cuppressocyparis leylandii* 'Castlewellan'. 12 *Cryptomeria japonica* 'Globosa Nana'. 13 *Juniperus chinensis* 'Variegata'. 14 *Cupressus arizonica* var. *glabra*.
15 *Chamaecyparis obtusa* 'Fernspray Gold'. 16 *Cryptomeria japonica*. 17 *Platycladus orientalis*.
18 *Pinus radiata*. 19 *Chamaecyparis pisifera* 'Boulevard'. 20 *Cupressus torulosa*.

conifers

The importance of evergreens becomes abundantly clear in winter. A permanent backdrop for the seasonality of bulbs, perennials and deciduous plants, conifers can provide the perfect solution to a winter garden, with many, such as the Leyland cypress (X *Cupressocyparis leylandii*), suitable for hedging. Some are great accent plants, punctuating the air with their vertical spires (such as *Juniperus chinensis* 'Spartan'), while others, such as the shore juniper (*J. conferta*), make superb ground covers, coping with just about any conditions.

Foliage varies from velvety green (like the Himalayan or Bhutan cypress, *Cupressus torulosa*) to the blue and grey of the Arizona cypress and blue spruce. Some are apricot, turning shades of reddish brown in autumn and winter as the cold intensifies; look for *Thuja occidentalis* 'Rheingold' and *Cryptomeria japonica* 'Elegans'.

winter
herbs, fruit & vegetables

The peace and calm of winter in the kitchen garden should be broken by some periods of hard work! Digging over the vegie patch, liming where appropriate and planting some cold-tolerant crops, such as lettuce and broad beans, is good exercise for gardeners.

Jump start spring!

Although most plants are hibernating, you can trick some plants, such as chicory and rhubarb, into early arrival by forcing them with covers. In late winter, to get a head start with warm season herbs and vegies, raise seedlings in protected greenhouses and on sunny windowsills and plant them out after frosts have finished. You can also purchase bare-rooted fruit trees and berry canes during their dormancy, saving money, and plant them out in winter. This gives them a chance to settle in before the growing season.

Rhubarb can be forced in late winter for an early spring harvest.

Herbs

Now the winter cold has set in, many herbs have either died down or gone completely, and that's when woody perennial herbs are most valued.

Rosemary, thyme, wormwood, bay laurel or sweet bay and some of the spices — such as cloves, nutmeg, cinnamon and cardamon — make fabulous additions to slow-cooked meals, and some can still be picked from the garden. Indoor sowing of leafy herbs and salad greens can help germinate early crops, and if you live in a mild area you can raise seedlings in cold frames and cloches.

Tarragon and wormwood

The genus *Artemisia* contains lad's love, absinthe, wormwood and tarragon. All are noted for their pungent foliage, feathery leaves and medicinal or herbal uses. They are excellent plants for dry sunny sites, where they can be kept trimmed to retain a neat shape or hedge.

The most valued species is French tarragon (*A. dracunculus* var. *sativa*) which has a delicate anise taste that is useful for flavouring asparagus, fish, poultry, pickles and vinegars, and is sometimes used as a substitute for garlic. Don't buy the Russian tarragon (*A. dracunculus* var. *inodora*) by mistake as its leaves can taste slightly bitter and it tends to grow a bit wild.

Other species include lad's love or southernwood (*A. abrotanum*), which acquired its name as an aphrodisiac and was sometimes called maid's ruin, and wormwood (*A. absinthium*) which is the chief ingredient in absinthe, an anise-tasting liqueur with a high alcoholic content. Roman wormwood (*A. pontica*) is also used to flavour vermouth.

Some cultivars of wormwood are grown for their ornamental foliage: these include *A. absinthium* 'Lambrook Silver' with deeply cut silver leaves, and *A.* 'Powis Castle' with feathery, silver-grey foliage.

All forms need to be consumed with extreme caution, as they contain a cumulative poison which is dangerous to the nervous system and makes them extremely useful in discouraging mice, moths, worms and many other pests.

Nutmeg

True nutmeg is *Myristica fragrans* but there are a few other plants worth noting for their similar flavour or scent. The nutmeg flower (*Nigella sativa*), related to love-in-a-mist, has black seeds that are nutmeg scented. Nutmeg bush (*Tetradenia riparia*) has nutmeg-scented leaves and pinkish flowers all through winter, making it an excellent shrub for the warm conservatory.

Many citrus fruits (left) are ready for picking in winter. In the most favoured areas where there is no longer risk of a hard frost and the soil is warming up, potatoes can be planted as winter is turning to spring (centre). The earliest sowings of brassicas (right) such as cabbages, broccoli, cauliflowers and Brussels sprouts can be made at the end of the season.

Mini greenhouse Use some glass jars to pot up leafy herbs on your windowsill for winter.

check list

jobs to do now

- In cold climates, you should lift mint and chives, then pot them and place them in a heated greenhouse.

- Citrus fruits growing out of doors can be fed in late winter with a balanced fertilizer. Pick up any fallen fruits. Spray with a suitable insecticide for scale if necessary.

- Peaches and nectarines are prone to a disease known as peach leaf curl. Control by spraying with a copper fungicide several times between mid- and late winter, before flower buds start to open.

- Deciduous fruit trees such as apples and pears can be sprayed with a dormant spray, such as tar-oil winter wash, to control overwintering pests.

- Thin apples and pears to form an open-centred shape.

- Grapevines need hard pruning. Cut out most of last season's wood to leave short 'three bud' spurs at 20 cm intervals along the main arms of the older stems.

- Spread well-rotted manure around the drip line of fruit trees. This is where the canopy finishes and feeder roots are plentiful, and where most benefit is received. Avoid building up manure and soil against the trunk as this can cause collar rot.

- Divide and plant rhubarb into rich soil. Rhubarb can be 'forced' by excluding light with straw or an upturned plastic bin.

- Tie the outer leaves of cauliflower over the curd to prevent discolouration of the heads.

- Lay out seed potatoes to encourage sprouting before you plant.

- Harvest Brussels sprouts, silver beet, cabbage, cauliflower and broccoli.

plant now

- Sow mustard and cress in succession through winter under glass or on a windowsill.

- Raspberries and other soft fruits are best planted in late autumn and winter when the plants are dormant. Cut the stems of raspberries back to about 30 cm to stimulate new shoots from the base.

- Rhubarb is planted from crowns in winter. Their large ornamental leaves make them an attractive feature in the garden bed.

- In mild regions you can make a start with vegetable sowings in the greenhouse to provide young plants for planting out in spring, for example brassicas, onions and leeks.

- Shallots can be planted in late winter or early spring. They are planted as small dry bulbs known as sets. The tips of the bulbs should be just visible above the soil.

- Asparagus crowns may be planted in late winter in mild areas, or in spring in colder regions.

- Buy seed potatoes and keep them in a cool, dark place for a few weeks so they sprout before planting time.

producing now

- Vegetables such as winter broccoli, winter cauliflower, winter cabbages, maincrop carrots, winter lettuce in a greenhouse or under cloches, leeks, parsnips, Swiss chard, swede or rutabaga (in mild winter areas) and winter spinach.

- Citrus are in fruit at this time of the year.

Frost protection If you live in a cold area, protect frost-sensitive seedlings by inverting a glass jar over each one.

bay **laurel**

Also known as sweet bay, this ancient plant has been held in high esteem for many centuries. The Latin name *nobilis* means famous, and in ancient times the Romans used bay leaves in wreaths to crown their poets and victors. Along with parsley and thyme, bay laurel is one of the essential elements of bouquet garni, and it also makes a handsome standard specimen. It has a slightly peppery flavour and can be used fresh or dried. The word 'laurel' has crept into the English language with phrases such as 'to rest on one's laurels' and 'look to one's laurels'. 'Laurel' literally means 'large glossy leaves' and is used to describe many plants, such as the mountain laurel (*Kalmia latifolia*), the English or cherry laurel (*Prunus laurocerasus*) and the spotted laurel (*Aucuba japonica*).

Vital statistics

Climate: *Laurus nobilis.*
Family: Lauraceae.
Climate: Cool to warm climate.
Colours: Creamy yellow flowers.
Height: Up to 12 m.
Planting time: Autumn.
Soil: Rich, well-drained soil with thick mulch to protect shallow roots.
Position: Full sun. Protect from cold winds for the first few years.
Planting spacing: 3 m.
Fertilizer: Liquid feed container specimens in spring.
Pests/diseases: Watch for sooty mould caused by scale insects.
Propagation: Layering in spring or semi-ripe cuttings in summer.
Storage: Dried leaves and flowers, essential oils, herb vinegar.

Did you know? Tradition has it that in the winter before the death of the Emperor Nero, despite the very mild weather, all the bay trees in Rome died.

blossoms, shade you from hot summer sunshine, produce delicious fruit and then, once the leaves fall, will allow welcome winter sunshine into your garden.

Select a spot where there is space for your fruit tree to grow unhampered. Avoid planting close to walls or fences, unless you are going to espalier it.

Short of space?

In small gardens fruit trees can be trained against sunny house walls and fences. If you grow them this way you need to pay a little more attention to pruning in order to maximize the yield. Patterns include:

1 Cordon, where a single stem is grown at an angle.
2 Fan, where several branches fan out from one point on the trunk.
3 Espalier, where the branches are trained horizontally from the trunk.

Even in the smallest garden you should be able to use one of these pruning methods to grow at least one, and possibly more.

If space is at a premium, you can also plant dwarf trees, such as miniature peaches and nectarines (there are several varieties), or pillar-like apple trees (generally known as Ballerina trees), which are perfect for narrow areas, such as garden beds edging driveways and paths.

Fruit trees can also be bought in a 'multigrafted' form. This simply means that a few varieties have been budded on to the one plant. This is often done with apples and pears, where several varieties are grafted onto the one tree (often called a 'family tree'). This looks great and saves space. If you have really tight parameters, grow a fruiting vine, such as a passion fruit or kiwi fruit, plants which are usually grown on a fence or pergola.

Fruit

It's good to grow your own fruit. One of life's little pleasures is the flavour of freshly picked fruit…delicious, because it can fully ripen on the tree, not in a box on its way to the fruit shop! Leftovers can be used for jams, jellies, chutney, relish, preserves and liqueurs.

Flowering peach blossoms.

Deciduous fruit trees

Winter is the best time for planting deciduous fruit trees. Depending on the climate, apples, pears, peaches, plums, nectarines and cherries are all easy to grow. A tree for all seasons, your deciduous fruit tree will give you delightful spring

PRUNING AN APPLE TREE

1 Neglected for some years, this apple tree has put its energy into producing wood instead of fruit.

2 Leave fruiting spurs.

3 Cut back to fruiting spurs.

4 Remove excess wood.

5 Remove the stubs of old bad cuts.

6 Remove old pruning wounds just above the ridge collar.

7 Remove branches butting against one another. Thin out the centre of the tree to let in the sun and air.

fruit care tip

Those plants that are traditionally sold as 'bare rooted' should be planted now while they are completely dormant (see page 414). Make sure there is no delay before planting as the bare roots will dry out very quickly. If you anticipate any delay, wrap the plants in damp hessian or heel them into the soil as a temporary measure.

Above: The espaliered design of this apple tree looks like a Jewish menorah, the eight-branched candelabrum that is an emblem of Judaism.

Opposite: Young apples ripening on the tree.

Very few, if any, fruit trees could be grown in these gardens because of the limited space available. However, by placing the trees along the garden walls and training them to grow in a more or less two-dimensional form, trees could be incorporated into the garden with relatively little loss of available space.

Gardeners in the more northerly regions of Europe soon found another benefit in espalier. Where the climate was cool and the summer short, the warm sunny microclimate directly adjacent to a south-facing wall permitted fruit trees to crop in one season, a result that could not be achieved with freestanding trees. Today, with our very small gardens, especially with new houses, growing fruits as espaliers is enjoying something of a revival.

A third benefit of growing fruit trees in an espalier form is that the open frame created by this method permits excellent light infiltration, with all parts of the tree exposed to direct sunlight. This results in a higher level of flowering, greater fruit production, and better colour development on the fruit. In addition, picking fruit from an espaliered tree is a simple process because of the small stature of these trees.

If you want to espalier a fruit tree, start with an apple or pear. These trees bear fruit on long-lived spurs and are probably the best for beginners. Stone fruits such as plums and cherries can also be espaliered, but many bear fruit on the shoots of the previous season's growth. This means that renewal pruning is necessary to ensure a continuous crop.

Espaliered fruit trees

Espalier is the art of training trees to branch in formal patterns, usually along a wall or on a trellis. The technique of espalier first became popular several hundred years ago in the walled gardens of medieval Europe.

That which one eats as the fruit of his own labor, is properly called food.

Proverb

Espalier design

There are a few basic designs that can be used. A T-shaped design (which looks like a Jewish menorah, pictured opposite) is a formal style. Another, very popular, formal style is to have a central trunk with pairs of branches trained horizontally on either side in tiers. The easiest design is probably an informal espalier where branches are not forced in any particular direction, but are simply trained along the wall. All of these are good for apples and pears. Cherries, plums and peaches are best trained as fans rather than as espaliers.

Tips for building an espalier frame

1 Establish a frame to work from. String heavy wire (12 or 15 gauge) from eyebolts on the wall or fence to provide a frame. Three levels of wire are usually sufficient for starting an espalier. The bottom wire should be at least 0.5 m from the ground, with the remaining wires spaced from 0.5 m to 1 m apart. Sturdy posts can also anchor a freestanding trellis into the ground and wires can be fixed to them. The trellis must be strong enough to support a heavy crop.

2 Plant the tree 15–20 cm from its support, ensuring that the graft union is at least 1 cm above ground level.

3 Tie the selected branches to bamboo canes with soft garden string; this keeps them straight. Over a few weeks, slowly lower the canes to the wire. Prune off branches that are not part of the design.

4 Rub off any flower buds. This permits the tree to direct its energy into productive growth until the espalier pattern is complete. No fruit should be allowed to develop until the framework growth is complete.

5 Tie new growth to bamboo canes and lower two branches to the wire, leaving one branch vertical. The next spring, prune this vertical branch to the height of the next wire, where new shoots will form to repeat the pattern.

6 Each year a new layer is formed, so that on a three-layered trellis, at least three years of growth are required to complete the effect, four years for four layers, and so on.

Cracked branches If you are bending a branch and it cracks, don't despair. A partially broken branch that is securely fastened to the frame will usually heal and grow normally.

PLANTING A BARE-ROOTED TREE

1 Dig a hole.

2 Take the root ball out of its protective covering.

3 Check that the roots are healthy.

4 Position the tree in the hole.

5 Backfill the soil around the tree.

6 Create a 'doughnut' ring around the plant to hold water.

7 Water it in.

8 The 'doughnut' retains the water and stops any run-off.

General tips on fruit growing

- All fruit needs full sunshine. In shade or semishade your tree will not yield well. It will lack vigour and be susceptible to disease and insect attack. Protect it from strong winds and it will grow better.
- Gardeners in temperate climates can grow many fruit trees: most popular are apples, pears, plums, cherries, peaches and nectarines. Soft fruits like gooseberries and blackberries are also widely grown.
- Position is everything when it comes to fruit. Avoid planting in low-lying patches which will encourage root rot and collar rot, and improve drainage either by adding manure and gypsum to your soil or by mounding the soil to elevate the bed.
- Regular water supply in the growing season is important for good cropping. Provide deep weekly watering in summer, if required, and a permanent mulch of garden compost or well-rotted manure.
- Gardeners in regions with mild winters should choose low-chill varieties of fruits such as apples and pears. Peaches and nectarines also do well in these regions.
- :For the home garden, wherever possible select plants that are self-fertile (that is, plants that don't need another variety with which to cross-pollinate).
- General maintenance includes feeding, watering, removal of weeds, pruning to shape, spraying when necessary and, of course, harvesting.
- Fan-trained peaches and nectarines (the best way to grow them) are pruned after fruiting by cutting back to new replacement shoots all shoots that have carried fruits.
- Apple trees and pear trees should be thinned in the centre to form an open vase shape. This lets in the sun and promotes heavy cropping.

DISEASES OF FRUIT TREES

1 Apple scab is a fungus which spreads more readily in warm, showery weather. Practise good hygiene by keeping the ground under your tree clean.

2 Although citrus affected by the fungus melanose look unappealing, the fruit is usually edible.

3 Mosaic virus, shown here on an apple tree, is spread through plant sap, so wash your hands, disinfect cutting tools and spray for aphids.

4 Foliage with peach leaf curl, a fungus which will weaken the whole tree if it is left unchecked.

- If growing fruit trees in grass, do not allow the grass to grow right up to the trunk, but leave a 1 m diameter circle of bare soil around the tree.
- Watch out for other critters like codling moth that may spoil your fruit. Take precautions early in the season so that your fruit remains edible until harvest.

The lemon-scented myrtle

If you love lemon fragrances, then citrus are not the only plants you can grow for this characteristic. The leaves of the lemon-scented myrtle (*Backhousia citriodora*) have a strong lemon fragrance. This Australian evergreen shrub or small tree has deep green shiny foliage which starts off red-green, and fluffy, cream-white flowers are produced in summer and autumn.

In frost-prone climates this frost-tender plant must be grown in an intermediate (temperate) conservatory, in a tub or large pot of acid, soil-based potting compost. Provide maximum light but shade from strong sun.

Water well in summer, far less in winter. Liquid feed the plant at four-weekly intervals during the summer. Trim lightly in spring to maintain a good shape.

Lemon-scented myrtle is delicious in both teas and curries.

Citrus trees

Citrus trees are popular home-grown fruits in warm temperate climates, but gardeners elsewhere can grow them in a conservatory. A citrus is a year-round tree with bright winter fruits which are a delicious source of vitamin C. The smell of citrus in bloom is always magnificent in spring and the aromatic fragrance of its foliage in summer is welcome too.

The following are the most popular citrus fruits as far as gardeners are concerned. Sweet oranges are perhaps the favourites, with 'Valencia' and 'Washington' (Navel orange) being familiar varieties. Sour or Seville oranges make excellent marmalade, as do kumquats, the hardiest citrus, which tolerates a low of -5°C. 'Clementine' is a well-known variety of tangerine or mandarin. Tangelos or ugly fruits are hybrids between mandarin and grapefruit. Lemons are probably next in popularity to oranges, with the variety 'Meyer' being well known. 'Eureka' is the standard commercial variety. Limes are often grown, especially the Indian lime, while grapefruits can also be grown by home gardeners.

Out of doors, citrus are best planted in the warmer months of the year. The three points to consider before planting are sunlight, drainage and feeding. All citrus love heat and water, as long as it drains away. It is a good idea to plant your citrus tree on a mound, with lots of organic mulch to keep its surface roots cool and moist. Fertilize regularly.

Clockwise from right: Tangelos, kumquats and the blossom of the 'Meyer' lemon.

Citrus care tips

- To produce good fruit reliably every year, all citrus trees need regular feeding and watering. You should feed your citrus in winter with a special citrus fertilizer if available, or with a complete general-purpose fertilizer. Make sure you water your tree first.
- Citrus are attacked by various pests including spider mites, scale insects, mealy bugs and aphids. Try washing these off with forceful jets of water. If this is not successful, spray with insecticide.
- Remove all grass and vegetation for a radius of at least 2 m around the tree trunk. Carefully cultivate the soil, avoiding any shallow roots, add the citrus fertilizer and mulch with cow manure, then water thoroughly.

Growing under glass

Several citrus fruits can be grown in a conservatory by gardeners in cool, frost-prone climates. Try sweet orange, sour or Seville orange, tangerine, lemon, lime, kumquat, and tangelo. They should produce fruit, but remember fruiting is not reliable under glass in a cool climate. Fruits can be grown in a conservatory with a minimum winter temperature of 7°C. Limes are better, with a minimum of 13°C. To produce fruit, warm temperatures (a minimum of 15°C) are needed for about six months after flowering.

Trees can be grown under glass all year round, in beds or borders, or grown in tubs and moved out of doors for the summer. Traditional tubs are the square wooden types in the Versailles style. Citrus trees do particularly well in tubs and could even be grown as standards if desired. Fill tubs with well-drained, soil-based potting compost. The trees need maximum light in winter

Oranges and lemons say the bells of St. Clement's.

English nursery rhyme

and good ventilation all year round. If the plants are still under glass in summer they will need shade from strong sun plus maximum ventilation, and damping down to provide humidity.

In a conservatory border, mulch plants in autumn each year with compost or well-rotted manure. In spring, apply a general-purpose fertilizer. Plants in containers should be fed with a liquid fertilizer every two weeks from spring to fall. Water citrus well in the growing period of spring and summer but far less in autumn and winter.

1 'Honey Murcott'
mandarin.

2 'Kaffir' lime.

3 Tangelo 'Minneola'.

4 'Eureka' lemon.

5 'Rio Red' grapefruit.

6 'Kaffir' lime.

7 'Seville' orange.

8 'Meyer' lemon.

9 Tangelo 'Minneola'.

10 'Meyer' lemon.

citrus

11 'Meyer' lemon.

12 Lemonade.

13 'Red Rio' grapefruit.

14 'Nagami' kumquat.

15 'Tahitian' lime.

16 'Meyer' lemon.

17 'Washington Navel' orange.

18 Australian or 'Calamondin' kumquat.

19 'Valencia' orange.

20 'Tahitian' lime.

21 'Tahitian' lime.

22 'Chinotto' sour orange.

blue**berries**

Blueberries are edible and ornamental, with ball-shaped flowers that develop into green berries before gradually turning blue. Blueberries are deciduous shrubs and the leaves take on fiery tints before they fall in autumn. Plants can be grown in a fruit garden or ornamental beds and also in tubs. They flower in spring and fruit in summer.

Vital statistics

Botanical name: *Vaccinium* species.
Family: Ericaceae.
Climate: In mild climates grow *V. ashei* varieties.
Culture: Best to plant two varieties for cross-pollination and therefore heavier crops.
Colours: Flowers white or pinkish, fruits blue.
Height: Growing to a height of up to 2 m.
Planting time: Late winter or early spring.

Soil: They must have acid soil and good drainage although they do enjoy moist conditions. Prepare the soil before planting with organic matter. Generous amounts of well-made compost will provide the plants with excellent nutrition. Do not add lime.
Position: In a sheltered position with full sun.
Planting depth and spacing: 1.5 m.
Fertilizer: Each spring with compost or rotted manure. Foliar spraying with seaweed fertilizer during the flowering period will assist with fruit set and supply necessary trace elements.
Pests/diseases: Birds love the fruit. Fruit fly can damage the skin.
Propagation: Easy by layering in spring.
Harvest and storage: The fruit develops in clusters of five to ten berries, which should be harvested five or six days after they have turned blue.

Vegetables

Winter conjures up images of
warm pies and pasties, hot soups
and baked potatoes.

The winter garden can supply many hardy
vegetables, such as leeks, maincrop carrots,
parsnips, rutabaga or swedes, mushrooms
(indoors), winter cabbages, winter
cauliflowers, sprouting broccoli, curly
kales, Brussels sprouts, Swiss chard, winter
spinach and overwintering lettuce
(outdoors or under glass).Why not select
some vegetables that look the part as well as
taste good, such as flowering cabbage or kale.

Lettuce (above) can be enjoyed all year round if suitable varieties are chosen.
A vegetable garden (below) can be formal and decorative.

PROPAGATING PLANTS INDOORS

Many vegetables can be started off from seed indoors in late winter for planting out in spring. Just follow these easy steps.

1 Fill a seed tray with compost and level it.

2 Firm the compost with a piece of board.

3 Sow the seeds evenly.

4 Sieve some compost over the seeds and water in.

5 Cover the tray with a sheet of glass.

6 To minimize temperature fluctuations, cover the glass with a sheet of paper.

7 Once the seeds have germinated, transplant the seedlings into larger trays or individual pots.

A potager

Luscious leafy vegetables such as cabbage, lettuce and spinach can be handsome plants, coming in a vast range of colours and textures. Blue-green, red or rich green cabbages, glossy green or reddish brown lettuces, rhubarb chard (Swiss chard variety), purple kohlrabi and purple Brussels sprouts are just a few that are perfect for dotting about flowers or adding structure to formal displays. Even parsley planted en masse looks great as a border.

Many herbs and vegetables have beautiful flowers in their own right. Runner beans have scarlet flowers in profusion and climbing peas have pretty white flowers that are edible. Nasturtiums have vibrant red, orange and yellow flowers, while lavender, chamomile, chives and borage will pretty up any boring vegie patch.

Better eat vegetables and fear no creditors, than eat duck and hide from them.

The Talmud

Buy some mature plants of flowering cabbages and kale from your local garden centre to brighten up the winter vegie patch. The bright pink and green or white and green foliage makes these interesting potted plants as well as ideal for planting out. The foliage is edible.

Grow flowering cabbages and kale in full sun, in free-draining soil. As with other members of the brassica family, you will need to keep an eye open for slugs and snails, plus caterpillars (cabbage worm).

Did you know? The French word *potager* means 'soup garden'.

1 To make the mushroom kit you'll need peat, lime, mushroom spore and a suitable container, such as an old wooden box, lined with plastic.

2 Moisten the peat with a little water until it feels damp all over and releases some water when you squeeze it.

3 Thoroughly blend the peat and lime together.

4 Spread the peat and lime to a depth of about 15 cm over the mushroom spore.

5 The completed mushroom kit, ready to be stored in a cool, dark place.

6 The fruiting bodies, or mushrooms, appear about four weeks later.

Mushrooms, toadstools and fungi

Mushrooms can be grown and harvested from kits all year round. The fruiting bodies of fungi, many types of mushroom are highly poisonous, so only experts should forage in the wild. A much safer bet is to plant your own. Fungal spore can be purchased for a whole range of varieties, with more of the exotic Asian types, such as shiitake and oyster, coming onto the market daily. All they need is a cool, dark place — such as a garden shed or cellar — in which to grow.

Clockwise from bottom left: Pink oyster mushroom, shiitake mushrooms (showing both underside and caps) and field mushroom.

Did you know? A truffle is a fungus that grows underground, under the shade of certain trees, especially pines and beech. They are normally sniffed out by specially trained dogs or pigs, and are an expensive commodity due to both their rarity and their exquisite perfume.

PLANTING SEED POTATOES

Potatoes are frost tender and should not be planted until the hardest frosts are over. This may be in late winter in mild areas but in most locations planting starts in early spring with the early varieties, continues in mid-spring with second earlies, and finishes in late spring with main-crop potatoes. They are grown from seed tubers (actually small tubers). In cool and cold climates with a short growing season the tubers are started into growth (known as chitting) before planting, to give them a head start.

1 Seed tubers are chitted in a cool, light, frost-free place. Stand them upright in trays (buds or 'eyes' uppermost) till they sprout.

2 Make a trench with a spade or hoe.

3 Create a wide, flat-bottomed or V-shaped 15 cm trench with a trowel.

4 Cut the seed potatoes into pieces so that each piece contains an eye.

5 Plant the pieces of seed potato in the trench.

6 Backfill the trench and lightly firm the soil.

rhubarb

Rhubarb is a perennial that is normally harvested in spring and early summer but it can be forced in late winter to provide stalks for picking in early spring. When rotating crops in the garden, rhubarb should only be lifted every five years or so as the crown, if left, will become big and produce lots of stems.

Vital statistics

Botanical name: *Rheum* x *cultorum*.
Family: Polygonaceae.
Climate: Temperate climates – not suitable for high temperatures.
Culture: Produces for five years or more if you lift it and divide it regularly.
Colours: Stems vary in the intensity of red depending on the variety; some may even be green.
Height: 1 m.
Planting time: Crowns any time from autumn to early spring. Seed sown in spring then planted out in autumn.
Soil: Most well-drained soils with added manure at planting time.
Position: Best in full sun.
Planting spacing: About 0.5 m apart.
Fertilizer: Complete fertilizer just before spring growth.
Pests/diseases: Sometimes suffers from crown rot or viruses.
Harvest: Spring and early summer. Only use the stalks, not the leaves as they are poisonous. For earlier stalks, cover crowns with 10 cm of straw in late winter and cover with an upturned bucket to exclude light.

rhubarb tarts

Chop 6 rhubarb stalks into lengths, toss in 75 g caster sugar, then put in a saucepan with 1 tablespoon orange juice. Cook gently with the lid on until just soft, then allow to cool. Fill 8 individual pre-baked pastry cases with mascarpone cheese and lay some rhubarb on top of each, then drizzle them with a little of the cooking juice. Makes 8.

Perpetual vegetables

Most vegetables are annuals and need replacing each season. There are a small number which are perennial – that is, they live for many years. Examples are asparagus, artichokes and rhubarb. Jerusalem artichokes can be kept going by saving a few tubers to replant in spring.

Some vegetables can be substituted for traditional types. Celeriac can be used as a substitute for celery, as the leaves and stems have the same flavour. Collards, types of kale, are leafy greens with a mild cabbage flavour. Swiss chard has thick stalks that are cooked as a vegetable and the leaves are used as spinach. There are varieties with coloured stems like the red rhubarb chard.

Companion planting

Grouping together plants that complement each other, thus reducing the need for chemical sprays and the overall incidence of insect and disease attack, is called companion planting. For example, plant French marigolds next to tomatoes: they secrete into the soil an enzyme or hormone that deters nematodes from infesting the roots of tomatoes, which are susceptible to nematodes.

Certain combinations of herbs and vegetables actually encourage better growth as well as repel predatory insects. Many herbs, especially those with fragrant foliage, encourage your garden to help itself by attracting beneficial insects (those that prey on pests).

For example, cucumbers enjoy growing with beans; peas go with radishes and nasturtiums; and chives and onions may be used around the garden to repel pests.

This table of companion plants will help you to plan your kitchen garden and reap the benefit of strong and healthy crops.

Top: Red-stemmed Swiss chard, known as rhubarb chard.

Bottom: The roots of tomatoes are susceptible to nematodes but marigolds secrete an enzyme which repels them.

vegetable planting guide

Aubergine
beans

Broad beans
potatoes, cucumbers,
cauliflower, cabbage

Cabbage family
potatoes, celery, dill,
chamomile, sage, mint

Carrots
peas, lettuce, chives,
onions, leeks, rosemary

Celery
leeks, tomatoes, French
or snap beans, cauliflower

Chives
carrots

Climbing beans
corn, summer savoury

Corn
potatoes, peas, broad
beans, cucumbers,
squash

Cucumbers
beans, corn, peas,
radishes

French or snap beans
potatoes, cucumbers,
corn, strawberries, celery

Leeks
onions, celery, carrots

Lettuce
carrots, radishes,
strawberries, cucumbers

Onions
beet, strawberries,
tomatoes, lettuce

Parsley
tomatoes, asparagus

Peas
carrots, turnips, radishes,
cucumbers, corn

Potatoes
beans, corn, cabbage,
horseradish, marigold

Pumpkins
corn

Radishes
peas, nasturtiums, lettuce,
cucumbers

Spinach
strawberries

Squash
nasturtiums, corn

Strawberries
French or snap beans,
spinach, borage, lettuce

Tomatoes
chives, onions, parsley,
asparagus

index

acknowledgments

Many people have contributed to *Dig*. First, my thanks go to Kay Scarlett, my publisher, for believing in my ability to fulfil her vision for such a gardening book, and allowing me so much freedom and scope. Next, to the exceptionally talented photographer Sue Stubbs, who has transformed the ordinary into the exceptional with her magic touch, styling, zest and flare. Her photographs have without doubt taken this book to another level. Also, to Marylouise Brammer, Vivien Valk and Sarah Baker who have coordinated everything, tied up loose ends, chased a million last-minute details and created the pages that you see.

I would also like to thank my babysitters, who have been an invaluable support during this project: Moira Rein, Adrian Sancataldo and Jennifer Harrison.

The publisher thanks the following individuals and organisations for supplying plants, fruit, vegetables and gardening supplies: Colourwise Nursery, Sydne, Australia, (02) 4566 6177; Cookshop Plus, Bowral NSW, (02) 4861 1105; The Digger's Club, 'Heronswood', Dromana VIC and the vegetable grower, Jarrod Ruch; Easy Care Gardening Inc., Turramurra NSW, (02) 9983 1644; Engalls Nursery, Dural and Epping NSW, (02) 9651 2735; Geranium Cottage Nursery, Galston NSW, (02) 9651 1667; Peter Hendrix, Golden Fruits, 'A' Shed, No. 3/4, Flemington Markets, Flemington NSW, (02) 9764 3799; Oasis Horticulture Pty Ltd, Winmalee NSW; Peppergreen in Berrima, Berrima NSW, (02) 4877 1488; Plant Growers Australia, (03) 9722 1444; John at Roy Cave & Son, Merchants of Strawberries, Exotic & Tropical Fruits, Stand 75, 'A' Shed, Flemington Markets NSW, (02) 9746 5265; Swanes Nursery, Dural NSW, (02) 9651 1322; Tesselaar Bulbs and Flowers, Silvan VIC, (03) 9737 9811, www.tesselaar.net.au; Keith Wallace Pty Ltd, Dural NSW, (02) 9651 4005.

The publisher also thanks the following for assisting with finding garden locations: Jonathan Garner, Puddleton, Designers, Builders & Carers of Unique Gardens, 0417 460 704; Judy Horton, Arthur Yates and Co, (02) 9763 9200; Riccardo Zanetti, Gardens by Zanetti, Landscape Design and Construction, Double Bay NSW, (02) 9327 6671.

Thank you to the following people for identifying plants: Tracey Armstrong, Information Officer, Mount Annan Botanic Gardens, Mount Annan NSW; Mark Engall, Engalls Nursery, Dural NSW; Greg Holt, Swanes Nursery, Dural NSW; Richard Johnstone, Information Officer, Mount Annan Botanic Gardens, Mount Annan NSW; Lisa Kinsella, The Digger's Club, Dromana VIC; John McGee, Oasis Nursery, Winmalee NSW; Greg Holt, Swanes Nursery, Dural NSW; Judyth McLeod, Honeysuckle Cottage Nursery; Sue Templeton, Unlimited Perennials, Lavington NSW; G R Warwick, 'Moidart', Bowral NSW.

photographic credits

Dell Adam 39.

Ben Dearnley/Jared Fowler 65 bottom, 96 bottom, 97 bottom, 320 bottom L, 406, 427.

Joe Filshie 35, 41 top and centre, 47 middle, 76 (top R), 78 L, 79 (middle and bottom rows), 81 R middle, 129 top L, 132 L, 139 bottom L, 141 (top two pix, fourth and fifth from top), 164 top L, 174 top centre, 188 top L, 257 top, 264 top, 268 centre L, 269 bottom R, 278, 290 centre and R, 291 R, 307 (R, second from bottom), 332, 333 bottom, 334 top L, 335 centre, 336, 342 R, 347 top L, 351 (third, fourth, fifth, seventh and ninth from top), 362, 366 top R, 375 top R, 384 L, 388 top R, 395 bottom, 396 top centre.

Denise Greig 37 bottom L, 95 top L, 178 bottom, 301, 317 (second and third from top), 323 bottom centre, 417 top R, 426 top.

Chris L. Jones 108, 186 L, 316, 320 bottom R, 322 (top and middle L), 324–5, 335 R, 409.

Jason Lowe 312 bottom L, 407 bottom R.

Brian McInerney 21 bottom, 22.

Andre Martin 244–5, 288–9 bottom, 333 top, 334 top R, 335 L, 335 R.

Luis Martin 23 bottom, 25 bottom.

© Murdoch Books Photo Library 16 top R, 27 bottom R, 51, 74 top, 95 bottom R, 231 bottom, 266 top centre, 267, 313 bottom L, 323 bottom L, 347 (top, second from R), 348 L, 351 (sixth from top), 399 top.

Tony Rodd 357.

Lorna Rose 16 bottom R, 17 top, 19, 26–7 centre, 27 top R, 28, 29 L, 31, 33 bottom L and R, 36, 37 bottom R, 38, 44, 45 top and centre, 53 R, 55 R, 56–7 (centre), 57 R (pix 1–9), 58, 60, 61 (all but third pic from top), 64, 65 top, 66, 67 (all but pix 1), 68 (all but middle R), 69–73, 74 bottom, 75 bottom, 78 R, 81 top L and R, 83, 87 bottom, 89, 90–3, 94 R, 95 (top R, bottom L), 96 (top, pix 1–4), 97 (top, pix 1–2), 98, 103, 104–5 top, 106 (all but deep etch), 109, 118 (top L, bottom L and centre), 117 top L, 119 R, 120 top, 124 top, 125 top and centre, 127, 129 R top and bottom, 130 top, 131 top, 132 R, 133, 136, 139 (top and bottom R), 140 top, 141 (third from top, bottom), 143 (top centre), 144–5, 150, 152, 153 top, 154–5, 164 R and bottom L, 165 bottom R, 167, 171 (top centre, bottom L), 172–3, 174 top L, 174–5 centre, 175, 176, 179 top, 180–1, 183, 184, 184–5, 185, 186 R, 187, 188 L centre, 189 R, 194 top, 195 top, 196, 198 bottom L, 199 R, 202, 204 centre and R, 205, 207, 208 (top L and centre L), 210, 211, 212, 212–13 centre top, 213 bottom, 214, 215, 216 L, 218 L centre and bottom, 218–19, 224 top L, 225 top R, 229 bottom, 230 bottom L, 235 top L and R, 242, 248–9, (centre top), 255, 259, 263, 264 centre L and R, 266 top L and R, 268–9 top centre, 272, 273 (top L and middle row), 274 centre, 281, 282 (top L, centre and R), 284–7, 289 (top L, centre and R), 291 L, 292–5, 296 top R, 297, 300, 302–3, 306, 307 bottom R, 310, 312 top L, 313 bottom R, 317 (top and bottom), 320 top L and R, 322 middle R, 323 top R and bottom R, 338–9, 340 (top L, R and centre), 347 (top, second from L, and bottom), 348 R, 350, 351 (first, second and eighth from top), 352 (far L, middle; centre), 354–6, 357 L, 358, 360 (top R), 361, 365 R, 367, 369 (top L, top R, middle R), 374, 375 L and bottom R, 378 (R, top and bottom), 380 top L and R, 381, 384 R top and bottom, 385 R, 386–7, 389 centre top, 390, 392, 394, 395 top, 398, 399 bottom, 400, 407 (top L and R, bottom L), 412, 415, 417 top L and bottom, 420, 421 bottom, 426 bottom.

Sue Stubbs cover, 4, 7, 8, 11, 12–14, 15 (top L and centre, bottom R), 16 (pix 1–3 L), 17 top, 18, 20, 21 (top, pix 4–6), 23 (top, pix 1–4), 24, 25 (pix 4–6 and 10–12), 26 L, 27 R centre, 29 R, 30, 32, 33 (top L, R and centre), 34, 37 top L and R, 39 bottom, 40, 41 bottom, 42–3, 45 bottom, 46–7 (centre), 47 bottom, 48–50, 52, 53 L, 54, 55 L, 56 L, 59, 61 (third pic from top), 62–3, 67 (pic 1), 68 middle R, 75 top L and R, 76 (all but top R), 77, 79 top, 80, 81 bottom, 82, 84, 86, 87 (top, pix 4–7), 88, 94 L, 99, 100–2, 104 bottom L, 104–5 (pix 1–4), 106 bottom R, 107, 110–16, 117 (R top, centre and bottom), 118, 118–19 centre, 120 (bottom, pix 1–3), 121–3, 124 bottom, 125 bottom, 126, 128, 130 bottom, 131 bottom, 134–5, 137, 138, 140 bottom, 142, 143 (top L, top R, bottom pix 1–3), 146–9, 153 bottom, 154 L, 155 R, 156–9, 161–3, 165 (top 3 pix and bottom L), 166, 168–9, 170, 171 (top L and R, bottom R), 174 bottom, 175, 177, 178 top, 179 bottom L and R, 182, 188 bottom L, 188–9, 190–3, 194 (bottom, pix 1–3), 195 (bottom, pix 1–2), 197, 198 top L and R, 199 L, 200–1, 203, 204 L, 208 top R and bottom L, 209, 213 R, 216 R, 217, 218 top L, 219 (pix 1–3 and bottom R), 220–3, 224–5 (centre top and deep-etched fruits on bottom), 226–8, 229 top, 230 top L and R, 231 top L and R, 232–4, 235 bottom R, 236–41, 243, 246–7, 248 L, 249 R, 251–3, 254, 257 bottom, 258, 260–2, 264 bottom, 265, 266 bottom L, 268 (top L, bottom L and R), 269 top centre and R, 270–1, 273 (top R and bottom row), 274 L and R, 275–7, 279–80, 282 (bottom pix, 1–4), 283, 288 top, 290 L, 291 centre, 296 (top L and bottom L), 298–9, 304–5, 307 (L and top 2 pix on R), 308–9, 311, 313 (herb teas), 315, 318–19, 321, 322 (bottom row), 326–31, 334 bottom, 340 bottom, 341,

342 (pix 1–3), 343–6, 347 top R, 352 (far L, top and bottom; far R), 353, 359, 360 (all but top R), 363–4, 365 (pix 6–8), 366 (all but top R), 368, 369 bottom R, 370–3, 376–7, 378 (L, pix 1–3; middle R), 379, 380 bottom, 382–3, 385 L top and bottom, 388 L and bottom R, 389 (top L and R, bottom R), 393, 396 (top L and R; bottom), 397, 401–5, 407 top centre, 408, 410–11, 414, 416, 418–19, 421 top, 423–5.

Pat Taylor 15 top R, 257 centre.

Mark Winwood 250, 413, 422.

The publisher would like to thank the following for allowing photography in their gardens: O Abbott, Huonville TAS: 78 L, 79 middle R, 81 R middle; Alstonville Tropical Fruit Research Station, Alstonville NSW: 216 L; Arizona Cacti Nursery, Box Hill NSW: 282 top L, 384 top R; 'Ashcombe Maze', Shoreham VIC: 90, 187 L; Auckland Regional Botanic Gardens, Auckland, New Zealand: 205 R; Australian Turf Research Institute: 57 (top; bottom 5 pix), 172; Sarah Baker and John Spence, Leichhardt NSW: 27 centre R, 124 bottom, 128 (top L, pix 1–2), 251 (pix 1–5); Bankstown Municipal Park, Bankstown NSW: 144 bottom, 150 R; Virginia Berger, Canberra ACT: 386 L top and bottom; Trevor Birley, Pymble NSW: 125 centre; G Boots, ACT: 28 L, 38, 69; Penny and John Boyd, Wahroonga NSW (Designer: Sue Montgomery): 68 top L; Brindley's Nurseries, Coffs Harbour NSW: 378 R top and bottom; Jenny Brown, Avalon NSW: 248–9 (centre top); 'Burnbank', Wagga NSW: 95 bottom L; 'Buskers End', Bowral NSW: 37 bottom R, 45 top R, 64, 141 (second from bottom), 143 (bottom, pix 1–3), 211 bottom L, 273 centre R, 354 top; Di Callaghan (design of pond), Sydney: 119 R; Camellia Grove Nursery, St Ives NSW: 79 (middle row), 388 top R; 'Cherry Cottage', Mt Wilson NSW: 91 top R, 386 R; Chinese Gardens: 37 bottom L; Chinese Growers, Botany NSW: 94 R, 235 top L; John Coco, Vineyard NSW: 242 L; Lynn Coddington, 'Wycombe', Armidale NSW: 70–1 top; Common Scents Nursery, Dural NSW: 293 top; Mr and Mrs Copes, Southern Highlands NSW: 199R; Corramilla Nursery, Browns Creek NSW: 61 (fourth from top), 67 (pic 6); E Cossil and T Carlstrom, Frenchs Forest NSW: 55 R; Cranebrook Native Nursery, Cranebrook NSW: 185 bottom, 292; 'Curry Flat', Nimmitabel NSW: 351 (eighth from top); Michelle Cutler and William Tocher, Tascott NSW: 342 R; Davidson's Wholesale Nurseries, Galston NSW: 365 R; Chris and Ruth Dimmock, Pennant Hills NSW: 86, 87 (top, pix 4–7), 360 (top, centre), 378 (R, middle); Mr Duke, Clare SA: 204 R; 'Dunedin', St Leonards TAS: 67 (pic 2), 97 (top, pic 2), 154–5; Janet Dunlop, Orange NSW: 392, 394 centre; Zeny Edwards, Turramurra NSW: 144 top L, 348 R; 'Elmwood', Exeter NSW: 164 top L, 351 (seventh from top); Engalls Nursery, Epping NSW: 417 top L; Erina Fragrant Garden, Erina NSW: 66 bottom, 73; 'Eryldene', Gordon NSW: 79 bottom L, 180 top R; Mrs Ailsa Ferguson, Killara NSW: 302 L, 381 L; Johnnie Felds, Marulan NSW: 120 top; Finches of Beechworth, VIC: 296 top R; Floriade, Canberra ACT: 268–9 centre top, 395 bottom; 'Foxglove Spires', Tilba Tilba NSW: 26–7 centre, 33 bottom R (and bottom pic), 70 bottom, 72 top, 211 bottom R; Jody and Lynton Frost-Foster, Tascott NSW: 336; D D Franklin: 268 centre L, 347 top L, 351 (third, fourth and ninth from top); Franklin Tea Gardens TAS: 47 middle; Peter Furner, Putney NSW: 56 L, 279 R; 'Galapagos Farm', Bruny Island TAS: 96 (top, second from L); Garden World, Keysborough VIC: 390 (middle); Mr and Mrs Gray, Wahroonga NSW: 141 bottom, 286 top R; Mr and Mrs Greene, Thornleigh NSW: 375 bottom R; Julia Hancock, Erskineville NSW: 132 R; Margaret Hanks: 36, 374; Harvey Garden, Gravelly Beach TAS: 141 (top, fourth from top), 264 top, 290 centre; Mr and Mrs Heckenberg, Mosman NSW (Design: Marcia Hosking, Glebe NSW): 130 top; 'Heronswood', Dromana VIC: 17 top, 369 top R, 380 top R; Diana Hill and David Potter, Ashfield NSW: 80 bottom L, 101 bottom, 115 bottom, 116 top, 121 bottom, 140 bottom, 143 top R, 148, 153 bottom, 154 L, 155 R, 156–7, 166, 178 top, 182 R, 193, 195 bottom (pix 1–2), 208 top R and bottom L, 280, 368 R, 411; 'Hillview', Exeter NSW: 317 top, 361 L, 367, 384 L, 398; Merv and Olwyn Hodge, Loganview Nursery, Logan Reserve, QLD: 284; E Hogbin, Mt Kuring-gai NSW: 407 top L; Jennie Holbbaum, Beecroft NSW: 67 (pic

9), 70 middle; I and J Howie, Orange NSW: 202; John Hunt, Kenthurst NSW: 67 (pic 5), 183 L; 'Kiah Park', Jaspers Brush NSW: 83 top, 136, 211 top, 291 L, 360 (top R); 'Kennerton Green', Mittagong NSW: 66 top R, 67 (pic 8), 338, 350, 352 (far L, centre), 412, 421 bottom; Meredith Kirton and Michael Bradford, Putney NSW: 14 top, 15 top L, 16 (pix 1–3 L), 17 bottom, 20 bottom, 47 bottom, 55 L, 59, 62–3, 76 (top L), 82, 102, 114 top, 115 (top 3 pix), 117 R centre and R bottom, 118 L centre and L bottom, 120 (bottom, pix 1–3), 121 (top, pix 1–6), 122–3, 128 top R, 131 bottom, 159 (R top and bottom), 170 bottom R, 171 top R, 194 (bottom, pix 1–3), 209, 217 top centre, 223 (top R and centre), 252 (pix 1–3), 270 top R, 273 bottom row, 321, 334 bottom, 341, 346, 366 (bottom pix 1–4), 379; Klerk's Nursery, Ingleside NSW: 64 L; Lawrences Plant Nursery, Mirboo North VIC: 420; Colin and Linda Lawson, Putney NSW: 179 bottom L and R; Mary Lidbetter, Berry NSW: 178 bottom; 'Lindfield Park', Mt Irvine NSW: 16 bottom R, 247 top centre, 262 bottom L, 266 bottom L, 269 top centre and R, 270 (top L and bottom, pix 1–5), 274 R, 275 (pix 1–4), 276 (top 2 pix), 290 L, 291 centre, 307 top R, 311 top L; 'Lorquon', Albury NSW: 96 top L; Elizabeth Luke, Mosman NSW: 179 top, 180 top L; Angus and Alison McIntosh, Deakin ACT: 274 centre; Robert and Carmela Machin, Putney NSW: 116 bottom, 117 top R, 143 top L, 170 top, 171 top L, 192 top and bottom L, 197, 213 top R, 219 (pix 1–3), 264 bottom, 279 top L and bottom, 396 top R, 397 (top L, R and centre); Garth and Sandy McIntyre, Mt Eliza VIC: 400; John Manents: 106 top; Menzies Nursery, Kenthurst NSW: 71 middle; Mercure Hotel, Heritage Park, Bowral NSW: 93; 'Merrygarth', Mt Wilson NSW: 287; Lorraine Meymouth, West Pennant Hills NSW: 171 bottom L; 'Moidart', Bowral NSW: 15 top centre, 26 L, 32, 33 top L, 34 bottom L, 37 top L and R, 39 bottom, 40, 41 bottom, 50, 53 L, 67 (pic 1), 68 middle R, 75 top R, 76 C and bottom rows, 79 top, 88, 99, 130 bottom, 161–3, 165 (top 3 pix), 199 L, 257 bottom, 265, 339, 396 top L, 410 top; Helen Moody, St Ives NSW: 75 bottom; Alice Morgan, Pymble NSW: 68 top R, 384 bottom R; 'Mossy Pines', Bermagui NSW: 95 top R, 109 top; Mt Tomah Botanic Gardens NSW: 91 bottom L, 96 (top, pic 4), 153 top; NSW Agriculture, Orange NSW: 320 top L, 415 (top and second from bottom); New Federation Daisies Colourwise Nursery: 152 R; 'Nooroo', Mt Wilson NSW: 80 top L, 244–5, 246 top R, 247 top L and R, 260–1, 262 (top, pix 1–6), 273 top R, 275 bottom L, 277 (top 4 pix), 282 (bottom, pix 1–4), 288–9 bottom, 296 top L, 307 (L and R, second from top), 308–9, 311 top R, 322 bottom L and centre; North Coast Regional Botanic Gardens, Coffs Harbour NSW: 194 top; E Ommaney, St Ives NSW (Ross Garden Design): 281; Noel Outerbridge, Alstonville NSW: 224 top L; Out of Town Nursery, Beechworth VIC: 64 R; Mr and Mrs Park, Canberra ACT: 66 top L, 340 (top L and centre); Parkers Nursery, Turramurra NSW: 297 centre; Paula Pellegrini, Randwick NSW: 15 bottom, 33 (top centre and R), 34 (top and bottom R), 138, 229 top, 258 top, 331 bottom R; Merrill and Kevin Pentergast, Ladysmith NSW: 300; 'Peppertrees', Berry NSW: 415 (second from top); Permaculture Institute, Tyalgum NSW: 426; 'Pinecrest', Leura NSW: 35, 278 centre; 'Pinehills', Bathurst NSW: 297 L, 356 L; Qualturf, West Ryde NSW: 57 (second and third from top); Rathmoy, Hunterville NZ: 19 bottom; Sue and Robert Read, Pennant Hills NSW: 14 bottom, 18, 20 (top, pix 1–3), 21 (top, pix 4–6), 23 (top, pix 1–4), 24, 25 (pix 4–6 and 10–12), 29 R, 52, 54, 61 (third pic from top), 75 top L, 77, 104–5 (pix 1–4), 107, 146–7, 149, 188–9, 198 top L and R, 204 L, 247 bottom R, 328, 330 L, 331 bottom L, 342 (pix 1–3), 343, 345 bottom, 359, 360 (top L; middle L and R), 371–3, 378 (L, pix 1–3), 393, 407 top centre, 408, 410 bottom, 414, 421 top, 423 top (pix 1–6), 424–5; Gita and Gunther Rembel, Middle Dural NSW: 282 top centre; Retirement Village, Castle Hill NSW: 235 top R, 242 R; J. Robb, Pennant Hills NSW: 257 top, 269 bottom R; Jill and Colin Roberts (ASGAP), TAS: 196 bottom R; 'Rose Cottage', Deviot TAS: 174 centre top, 188 top L, 396 top centre; Linda Ross, Kurrajong NSW: 30, 42–3, 126, 177, 217 (top L and R, bottom pix 1–3), 220, 222, 224–5 (papaya, persimmon, tamarillo, lychees, mangosteen), 226–8, 230 top L and R, 231 top L and R, 234 R, 239, 243 R, 274 L, 275 R, 368 top L and bottom L, 369 bottom R; Ross Roses Nursery and Garden, Willunga SA:

133 R, 204 centre; Janet and Lee Rowan, Newcastle NSW: 58, 68 bottom R; Royal Botanic Gardens, Melbourne VIC: 180 bottom, 375 top L; Royal Botanic Gardens, Sydney NSW: 28 R, 57 (fourth from top), 66 top centre, 67 (pic 3), 68 bottom L, 97 top L, 129 bottom R, 144–5, 164 R, 171 top centre, 173, 175 R, 187 R, 188 L centre, 189 R, 218 L centre and bottom, 218–19, 229 bottom, 259, 264 centre L, 272, 273 top L, 286 bottom L, 289 top L; 'Runnymede', Newtown, Hobart TAS: 290 R; Ruston's Roses, Renmark SA: 208 top L; Jan and Pirrie Sargent, Miallo QLD: 212–13 centre top; Dora Scott, Wahroonga NSW: 65 top, 98, 175 centre, 176, 218–19 centre, 266 top R, 313 bottom R, 323 bottom R; Maggie Shepherd, Canberra ACT: 56–7 centre, 141 (third from top), 369 R middle, 'Shirley', Monaro NSW: 96 (top, second from R); 'Silky Oaks Lodge', Mossman QLD: 213 bottom; Cliff Smith, Riverstone NSW: 131 top, 417 bottom; Mrs Smith, Orange NSW: 67 (pic 4), 361 R; Derek and Karyn Sprod, Netherby SA: 198 bottom L, 205 centre; John Stowar, Mt Murray NSW: 140 top; 'Strathrook', Orange NSW: 103; Swane's Nursery, Dural NSW: 92 bottom, 358; Tasman Bay Roses, Motueka, New Zealand: 289 top R; Pat Taylor, Pymble NSW: 369 top R, 390 bottom L; 'The Folly', Chewton, United Kingdom: 196 bottom L; The Hedgerow Roses, Tumbarumba NSW: 45 centre, 208 L middle, 390 bottom R; The Lilian Fraser Garden, Pennant Hills NSW: 80 top R, 329, 330 R, 331 (top L, R and centre), 340 bottom, 344, 345 top, 347 top R, 352 (far L, top and

bottom; far R), 353, 385 L top and bottom, 389 top L and R; 'The Orangerie', Stirling SA: 19 top; The Rose Garden, Watervale SA: 205 L; Douglas Thompson, Killara NSW: 118 top L, 118–19 centre, 251 L, 283, 370, 403; Ann Thomson Garden Advisory Service, St Ives NSW: 47 top, 81 top L and R, 389 top centre, 394 top; Murray Thomson, Woollahra NSW: 340 top R; 'Tintagel', Mittagong NSW: 109 bottom, 323 top R, 407 top R; 'Titoki Point', Taihape, New Zealand: 214, 352 centre; Tomar House, Rosevears TAS: 129 L; A and R Tonkin, Orange NSW: 67 (pic 10); 'Tregamere', Te Awamutu, New Zealand: 104–5 top; Tropical Fruit World, Duranbah NSW: 225 top R, 230 bottom L; 'Vireya Vale', Mt Pleasant NSW: 78 R; Wagga Botanical Gardens, Wagga NSW: 33 (bottom L), 106 (bottom centre), 174–5, 295 R; 'Willows End', Killara NSW: 291 R; Sandra Wilson, Epping NSW: 152 bottom L; 'Winterwood', Mt Tomah NSW: 31 top; Woodlyn Nurseries, Fiveways VIC: 44, 255 top R, 347 (top, second from L), 351 top, 380 top L, 381 centre; 'Woodridge', Berrima NSW: 333 bottom; Yellowrock Nursery, Yellowrock NSW: 391 top.

Although every care has been taken to trace and acknowledge copyright, the publisher apologises for any accidental infringement where copyright has proved untraceable. The publisher would be pleased to come to a suitable arrangement with the rightful owner in each case.